Intermediality and Storytelling

Narratologia

Contributions to Narrative Theory

Edited by
Fotis Jannidis, Matías Martínez, John Pier
Wolf Schmid (executive editor)

24

De Gruyter

Intermediality and Storytelling

Edited by
Marina Grishakova
Marie-Laure Ryan

De Gruyter

This publication has been supported
by the Estonian Science Foundation (Grant 7166)

ISBN 978-3-11-023773-3
e-ISBN 978-3-11-023774-0
ISSN 1612-8427

Library of Congress Cataloging-in-Publication Data

Intermediality and storytelling / edited by Marina Grishakova, Marie-Laure Ryan.
p. cm. – (Narratologia. contributions to narrative theory ; 24)
Includes index.
ISBN 978-3-11-023773-3 (alk. paper)
1. Mass media. 2. Narration (Rhetoric) 3. Discourse analysis, Narrative. 4. Intermediality. 5. Digital media – Influence. 6. Mass media and the arts. I. Grishakova, Marina. II. Ryan, Marie-Laure, 1946–
P96.N35I67 2010
302.23–dc22
2010039209

Bibliographic information published by the Deutsche Nationalbibliothek

The Deutsche Nationalbibliothek lists this publication in the Deutsche Nationalbibliografie; detailed bibliographic data are available in the Internet at http://dnb.d-nb.de.

Printing: Hubert & Co. GmbH & Co. KG, Göttingen
∞ Printed on acid-free paper

Printed in Germany

www.degruyter.com

Contents

Editors' preface

Like a rock thrown into a quiet pond, the concept of narrative, introduced on the intellectual scene by French structuralists, has generated a series of ripples that expand its relevance from language-based, book-supported literary fiction to other disciplines (discourse analysis, medicine, theology, law, history), to other semiotic modes (visual, aural, kinetic, interactive), and to other technologies (painting, photography, TV, film, the computer). The last two expansions form the object of intermedial storytelling.

The study of the storytelling abilities of different media has not awaited the technological explosion of the 20th century, nor indeed the development of a scholarly concept of medium. Plato's distinction between mimetic and diegetic modes of storytelling and Lessing's reflections on the expressive power of temporal and spatial art forms can be regarded as foundational for the study of narrative mediality. So does, in the 20th century, the work of Walter Ong (1982), a disciple of the media guru Marshall McLuhan, who investigated the impact of orality, writing, and print technology for narrative form. Intermedial narratology still lags behind literary narratology and the study of language-based narrative in various disciplines, but it is fast gaining ground, thanks in large part to the rapid expansion in the past twenty years of digital technology as a new narrative medium. The "digital turn" in the humanities (to adopt a terminology that has also produced the "linguistic turn" of structuralism and the "narrative turn" of interdisciplinary studies) has not only directed attention to what has come to be known as "new media," it has also, just as importantly, led to a reassessment of the configuring impact of older media for thought, narrative and the processing of information (a processing which would be called "reading" in an approach that privileges written language). The digital scholar N. Katherine Hayles (2002:28) has called for instance for a "media-specific analysis" of texts which takes into consideration what she calls the "materiality of the medium"—a term by which she means the physical support of inscription.[1] Thanks to this kind of approach, the

1 The drawback of this focus on "materiality" is that it ignores ephemeral physical manifestations, such as the spoken word. Hayles has been exclusively concerned with print and digital writing.

book, an object long taken for granted, has been rediscovered as a "technology" that affords unique forms of cognitive processing, while writing has emerged as a mode of expression capable of combining the visual and the linguistic, which means, the spatial and the temporal, by turning the disposition of graphemes on a page into a signifying device.

Yet for all its present popularity, the concept of medium remains strangely ill-defined.[2] What for instance is the medium of Jane Austen's novel *Pride and Prejudice*: is it language, is it writing, or is it the book? All three of these conceptions of medium have an impact on what kind of story can be told, though studying the importance of the book or of writing as a medium for *Pride and Prejudice* will not differentiate this particular novel significantly from most other novels. Focusing on its handling of language, by contrast, will result in a much more individuated analysis, since all uses of language are original, unique to the work. It is only when *Pride and Prejudice* is regarded as a member of the homogeneous class of standard novels, and is contrasted to experimental uses of the book or of typography, that its bookishness and graphic appearance become significant features. What this means for the study of narrative mediality is that if we want to capture the specific narrative power of whole media, we must often treat individual works as representative of an entire class. Yet we should not ignore the ability of individual works to expand the expressive potential of their medium by revealing possibilities that had remained so far unexploited. An example of this phenomenon is the creative uses of visual elements, such as photographs, maps, and sketches in recent novels. As we hope to show in this book, the close reading of individual works can be as fruitful for the study of narrative mediality as the general discussion of a type of medium.

Among the seven or eight definitions of medium offered by most dictionaries, the most useful to the study of storytelling media are the technological (a channel for long-distance communication) and the artistic (the material or form used by an artist, composer or writer). If medium is to acquire narratological relevance, it is as a "language" with a specific storytelling power, which means, as a basically semiotic phenomenon. While verbal language, sound and images are inherently semiotic phenomena, technologies are not. This is not to say that they do not affect narrativity: a channel of transmission can be visualized as a conduit of a certain shape that allows only certain objects to pass through. Actually, most media of transmission allows the passage of stories that were configured for other

2 And so does its English form: while the correct Latin form is *medium* (sing.), *media* (plur.), some scholars use the plural *mediums*, and others use *media* in the singular.

media: for instance, a film shown on television or a book on Amazon's Kindle reading machine. But channel-type media can also give rise to a distinct type of narrative that takes advantage of their distinct affordances. When this happens, the distinction between medium as semiotic phenomenon and medium as channel of transmission disappears, and technology acquires genuine narratological significance.

* * *

The present book is titled *Intermediality and Storytelling*. This choice requires some explanation. While the concept of medium has become very prominent in narratology, there are so many candidates available to refer to the relations between narrative and media that terminology has become a true nightmare: what, if any, are the differences between transmediality, intermediality, plurimediality, and multi-mediality (not to mention multimodality)? This terminological fuzziness extends to the project we are undertaking: should it be called multimedial, transmedial, intermedial, or simply "media-centered" narratology? Our intent in choosing intermediality for the title of this volume is to cast the net of the relations between narrative and media as widely as possible. As Werner Wolf (2008) observes, intermediality can be conceived in a broad and in a narrow sense. In its broad sense, the one we endorse here, it is the medial equivalent of intertextuality and it covers any kind of relation between different media. In a narrow sense, it refers to the participation of more than one medium — or sensory channel — in a given work. The opera, for instance, would be intermedial through its use of gestures, language, music, and visual stage setting. If intermediality is interpreted in a wide sense, other terms must be forged to differentiate its diverse forms, including a new term for the narrow sense. Wolf (2005) suggests "plurimediality" for artistic objects that include many semiotic systems, though "multimodality" has recently become widely used; "transmediality" for phenomena, such as narrative itself, whose manifestation is not bound to a particular medium; "intermedial transposition" for adaptations from one medium to another; and "intermedial reference" for texts that thematize other media (e.g. a novel devoted to the career of a painter or composer), quote them (insertion of text in a painting), describe them (representation of a painting through ekphrasis in a novel), or formally imitate them (a novel structured as a fugue). The importance of Wolf's catalog lies more in its spirit than in its letter: that is, in its distinction of the various types of relations between media and narrative, rather than the exact name given to these relations. In the name of this spirit, we have not tried to impose uniformity on the terminology used by our contributors, as long as they make their usage clear.

The essays collected in the following pages expand the project of the 2004 collection *Narrative Across Media* by covering a wider variety of storytelling media: photography, television, and blogs now receive their due, together with film, literature, musicals, comics, computer games and advertising — a form of discourse (rather than a medium proper) that makes use of multiple media. But *Intermediality and Storytelling* also innovates with respect to the earlier collection through its focus on two phenomena which have received considerable critical attention in the intervening years. The first is multimodality. Though narrative most certainly originated in oral storytelling — verbal language remaining by far the most powerful mode of signification for the representation of what makes a story a story, namely interactions between humans and between humans and the world — it is safe to assume that it has always relied on the many resources of face-to-face communication: sound, gestures, and facial expressions. From its very beginning, then, narrative performance has been a multimodal phenomenon. Later on came images, moving pictures and music. Though monomedial forms are perhaps the most heavily represented in Western cultures, thanks to the importance of language-only books, they are by no means the norm. The other feature that singles out this collection within the growing field of media studies is the focus of several of its chapters on what may be called a generalized form of ekphrasis: namely the representation of media, of types of signs, or of modes of perception within a work of another medium that relies on other types of signs.

* * *

The collection opens with Marie-Laure Ryan's paper "Fiction, Cognition, and Non-Verbal Media." Ryan examines critically the extension of the concept of fiction beyond its literary homeland. She argues that theory of fiction should be more than a taxonomic tool that would help to separate fiction from nonfiction: it should provide an access to the pragmatic and cognitive dimensions of fictionality and tell us something about the nature of fictional experience as well as about the cognitive relevance of fiction. Ryan discusses fictionality in literature, film, painting and other media and introduces the notion of indeterminacy to refer to a suspension of the judgment of fictionality.

Brian McHale and William Kuskin explore narrativity in comics. McHale uses Martin Rowson's parodic graphic-novel adaptation of T.S. Eliot's quasi-narrative poem, *The Waste Land,* as a case study to show how various forms of narrative and poetic segmentivity interact in this complex multimodal text. By integrating comics and graphic novels into twentieth-century literary history, Kuskin presents these genres as part of a specifically literary reassessment of the book medium. He argues that the importance of comics narrative lies not in its exclusivity but in its generality, in what it can teach about the medium of the literary book in the increasingly crowded field of narrative technologies.

Jason Mittell and Paul Cobley discuss the narrative techniques that storytelling media use to control viewers' cognitive and emotive reactions. Mittell examines television storytelling strategies in the light of contemporary understanding of the mechanics of memory. He does so by identifying the narrative techniques that TV serials exploit to engage viewers and enable long-term comprehension that transcends the division of the show into weekly episodes and annual seasons. The paper describes some of the techniques that television uses to cue previous events while still maintaining the possibilities of suspense and surprise. Cobley analyzes a series of audio-visual narratives from film and television, arguing that, in the wake of 9/11, they have intensified a sense of anxiety that has always been part of narrative. The post-9/11 narratives discussed in the paper articulate this anxiety through themes of surveillance and conspiracy that inspire a 'desire to know' of paranoid proportions.

The next two chapters are devoted to non-standard types of film. Samuel Ben Israel's paper provides a new perspective on films with multiple protagonists by introducing an approach borrowed from social psychology. Ben Israel argues that multi-protagonist films not only diverge from classical narration in various ways, but that in these deviations another kind of narration emerges, a relational narration that corresponds to a new social and philosophical conception of man in Western societies. Per Krogh Hansen examines the narrativity of musical films, a genre in which story is told through dialogue and acting, as well as through music, singing and dancing, without privileging any of these modes. By investigating how a story emerges from a simultaneous, interactive process of 'talking, singing and dancing', this paper provides a model of the functioning of narrative in musical films – and in multimodal texts in general.

In their contribution on photo narratives, Jan Baetens and Mieke Bleyen take issue with the essentialist view of the photographic medium as anti-narrative or a-narrative, and sketch a method for a narrative reading of photography, both in single and multiple images. In their analysis of the photonovel — a genre characterized by the presence of fictionality, sequentiality, and words, Baetens and Bleyen highlight its management of the blank areas of the photographic image as spaces where text can be inserted. They also present a close narrative reading of a wordless sequence of photographs: *Aujourd'hui*, a work by the Belgian photographer Marie-Françoise Plissart. Meanwhile, Markku Lehtimäki focuses on the American documentary *Let Us Now Praise Famous Men* (1941), a work that combines prose by James Agee and photographs by Walker Evans, as an example of a narrative that calls into question its own representational practices. Lehtimäki shows how the work shakes the readers' preconceptions by problematizing the relationship between the multimodal text and the harsh realities of the actual world.

Ruth Page's and David Ciccoricco's papers deal with new media. Page argues for a paradigm shift in the study of digital narratives that incorporate not only literary texts, but also online storytelling from 'everyday' domains. Her analysis integrates methods used for conversational stories (sociolinguistics and discourse analysis) with literary-theoretical considerations, two approaches often kept separate in narrative studies. Given its dual focus on text and talk, the essay revisits the central concept of *interactivity* in the light of the computer mediated user interactions that typically accompany web 2.0 platforms. Analysis of particular examples is taken from personal blogs, social networking sites, discussion forums and fanfiction. Ciccoricco's paper examines the narrative mechanics of the video game *God of War* (2005). Drawing on theoretical concepts from literature, film, and game studies, Ciccoricco demonstrates how gameplay influences narrative mechanics and how narrative complexity can be created in an interactive environment, despite the limitation of the player's choice of actions to what can be easily simulated by the game controls: mostly moving, fighting and collecting objects. His paper demonstrates that a narrative-theoretical framework can be applied to video games without losing sight of the specificity of gaming experience.

Elsa Simões Lucas Freitas analyzes a multimodal advertising campaign whose aim is to promote a public service television channel. When this campaign uses television, the medium that divulges the advertising message is, simultaneously, (1) the channel used for conveying it and (2) the object of the advertising message. Due to the effective conflation of narrative functions, the medium becomes the story. The analysis of the multimedia campaign provides new insights into the phenomena of intermediality, narrative and storytelling.

Alison Gibbons' case study is Mark Z. Danielewski's (2000) *House of Leaves*, a graphically complex novel whose multimodal design demands intense reader activity. Using a cognitive-poetic and text-world approach, the article suggests that such active participation creates what the author calls a *figured trans-world*, a textual world that not only invites readers to identify with the characters, but, in addition, dramatizes their role as readers by inviting them to play a corporeal role. According to Gibbons, the figured trans-world crucially accounts for both the readers' self-awareness of the book as object and their heightened involvement with the narrative in a literary experience that might itself be termed intermedial.

Marina Grishakova's paper draws on W. J. T. Mitchell's concept of "metapicture" and on W. Nöth's distinction between "metapictures" and "self-referential pictures". Grishakova introduces the concept of "intermedial metarepresentation" to refer to the intermedial and intersemiotic transfer within verbal and visual media. Intermedial metarepresentation combines self-referentiality with metadescription and reflects the semiotically mixed character of media. In verbal narratives, tension between the iconic and symbolic components of the medium arises from the dissociation of the "performative" (telling) and "cognitive" (showing) aspects of narration; in visual narratives, it becomes manifest due to discrepancy between images and verbal elements.

While maintaining a bi-focal attention to intra-textual multimodality and to transtextual relations between media, the papers demonstrate how intermedial and narrative studies may be mutually enriching and how the very process of semiotic mediation simultaneously imposes constraints and engenders growing complexity in the domain of storytelling practices.

Marina Grishakova, Marie-Laure Ryan

References

Hayles, N. Katherine (2002). *Writing Machines.* Cambridge, Mass: MIT Press, 2002.

Lessing, Gotthold Ephraim (1984 [1766]). *Laocoön: An Essay on the Limits of Painting and Poetry*, trans. and intro. E. A. McCormick. Baltimore: The Johns Hopkins University Press.

Ong, Walter J. (1982). *Orality and Literacy. The Technologizing of the Word.* London: Routlegde.

Ryan, Marie-Laure, ed. (2004). *Narrative Across Media: The Languages of Storytelling.* Lincoln: University of Nebraska Press.

Wolf, Werner (2008). "The Relevance of Mediality and Intermediality to Academic Studies of English Literature." In: A. Fischer and M. Heusser (eds.). *Mediality/Intermediality, Swiss Papers in English Language and Literature.* Tübingen: Gunter Narr Verlag, 15–43.

– (2005). "Intermediality," "Music and Narrative," and "Pictorial Narrativity." In: D. Herman, M. Jahn and M.-L. Ryan (eds.). *The Routledge Encyclopedia of Narrative Theory.* London: Routledge, 252–56, 324–29, and 431–35.

Marie-Laure Ryan
(University of Colorado at Boulder)

Fiction, Cognition, and Non-Verbal Media

The concept of fiction is as difficult to define technically as it is easy to grasp intuitively. The layman's interpretation is easily captured by the definition of the online encyclopedia Wikipedia: "Fiction (from the Latin *fingere*, 'to form, create') is storytelling of imagined events and stands in contrast to non-fiction, which makes factual claims about reality." This is followed by a list of all the genres of fiction: novels, short stories, fables, fairy tales, and beyond literature: films, comics and video games. If it is that simple to define fiction, this is very bad news for the philosophers and literary theorists who have sweated over the problem for the past 20 years. Aren't they trying to reinvent the wheel?

Fortunately for the theorists and philosophers, Wikipedia's definition leaves many questions unanswered. A truly meaningful theory of fiction should be more than an instrument by which to sort out all texts into fiction and non-fiction: it should also tell us something about how we experience these texts, what we do with them, why we consume them, and why it is important to make a distinction between fiction and non-fiction. It should, in other words, have a phenomenological and a cognitive dimension.

By cognitive dimension I do not mean that a theory of fiction should rely on cognitive science in a technical sense. This paper will not deal with how neurons fire in the brain when we experience fiction, nor with the importance of the creation of fictional worlds for the life of the mind, even though it is a topic of prime importance.[1] What I mean with cognitive dimension is that the judgment "is it a fiction" must influence the use of a text or the interpretation of a behavior. Here are three cases where these responses depend crucially on the judgment of fictionality.

The first example comes from a famous fictional character, the comic book hero Tintin, but we can imagine that the events happened in real

---

1 See Schaeffer 1999, Dutton 2008 and Boyd 2009 on the importance of fiction for the life of the mind.

life, rather than being part of a story. In *Cigars of the Pharaoh*, Tintin hears a woman being savagely beaten in the Sahara desert. A good boy scout that he is, he rushes to her rescue, but instead of being thanked for his chevaleresque behavior, he discovers that he has stumbled upon a movie set, and he must suffer the anger of the entire film crew. The action was feigned, and the participants were actors playing a role.

Whereas the failure to recognize fiction in the Tintin story is due to honest mistake, the 1999 movie *Blair Witch Project* deliberately seeks to produce misidentification. The film was presented on an advertising Web site as the content of the camera of three young people who were investigating reports concerning a witch and who were found dead in a forest in Maryland. Needless to say the advertisement was a hoax: the film was not an authentic document discovered *post-mortem*, but a simulation filmed by the actors themselves. A spectator who believes the Web site will watch the movie with much greater horror than a spectator who knows how the film was made.

In literature, the importance of the judgment of fictionality is demonstrated by a novel titled *Marbot: A Biography* (1981; Engl. trans. 1983) by the German author Wolfgang Hildesheimer. The novel tells the life of Sir Andrew Marbot, a nineteenth century British intellectual who frequented German and English romantic poets and published several books about aesthetics. The seriousness of the scholarship is demonstrated by footnotes and an index, and the authenticity of the hero is attested by illustrations, such as a photograph of Marbot's ancestral castle, his portrait by Eugène Delacroix, and the portrait of his mother by Henry Raeburn. The text makes no use of the narrative techniques typical of the novel, such as representations of the private thoughts of characters, and it uses hypothetical constructions to distinguish speculative interpretations from verifiable reports of facts. All these features fooled some early critics into taking the text for a genuine biography, especially since Hildesheimer had previously penned a Mozart biography. But Sir Andrew Marbot is an invented character, and the text is a fiction. A reader who mistakes the text for a biography may be tempted to look up Sir Andrew Marbot on Wikipedia, to search for his works in the catalog of a library, or even to write a dissertation about him. By contrast, a reader who correctly identifies the work as a novel will be entertained by the author's clever imitation of scholarly writing.

What the case of Marbot demonstrates is that one cannot always tell whether or not a text is a fiction by inspecting the text. There are admittedly what Dorrit Cohn (1999) calls "signposts of fictionality," and these signposts concern form as well as content: a text that makes heavy use of stream of consciousness, or that starts with "once upon a time," or that tells about a prince being turned into a toad is likely to be a fiction. But these signposts are optional.[2] While a text of non-fiction cannot use fictional devices without losing its credibility, a fictional text can always imitate non-fiction. It follows that fictionality is not a semantic property of texts, nor a stylistic one, but a pragmatic feature: a feature that tells us what to do with the text.

Philosophical approaches to fiction

Modern literary criticism (by this I mean the tradition of academic criticism that started in the twentieth century) was slow to discover the importance of the concept of fiction. It wasn't until the seventies that philosophers of the analytic school discovered fiction as a topic of interest. They were not particularly interested in the experience of literature and in the appreciation of works of art: what mattered to them were the truth conditions of sentences that refer to fictional individuals, such as Anna Karenina and Santa Claus. But this problem could not be divorced from the attempt to capture the nature of fiction through formal definitions.

Theories of fiction can be divided into two classes: those that take language-based storytelling as their starting point, and those that are neutral with respect to medium and narrativity. Among the approaches that treat fiction as a form of verbal storytelling are those of the philosophers John Searle, David Lewis, and Gregory Currie.

For Searle (1975), fictionality is an operator that affects the speech act of assertion. An assertion is a speech act that commits the speaker to telling the truth. But in fiction, the author only pretends to make assertions, or imitates the making of assertions. This act of pretense relieves the author of the responsibility to fulfill the sincerity conditions that relate to assertion: having evidence for the truth of the asserted proposition p, and believing the truth of p. Searle distinguishes a deceptive from a non-deceptive form of pretense, the first corresponding to lies, and the

---

2 In her discussion of the signpost of fictionality, Cohn (1999: 117) shrewdly observes that the example that Searle (1975: 325) chooses, reportedly at random, to show that "[t]here is no textual property, syntactic or semantic, that will identify a text as a work of fiction" flagrantly disproves his case: "Ten more glorious days without horses! So thought Second Lieutenant Andrew Chase-Smith recently commissioned in the regiment of King Edwards Horse, as he pottered contentently in a garden on the outskirts of Dublin on a sunny Sunday after-noon in April nineteen-sixteen." (From Iris Murdoch, *The Red and the Green*). The report of inner life discredits this passage from being non-fiction. But I think that this unfortunate example does not invalidate Searle's claim, because he is speaking of necessary properties.

second to fiction. Though the language of fiction is often indistinguishable from the language of nonfiction, readers are protected from taking the textual statements as genuine information by their recognition of the author's act of pretense. Insofar as fictionality is determined by the author's intent, a text cannot pass from nonfiction to fiction or vice versa. The notion of fiction as pretense has been widely accepted, but Searle's account is problematic in its handling of the statements within fiction that refer to real-world entities. According to Searle, Conan Doyle pretends to make assertions when he refers to Sherlock Holmes, but he makes serious assertions when he refers to London. It is hard to reconcile this patchwork of fiction and nonfiction with the homogenous impression that the world of the Sherlock Holmes stories makes on the reader. Moreover, the "pretended assertion" analysis remains ambiguous as to who is doing the pretense: Searle claims that in the case of a fiction told by a heterodiegetic, invisible narrator (what followers of Ann Banfield would call the no-narrator type of fiction), the author pretends to be a version of himself who believes in the truth of the story, while in the case of homodiegetic narration, the author pretends to be a radically different individual. While it is indeed much more difficult for authors to distanciate themselves from the views of anonymous heterodiegetic narrators than from the judgments of individuated ones — the narrator's personality acting as a shield — this analysis could lead to the questionable view that readers project the individuating features of the author unto heterodiegetic narrators. Finally, the idea of "pretended assertion" should be extended to "pretended speech act" if the theory is to account for the rhetorical questions and mock commands to the reader that pepper fictional discourse.

Another philosopher of the analytic school who addressed the issue of fictionality is David Lewis, the most prominent theorist of the plurality of worlds. For Lewis (1978), fiction is a story told as true about a non-actual possible world by a narrator situated within this other world. A nonfictional story by contrast is told as true about our world by one of its members. The difference between fiction and nonfiction is consequently a matter of reference world.

In Lewis' model, possible worlds stand as various distances from the actual world, depending on how many propositions take a different truth value in each world. The close worlds will contain many individuals who have counterparts in the actual world (for instance, the world of Tolstoy's *War and Peace*), while the remote worlds will have an entirely different population (the world of J.R.R. Tolkien's *Lord of the Rings*). Counterparts of the same individual can have different properties in each possible world: for instance, the Napoleon of a historical novel could say things that he never said in reality or even win the battle of Waterloo. This idea of counterpart relation solves the problem encountered by Searle when the text refers to actual entities. For Lewis, the world of the Sherlock Holmes stories is not created by a mixture of fictional and nonfictional statements, but by a fully fictional discourse that describes a possible world linked to the actual world through many counterpart relations. But since counterparts are not exact copies of each other, the author of the Sherlock Holmes stories is fully free to modify the geography of London or the biography of Napoleon.

While Searle describes fiction as a particular modality of the speech act of assertion — this is to say, as a meta-speech act — Gregory Currie (1990) regards it as an alternative to assertion. His definition of fictionality is formulated through a model inspired by Searle's analysis of the speech acts of assertion, command and promise, and by the philosopher H. Paul Grice's account of meaning in language. According to Currie, a speaker S performs the illocutionary act of uttering fiction if S utters a proposition P to an audience A with the intent that

(1) A would make-believe P
(2) A would recognize S's intention of (1), and
(3) A would have (2) as a reason for doing (1).[3]

The principal merit of this analysis is to open up the definition of fiction from a purely logical to a cognitive and phenomenological account by introducing the important notion of make-believe. But make-believe is not a distinct type of speech act, it is a use of the imagination that manifests itself in a wide variety of human activities: not only in storytelling, but also in dramatic acting, in playing with dolls or toy soldiers, in wearing masks and costumes, in adult role-playing games such as Dungeons and Dragons, and of course in those computer games where players identify with an avatar. Currie regards fictional make-believe as a subset of this larger class of make-believe (1990: 71). For him, storytelling illustrates fictional make-believe, while playing with dolls and toy soldiers would illustrate the nonfictional form.

For Kendall Walton, by contrast, all make-believe is in essence fiction, and all fiction is make-believe. This postulate enables him to propose a truly medium-free theory of fiction. As Walton declares, "not all fiction is linguistic. Any adequate theory of fiction must be able to accommodate pictorial fictions, for instance, as well as literary ones." (1990: 75). Walton's central thesis is that "in order to understand paintings, plays, films,

3 This is a somewhat simplified formulation. I have left out the specifications that are not directly relevant to my presentation of Currie's approach.

and novels, we must look first at dolls, hobbyhorses, toy trucks and teddy bears" (1990: 11). In their games of make-believe, children takes objects and pretend that they are something else: for instance, a doll is taken by the players for a baby, a toy soldier for a real soldier, and a certain tree for the jail in a game of cops and robbers. By standing for something else, the objects manipulated by the players become what Walton calls "props in a game of make-believe." The function of a prop in a game of make-believe is to encourage the play of the imagination.

Walton's notion of "game of make-believe" thus involves two distinct features: taking something as something else; and inspiring the imagination rather than conveying information. Both of these features can be applied to narrative literature as well as to children's games: readers pretend that the text written by the author is the discourse of a fictional narrator, and they use this discourse to construct the mental image of an imaginary world, just as children pretend that a certain stump is a bear, and use the stump to imagine a world where they are being chased by ferocious animals.

My own approach to fiction is a blend of ideas inspired by all these theories. Like Walton, I regard fiction as a mode of representation; this is to say, as an essentially mimetic activity. It is common to talk about an opposition between fiction and reality, and also about an opposition between representation and reality. Some theorists, especially those influenced by post-modern theory, conclude that every representation and every narrative is a fiction. I call this stance the "Doctrine of Panfictionality" (Ryan 1997). But the association of fiction and representation on the basis of their common opposition to reality rests on a fallacious symmetry. If we look at the three examples of fiction that I gave above, namely *Tintin*, *Blair Witch* and *Marbot*, only the *Tintin* example opposes directly fiction and reality. Tintin must decide if the events he is observing are pretended or if they really count. The contrast pits represented actions against real actions, and fiction designates the act of representing actions. But in the other two examples, *Marbot* and *Blair Witch*, fictional representation is not opposed to reality, but rather to another type of representation: we must decide if the author of *Marbot* represents a real or an imaginary person; and if the movie footage of *Blair Witch* captures real or simulated events. The notion of pretense, or make-believe, allows us to bring *Tintin*, *Blair Witch* and *Marbot* under a common denominator. In *Tintin*, fiction consists of pretending to perform actions as opposed to performing these actions for good, while in *Marbot* and *Blair Witch*, fiction consists of pretending to represent reality, as opposed to representing reality. In contrast to the Doctrine of Panfictionality, this account recognizes both a fictional and a non-fictional mode of representation.

Why do people care about "pretending to represent reality"? If fiction matters to us, it is because it evokes a world to the imagination, and the imagination takes pleasure in contemplating this world. But even though fiction represents a foreign world, it represents this world as if it were actual, using in language the indicative rather than the conditional mode. By taking the appearance of factuality, it asks its users to transport themselves in imagination into this foreign world. I call this act of transporting oneself fictional recentering (Ryan 1991: 21–23).

Recentering should not be confused with another phenomenon associated with fiction, namely the phenomenon of immersion. Whereas recentering is a logical operation which we deliberately perform whenever we read (or watch) a work of fiction, immersion is an experience created by artistic devices. The text must be able to bring a world to life, to give it presence and to capture our interest in a story. All fictions require recentering to be properly understood, but only some of them turn recentering into immersion. This lack of immersivity can be a matter of artistic failure, but it can also be a deliberate effect. Many postmodern texts try to block immersion through the use of self-referential devices that remind the reader of the constructed nature of the fictional world. Conversely, immersion is not restricted to fiction. I can be immersed in a true story without having to recenter myself into a foreign world.

When recentering takes place, the text is no longer regarded as making statements about the real world, or at least, not directly,[4] and the fictional world is contemplated for its own sake. It would seem that recentering occurs whenever a text describes an imaginary world, but this is not the case. When I make a counterfactual statement, for instance "If Napoleon had not invaded Russia he would not been exiled on St Helena," I invoke an imaginary state of affairs, but my purpose is to say something about the real world: namely that invading Russia was a critical mistake of Napoleon. By making this statement I remain centered in reality. The same is true of the practitioners of the genre known as counterfactual history (Ferguson 1999). When historians speculate about other directions that history could have taken, they present these alternative histories from the point of view of a member of the real world, and they do so in order to evaluate the decisions of the people who control the course of history. The non-fictional variety of counterfactual history

4 In the equivalent of an indirect speech act, a fictional text can suggest that its moral, or its general statements (of the form: all x) are valid not only in its own world, but in the real world as well. This is a case of double reference. Statements concerning individuals (there is an x, such as…), by contrast, cannot participate in this double reference.

must however be distinguished from its fictional counterpart, the novel of alternate history (Hellekson 2001). A good example of this genre is Philip Roth's novel *The Plot Against America* (2004), which represents an America where Charles Lindbergh is elected President in 1940, supports the Nazi regime, and takes humiliating measures against the Jewish population. In counterfactual fiction there are no formal markers of irreality, and the reader pretends that the imaginary situation really happened.

Extending concept of fiction to other media

The importance of the judgment of fictionality lies in the fact that it determines with respect to which world the information transmitted by the text should be evaluated. If the judgment says fiction, this information concerns a non-actual possible world, where it is automatically true (unless the narrator is judged unreliable), since the world is created by the text. If the judgment says "non-fiction," the information describes the actual world, but since this world exists independently of the text, it can be either true or false with respect to this world. The judgment of fictionality is most important for language, because language articulates clearly defined propositions that make a truth claim, and truth value is evaluated with respect to a specific world. For instance, "Emma Bovary committed suicide by taking arsenic" is true in the world of Flaubert's novel but false in our world; while "Napoleon died on St Helena" is true in our world, and in many fictional worlds, but false in the novel of Guido Artom *Napoleon is Dead in Russia* (1970).

Images present a much more problematic case for the theory of fictionality because, as Sol Worth observed (1981), they are unable to make propositional acts with unambiguous content. Think of the sentence: "The cat is on the mat." It has a well-defined argument — cat; through the definite article, it picks a specific referent — this cat, no other; and its predicate tells us that it is about a specific property of the cat: being on the mat, not about its color or its breed or how much of the mat the cat's body is covering. The message of a picture representing a cat on a mat is much fuzzier. The spectator will certainly identify the image as representing a cat, but instead of reflecting on the fact that the cat is on the mat he may pay attention to the green eyes of the cat, to its long fur, to the fact that the cat is looking at the photographer, and so on. The picture shows a cat by showing many of its visual features, but unlike language, it does not unambiguously force some of these features to the attention of the spectator at the expense of others. We know what the picture shows, but we can't tell exactly what it says, because saying requires an articulated language with discrete signs.[5]

If the image is a photograph and not a painting, however, it will say something much more specific. Because photography is a mechanical method of capture, it bears witness to the existence of the cat and to its presence in front of the camera. An image obtained by mechanical means is not only an icon bearing a visual resemblance to an object, but also an index related to its referent through a causal relation: the mark on a sensitive surface of the patterns of light reflected by the object. This is why Roland Barthes wrote: "The photograph is literally an emanation of the referent… Discourse combines signs which have referents, of course, but these referents can be and are most often 'chimeras.' Contrary to these imitations, in Photography I can never deny that *the thing has been there*" (1981: 80).

The same, of course, holds for film and videos. Thanks to their technological objectivity, photos and movies offer a much more convincing testimony of the objects or events they represent than images created by the human hand, or even verbal descriptions. We need only think of the importance of the video tape in the Rodney Clark affair, or of the scandal created by the photos showing prisoners being humiliated at the Abu Ghraib prison in Baghdad. Photo and film may admittedly be manipulated, in which case they will not give a reliable testimony of the existence of their referent or of its presence in a certain place at a certain time. A manipulated photo or film is the equivalent of a lie in language, unless the manipulation is meant to be recognized. But it is precisely the ability to make truth-functional statements that make it possible for a type of signs to either lie, tell the truth….or be used as fiction.

Fiction and film

If there is one medium besides language for which the distinction between fiction and non-fiction is unanimously considered relevant, both by theorists and by the public at large, this medium is film. The relevance of the distinction comes from the fact that film can be used to convey truths about the real world. In a documentary film the camera captures two types of events: first, events that happened in the world independently of their being filmed, for instance rescue efforts after an earthquake, and

5 The expressive — and narrative — power of pictures can however be enhanced by segmenting them into discrete units, as is the case in comics.

second, events staged for the camera, in which people perform real actions, or speak in their own name without playing a role, for instance a basket-weaver demonstrating her trade and talking about her life. Fiction film, by contrast, captures simulated events that do not count in the real world, namely the role-playing of the actors, and it relies on the pretense that the actors really are the characters.

The distinction between make-believe and behavior that counts also affects photography, even though the fictional use of photography is much less widespread than the fictional use of film. But the work of the Victorian photographer Julia Margaret Cameron illustrates the difference: one of her photographs, titled "King Lear and His Daughters," captures actors who impersonate the characters of Shakespeare's drama, while another, "Alfred, Lord Tennyson," represents a historical character. From the portrait of Lord Tennyson we can derive information concerning the real world — how the poet looked like — but the King Lear picture only helps us imagine the non-actual world of Shakespeare's drama.

Virtually every theorist of fiction and every theorist of the cinema will agree that when we watch a film we imagine that the actors are the characters. But this observation does not exhaust the question of what exactly we pretend to be doing when we watch a film. Here we have a choice between two possibilities.

The first is to extend to film the analysis that describes our experience of language-based storytelling. In the medium of language, we do not perceive events directly, but rather read or hear a report of events by a narrator. We do not merely imagine that p and q happened, but that a narrator reports p and q to any audience, and sometimes we suspect that p and q were not exactly as reported. If we extend this analysis to film, when we watch a film we do not imagine that we are witnessing events, but rather, that somebody is showing us the events through the medium of film. In other words, when we watch a fiction film, we imagine that it is a kind of documentary film, and that the images on the screen are just that — images captured by a camera. Or less literally, we imagine that the fiction film is a story told by a narrator using certain visual devices, and that this narrator is distinct from the actual filmmaker(s), since he is showing as true what we know to be simulated. In this view, fiction film involves in make-believe a storyteller, just as literary fiction involves a narrator. There is a whole school of film critics who endorse such a view: Seymour Chatman (1990), François Jost and André Gaudreault (1990), and even Christian Metz (1970), who coined the term "Grand Image Maker" to designate the filmic equivalent of the narrator.

The alternative to a narrator-based conception of film is to claim that film presents life unmediated. This is, in its broad lines, the view defended by David Bordwell (1985) and Gregory Currie (1995). This approach does away with the concept of a filmic narrator, and treats the spectator as an eye, or as a consciousness directly focussed on the scene of the action. In drama, this is known as the missing fourth wall: nobody "shows" the events on the stage to the spectator, the spectator just happens to see them, as if he were looking through a hole in the wall. While the narrator-based approach regards the fiction film as some kind of imaginary equivalent of the documentary film, this approach drives a wedge between the two. When we watch a documentary, we are aware that the events were captured on film by a camera, and this knowledge is what gives the documentary its testimonial value. What we watch is not the events themselves, but the recording of these events by technological means, a recording that brings proof that the events really happened. But when we watch a fiction film, according to the direct perception analysis, the medium disappears from our mind; it is not part of our game of make-believe that somebody filmed the events.

I personally prefer this approach to the idea of a filmic narrator, but the idea that the spectator pretends to observe life unmediated is not free of problems. As Gregory Currie has argued (1995: 170–79), we should not cast the spectator into the role of a hidden observer who witnesses the events, because this would lead to unnatural assumptions. For instance, if the spectator plays the role of an observer, a movie could not suggest that a murderer enters a house without being seen by anybody. When a film shows a close-up of lovers, the spectator certainly does not imagine that he is spying on the characters and that he is located a few inches away from them. And since in film image and sound often come from different sources, for instance in the case of extradiegetic music or voiced-over narration, the observer would have to be split in two in order to apprehend both the image and the soundtrack. I cannot think of an entirely satisfactory solution to this problem; the best answer I can come up with is to say that the spectator does not pretend to be a flesh-and-blood observer located on the scene, but rather sees himself as disembodied consciousness that moves around the fictional world as freely as the camera.

Fiction in painting

I have already stressed the main reason for the questionable status of the concept of fiction in man-made pictures: they lack the ability of language to make precisely identifiable truth claims; and they lack the ability of mechanical methods of capture to bear witness of the existence of what they show. The problematic character of the idea of pictorial fictionality is demonstrated by the variety of responses that the question has generated.

The most radical position is that of Kendall Walton. For Walton, fictionality in the visual domain is synonymous with pictorial representation: "Pictures are fictions by definition" (1990: 351). Why does Walton claim that all pictures are fictional? Let's recall that for him a fiction is a "prop in a game of make-believe." In the case of pictures, the game of make-believe consists of pretending that we are directly seeing the depicted object. For instance, if I see a picture and I identify it as the picture of a ship, I imagine that I am seeing a ship, even though I know that I am facing a canvass covered with paint. My game of make-believe consists of identifying the various features of the ship: this is the hull, this is the mast, this is the sail, etc. As soon as we identify a shape as the shape of an object, we engage in a game of make-believe, since we know that the shape is not the object that it depicts.

Walton's position encounters two problems. First, it may be true of paintings done in a realistic style that we imagine facing the represented object and seeing it directly; but in other cases, for instance with representations done in a very sloppy or schematic style, we will process the image as the sign of an object, rather than directly as an object, because they do not convey a sense of its presence. We may say of a schematic representation "this is a ship," but we really mean "this represents a ship."

Second, this treatment of pictorial fictionality creates a deep asymmetry between visual and language-based representation. In the case of language-based representations, Walton distinguishes fictional ones, which give rise to make-believe, and non-fictional ones, which give rise to belief. In language, "fictional" designates a particular mode of representation. But in the case of the visual arts, "fictional" becomes synonymous with representation itself. Now if all pictorial representations are fictional, the diagnosis of fictionality becomes automatic, and it does not carry cognitive consequences. Why not then admit that fictionality does not matter in painting?

This is the position taken by the Swiss theorist and artist Lorenzo Menoud (2005). For Menoud, fictionality depends not only on the ability to convey truths, but more fundamentally, on the ability to tell stories. Since narrative is about the evolution of a world in time, the only media capable of fictionality are those that present a temporal dimension, namely: language, the theatre (including mime and dance) and the cinema. Pictures cannot be fictional, because their static nature makes them unable to represent changes of state. It is consequently pointless to raise the issue of fictionality in painting and photography. The problem with this interpretation is that pictures are not entirely devoid of narrative ability.

A series of still pictures can very well be used to tell a story, even without language, as we see with some comics and sequences of paintings. Even an isolated picture can suggest a story if it captures what Lessing (1984) called a pregnant moment: a moment that suggests both a past and a future.

Yet another conceivable solution to the problem of pictorial fictionality is to regard the domain of painting as more or less evenly divided between fiction and non-fiction, with every individual picture falling on one side of the border. This approach rests on the notion of reference world. Just as language-based texts can represent either the real world or an imaginary world, so do visual representations: "View of Delft" by Vermeer can be said to convey information about the real world Delft, while "Swans Reflecting Elephants," a painting of a fantastic landscape by Salvador Dali, only pretends to represent reality: it inspires make-believe rather than belief. This is the position taken by Gregory Currie (1990) and by the French theorist Jean-Marie-Schaeffer (1999). For Currie, a painting of a unicorn will be fictional if it suggests that unicorns exist in the world of the painting, and if the painter does not believe in unicorns. On the other hand, the portrait of the Duke of Wellington by Goya is non-fictional, because it captures the artist's perception of the Duke; this means that the spectator can use it to gather information about what the Duke of Wellington looked like. In this interpretation, the painter records faithfully what he sees, and his eye and brush function as a kind of photographic camera. But Currie encounters difficulties with the portrait of Henry Kahnweiler by Picasso, an image done in a Cubist style that bears only the slightest resemblance to a human being. Currie (1990: 40–41) suggests that the appearance of the portrait is a kind of metaphorical representation, the visual equivalent of describing a real person by saying that he was a "giant," or an "angel," or a "greedy vulture." But later he admits that we cannot derive any kind information about Henry Kahnweiler's appearance from this portrait. Would a fictional explanation do better? We could perhaps say that the painting is a fictional representation of a counterpart of Henry Kahnweiler in a non-actual possible world, just as the novel *War and Peace* represents a counterpart of Napoleon in a world where Pierre and Natasha exist? This interpretation does not offer a viable solution either, because we would have to imagine that in this possible world Kahnweiler is flat and broken up into a hundred of little pieces. Regarding this portrait as a fiction is no more satisfactory than regarding it as non-fiction.

The three approaches to pictorial fictionality discussed so far do not exhaust the field of possibilities. I would like to defend a fourth position: some pictures are fictional, some are non-fictional, and for some of them the decision is irrelevant.

There is a whole class of pictures for which the judgment of fictionality makes sense, because these pictures are illustrations of texts that are themselves either fictional or non-fictional. For instance, the illustrations of a guidebook for the identifications of birds or flowers are clearly non-fictional: we use them to gather information about the real world. On the other hand, the illustrations of a fairy tale display an imaginary world for its own sake. In all these examples, pictures inherit their fictionality from a text, and the analysis of language-based fiction applies indirectly to them. But this criterion does not work very well for paintings that illustrate stories told to be believed, such as Biblical narratives. Consider a nativity scene from the Italian Renaissance. Is it fictional of factual? We could say that it is fictional because the painter used his imagination, or we could say that it is non-fictional because the painter meant it as the illustration of a story told (or received) as true. But in this case the question of fictionality does not really seem to matter: we will not look at the picture differently if our particular theory makes us decide one way or another.

Rather than inheriting fictionality from a text, some pictures could be considered fictional by analogy with the fictionality of language, film and drama. Here the common denominator is the notion of game of make-believe. A painting will be considered fictional if it represents models who are playing a role. Conversely, we could say that when the models pose as themselves, the image documents the appearance of the model, and it can be considered non-fictional. In both cases, the image must be done in a reasonably realistic style to allow a judgment of fictionality. By this standard, a portrait of Simonetta Vespucci by Botticelli titled "Portrait of a Woman" is non-fictional, but a portrait of the same model where she poses as the Virgin Mary would be fictional.

Does this mean that in non-fictional painting artists represent their perception, and in fictional painting they pretend to do so? The trouble with this analysis is that because artists only represent their perception to some degree, the judgment of fictionality becomes highly subjective and no longer depends on a reasonably clear-cut authorial intent, as it does in literature.

Another problem with this idea is that many paintings, because of their style, cannot be regarded as a record of perception, whether genuine or faked. When we look at the "portrait" of Henry Kahnweiler, we do not think: "this how Henry Kahnweiler appeared to Picasso," but rather: this is what the sight of Henry Kahnweiler inspired to Picasso's imagination. The painting is neither a record of perception, nor a make-believe record of perception. It is just a image. With such a painting, it is not necessary to decide whether it represents our world or another world, because such a judgment does not carry any cognitive consequences.

A very large number of man-made pictures fall into this no-man's land between fiction and nonfiction. We appreciate them without asking ourselves any questions about their relation to reality. The spectator does not run the risk of misinterpreting them by relating them to the wrong world, and if this risk does not exist, there is no need to make a judgment of fictionality. Even when a painting presents itself explicitly as a representation of a real-world referent, as is the case with Vermeer's "View of Delft" or the Duke of Wellington portrait by Goya, we don't care about its documentary value when we look at it as an *artwork*. If Vermeer had added features to the skyline of Delft for purely compositional reasons, if Goya's portrait of Wellington were not faithful to the model, this would not affect our appreciation of the art of the painter. Similar liberties would not be forgivable in the text of a historian about either Delft or Wellington. The aesthetic attitude toward a painting makes the diagnosis of non-fictionality irrelevant. The same could perhaps be said of language-based texts; when we read Rousseau's *Confessions* as a literary work, we are much more forgiving toward its potential inaccuracies than when we read it as a historical document. But the main difference between painting and language-based texts is that only some texts, but almost all paintings are created as aesthetic objects. This means that almost all paintings, but only some texts, invite us to cancel the importance of the question of accuracy with respect to reality.

Indeterminacy in various media

Painting is not unique in producing works that lie outside the dichotomy of fiction and nonfiction. All media present a zone of indeterminacy. The size of this zone varies from medium to medium, depending on the ability of this medium to articulate precise truths and to narrate a story. In language, fictional and nonfictional uses are roughly of equal importance, but the indeterminate zone is minimal. It is occupied by concrete poetry, or by some lyrical poems, especially by poems that make general rather than particular statements. When I read Baudelaire's poem "Les chats," for instance, I do not need to decide whether the cats described in the poem belong to the actual world or to a fictional world, and whether the poet plays a role or speaks in his own name. I am not alone in questioning the fictional status of poetry: Käte Hamburger (1968), one of the pioneers of the modern theorization of fiction, considered lyric poetry to be what she called a "Wirklichkeitsaussage," a discourse about the real world, rather than a fictional genre. I will not go as far as Hamburger — I call some poems, but not all of them, fictionally indeterminate. We cannot ascribe the entire lyrical genre to either fiction or non-fiction, as we can with the genre "novel"[6]: when it comes to fictionality, poems should be judged on an individual basis.

In film, fiction is more widespread than documentary, and it is hard to find cases that fall in the middle. The indeterminate zone could perhaps be represented by certain artistic montages of images recorded from real life that do not tell a story. Photography is mostly non-fictional. I will place in the no man's land a picture strongly manipulated by Photoshop or a collage of different images. Abstract works, whatever their medium, will always fall in the indeterminate zone, since both fictionality and non-fictionality presupposes a mimetic dimension. Media such as architecture and music, which are unable to articulate propositions, will fall entirely in the indeterminate zone, unless they present an inherited fictionality. This will happen when they illustrate a fictional text, as do Cinderella's castle at Disneyland or the symphonic poem *The Sorcerer's Apprentice* by Paul Dukas. On the other hand I would not call Tchaikovsky's *1812 Overture* non-fictional, even though it refers to historical events, because it does not make precise and verifiable statements about these events.

Conclusion

In conclusion I would like to return to the question of the relations between fictionality and narrativity. There is no doubt that language-based narrative is the cradle of the theory of fictionality. Some time between the eighteenth and early twentieth century, the notion of fiction became a recognized category in Western cultures, arguably as the result of dual causes: the rise of the novel as the most prominent form of literature, and the importance of the notions of truth and falsity in these cultures. In earlier times, people were not concerned with fiction and its poorly defined opposite of non-fiction, but rather, with poetry, and within poetry, with the three classical genres of epic, drama and lyric.[7]

Once the concept of fiction took roots in Western culture, it quickly grew branches that stretched beyond its original domain of application. Since invented stories exist in all cultures, the concept was easily extended

---

6 I write this fully aware of the existence of a genre called the "nonfiction novel" or "true fiction." Insofar as authors are not asked to provide documentation for their claims, it still abides by the convention of a fictional contract.

7 The lack of a culturally recognized category equivalent to our concept of fiction does not mean that the members of this culture are unable to distinguish stories told as true about the real world from stories about imaginary worlds; it rather means that other taxonomic criteria are considered more relevant.

to older forms of narrative native to cultures that did not make use of the concept of fiction: forms like fairy tales, legends, jokes, tall tales, fables, and epic poetry. Even myths were occasionally treated as fiction, even when in their culture of origin they were told as sacred truth and not as invented stories.

Another expansion was toward what Plato called mimetic forms of storytelling. Plato distinguished two ways of presenting stories: in the diegetic mode the story is reported, while in the mimetic mode the story is directly shown. Since both modes are capable of presenting invented stories,[8] there is no reason to limit the concept of fiction to the diegetic mode. Through its extension to drama and to film, the concept of fiction became emancipated from language.

During the twentieth century, literary authors started producing prose texts that subverted narrative structures, but were still a product of the imagination. Narrativity thus became an optional feature of fiction. For instance, many of the texts gathered by Jorge Luis Borges under the title *Ficciones* (1962) do not tell stories. They consist instead of philosophical reflexions, of descriptions of imaginary books, or of ethnographic accounts of non-existing cultures. Another example of non-narrative fiction is Samuel Beckett's novel *The Unnamable* (1965), which represents the thoughts that pass through the mind of a speaker. Since it does not assert anything about the external world, it does not tell a story.

When philosophers invoked pretense and make-believe to explain the nature of fiction, they created a bridge between literature and games. On one hand, games of make-believe were recognized as an activity that represents the same spirit of play as fictional storytelling, maybe even as the ancestor of literary fiction; on the other hand, role-playing games such as Dungeons and Dragons or computer games became widely recognized as a form of fiction. Whenever a game creates a concrete world and invites the players to play a role in it, it becomes a fiction.

Once a theory has been elaborated, there is a strong tendency to expand its domain of application. If narrativity could become an optional feature of fiction, if language could become optional, why not go all the way and look for manifestations of fictionality in non-verbal media of very limited narrativity, such as painting, or even architecture and music?[9] But these applications of the concept of fiction no longer correspond to culturally recognized modes of classifications. The general public cares

8 It is dubious that the mimetic mode can function non-fictionally: in the theatre, for instance, the mere fact that characters are impersonated by actors makes the performance fictional, even when the story is "true to life."

9 See for instance Rabinowitz 2004 for the claim that music can be fictional.

about fictionality in film and verbal texts; but it is only the theorists who ponder fictionality in painting, architecture and music. The further the notion of fiction is stretched from its original domain of language-based narrative, the more this stretching becomes a purely theoretical game, and the less it corresponds to cognitively meaningful judgments. This is why the zone of undecidability grows, as we extend the notion of fictionality to more and more art forms and to more and more media.

As we play the game of theoretical expansion, we should avoid two strategic errors. The first is to try to fit all media into a rigid mold inherited from language-based narrative. This is what happens when one regards visual media such as film as the discourse of a fictional narrator. This approach provides a solid definition of fictionality, but it ignores the particular nature of each medium. The second *caveat* is to completely re-design criteria of fictionality, as we adapt the concept to new media. This is what happens when Walton claims that all pictures are fictional by definition, but makes a distinction between fictional and non-fictional representation in language. Such an approach respects the differences among media, but at the cost of a unified conception of fictionality.

How then can we reconcile the centrality of language-based narrative for the phenomenon of fiction with the idea that fiction can appear in other forms and media? I propose to start from an account of fictionality in language-based narrative, and to expand it by analogy to other cultural artifacts but without insisting on a literal or on a complete equivalence. There will be prototypical and marginal forms of fictionality, depending on how many features they share with the prototypical case of language-based narrative. Since an analogy requires only partial resemblance between its two terms, not a complete identity, this proposal avoids the problems of the first and the second approach: unlike the first, it respects the particular nature of each medium; and unlike the second, it attributes common features to both the typical and marginal forms. These features are those that truly make a cognitive difference: pretense, make-believe and the display of an imaginary world for its own sake.

References

Artom, Guido (1970). *Napoleon is Dead in Russia*. Trans. Muriel Grindrod. New York: Atheneum.

Banfield, Ann (1982). *Unspeakable Sentences: Narration and Representation in the Language of Fiction*. London: Routledge & Kegan Paul.

Barthes, Roland (1981). *Camera Lucida. Reflections on Photography*. Trans. Richard Howard. New York: Hill and Wang.

Beckett, Samuel (1965). *Three Novels: Molloy. Malone Dies. The Unnamable.* New York: Grove Press.

Bordwell, David (1985). *Narration in the Fiction Film.* Madison: University of Wisconsin Press.

Boyd, Brian (2009). *On the Origin of Stories: Evolution, Cognition, and Fiction.* Cambridge, Mass.: The Belknap Press of Harvard University Press.

Borges, Jorge Luis (1962). *Ficciones.* Ed. Anthony Kerrigan. New York: Grove Press.

Chatman, Seymour (1990). *Coming to Terms: The Rhetoric of Narrative in Fiction and Film.* Ithaca, N.Y: Cornell University Press.

Cohn, Dorrit (1999). *The Distinction of Fiction.* Baltimore: The Johns Hopkins University Press.

Currie, Gregory (1990). *The Nature of Fiction.* Cambridge: Cambridge University Press.

– (1995). *Image and Mind. Film: Philosophy and Cognitive Science.* Cambridge: Cambridge University Press.

Dutton, Denis (2008). *The Art Instinct: Beauty, Pleasure, and Human Evolution.* New York: Bloomsbury Press.

Ferguson, Niall, ed. (1999). *Virtual History: Alternatives and Counterfactuals.* New York: Basic Books.

Gaudreault, André, and François Jost (1990). *Le Récit cinématographique.* Paris: Nathan.

Hamburger, Käte (1968). *Die Logik der Dichtung.* Stuttgart: Klett.

Hellekson, Karen (2001). *The Alternate History: Refiguring Historical Time.* Kent, OH: Kent State University Press.

Hergé (1975). *Cigars of the Pharaoh.* Boston: Little, Brown.

Hildesheimer, Wolfgang (1983). *Marbot: A Biography.* Trans.Patricia Crampton. New York: G. Braziller.

Lessing, Gotthold Ephraim (1984). *Laocoön: An Essay on the Limits of Poetry and Painting.* Trans. Edward A. Mc Cormick. Baltimore: The Johns Hopkins University Press.

Lewis, David (1978). "Truth in Fiction." *American Philosophical Quarterly* XV: 37–46.

Menoud, Lorenzo (2005). *Qu'est-ce que la fiction?* Paris: Vrin.

Metz, Christian (1974). *Film Language: A Semiotics of the Cinema.* Trans. Michael Taylor. New York: Oxford University Press.

Rabinowiz, Peter (2004). "Music, Genre, and Narrative Theory." In: Ryan, Marie-Laure (ed.). *Narrative Across Media.* Lincoln: Nebraska University Press, 305–28.

Roth, Philip (2004). *The Plot Against America.* Boston: Houghton Mifflin Co.

Ryan, Marie-Laure (1991). *Possible Worlds, Artificial Intelligence, and Narrative Theory.* Bloomington: Indiana University Press.

Ryan, Marie-Laure (1997). "Postmodernism and the Doctrine of Panfictionality." *Narrative* 5.2: 165–188.

Schaeffer, Jean Marie (1999). *Pourquoi la fiction*? Paris: Seuil, 1999.

Searle, John (1975). "The Logical Status of Fictional Discourse." *New Literary History* 6: 319–32.

Walton, Kendall (1990). *Mimesis as Make-Believe, On the Foundations of the Representational Arts.* Cambridge, Mass: Harvard University Press.

Worth, Sol (1981). "Pictures Can't Say Ain't." In: Gross, Larry (ed.). *Studying Visual Communication.* Philadelphia: University of Pennsylvania Press, 162–184.

Brian McHale
(The Ohio State University)

Narrativity and Segmentivity, or, Poetry in the Gutter

The general subject of this paper is how narrative interacts with other forms of organization in complex "mixed" texts. Narrative theory tends to treat non-narrative organization in narrative texts as supplemental, a little "something extra," auxiliary to narrativity; and it does so even in cases of mixed or hybrid texts, such as narrative poems or graphic novels, in which narrativity competes with other forms of organization, or may even be subordinated to them. I want to argue that this sort of interaction should be regarded not as incidental to narrative theory, but rather as a dimension of narrative form that a sufficiently capacious theory should be able to accommodate.

The interaction between narrative and non-narrative organization becomes especially visible whenever textual materials undergo transformation into a different form — for instance, in cases of *translation* and *adaptation.* Elsewhere I have investigated from this perspective a case involving multiple translations of the "same" (verse) narrative; here I will consider one particularly complex case of cross-media adaptation. First, however, a few theoretical tools need to be placed in readiness for use.

1.

Contemporary narrative theory has paid relatively little attention to narrative poetry,[1] and as a consequence the interaction between narrative organization and the poetic organization of texts remains woefully undertheorized. This is no minor oversight, considering the cultural importance of the corpus involved, not to mention its sheer size. After all, a great many poems, including some of the most highly valued texts in the canons of world literature, narrate or imply stories. To overlook poetic narrative is

1 There are honorable exceptions to this rule, such as the work of Peter Hühn and his colleagues on narrative in lyric poetry; see Hühn 2004 and 2005; Hühn and Kiefer 1992.

to overlook an indispensable corpus. Moreover, the interaction of narrative and poetic form in narrative poems is in many ways paradigmatic for other interactions in "mixed" texts (as we shall see), so the neglect of narrative poetry also threatens to impede progress in theorizing other transgeneric and trans-media interactions.

Narrative theory's neglect of poetry means, among other things, that it isn't even clear how we should characterize the *parties* to the interaction: what exactly is interacting with what? If we assume that what makes a narrative a narrative is its quality of *narrativity* (however that might be defined)[2], then what is its opposite number, the quality that makes a poem a poem — poetry's *dominant*, as narrativity is narrative's dominant? Presumably, it is *this* quality, whatever it might be, that narrativity interacts with in a mixed text of narrative poetry.

One particularly compelling answer has been offered by the poet and critic Rachel Blau DuPlessis, and corroborated independently, in somewhat different terms, by John Shoptaw. Poetry, according to DuPlessis, is defined by the criterion of *segmentivity*; segmentivity is poetry's dominant, as narrativity is narrative's. Segmentivity, "the ability to articulate and make meaning by selecting, deploying, and combining segments," is "the underlying characteristic of poetry as a genre." Poetry is *segmented* writing, "the kind of writing that is articulated in sequenced, gapped lines and whose meanings are created by occurring in bounded units [...] operating in relation to [...] pause or silence." Segments come in a variety of kinds and sizes, ranging from words, or even just letters, which may "hang alone in an open space," through lines, up to "larger page-shapes" such as stanzas or other configurations of language and spacing. The ends of segments may be signaled by special devices, or not:

> Line terminations may be rounded off by rhyme, or by specific punctuation marks, but they are basically defined by *white space*. Recurrent patterns of parallel sounds (rhyme) are not necessary to mark line ends, though rhyme is popularly taken to indicate poetry (or its lack), a fact which should actually draw our attention to the crucial importance of articulated segments in the definition of poems.

Segments of one kind or scale may be played off against segments of another kind or different in scale; for instance, "Sentence or statement may be draped, or shaped, across a number of lines," as in traditional *enjambement*. In general, DuPlessis concludes, "The specific force of any individual poem occurs in the intricate interplay among the 'scales' (of

2 See, for instance, Fludernik 1996: 20–43; Herman 2002: 85–113; McHale 2001; Prince 1982 and 1999; Ryan 1992; Sternberg 1992.

size or kind of unit) or comes in 'chords' of these multiple possibilities for creating segments."

Shoptaw's name for what DuPlessis calls segmentivity is the more traditional-sounding term *measure*. Like DuPlessis, however, Shoptaw is committed to accommodating formally radical, "free" and even "prosaic" poetry alongside traditionally metrical, lyrical, and figurative kinds, so his definition of measure is more capacious than the traditional sense of measure as meter. Shoptaw defines a poem's measure as "its smallest unit of resistance to meaning" (212). Measure determines where *gaps* open up in a poetic text, and a gap is always a provocation to meaning-making. It is where meaning-making is interrupted by *spacing*, where the text breaks off and a gap (even if only an infinitesimal one) opens up, that the reader's meaning-making apparatus must *gear up* to overcome the resistance, bridge the gap and close the breech.

Shoptaw specifies the scales or levels of measure that are possible in poetry. Poetry can be *word-measured*, as it is, for instance, in certain modernist one-word-per-line poems, such as William Carlos Williams's "The Locust Tree in Flower"; it can even be measured at the level of the *letter*, as in modernist experiments like e.e. cummings' poem "r-p-o-p-h-e-s-s-a-g-r." Poetry can be measured at the scale of the *phrase*, as it is, for instance, in Emily Dickinson's poetry; it can be measured at the scale of the *line*, as it normally is in most lyric poetry; it can be measured at the level of the *sentence*, as in prose-poetry or in the Language poets' practice of the "New Sentence"; and it can be measured at the level of the *section*, as in sonnet cycles or in sequences like *The Waste Land* (about which I will have much more to say below). It can also be measured (though Shoptaw never explicitly says so) at the level of the *stanza*, as in stanzaic narrative forms such as *ottava rima* or the Spenserian stanza. What DuPlessis calls "chords," Shoptaw characterizes in terms of the counterpoint of *measure* and *countermeasure*. Poetry that is predominantly measured at one level or scale — say, the level of the *line* in Milton's blank verse, or of the *phrase* in Dickinson's poetry — may be countermeasured at other levels or scales: in Milton's case, that of the *sentence*, counterpointed against his blank verse lines; in Dickinson's, the levels of *line* and *stanza*, counterpointed against her poetry's predominant phrase-segmentation.

This concept of countermeasurement, or of "chords" of segments, gives us a convenient tool for beginning to talk about the interaction of narrativity and segmentivity in narrative poems. Narrative, too, is segmented writing, in a sense, though it is not dominated by segmentivity, as poetry is. Story may appear continuous, a "flow" of events, but if one only turns up the magnification high enough, sequence dissolves into the granularity of kernels and catalyzers (or bound and free motifs, depending upon one's terminology). On the level of discourse, narration is segmented into multiple, shifting voices, while point of view is segmented by constant micro-shifts of focalization. Time in narrative is measured or segmented, speeding up or slowing down from segment to segment, or shifting from present-time to flashback to flashforward, or from singulative to iterative mode. Narrative space, too, is segmented, as is narrative consciousness. Everywhere in narrative, at all levels, the continuous and "smooth" can be broken down into the segmented or measured, and gaps abound, of various kinds, on all levels. In poetic narratives, narrative's own segmentation interacts with the segmentation "indigenous" to poetry to produce a complex counterpoint among segments of different scales and kinds — "countermeasurement," in Shoptaw's terminology; "chords," in DuPlessis's.

Elsewhere (McHale "Beginning") I have demonstrated how segmentivity and narrativity interact in four English-language translations of the "same" narrative episode from *The Iliad* of Homer. In this episode, from Book XVI of the poem, Achaeans and Trojans battle literally over top of the corpse of the slain Trojan hero Sarpedon, while on a different plane of action, Zeus debates with himself whether or not to allow the Trojan Hector to kill the Achaean Patroclus. Each of the four translators — George Chapman (early seventeenth century), Alexander Pope (early eighteenth century), and Richard Lattimore and Christopher Logue (both mid- to late-twentieth century) — must decide how to deploy the shifts of focalization in this passage relative to the segmentation of their chosen verse-measure: long-lined rhyming "fourteeners" in Chapman's case, closed heroic couplets in Pope's, long-lined free verse in Lattimore's, and shorter-lined free verse, eccentrically divided into sections, in Logue's. Narrative segmentation and poetic segmentation interact differently in each of these versions. Line is countermeasured against sentence in Chapman's and Lattimore's versions (albeit somewhat differently in each), and they both leave the focalization of this episode ambiguous; not so Pope, in whose version line and syntax strictly coincide, and the decisive shift in focalization from battling humans to Zeus occurs *between* lines; while Logue also decisively shifts the focalization, but uses the spacing between *sections* of lines to do so. Each version measures and countermeasures differently, both with respect to poetic form and with respect to the articulation of narrative; each sounds a different chord of segments.

2.

Segmentivity is not limited to verbal art. There are obvious analogues to the segmentation of poetic narrative in *visual* narrative forms, for instance in cinema. Cinematic narrative partly coincides with, but partly counterpoints the rhythm of film segmentation, its pattern of editing or montage. A cut in a movie is roughly analogous to the gap between one poetic segment or unit of measure and the next, and as we know from Shoptaw, it is when a gap opens that we are provoked to intervene and bridge the gap by *making meaning*. Infinitesimal though it may be, the space between one shot and the next is one of the places where meaning is made in cinema. In some cinema traditions, notably in classic Hollywood cinema, the cut is designed to be as invisible as possible, and the viewer's constructive role to be as automatic and subliminal as possible; in other traditions, especially those influenced by Eisenstein's aesthetics of montage, the cut is meant to be conspicuous, and viewers are called upon to intervene more actively to make meanings. An example of the latter kind of cinematic meaning-making is the famous match-cut in Kubrick's *2001: A Space Odyssey* (1968), where, from one frame to the next, the ape-man's bone weapon, flung into the air, is replaced by a space-shuttle in free fall. The film's entire meaning, it could plausibly be argued — its concepts of time and evolution, its reflection on technology and futurism, and so on — all hinge on that one match-cut.

Instead of narrative cinema, however, let me turn to another, perhaps more obvious analogue of poetic segmentation, in a different medium — "sequential visual art," or comics. Just as the spacing between segments or units of measure provokes meaning-making in poetry, and just as the cut or edit does (more or less conspicuously, more or less subliminally) in movies, so it is the space between the panels that mobilizes meaning-making in comics. Scott McCloud, in *Understanding Comics* (1993), a poetics of comics in comic-book form, emphasizes the crucial function of the blank space that separates one panel in a comic-book from the next, called in comics-speak the *gutter*. "Despite its unceremonious title," McCloud writes, "the gutter plays host to much of the magic and mystery that are at the very heart of comics. Here in the limbo of the gutter, human imagination takes two separate images and transforms them into a single idea" (66). McCloud illustrates the concept of the gutter with two juxtaposed panels: on the left, an image of a man shouting "Now you die!!" as he threatens another man with an ax; on the right, a city skyline at night, over which the cry, "Eeyaa!" sounds. Every read will infer that a murder has been committed, though we are shown no image of it; the murder occurs in the gutter, as it were, and we readers are accomplices to it. The gutter is the reader's domain; it is here that we perform acts of "closure" that allow narrative to jump the gap between one panel and the next. "There's something strange and wonderful that happens in this blank ribbon of paper," McCloud writes. "Comics ask the mind to work as a sort of in-betweener — filling in the gaps between panels as an animator might" (88). "Several times on every page," he continues, "the reader is released — like a trapeze artist — into the open air of the imagination... then caught by the outstretched arms of the ever-present next panel!" (90).[3]

To sample the sort of gap-filling work that we are routinely called on to do "in between" the panels of comics, consider Figure 1, a wordless page from a graphic novel. Though this sequence is a good deal more enigmatic than the ax-murder between the panels of McCloud's example, I think it still remains perfectly legible. We see two men in a vacant landscape, the one nearer to us holding out a cricket in his hand, the man further away gesticulating as though giving a speech. Between the first and second panels, the men move apart; between the second and third, the man in the hat approaches the other man, who has fallen to his knees; between the third and the fourth, the kneeling man lurches to his feet; between the fourth and the fifth, he topples full-length to the ground. Easily negotiating the gutters between the panels, we connect up these segments into a coherent (if somewhat mysterious) narrative sequence.[4] There is nothing special about this; apart from the absence of words to help us along, this page reflects a normal comics reading experience.

What *is* special about this example, however, is that it comes from a graphic-novel adaptation of a narrative poem (or let's say, more circumspectly, a *quasi*-narrative poem). This is a page from Martin Rowson's 1990 adaptation of T.S. Eliot's modernist poem, *The Waste Land* (1922). Now, adaptations of "classic" prose narratives in comics form are hardly a novelty — there is even a graphic-novel version of Proust's *Recherche* — but adaptations of poetry are few, so Rowson's adaptation of Eliot gives us a rare opportunity to reflect a little on the possible parallels between segmentation in narrative poetry and segmentation in comics.[5]

---

3 See Berlatsky, whose account of McCloud's poetics of the gutter is akin to my own; however, Berlatsky is mainly concerned with *frames* and *framing* (in both the physically liminal and the cognitive senses of those terms), not with *gaps* and *spacing*, as I am.

4 We also register a change of focalization, a shift from an objective to a subjective point of view, in the last two panels: we view the falling man more or less from the perspective of the man in the hat.

5 On Rowson's *Waste Land*, see Tabatchnik 2000, especially 84–5, where the author anticipates the analysis in terms of McCloud's poetics of the gutter than I am undertaking here. I would also like to acknowledge Paulo Campos, whose unpublished paper, "Whodunit?

Figure 1. Image from *The Waste Land* by Martin Rowson (Rowson 1990, unpaginated). Copyright © 1990 Martin Rowson. All images reproduced by permission of Rogers, Colerdige & White Ltd.

As it turns out, Rowson's adaptation is actually quite complex, and we will need right at the outset to give a little consideration to some of the many dimensions of its complexity. First of all, the original on which it is based, *The Waste Land,* is a highly prestigious canonical text — more than canonical, *hyper*-canonical, among the *most* canonical texts of the mod-

---

The Strange Case of Eliot and the Annotated Poem," deals in part with Rowson's *Waste Land.*

ernist era, along with Joyce's *Ulysses*. To recast such a text in the popular medium of comics must inevitably result either in inadvertent *kitsch* or deliberate *parody*; in Rowson's case, it results in parody. An act of cultural iconoclasm, evidently malicious in intent and animated by a spirit of resentment,[6] Rowson's *Waste Land* nevertheless is a *serious* parody. As with all serious parodies, in the process of parodying the original the parodist also illuminates and clarifies aspects of its poetics.[7]

One aspect that Rowson illuminates is the *narrative* dimension of *The Waste Land*. A moment ago, I backtracked and characterized *The Waste Land* as a "*quasi*-narrative" poem; another critic calls it a "poetic *anti*-narrative" (Kinney 180). However you want to characterize it, *The Waste Land* bears an oblique and difficult relationship to forms of narrative coherence, and to the tradition of narrative poetry. Rowson's graphic-novel adaptation in effect *narrativizes The Waste Land*. In other words, Rowson takes a text that, like many other modernist and avant-garde texts, is only sporadically, obliquely and problematically narrative, and supplies the missing or "lost" narrative elements.

"Lost" is the operative word here, since, as we know, the poem in its original version — before Ezra Pound undertook to edit it — contained much more continuous narrative than the published text of 1922. As we learn from the invaluable *Facsimile and Transcript* of the *Waste Land* manuscript, the poem was drastically "de-narrativized" in the course of its collaborative composition by Eliot and Pound. Three long passages of connected narrative were eliminated altogether, and other narrative passages rendered elliptical by editing. The result of all this cutting was drastically to shift the proportions of the poem away from narrative and toward lyric, and to open gaps where there previously had been none, or to widen and deepen the gaps that had been there all along.

---

6 See Rowson's own account of his motives, in *The Independent on Sunday*: "Personally, I'm still of the opinion that Eliot's *Waste Land* is obscurantist, mawkish, constipatedly pious, elitist, inconsistent, miserable over-rate nonsense which wouldn't look out of place on the inner sleeve of one of Led Zeppelin's later albums."

7 Parody serves invaluable heuristic and pedagogical functions, at its best rendering visible features and patterns that might otherwise pass unnoticed, taken for granted; defamiliarizing what is too familiar, it casts an alienating light on what passes for "natural." It was with this sense of parody's value in mind that Viktor Shklovsky once called Sterne's *Tristram Shandy* "the most typical novel in world literature" (170). Obviously, he did not mean that most novels, or even very many of them, resemble *Tristram Shandy*, but that, in parodying the conventions of the novel, *Tristram Shandy* laid those conventions bare for our examination, as in a sort of x-ray. Coincidentally — or perhaps not coincidentally at all — Martin Rowson is also the author of an astonishing graphic-novel version of *Tristram Shandy* (1996).

This loss of narrative coherence seems to have provoked an anxious reaction in Eliot himself. This is how I choose to understand Eliot's notorious annotations, appended to the end of the poem: not as "filler" for a manuscript that was a little too slim to be published as a separate book,[8] nor as an attempt to educate or bully his readers, or to condescend to them, but as compensation for lost narrativity. Eliot's notes seek to restore at a different level the narrative bridges that had been destroyed in the editing process.[9] In the first of these notes, Eliot refers us to Jessie Weston's *From Ritual to Romance*, indicating that his fragmentary narrative should be filled out or completed using materials from Weston's narrative. In effect, *From Ritual to Romance* frames *The Waste Land*, supplying the master-narrative within which Eliot's poem is inscribed. In another note, perhaps the most notorious of them all, to line 218 of the poem, Eliot informs us that the mythological figure of Tiresias, "although a mere spectator and not indeed a 'character', is yet the most important personage in the poem, uniting all the rest [...] What Tiresias *sees*, in fact is the substance of the poem" (125). This note seems to invite us to reconstitute a narrator/focalizer for the poem, and thus to take the first steps toward recovering its "lost" narrative continuity. A number of the poem's commentator's have been willing to follow Eliot's lead here by interpolating a protagonist to whom the poem's experiences could occur, in effect recasting *The Waste Land* as the "adventures of Tiresias."[10]

---

8 For an account of the complex history of *The Waste Land*'s publication, see Rainey 1998: 77–106.

9 Another way to approach this would be to ask whether the gaps in *The Waste Land* are located primarily at the level of *story* or at the level of *discourse*; if the latter, then presumably the "lost" story materials could be reconstructed, but if the former, then there is no story-level coherence to be recovered in any case. The answer, I think, is *both*: *The Waste Land* is certainly incoherent at the discourse level, but it is also incoherent at the story level, more so in the edited version, perhaps, than in the original manuscript, but the original version is already drastically "deficient" as story. It is this deficiency of coherence at the story level that Eliot's notes and cross-references seek to redress.

10 Of these, the most egregious is surely Calvin Bedient, whose narrativization of the poem I can't resist quoting: "The plot itself might be Bunyanized [*i.e.*, allegorized] as follows: After suffering a loss of Romantic belief in the vicinity of the Hyacinth Garden, Pilgrim, hearing a voice reproach him with being the Son of man, and uncertain of his way, visits the fortune-telling booth in Vanity Fair, and is warned to Fear Death by Water. Heeding this baneful advice, he walks round and round in Hell in the Unreal City, where only the crowds flow, sharing their quiet desperation. He marries Belladonna, the Lady of the Rocks — a fiery Medusa who turns his penis to stone — and wanders the banks of the Thames, a voyeur of the slimy rats' bellies, cigarette ends, horny London traffic, typists scarcely forced. At length, no longer able to bear the absences of the Hanged Man, weary of the Blind Seers and Fake Goddesses of Vanity Fair, he ascends the Mount of Voluntary Dryness, praying for rain. Successfully meeting the challenge of the Perilous Chapel, he receives a sign of acceptance from the Heavens, and with Divine Help gathers wisdom

Rowson declines this particular narrativizing gambit of Eliot's, and instead narrativizes *The Waste Land* differently, against the grain. He does so by "translating" it into the genre-code of hardboiled detective fiction and film. Here, then, is yet another dimension of this adaptation's complexity: it involves not just *two* media, verbal art and graphic novel, but also a *third*, the movies. Rowson draws narrative and visual motifs from the entire hardboiled detective genre, but especially from John Huston's film *The Maltese Falcon* (1939), based on a novel by Dashiell Hammett (1930) and Howard Hawks's *The Big Sleep* (1946), based on a Raymond Chandler novel (1939). Rowson narrativizes Eliot's poem by interpolating a protagonist — a West Coast detective named Chris Marlowe — and a conventional detective-story plot involving the search for a lost object — the Holy Grail itself, in fact. In other words, he overlays the plot of *The Maltese Falcon* with elements of Eliot's mythological sub-texts.[11]

Now finally we are in a position to glimpse the full complexity of Rowson's adaptation. One consequence of "triangulating" among three different media — poetry, comics and movies — is that *several* different kinds of segmentation or spacing are potentially relevant, and may be coordinated or counterpointed with one another. The original poetic text of Eliot's *Waste Land* involves one kind of segmentation; the comic-book medium in which Rowson recasts the poem involves another kind of segmentation; while the cinematic medium to which the comic-book alludes visually and thematically potentially introduces yet another kind of

---

for a further purification. At the end, he sits fishing on the Shore of Beatitude, the Arid Plains safely behind him, his line baited for God-food" (Bedient 1986: 60). For skeptical views of Bedient's and others' narrativizations of Eliot's poem, see Litz 1973: 6; Brooker and Bentley 1990: 6.

11 The conjunction of *The Waste Land* with the hardboiled detective genre is less arbitrary and whimsical than it might first appear. First of all, Eliot belonged to the same generation as the founders of the hardboiled detective genre: Eliot and Raymond Chandler were exact contemporaries (as Rowson observed in his *Independent on Sunday* piece), while Dashiell Hammett was only a few years younger. Hammett's first hardboiled detective stories appeared in the pulp magazine *Black Mask* in 1922 and 1923, exactly contemporaneously with *The Waste Land*, first published in Britain in October 1922, and in the United States in November, with book versions appearing in December in the States and in Britian in 1923. It is a little hard to imagine which bookstore or newstand would have carried *both* the December 1922 *Black Mask*, containing Hammett's first hardboiled detective story, and the November 1922 issue of *The Dial*, containing the first American publication of *The Waste Land*; nevertheless, from a strictly chronological point of view, it's not out of the question. Such synchronicities aside, hardboiled detective fiction can be seen to reflect the same experience of modernity as high-modernist texts like Eliot's; as Paula Geyh writes, "hard-boiled detective fiction represents the popular version of literary modernism" (2001: 26). Besides Geyh, see also Christianson; Eburne. Of these three, only Christianson seems to have been aware of Rowson's graphic novel, and even he encountered it too late to take it into account, mentioning it only in the very last note of his article.

segmentation. We might even want to take into account the intrinsically "gappy" nature of the detective story itself, a genre that is characterized by the opening and filling of narrative and epistemological gaps — a genre that asks the question, *whodunit?*

In the interests of keeping complexity within manageable limits, however, I propose to consider here only the relationship between poetic segmentation, on the one hand, and the poetics of the gutter on the other. Let's begin with Eliot's original poem. As we recall from Shoptaw, *The Waste Land* is the paradigmatic example of a poem measured at the level of the *section*; in other words, it is segmented into groups or blocs of lines, and it is the discontinuity between sections, and the relationships among them that drives meaning-making in the poem. *The Waste Land* is divided into five sections of unequal length, each separately numbered and titled. Moreover, each titled section is in turn divided into several sub-sections which differ from each other formally and in terms of the narrative situations they express or evoke.

Let's consider only the poem's first section, "The Burial of the Dead" (Eliot 135–7).[12] Leaving aside content for the moment, visual inspection alone tells us that "The Burial of the Dead" is divided into at least four segments by three white spaces — in effect, the equivalent of gutters in comics. The second of these segments is further sub-divided into three by the intrusion of a quatrain that is visually distinct — deeply indented, italicized — and even linguistically distinct (German instead of English).[13] One section-division is *not* indicated visually: the one between lines 7 and 8, where both form (line-length, rhythm) and content change abruptly, but without any corresponding spatial gap.

Each segment differs from the others in speaker, characters, and narrative situation. The first segment (ll. 1–7) offers gnomic or proverbial sayings in a collective voice ("us"), and seems to lack a narrative situation altogether:

> April is the cruellest month, breeding
> Lilacs out of the dead land, mixing
> Memory and desire, stirring
> Dull roots with spring rain.

---

12 I will not reproduce the entire section here, not only because it is widely available, but also because of the prohibitive cost of permissions.

13 In the first published edition of 1922, this interpolated quatrain is set off by white space from the blocs of lines the precede and follow it; in the layout found in Eliot's *Complete Poems and Plays, 1909–1950,* these framing white spaces have been eliminated. I am grateful to Murray Beja for calling this difference to my attention.

In the second (ll. 8–18), a woman evidently named Marie reminisces about her aristocratic childhood:

> And when we were children, staying at the archduke's,
> My cousin's, he took me out on a sled,
> And I was frightened.

The third segment (ll. 19–30) is set in a desert landscape:

> … you know only
> A heap of broken images, where the sun beats,
> And the dead tree gives no shelter, the cricket no relief,
> And the dry stone no sound of water.

Next comes the German quatrain (ll. 31–4), actually an excerpt from Wagner's *Tristan und Isolde*, evoking the narrative situation of that opera; another fragment from *Tristan* appears in line 42. In lines 35–41 appear memories of what seems to have been an erotic encounter with someone called the "hyacinth girl." After the next gap or gutter comes a rather fully narrativized scene (ll. 43–59) involving a reading of the tarot cards by the fortune-teller, Madame Sosostris. Finally, after yet another gutter, the section ends with a scene on the streets of London (ll. 60–76), where the speaker accosts an acquaintance named Stetson, and asks him cryptic questions:

> "That corpse you planted last year in your garden,
> "Has it begun to sprout? Will it bloom this year?
> "Or has the sudden frost disturbed its bed?

This is the disjointedly narrative material that Rowson adapts in the first nine pages of his graphic novel. He begins by creating a framing situation with no precedent in Eliot's poem, one borrowed from the hardboiled detective genre: the private detective in his office, receiving a potential client and listening to her story (see Figure 2).

Rowson recognizes that the first seven lines of the poem and the next eleven belong to different situations, even though they are not separated visually; so he distributes them to different speakers, assigning the first seven lines to his detective Marlowe's *voice-over narrative* (another detective-movie convention), the other eleven lines to the client, Countess Larisch — she becomes the "Marie" of the childhood reminiscence.

How is one to negotiate the gap or gutter between the poem's first undivided bloc of lines, which ends with Marie and her cousin the archduke in the mountains, and the beginning of the second bloc, set in the "red rock" desert? Rowson does so by producing a *narratological* shift: from the external scene to an *internal, mental* one, and from the present moment to one in the past. While half-listening to his client's story, Marlowe

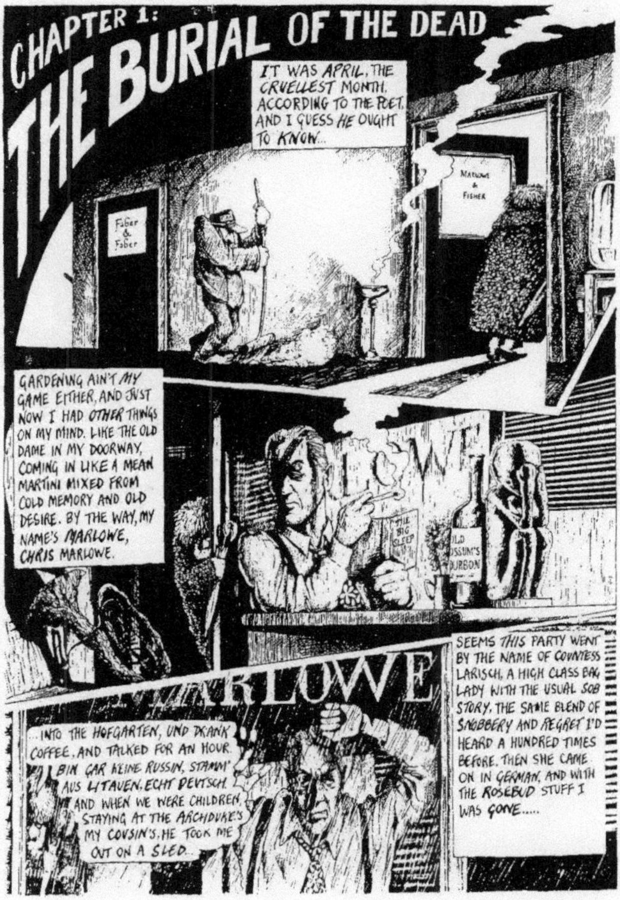

Figure 2

flashes back to the last time he saw his partner Miles, who is now dead, at a burnt-out casino in a desert town (see Figure 3).

The transition itself occurs at the top of the new page, in a triangular panel crowded into the upper left-hand corner — or better, it occurs as we cross the *gutter* between that panel and the next, accompanied by the voice-over narrative that helps us motivate the shift in visual imagery. In the panel at the bottom of the page, Rowson assigns lines 19–20 of the poem to the voice of Miles — "What are the roots that clutch, what branches grow/ Out of this stony rubbish?" — and he illustrates line 22 — "A heap of broken images." We have already looked at the next page (see

Figure 3

Figure 1), where Rowson's panels coincide very closely with Eliot's *line*-measurement of his material, with each panel corresponding to one, two, or at most three lines of Eliot's poetry.

On the following page, the transition to Eliot's next segment occurs once again in the upper left-hand corner, as Marlowe returns from his flashback to the present scene in his office (see Figure 4).

Countess Larisch is still there, still talking, and the quatrain from Wagner is assigned, plausibly enough, to her voice. The transition that follows is one of the purest examples of "closure," in McCloud's sense: we leap from one scene to the next, from Marlowe's office to a rainy street-scene, across the width of the gutter, filling in the intervening events our-

Figure 4

selves. As usual, however, the voice-over helps us close the gap, informing us that the Countess has hired Marlowe to recover a lost object (he's not sure exactly what). Out on the street, Marlowe encounters the hyacinth girl, who claims to have known him in the past, and who sings the detached line from *Tristan.*

I omit the next page, where Rowson digresses from *The Waste Land* to scenes from other poems by Eliot ("The Love Song of J. Alfred Prufrock" and the quatrain poems about Sweeney). The following two pages illustrate the scene of the tarot reading at Madame Sosostris's (see Figure 5).

Initially, Rowson follows the order of Eliot's scene rather faithfully, almost line-by-line, but as the scene progresses he diverges from Eliot in

Figure 5

order to prepare for the next, rather elaborate transition (see Figure 6). Why does this transition need to be so elaborate? Rowson has complicated matters for himself, spatially, by making his protagonist a West Coast detective, but needing to relocate him to London, where Eliot's poem is mostly set. Even without introducing this arbitrary complication, however, the poem itself already has plenty of abrupt spatial displacements of its own, as we have seen: from the mountains to the desert, from the desert to the hyacinth garden, from the garden to the scene of Madame Sosostris's fortune-telling, and still to come, from this indoor scene to London Bridge. This time Rowson solves his spatial problem not by introducing

Figure 6

a flashback, but by recourse to conventional narrative motifs of the hard-boiled genre. While attending the session at Madame Sosostris's, Marlowe is served a drugged drink; he is loaded unconscious into a packing-crate, then flown to London. Note the panel in the lower right-hand corner showing the map of the plane's itinerary from Los Angeles to London, a cliché of adventure movies from *Casablanca* (1942) to *Raiders of the Lost Ark* (1981) and beyond.

This panel, in effect, corresponds to the gap or gutter between Eliot's next-to-last segment and the last one. At the top of the next page Marlowe awakens on a street in London (see Figure 7).

Figure 7

The panels on this page illustrate the visual and auditory material in Eliot's lines 61–8. On the next page comes the encounter with Stetson (see Figure 8), which Rowson converts into a classic chase-scene, borrowing his visual imagery this time not from *The Maltese Falcon* or *The Big Sleep* but from Carol Reed's *The Third Man* (1949).

The example of Rowson's *Waste Land* adaptation is so complex that conclusions are hard to draw. Nevertheless, I can venture a few tentative generalizations. First of all, Rowson's adaptation confirms what we already knew, namely that the *principle* of segmentivity organizes *both* poetic texts and "sequential visual art" (McCloud's definition of comics), even though the *kinds* of segmentivity differ. Secondly, this difference in kinds of segmentivity means that Rowson often segments his version in

Figure 8

different places than Eliot does; he *re*-segments *The Waste Land*, filling in where Eliot left gaps, and opening gaps where Eliot's text was continuous and unsegmented. Rowson throws a narrative frame around the poem, re-framing it; he creates new characters, and distributes the poem's lines among them; he introduces flashbacks to motivate certain discontinuities in the poem, and spatial displacements to motivate others. In other words, he narrativizes the poem, and in doing so he fills in some of the gaps that Eliot left.

But narrativizing also opens gaps, especially when one narrativizes using the comics medium. Rowson's narrative, like *all* comics narratives, is full of gaps — literally full of gutters, in-between spaces where the work of closure is left to the reader. Rowson's *Waste Land* is at least as full of gaps as the notoriously "gappy" poem that he is narrativizing. Nevertheless, we cannot map the gaps of Eliot's *Waste Land* one-for-one directly onto the gutters of Rowson's version; one version is not *homologous* with the other. But the two versions *are* analogous: Rowson's comic-book is gappy just as *The Waste Land* is gappy, though sometimes in different places. Here, then, is one reason why Rowson's parody is such an illuminating one: despite the manifest indecorousness of coupling a hyper-canonical poem like *The Waste Land* with a low-art medium such as comics, the analogy between them proves to be a sound one — the "fit," it turns out, is surprisingly good.

Both Eliot's verse *Waste Land* and Rowson's comics adaptation of it are mixed or hybrid texts in which narrativity and segmentivity interact, though they interact differently in each case. The narrativity of Eliot's text is weak or muted, implied by the poem's ancillary materials (its infamous notes) but present only obliquely in the text proper. Here segmentivity — measurement at the level of the line and especially of the section — dominates. Rowson's adaptation narrativizes *The Waste Land*, restoring its "missing" or effaced narrative, though the story it restores is a different one than we might have inferred from Eliot's notes. Rowson also *re-segments* Eliot's poem in the process of adapting it as a comic book, using the gutters of the comics medium analogously to the way Eliot used spacing in the verbal medium. Here, though the hybridity of Eliot's original is preserved, narrativity and segmentivity are much more evenly balanced than in the verse *Waste Land*, and it would be difficult to say which is dominant.

One surprising finding of this analysis is that comics appear to be more akin to poetry, even to prestigious avant-garde poetry, than we might have supposed. Comics, too, like poetry, are measured and countermeasured; they sound chords of segments. And comics, also like poetry, elicit meaning in the place where meaning stalls out — in between, in the gutter.

References

Bedient, Calvin (1986). *He Do the Police in Different Voices:* The Waste Land *and Its Protagonist.* Chicago: University of Chicago Press.

Berlatsky, Eric (2009). "Lost in the Gutter: Within and Between Frames in Narrative and Narrative Theory." *Narrative* 17.2: 162–87.

Brooker, Jewel Spears, and Joseph Bentley (1990). *Reading* The Waste Land*: Modernism and the Limits of Interpretation.* Amherst MA: University of Massachusetts Press.

Christianson, Scott R. (1990). "A Heap of Broken Images: Hardboiled Detective Fiction and the Discourse(s) of Modernity." In: *The Cunning Craft: Original Essays on Detective Fiction and Contemporary Narrative Theory,* ed. Ronald Walker and June M. Frazer. Macomb IL: Yeast Printing, 135–48.

Duplessis, Rachel Blau (1996). "Codicil on the Definition of Poetry." *Diacritics* 26. 3/4: 51.

Eburne, Jonathan P. (2003). "Chandler's Waste Land." *Studies in the Novel* 35.3: 366–82.

Eliot, T.S. (1971). *The Waste Land: A Facsimile of the Original Drafts including the Annotations of Ezra Pound,* ed. Valerie Eliot. London: Faber and Faber.

Fludernik, Monika (1996). *Towards a 'Natural' Narratology.* London: Routledge.

Geyh, Paula E. (2001). "Enlightenment Noir: Hammett's Detectives and the Genealogy of the Modern (Private) 'I'." *Paradoxa* 16: 26–47.

Herman, David (2002). *Story Logic: Problems and Possibilities of Narrative.* Lincoln: University of Nebraska Press.

Hühn, Peter (2005). "Plotting the Lyric: Forms of Narration in Poetry." In: *Theory into Poetry: New Approaches to Poetry*, ed. Eva Müller-Zettelman and Margarete Rubik. New York: Rodopi.

– (2004). "Transgeneric Narratology: Application to Lyric Poetry." In: *The Dynamics of Narrative Form: Studies in Anglo-American Narratology,* ed. John Pier. Berlin and New York: de Gruyter, 139–158.

Hühn, Peter and Jens Kiefer (2005). *The Narratological Analysis of Lyric Poetry: Studies in English Poetry from the 16th to the 20th Century*, transl. by Alastair Matthews. Berlin and New York: de Gruyter.

Kinney, Claire Regan (1992). *Strategies of Poetic Narrative: Chaucer, Spenser, Milton, Eliot.* Cambridge: Cambridge University Press.

Litz, A. Walton (1973). "*The Waste Land* Fifty Years After." *Eliot in His Time: Essays on the Occasion of the Fiftieth Anniversary of* The Waste Land, ed. A. Walton Litz. Princeton NJ: Princeton University Press.

McCloud, Scott (1993). *Understanding Comics: The Invisible Art.* New York: HarperCollins.

McHale, Brian (2001). "Weak Narrativity: The Case of Avant-Garde Narrative Poetry." *Narrative* 9.2: 161–67.

Prince, Gerald (1982). "Narrativity." In: *Narratology: The Form and Functioning of Narrative.* Berlin: Mouton, 145–61.

– (1999). "Revisiting Narrativity." In: *Grenzüberschreitung-engen: Narratologie im Kontext/ Transcending Boundaries: Narratology in Context*, ed. Walter Grünzweig and Andreas Solbach. Tübingen: Gunter Narr, 43–51.

Rainey, Lawrence S. (1998). *Institutions of Modernism: Literary Elites and Public Culture.* New Haven: Yale University Press.

Rowson, Martin (1999). "Martin Rowson recalls his wrangles with the Eliot estate over his version of *The Waste Land.*" *The Independent on Sunday.* 12 December 1999. http://www.independent.co.uk/arts-entertainment/books-stealing-toms-plunder-this-on-two–1131983.html. Last accessed 25 August 2009.

– (1990). *The Waste Land.* New York: Harper and Row.

Ryan, Marie-Laure (1992). "The Modes of Narrativity and Their Visual Metaphors." *Style* 26.3: 368–87.

Shoptaw, John (1995). "The Music of Construction: Measure and Polyphony in Ashbery and Bernstein." In: *The Tribe of John: Ashbery and Contemporary Poetry,* ed. Susan Schultz. Tuscaloosa: University of Alabama Press, 211–57.

Sternberg, Meir (1992). "Telling in Time (II): Chronology, Teleology, Narrativity." *Poetics Today* 13.3: 463–541.

Tabatchnik, Steve (2000). "The Gothic Modernism of T.S. Eliot's *Waste Land* and What Martin Rowson's Graphic Novel Tells Us about It and Other Matters." *Readerly/Writerly Texts* 8.1/2: 79–92.

William Kuskin
(University of Colorado at Boulder)

Vulgar Metaphysicians: William S. Burroughs, Alan Moore, Art Spiegelman, and the Medium of the Book

Current critical opinion regards comics as a unique medium.[1] The classification suggests comics' special authority and offers a governing definition: based in the assembly of individual cartoon panels into narrative strips, strips into pages, pages into pamphlets, and pamphlets into books, the medium of comics is defined by sequence.[2] In the short term, this emphasis has served comics studies well, creating a field of popular and academic writing with an increasingly defined history and terminology. Obviously, comics differs from prose and poetry; nevertheless, the claim that it is a unique medium obscures the ways in which it participates in literary form, creating a problem that cuts both ways: once it is established that comics is *sui generis*, it is easy to pass over its relationship to established modes of literary experimentation; just so, once isolated from the literary canon, it is easy to dismiss comics as *merely* a popular form of entertainment of no great historical significance. Further, by defining comics as a medium of unique semiotic codes, it is easy to imagine that the physical medium does not matter, easy to imagine that a comic book is essentially a vehicle for a story told with pictures, interchangeable with a storyboard for a film or webpage on a screen. Yet if the term media emphasizes any one point, it is

---

1 I wish to thank Austin Trunick of DC Comics and Kathryn Barcos of the Steven Barclay Agency for help in securing permissions for the visual images.
I review comics criticism in Kuskin 2008: 5–12; see also Chute and DeKoven 2008.

2 The main source for this definition in American comics studies is Will Eisner's *Comics and Sequential Art: Principles & Practice of the World's Most Popular Art Form* (2005), elaborated by Scott McCloud in *Understanding Comics: The Invisible Art*, where he defines comics as "juxtaposed pictorial and other images in deliberate sequence intended to convey information and/or to produce and aesthetic response in the viewer" (1994: 9). Thierry Groensteen's 1999 *Systѐme de la bande dessinѐe*, translated for English readers as *The System of Comics* (Groensteen 2007), provides the most detailed working out of the relationship between sequence, medium, and semiotics.

the interconnected nature of its various registers — cultural dissemination ("the media"), technology ("the new media," "the Gutenberg Galaxy"), and semiotics (language, image, sound) — and so I argue that rather than a pure form, the importance of comics narrative lies in its insistent impurity: as much as comics rely on books and tropes, they are literary; as much as they are relentlessly popular, they recall that literature itself is embedded in and produced by an entertainment economy. In this impurity, comics recall the vulgar poetics inherent in all literary production.

Amazingly, the literary history of comics and graphic novels remains to be told.[3] One place to begin such a telling, for Anglo-American comics at least, is with the 1986 trifecta: Frank Miller's *The Dark Knight Returns*, Alan Moore and Dave Gibbons' *Watchmen*, and Art Spiegelman's *Maus: A Survivor's Tale, Volume 1, My Father Bleeds History*. Serialized in or before 1986, these three texts appeared within months of one another and still assert a defining shape over contemporary comics. In this essay, I begin with two specific pages of *Watchmen*, the first for its evocation of sequence and trope through the comics grid and the second for its literary allusions, particularly to the work of William S. Burroughs. I then turn to a page of Burroughs' experimental novel, *The Soft Machine*, to discover in it the same combination of linguistic and visual codes as in *Watchmen*. Taken together, these three pages illustrate an essential point for late twentieth-century literary fiction, one often claimed for comics alone: the book is a composite medium for time travel. Rather than understanding comics as either a new medium of high art or a herald announcing the final demise of literature in the roiling noise of pop culture, then, I suggest we recognize comic books as literary objects and in doing so allow them to expand our understanding of literature in general. Thus, my main thesis in this essay is that comics neither defines a new medium nor is defined by narrative sequence but is intertwined with prose and poetry in the specifically literary formulation of the medium of the literary book, *graphia*.

Burroughs' work also appeared in an important comics series of the mid–1970s, Art Spiegelman and Bill Griffith's *Arcade: A Comics Revue*, the fourth issue of which contained an early excerpt from his novel *Cities of the Red Night*, illustrated by that most notorious of underground comix artists, S. Clay Wilson.[4] *Arcade* comes at the tail end of the 1968–1974 underground scene, and in it Spiegelman sets out a specifically literary

3 Though there are a number of excellent histories of comics, none connect comics to modern literature in any detail. For an insightful discussion of the relationship between comics and literature, see Baetens 2008. For a counter point, see Meskin 2009.

4 For underground comix see Estren 1974, as well as the excellent 2-in–1 anthology, Donahue, et. al. 1981; for Wilson, see Rozanski 2009.

agenda for comics, which I read through the back cover of issue two. Where *Arcade* was experimental, Spiegelman's self-proclaimed conservative approach in *Maus* allowed him to move to *The New Yorker*, a powerful venue for cultural authority (Spiegelman 2007: 36). This move is related to the advent of the graphic novel, which signals an exchange in the terms of authority by which comics travel, a sleight of hand in which comics' authority is bolstered at the expense of its literary and book history. In elaborating the unique nature of comics as a medium to the neglect of its literary and bookish connections, almost all the current monographs on comics happily buy into this confidence game, whether they accept the term "graphic novel" or not. In contrast, mainstream superhero comics, following Frank Miller, have brokered no such deal and are instead increasingly moving into new media forms, into films and digital downloads, largely at the expense of page design.

My overall claim is, therefore, threefold: first, I argue that comics and graphic novels are literature, and that this recognition forces us to reconsider the purity of our categories of analysis. In this essay, my work toward this point is chiefly historical, and I endeavor to show how the status of the contemporary graphic novel has evolved in concert with twentieth-century experimental literature. My second point occupies a broader parameter: literary books have always been multi-modal in that their physical structure is intimately connected with their figural structure, and this obviates any sense that content — be it words, images, or some combination thereof — can be extracted from one medium and embodied in another without a powerful shift in meaning. Comics make this plain, but only as the exception that proves the rule. My term, graphia, attempts to name this rule of the literary book. On the broadest level, my third point in this essay is that it is a commonplace to view the book as an outmoded vessel, its contents either rarefied by artistic privilege and history or deserving of refurbishment through a new technological presentation. Comics renew the book through their vulgarity, their tradition of experimentation outside the borders of generic category and critical refinement. Literary studies, grappling as it is with the relationship between the literary artwork as a formal abstraction and the significance of media, are in a unique position to read the vulgar metaphysics of the book.

Watchmen is in many ways about the temporal dimensions of the book. This theme emerges from its reflections on comic book history and form, reflections that permeate its plot so completely that it contains a kind of primer on comics history. For example, at first glance the main characters appear original to Moore, but they are in fact carefully revised versions of the Charlton Comics line of superheroes, purchased by DC in 1983 (Moore and Gibbons 2005). The characters are indebted to these companies within the plot: one claims his inspiration from the historically true first appearance of Superman in *Action Comics*, also a DC franchise; another is raised in a orphanage named the Charlton Home; the two super teams in the book, the Minutemen and the Crimebusters, align with the two major periods of comic book history, the Golden Age and the Silver Age. This mixing of archive and invention continues throughout: the heroes suffer the "Keane Act," a governmental ban on certain types of superheroes and a seeming allegory for the 1954 US Senate subcommittee hearings that banned certain types of comics; a minor character reads a fictional pirate comic, "The Black Freighter," attributed to the publishing house EC, a company explicitly targeted by the Senate investigation.[5] The panels of "The Black Freighter" are woven into *Watchmen's* larger story, and the illustrator appears in a photograph of the actual EC comics creator, Joe Orlando. Rather than a historical novel, which might run history and fiction parallel, *Watchmen* overlaps them in a kind of spiral, so that the allusion to one leads back to a point about the other: for example, at *Watchmen*'s conclusion, the horrible octopus-monster that destroys Manhattan harkens back to another telepathic earth-threatening invertebrate, Starro the Conqueror of the first appearance of DC's main superhero team, the *Justice League of America* (Fox, et al. 1992). In *Watchmen*, this monster is created by a fictional comic-book writer and illustrator working in collaboration with geneticists and special effects experts, as if to suggest the power of comics to impact the world even as it shapes *Watchmen*'s plot. When we meet the one true superman of the book, Dr. Manhattan, he is attempting to validate some sort of "supersymmetrical theory" (Moore and Gibbons 1986: I.23), and in that *Watchmen* continually challenges its audience to grapple with the possibility that all its various details — all its interpellations and references, all its tricks of layout and color, all its shifts in narrative voice and line — balance out neatly in its imaginative universe, it invites its readers to search for such a theory as well. In this way, the answer to the refrain that appears in fragments of graffiti throughout *Watchmen*'s plot and finally emerges as the entire book's postscript — "Who watches the watchmen?" — is the reader.

Dr. Manhattan makes this challenge explicit by asking his estranged lover, Laurie Juspeczyk, to rise to his perspective at the end of Chapter IX (Moore and Gibbons 1986: IX.23; figure one). "Laurie, you complain, perhaps *rightly*, that I won't see existence in human terms," he grants in the first panel of the page, continuing, "but you yourself refuse to consider *my* viewpoint, letting your emotions *blind* you. *Look* at yourself: angry,

5 For the Senate Subcommittee investigation see Nyberg 1998.

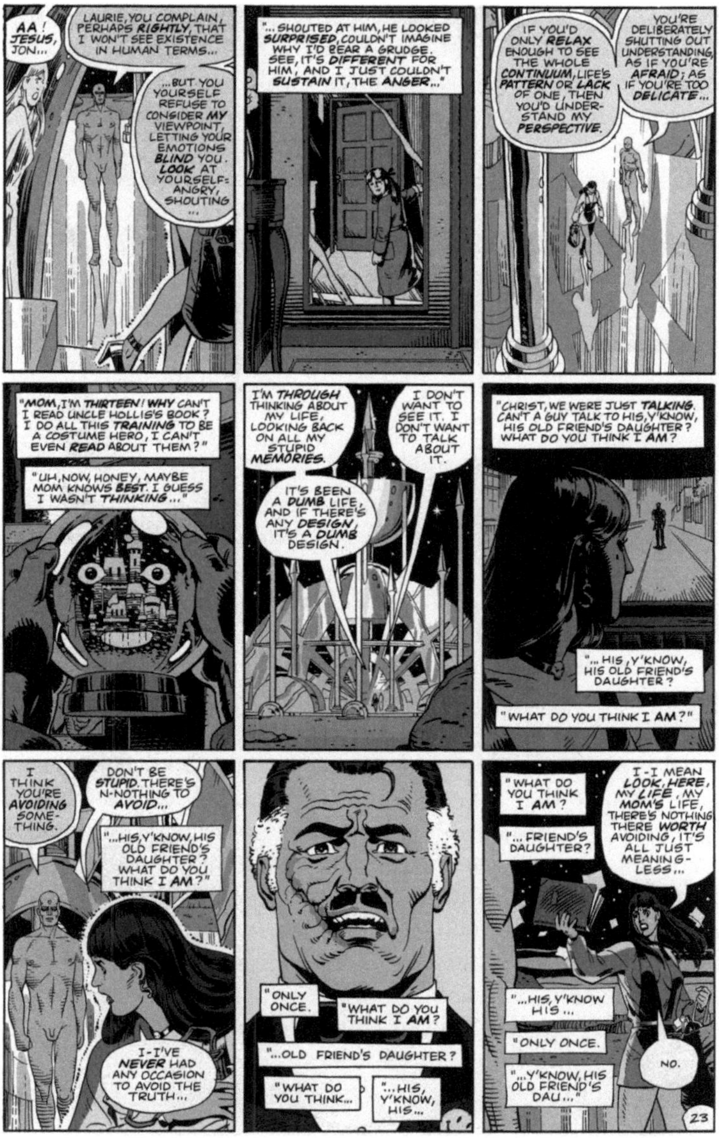

Figure 1: The Comics Page as Metonymic Space. "The Darkness of Mere Being." (Moore and Gibbons 1986: IX.23. By permission of DC Comics). See the color illustration on page 335.

shouting…." Dr. Manhattan's perspective is complex, to say the least. The accidental creation of an experiment in atomic disintegration, he is fated to understand time as a nonlinear whole, a solid object rather than a progressively unfolding chronological sequence. Earlier in the chapter Dr. Manhattan tells Laurie, "time is *simultaneous*, an intricately structured *jewel* that humans insist on viewing one edge at a *time*, when the whole *design* is visible in every *facet*" (Moore and Gibbons 1986: IX.6). In that he sees time as an object, Dr. Manhattan's perspective is similar to the reader's, who can perceive the whole page at one glance and the entire narrative in one turn through the book. So, Mark Bernard and James Bucky Carter have nicely observed that he is "a metaphor for the art of the graphic novel in itself as well as for the graphic novel experience" (Bernard and Carter 2004).[6] In panel three of page twenty three, Dr. Manhattan cautions Laurie not to read her life as a sequence of parts, but to "see the whole *continuum*, life's *pattern* or *lack* of one." If Dr. Manhattan is a metaphor for the graphic novel experience, he is a metaphor that insists upon synecdoche, that suggests the simultaneous understanding of an orderly sequence.

When Dr. Manhattan challenges Laurie to consider his viewpoint, he asks her to "look at herself" and thus drives these themes of reading and reflection to an almost recursive tautology by inviting a comic-book super heroine to reflect on her place in the comics page. Throughout *Watchmen*, Moore and Gibbons organize the page according to the traditional nine-panel grid, the iambic pentameter of comic book schemes. In this particular instance they arrange the grid into a patchwork of alternating color palettes. The immediate conversation between Dr. Manhattan and Laurie appears in pink panels, fitting because it occurs, as it does, on Mars. These establish a narrative sequence keyed to the time it takes the characters to speak their dialogue as they make their way across the glass floor of Dr. Manhattan's Mars Tower. In contrast, the odd-colored panels are reproduced from the chapter's previous pages: in the first tier, panel two derives from a story of Laurie's childhood on page seven; in the second tier, panel one comes from the same story as it is told on pages six and seven, and panel three appears in Laurie's first encounter with the grizzled vigilante-turned-assassin, the Comedian, on page sixteen; finally, in tier three, panel two is from page twenty-one, Laurie's drunken confrontation with the Comedian when she is an adult. Thus, the odd-colored panels disrupt the governing narrative sequence implied by the pink panels while maintaining the larger sequence of the nine-panel grid.

---

6 For Alan Moore in general, see Di Liddo 2009.

The text draws still more narratives onto the grid. Panel four, the panel of the snow globe reflecting a young Laurie's face, appears in three textual variants over the course of the chapter: on page six, the image carries no prose at all; on page seven, it undergirds Laurie's narration of an event in early childhood ("I lifted it, starting a blizzard. I knew it wasn't *real* snow, but I couldn't understand how it fell so *slowly*. I figured inside the ball was some different sort of *time. Slow* time"); and on page twenty-three, it supports two boxes of dialogue lifted from page twelve, an entirely different scene in which an adolescent Laurie, her mother, and a retired superhero, Hollis Mason, argue about his memoir. Here Laurie whines to her mother, Sally, "'*Mom*, I'm *thirteen*! *Why* can't I read Uncle Hollis's book? I do all this *training* to be a costume hero, I can't even *read* about them?'" Mason, recalling his narration of Sally's rape by the Comedian, mutters, "Uh, now, honey, maybe mom knows *best*. I guess I wasn't *thinking*....'" Similarly, the boxed text in panels six through nine combine lines spoken by the Comedian to a sixteen-year old Laurie on page sixteen and a drunken Laurie on page twenty one. The page thus connects four temporally distinct narratives (the present on Mars; Laurie's childhood, adolescence, and adulthood) through no less than four separate operations. In the first, it creates a governing rhythm through the progression of pink panels. In the second, it wedges into this sequence a number of individual panels from earlier narratives in the chapter. In the third, it overlays this halting rhythm with textual references that also reach back into the chapter. In the fourth, these references connect to one another, writing a subtext about the Comedian's importance. In each case, these fragments are incorporated through some species of metonymy: metalepsis (the character within the page is invited to read the page), synecdoche (the single panel represents the whole page of panels), change of name or metonymy proper (the first-person dialogue changes to omniscient narrator in the transposition from balloon to narrative box), and juxtaposition (the panels laid side by side, the words layered on top of the images). These figurations appear at first to be Laurie's memories, but they equally illustrate Dr. Manhattan's awareness of time. Paradoxically, then, as Laurie reflects on her own perspective, she achieves Dr. Manhattan's.

Page twenty-three is thus a poem on reflexivity.[7] In this, it is both a statement of human psychology and of narrative density. It relies upon sequence but is also strongly coherent in ways that sequence alone cannot explain, literally illustrating its thematic unity through a series of reflec-

---

7 Rocco Versaci (2007:12) argues that this self-reflexive quality is fundamental to comics.

tions and backward glances as well as through narrative and trope.[8] When Laurie looks at herself figuratively, she actually sees her reflection in the snow globe, itself a metaphor for the self-contained world of fiction she inhabits. Laurie comes to a powerful realization — that the Comedian is her father — by reading the text of her own past, and this is itself a metonym (the name "rapist" is changed to "father"), which occurs at the same time as the reader realizes that the page's subscription to sequence is also a subscription to figuration. And so the page's central panel depicts a multidimensional object, Dr. Manhattan's Tower, that stands for his jewel of time and for the comics page itself.

Moore and Gibbons explore the multidimensional nature of the comics page throughout *Watchmen*. For example, the title page of Chapter XI appears as an object lesson in the power of sequence (figure two). A variant of the nine-panel grid, this page's pace is modulated through the size and shape of its panels. The first panel begins with an extreme close up of Adrian Veidt's Antarctic greenhouse, one so extreme that it is initially impossible to tell what is being shown, impossible even to discern that the white space is snow. Panels two, three, and four widen the aperture of view by moving horizontally backwards so that as each panel delivers more visual information, their identical size, shape, and layout create a quick but even tempo. Panels five and six maintain this pattern but stall the visual revelation, building a sense of frustration into the pacing, which the final tier alleviates by presenting a panorama that concludes the page with a rush of visual information that actually slows the reader's pace. The page's resolution comes at the cost, then, of rhythm and detail. Moore and Gibbons use this motif throughout *Watchmen*: the very first page of Chapter I uses the same layout to a similar effect. It too begins with an extreme close up, this time of the blood-splattered smiley-face button lying in the gutter, and it too moves progressively backward, this time vertically, so that by the final tier we stand just over a police detective many floors above the street, able to see the entire four-lane avenue below (as well as his bald pate) but not that single telling clue. These pages stage a tension in perspective between context and detail largely through sequence alone,

---

8 In *Understanding Comics*, Scott McCloud details six kinds of sequential transitions. The form that accommodates the transition from Laurie and Dr. Manhattan to the abrupt image of the Comedian in tier three, is category four, Scene-to-Scene, "which transport us across *significant distances* of *time* and *space*" (1994: 71). But this is only one way of describing the action and is married to a kind of progressive narrative that doesn't capture the figurative aspects of Laurie's memory and Dr. Manhattan's perception. The notion of metonymy, I argue, describes the use of juxtaposition here with a fluidity better suited to this situation; see also Kukkonen 2008.

Figure 2: Sequence and Synthesis. "Look On My Works, Ye Mighty..." (Moore and Gibbons 1986: XI.1. By permission of DC Comics).
See the color illustration on page 336.

a tension *Watchmen* pursues by exploring each character's perspective in a different chapter. "Who watches the watchmen?" is essentially a question of the moral implications of this tension in reading, of the overwhelming nature of context and the blindness of intense focus.

Still, sequence is only one aspect of this page. We can see this in Veidt's description of "multi-screen viewing," his practice of watching a grid of televisions for upcoming economic and political trends, and clearly a parallel to our own view of the multi-paneled page. Returning to the first panel, Veidt's prose promises "an observation," but the panel illustrates nothing; it is *tabula rasa*, a blank page. The second panel pulls back to reveal splashes of color obscured by what now appears to be a blanket of snow. This new panel invites us to reread the previous panel, and though the text of the new panel has nothing to do with its own visual scene, they explain one another nicely: Veidt's mention of "an impending world of exotica glimpsed only peripherally" becomes our glimpse of the splay of color in the center of the panel and in its top right-hand corner. In panel three, he introduces "abstract or impressionist painting," which again forces us back to the previous panel while putting us in mind of the fine arts as we search out its shape in this new panel. Darting between these two panels, we too find that meaning is "transient and elusive, [and] must be grasped *quickly*." And so his claim that "an emergent *worldview* becomes gradually *discernible* amidst the media's *white noise*" in panel four becomes our gradual discovery of the dome amidst the white blanket of snow. Throughout the page, Veidt lists off all kinds of plastic media — writing, painting, television, music, animation — and as the concave glass face of the dome recalls the CRT screen, it conspires to a metaphor for the way superficial representation — the flat page, the canvas, the TV screen, film, digital tape, and the bristol board — figures depth, the butterfly flickering within. In a sense, then, the page lays all these arts before us, as if to say that comics are beyond a single discipline, and with this it is tempting to succumb to the facile view of comics as some sort of hybrid between word and image. Yet the entire page is undergirded by the powerful quotation from Percy Shelley's poem, "Ozymandias" — "Look on my works, ye mighty..." — which draws a final parallel between Veidt's Antarctic green house covered by snow, and the "colossal wreck" of Shelley's poem covered by sand. Indeed, the title is so large that it influences the reader from the start, so that the page doesn't really present a sequential narrative at all so much as a unified statement, which the reader then investigates less according to the rhythm of panels, and more stage by stage, taking in the whole and then the parts. Without the allusion, the page remains interesting but also limited, trapped in its own blindness of sequential movement. With the allusion, the page is neither poem of sequence nor hybrid of drawing and writing so much as a synthetic statement on the way art transcends individual renown and grapples with time — the microcosmic time of reading and the macrocosmic time of history. Its thesis leaves off just at the ellipses, just at the precipice of despair at human mortality. Again, a single mode of perception is never enough in *Watchmen*, and if we shift our own view ever so slightly, we can see that the odd shape of the snowfall in panel two of the title page to Chapter XI is the same shape as the blood stain on the smiley-face badge and the same shape as the disintegrating bodies at the end of the chapter (Moore and Gibbons 1986: XI.28). This operation works not through analogy (a butterfly is like a bloodstain or a holocaust) but by juxtaposition (we must read across the text), not by metaphor but by metonymy.

Though its force is often overlooked, metonymy is the central trope for the technology of the book. In the second panel on the page, Veidt notes that his process of watching a grid of televisions is "seemingly anticipated by Burroughs' *cut-up* technique." Burroughs is useful to an understanding of *Watchmen*, not just because Moore is a professed reader of his texts (Baker 2005: 16–9; Baker 2007: 68), but because, as Robin Lydenberg argues, Burroughs writes with "an insistent literalness, the condensation or displacement of the whole by the part, the tendency to reduction and amputation, … all stylistic effects which link Burroughs' style with metonymy" (1987: 31). Lydenberg refers to this as "metonymic dismemberment," a technique exemplified by the cut up (1987: xi). In its most basic execution, the cut up is the process of cutting an existing page into four quadrants, rearranging the parts into a new pattern, and typing up the results in a new lineation (Burroughs and Gysin 1978: 14). Burroughs first gestures to the cut up in the "*Atrophied Preface*" to *Naked Lunch*, where he announces "you can cut into *Naked Lunch* at any intersection point…," implying that the cut up belongs more to the province of reading than of writing (Burroughs 2001a: 187). Oliver Harris argues that Burroughs was using cut ups as early as 1951 to revise the "Junk" manuscript (Burroughs 2003: xxvii), but Burroughs himself attributes the realization of the cut up as a compositional technique to Brion Gysin, who came upon it after the publication of *Naked Lunch* while Burroughs was in London being treated by Dr. Dent for heroin addiction. In *The Third Mind*, Gysin recalls,

> While cutting a mount for a drawing in room #15 [of the Beat Hotel in Paris], I sliced through a pile of newspapers with my Stanley blade and thought of what I had said to Burroughs some six months earlier about the necessity for turning painters' techniques directly into writing. I picked up the raw words and began to piece together texts that later appeared as "First Cut-Ups" in "Minutes to Go." (Burroughs and Gysin 1978: 43–4)

Gysin slices through text with his Stanley blade; he works with "raw words," literally carving them from their original context; he does not write his texts, but pieces them together as a collage. Burroughs explored the cut up and its complementary technique, "the fold in," most prominently in *The Nova Trilogy*. These three experimental novels — *The Soft Machine, The Ticket that Exploded*, and *Nova Express*—derive from the word-hoard manuscript, the six or seven hundred pages Burroughs produced between 1953 and 1958 and from which he distilled *Naked Lunch* (Murphy 1997: 103; Loranger 1999). In effect, the four novels constitute a massive cutting into that manuscript, a rereading that becomes a rewriting, and so Burroughs constructed the trilogy out of itself, cutting it against its own passages, pouring into it existing literature such as Franz Kafka's *The Trial*, T. S. Eliot's *The Waste Land*, and William Shakespeare's *The Tempest*, and, especially in *The Ticket that Exploded*, splicing in transcripts of tape recordings. Burroughs asserts that spontaneity is crucial to his writing process: "you cannot will spontaneity," he observes, "but you can introduce the unpredictable spontaneous factor with a pair of scissors. It is experimental in the sense of being *something to do*. Right here write now… all writing is in fact cut-ups" (Burroughs and Gysin 1978: 29–32). This emphasis on the scissor's randomness obscures Burroughs' authorial control, his power over what to cut and what to let stand, over whether to leave words intact or fragmentary, and over how much to smooth and punctuate the result in retyping it. In fact, Burroughs disliked the cut ups in the first edition of *The Soft Machine* so much that he reworked the text after its initial publication in 1961, introducing a more coherent narrative structure for the 1966 edition. The sign of reading and spontaneity, the cut up is also the mark of writing and revision.

The Nova Trilogy features cut ups within its plot. Take, for example, the "Where You Belong" chapter of *The Soft Machine*. This begins as a story in which Burroughs' first-person narrator takes a corporate job ("Most distasteful thing I ever stood still for," Burroughs 1966: 154) with the media conglomerate, the Trak News Agency. Trak controls people through narrative ("We don't report the news—We write it," Burroughs 1966: 152), and the narrator is quickly folded into their structure ("And next thing I know they have trapped a grey flannel suit on me and I am sent to this school in Washington to learn how this writing the news before it happens is done"). He ends up cutting it up. In the revised, 1966 Grove Press edition of the *Soft Machine*, this cut up takes place on page 153 (figure three). The page initially appears organized according to the protocols of any printed novel, with neatly justified margins and clear paragraphs breaks. So, the first line carries over from the facing page, continuing the description of Trak's IBM machine by explaining how it processes sub-

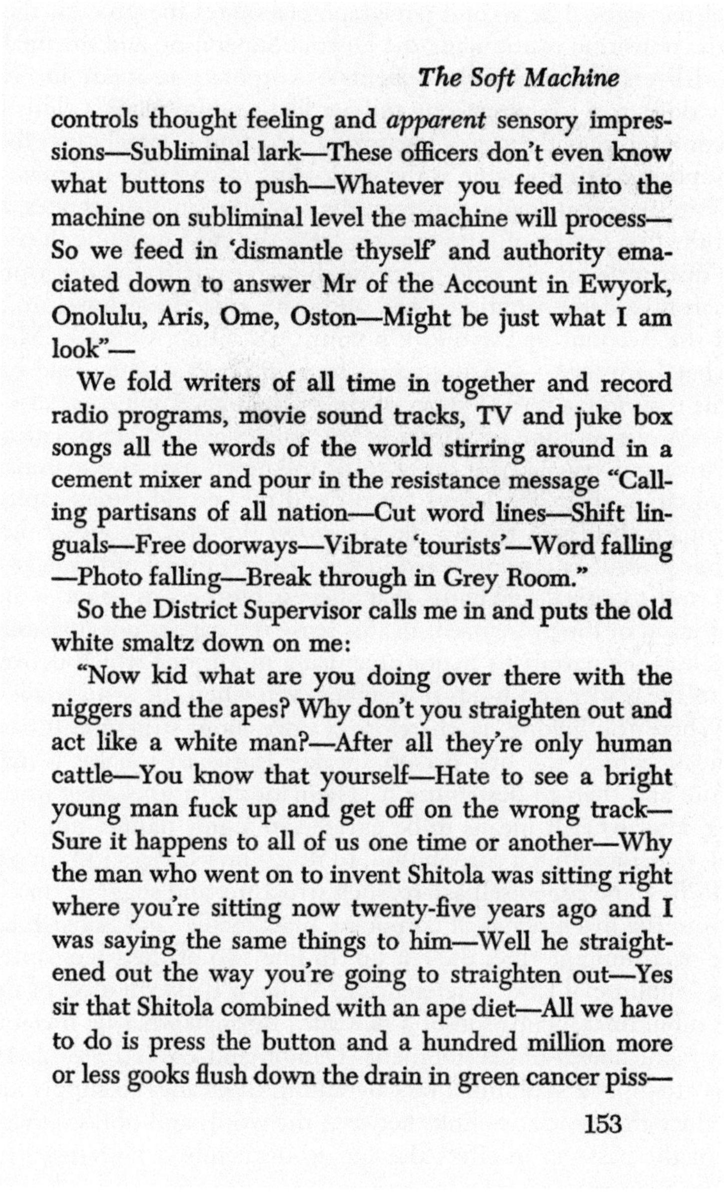

The Soft Machine

controls thought feeling and *apparent* sensory impressions—Subliminal lark—These officers don't even know what buttons to push—Whatever you feed into the machine on subliminal level the machine will process—So we feed in 'dismantle thyself' and authority emaciated down to answer Mr of the Account in Ewyork, Onolulu, Aris, Ome, Oston—Might be just what I am look"—

We fold writers of all time in together and record radio programs, movie sound tracks, TV and juke box songs all the words of the world stirring around in a cement mixer and pour in the resistance message "Calling partisans of all nation—Cut word lines—Shift linguals—Free doorways—Vibrate 'tourists'—Word falling—Photo falling—Break through in Grey Room."

So the District Supervisor calls me in and puts the old white smaltz down on me:

"Now kid what are you doing over there with the niggers and the apes? Why don't you straighten out and act like a white man?—After all they're only human cattle—You know that yourself—Hate to see a bright young man fuck up and get off on the wrong track—Sure it happens to all of us one time or another—Why the man who went on to invent Shitola was sitting right where you're sitting now twenty-five years ago and I was saying the same things to him—Well he straightened out the way you're going to straighten out—Yes sir that Shitola combined with an ape diet—All we have to do is press the button and a hundred million more or less gooks flush down the drain in green cancer piss—

153

Figure 3: The Novel as Cut Up. "Where You Belong" (Burroughs 1966: 153).

liminal messages. The second paragraph elaborates the process, the third is a brief transition introducing the District Supervisor, and the final paragraph delivers his rant on the benefits of corporate structure for identity ("Why don't you straighten out and act like a white man?"). This layout is so common that the page's organizing structure is largely invisible, the paragraphs barely noticeable as the scaffolding of narrative progress. As we enter into these paragraphs, however, the organization disintegrates. In line five of the first paragraph, the narrator feeds the IBM machine the instructions "dismantle thyself" and the prose shifts from narrative description to non-narrative demonstration: "and authority emaciated down to answer Mr of the Account in Ewyork, Onolulu, Aris, Ome, Oston — Might be just what I am look —" The passage looks paratactic when read quickly, but this is simply a formal effect of the printed page, which asserts unity. Page 153's organization is ultimately less syntactical and grammatical than associative and visual, a cut up of some unknown narrative material with a list of cities, their first letters cut off and the second letters capitalized. The cut up thus goes from a device *within* the plot to one *of* the plot, and so it presents a tension between the material forms of the page — the layout and marginal apparatus that suggest business as usual — and the organization of the prose itself. In this sense the page is not invisible at all so much as the narrative's major organizing motif, one which delivers the story to the reader and holds it together even when the syntax falls apart.

"Where You Belong" is, therefore, a story about structure. It describes a scene in which the first-person speaker learns to inhabit a narrative structure and then to destabilize it. Thematically, it asks after where you belong, after what it means to be encased in a grey flannel suit, to go to school, to exist within a corporation, to read a novel. Page 153, in particular, asks how the page itself asserts such structure, and suggests that liberation from the machineries of corporate, mass media, and bookish law lies in one overriding gesture: the cut up. In line two of the page, Burroughs inserts "Subliminal lark," a reference to William Blake's notion of the *lark* as the subliminal incubation of a new idea through what he imagines are twenty eight phases of development (Damon and Eaves 1988: 234). The cut up attempts a subliminal lark by asking the reader to supply closure, to produce the associative links between the words and phrases that make sense of the passage. In effect the cut up dismembers narrative structure to invite the reader to take an active part in the creation of the story. A device forever on the boundary between reading and writing, the cut up makes the reader complicit in literary production.

We can see this effect best in the second paragraph, which begins with a straight narrative account of the work at Trak ("We fold writers of all time in together and record radio programs, movie sound tracks, TV and juke box songs") but then goes through the same disintegrative process as the first. For all intents and purposes, the punctuation evaporates by line three to create a breathless rush ("songs all the words of the world stirring around"). By the end of line four, this becomes so garbled that the passage's explanation of the resistance message ("pour in the resistance message") bleeds directly into the message itself ("'Call-ing partisans of all nation'"). From this point on, the paragraph introduces material that appears throughout the trilogy. "Word falling — Photo falling — Break through in Grey Room" is a kind of catchphrase Burroughs inserts in part or as a whole at various points in the trilogy, and the entire resistance message appears in a mildly scrambled form in the "Uranian Willy" chapter of *The Soft Machine* when Pilot K9 engages the Nova Mob in aerial combat, and in the chapter, "Combat Troops in the Area" in *The Ticket That Exploded*. In this chapter, the resistance message knits together three distinct narratives: one of K9 in combat with the insect people of Minraud, a second of a young street boy named Kiki, and a third of a sexual encounter between Bill and John in a St Louis workshop (one that later turns out to be an investigation in tape-recording cut ups). Each of these narratives share the "Photo falling — Word falling" phrase, which the chapter explains allows its characters to shift from one narrative to another. So, K9 is instructed that if his galactic shock troops are forced to fall back, "the operation of retreat on this level involves shifting three-dimensional coordinate points that is time travel on association lines — Like this:," at which point the narrative immediately shifts from K9's briefing to a cut up of Bill and John's affair (Burroughs 1967: 111). The cut up thus organizes *The Nova Trilogy* through metonymy, and its characters use the juxtaposition of its phrases to teleport across its chapters and volumes. In fact, they use it to shift identities in the same manner: the first person speaker of "Where you Belong," so evidently Burroughs at the start, is named Inspector J. Lee of the Nova Police by the last novel, *Nova Express*. Lee, of course, is Burroughs' mother's maiden name, and his occasional pen name. Metonymy: just as the narrative shifts along the associative lines developed through the reiteration of individual semantic units at different moments, the characters, if not the author, change names as the narrative structure requires.

In this emphasis on repetition and proximity, it is hard not to read page 153 of *The Soft Machine* according to the protocols of *Watchmen*. For each of its phrases, each appearance of the resistance message, acts as a modular part of the narrative, the prose equivalent of one of Gibbons' panels. This similarity is obvious because Burroughs' technique of metonymic dismemberment strips away the structural apparatus of grammar, punctuation, and narrative, reducing the page to an instance of sequential possibilities and the book itself to a database waiting for the reader to create associative links between it parts. We can see the parallel particularly well in Chapter IV of *Watchmen*, "Watchmaker," the chapter in which Dr. Manhattan first retreats to Mars. There, he begins to question the possibility of a prime mover, a watchmaker, who sets the universal design in motion. Contemplating a photograph of his lost human form, he remarks "I'm tired of looking at the photograph now. I open my fingers. It falls to the sand at my feet. I am going to look at the stars. They are so far away, and their light takes so long to reach us.... All we ever see of stars are their old photographs" (Moore and Gibbons 1986: IV.1). So, too, in the last panel of Chapter IX, page twenty three, Laurie waves her mother's scrapbook in the air, the photographs and clippings falling around her. These many photos are abstracted from their context but remain tethered to their meaning, like the light of a star communicating its existence through time and space. "Word falling — Photo falling" — in both *Watchmen* and the *Nova Trilogy* words and images are time-specific packets information that can be materially juxtaposed in different contexts. Dr. Manhattan, Laurie, Veidit, Inspector Lee, Pilot K9, Bill and John, as well as their readers are thus time travelers of a sort, able to recapture the narratives of lost time or read narratives of the future by recognizing the metonymic relationship of words and images to their contexts within the structure of the book.

The same is true for the authors. Burroughs frequently reports that cut ups allow him to see into the future (Burroughs and Gysin 1978: 3, 96; Burroughs 1974: 27–56). Moore, in describing his own latest prose novel, suggests time is a permanent structure:

> But time, if I understand it correctly, isn't actually passing, except in our perception of it. In fact, as far as I understand it, every moment in the universe, from its most remote past to the most distant future, is all happening at once in some permanent, eternal kind of globe of space time in which the beginning and end of the universe are both there at the same time, along with every tiny moment in between, including all those moments which made up our lives. (Baker 2007: 58)

Here, then, is the jewel that Dr. Manhattan describes to Laurie, the snow globe that Laurie finds in her memory, the Antarctic dome that Veidt lives in, as well as the pages that Gysin cuts into and that Burroughs assembles. Indeed, what is this jewel of time, this globe of space time that Burroughs and Moore describe if not a metaphor for the book?

Watchmen, no less than the *Nova Trilogy*, is about the temporal dimension of the book, about the ways books evoke time within their plots and act as time machines for their readers. "Where You Belong" in particular asks after how we read this multidimensional structure of the book, as a readerly object unto itself or as a writerly form spiraling outward. On the one hand, it suggests that *The Nova Trilogy* is entirely self contained, its associative links bound to one another as tightly as the novels are bound by their covers. In such a conception, the resistance message is the part that stands for the whole, the telling phrase that allows the characters to shift coordinates from narrative to narrative and the reader to make sense of the various sequences. In this vein, Burroughs himself explains in an interview conducted shortly after the publication of *Nova Express* that "Break through in Grey Room" is essentially the trilogy's conclusion: "the nova police have made a break-through past the guards and gotten into the darkroom where the films are processed, where they're in a position to expose negatives and prevent events from occurring" (Murphy 1997: 130). Accordingly, the cut up delivers the final triumph of the resistance, the fragmentary radio instructions to burst into the corporate studio and the crucial passage that resolves the trilogy. On the other hand, the book is itself a portal, a window on its own narrative of production. In this, "Word falling — Photo falling" defines the very technique by which the passages are made, the arbitrariness of Gysin's Stanley blade and of Burroughs' various cut ups and fold ins. Gysin even uses the phrase "Word falling — Photo falling — Break through in Grey Room" to gloss his time with Burroughs at the Beat Hotel during the final edit of *Naked Lunch*, when Burroughs was attempting to shake his addiction while pounding out new passages of text, reviewing galley proofs, improvising characters out loud, and Scotch taping photographs throughout the room (Burroughs and Gysin 1978: 43). Given these two possibilities — Burroughs' tidy explanation of breaking into the editorial suite that ties up the trilogy; Gysin's understanding that this is room #15 of the Beat Hotel, the center of operations for the word-hoard manuscript — the Grey Room is both the Nova Mob's control hub and the place where Burroughs unmasks the control process, and cutting up is simultaneously the technique of writing the news and of destabilizing it, the white noise and the subliminal message encoded within, the narrative's form and its content. N. Katherine Hayles notes that in Burroughs' works "the observer cannot stand apart from the systems being observed" (1999: 221), and this is true for the reader as well, who is pulled into the soft machine of the book as an active agent. The medium is the message: fitting the logic of metonymy, the cut up renames the act of literary creation as the physical act of writing, substituting for the imaginary space of fiction the material space of the book. In doing so it illustrates its characters moving through the book by associative channels, and asks that its readers do the same or be consumed by the various threats it describes: the insect people of Minraud, the grey flannel suit, and linear narrative.

Watchmen asks its reader to appreciate the formal structure of the book in much the same way as *The Soft Machine*. Moore discusses the material nature of reading in an interview from 2002:

> With a comic, you have a medium where the reader is very much in control of the material. Somebody reading *Watchmen* can pause and take as long as they want to look [sic] one of Dave Gibbons' panels. They can wait until they've spotted every little detail in the background. Or, if they pass on more quickly, they've got the liberty if, in a few pages time, they suddenly find some line of dialogue, some image, that seems perhaps to resonate with something that they saw a couple of pages back, they can flip back a couple of pages and they can say, "Ah, yes, this piece of dialogue *does* relate to that piece of dialogue a couple of pages ago." (Baker 2005: 61)

As Moore implies, the ability to participate in narrative composition through reading, to observe different temporalities on one page, is frequently claimed as exclusive to comics. Yet elsewhere he is expansive about immersing himself in Thomas Pynchon's *Gravity's Rainbow* at just such a pace and about studying Gabriel García Márquez's narrative structure (Moore 2007: 5–15). Here, then, is the very process of reading *The Nova Trilogy*, one that takes the book not as a fixed sequence but as an object the reader moves within, which allows sections to be folded against one another and configured into different arrangements. This mode of reading is less a function of the comics page than a process common to all who read books according to *slow time*, the powerful mode of reading the self-contained universe — the snow globe — of the book. Its central mandate is the cutting into the text; as Burroughs says, it is reading as *something to do,* as a manipulation of a preexisting material form that produces an original composition, a composite text in which the reader's imagination combines with the art object toward a new interpretation. The literary book thus invites the reader to achieve figuration through a synthesis between language and technology.

Let me be clear. Superficially, comics and prose or poetic literature appear significantly different. Yet, when we take the time to close read their operations, we find they work according similar mechanisms. For whatever the medium of comics does, it does through the medium of the book. "One of the things that is wonderful about comics," Art Spiegelman reminds us, "is that comics are a printed medium" (2007: 32). To my mind, this observation should make us question whether the definition of comics as a sequential medium or of literature as a medium of language are sufficient. For if it is true that comics are defined by sequence, this truth strikes no essential difference from manuscript and printed books, a format that parallels the sequential nature of language with the sequencing of pages. All books depend upon sequence, which they invite readers to manipulate, and all books demand their readers process visual information, the *mise-en-page*, in the construction of meaning. To say, then, that Dr. Manhattan is a metaphor for the comics page, and experience underestimates the closeness of, and Moore's debt to Burroughs' technique, and the power of the book overall. To say, too, that *The Soft Machine* works through the medium of literature because it uses language, obscures its deep relationship to the physicality of the cut up. Both the *Nova Trilogy* and *Watchmen* specifically discuss a range of technological media — computers, television, music, film — but their material substrate, their medium, is the book. As a medium, the book has specific figural tendencies — its ability to assemble serialized installments into a convincing whole; its tendency to draw the reader into its imaginative world; its readiness to imply a whole greater than its material parts; its capacity to stand in for the author — that cluster around metonymy. The recognition that the book's material form is deeply semiotic and that its semiotic codes are deeply material should frustrate any categorical description that relies on only one sense of media. So, I suggest a new term, *graphia*, as a way of acknowledging the interplay of media-as-technology and media-as-semiotic-code that occurs in the literary book.

Burroughs was famously interested in multimedia experimentation and cut up newspapers, diaries, drafts, printed literature, film, and audio transcripts (sometimes made from multiply spliced tape recordings). He recorded "Where You Belong" at least three times, cutting and splicing tapes of his reading to create very different iterations (Burroughs 1995; Burroughs 1998; Burroughs 2001b; Hayles 1999: 216). With Gysin, he experimented with computer-generated patterns of words (Burroughs and Gysin 1978). He produced illustrated fiction as well: Gysin provided pictures for *Exterminator!* and *The Third Mind*, and S. Clay Wilson illustrated his book of short fiction, *Tornado Alley* (1989), as well as a chapter from *Cities of the Red Night* (1981), which appeared in *Arcade: The Comics Revue* #4 (1975).[9] Edited by Art Spiegelman and Bill Griffth, and published by the underground comix house, The Print Mint, *Arcade* ran for seven issues from the spring of 1975 through the fall of 1976. Five of the seven covers were illustrated by the most recognized figure of the underground comix movement, R. Crumb, and in many ways this announces *Arcade*'s agenda. Spiegelman explains, "at the time underground comics were going through a recessionary cycle, and we just wanted to have a life raft that everybody

9 Titled "Fun City in Ba'dan" (Burroughs and Wilson 1975), this appears in a somewhat shorter version as the chapter "Please to use Studio Postulated to You" (Burroughs 1981: 266–71). In *Cites of the Red Night* all the characters who are writers employ illustrators; see 103, 167, and 173.

could climb on to" (Spiegelman 2007: 22). *Arcade* is unique among the underground anthologies, however, not simply because Burroughs appears within it, but because, as Mr. Les Hancock of New York, New York, comments in the letters column to issue three, "it's *edited*."

Spiegelman and Griffith are clear about this difference from the start. They introduce the first issue with a comics-format editorial featuring the pair of them at a shooting gallery arcade. Between shots Spiegelman lays out the program: "Arcade is gonna be a comics magazine for *Adults!* We'll have *culture* with a minus and *entertainment* with a plus!.. We've got … *Humor! Satire! Pulp Adventure! Slices of Life!! Experimentation!!* And *Irrational Behavior!!* It's the best of the *New* comics …. And the best of the *Old!* Every ish we'll unearth a great blast from the past!" (Spiegelman and Griffith 1975: 4). As they run out of bullets, Griffith adds, "*Plus*, each issue will include lavishly illustrated fiction and articles." Over the course of the seven issues, Spiegelman and Griffth become increasingly harried by deadlines and publication woes, but throughout *Arcade*'s run they aim for a literary, if not pedantic, editorial plan so that rather than claiming that comics' cultural authority stems from its status as a unique medium, they present it as organically connected to literary history and an expression of contemporary fiction.

Spiegelman's own work in *Arcade* tends toward short, experimental pieces. The back cover of *Arcade* #2 features the one-page strip, "Day at the Circuits," which illustrates the complexity of the grid in a way comparable to Moore and Gibbons (Spiegelman 1975; figure four). The composition is a gag about the recursive nature of drinking and depression, which it accomplishes by exploiting the recursive nature of the page. A box in front of the title announces the problem from the start: directing the reader to follow the arrows, it contains a logo in which the exemplary pointer connects head to tail as in an infinity sign. The action of the page begins, like so many jokes, with two characters in a bar: Slim moans, "I only drink to keep from getting so damn depressed!," and Bruiser sympathizes, "Ah-things ain't so bad! What's gotcha down?" From there the reader is faced with a choice, but no matter the decision, Slim ends up repeating the same line, "I'm depressed because I drink so much!... It's destroying my liver!" The reader is invited to follow on but ultimately must return to the first panel and begin the circuit again. The page makes a complex use of color to this end as well. The first panel is lavishly colored and the rest of the page is set in two dominant tones: with the exception of the center panel, the bottom half is largely pink and the right hand column begins as blue before fading to pink. The colors sketch the page's argument: life is initially vibrant but rapidly becomes monochromatic; any immediate escape from the blues at best degenerates into a rose-colored

Figure 4: Recursion and Page Layout. "Day at the Circuits" (Spiegelman 2008. Originally printed in Spiegelman 1975. By generous permission of Art Spiegelman). See the color illustration on page 337.

inebriation in which the same old tavern looks different, until one realizes the stark reality of Bruiser's conclusion, "Well, why doncha just slash yer wrists." Even the title puns on the inescapable nature of life's monotony, so that instead of a day at the circus that would alleviate life's misery, the page is a poem that leaves its reader circulating the grid on the edge of despair.

"Day at the Circuits" presents a world in a bubble, entirely contained by the live area of the page. Its humor is aimed at exactly the kind of reading Laurie learns in Chapter IX of *Watchmen* — that linearity is only one way to read, that the comics page is understood through juxtaposition and association, that it must be read according to *slow time* — and it comes to the same conclusion as Burroughs: that to undermine linear fiction is still to participate in the word-image system; there is no short-circuiting the soft machine. Bruiser keeps suggesting the wisdom of a linear reader — "Don't talk in circles!," "All these stupid dumps look alike!," and "Let's get outa this dump!" — but to no avail. In fact, the more mechanical the reader, the more definitive the quagmire: even if the reader insists on making it to the last panel of the bottom tier, she is back in the same tavern by different means. That is, even though she has progressed sequentially, the image returns her to the start by a visual analogy. The page plays with sequencing to defy narrative progression, creating a primitive sort of time travel for its characters, and its final recourse is simply to appreciate, as Dr. Manhattan might say, the whole *continuum of the page* — life's *pattern* or *lack* of one. Comic books are often taken as a dodge for serious reading, ostensibly because they present less text than a novel or short story, but the message created by page after page is that the only recourse to a pervasive despair is the slow aesthetic of literary interpretation.[10]

Spiegelman followed *Arcade* with two significant editorial projects: his 1977 collection, *Breakdowns*, and *RAW Magazine*, which he edited with Françoise Mouly from 1980 through 1991. Both are concerned with establishing cultural authority for comics. Advertised in the last issue of *Arcade*, *Breakdowns* reprinted much of Spiegelman's work from that series with selections from a few of his other underground publications. If *Breakdowns* consolidates Spiegelman's work in the underground movement, *RAW* turns away from it to achieve what *Arcade* only plinked at: Spiegelman explains that *RAW* is "a literary magazine, it uses comics instead of seas of type as its way of communicating. Any artist who's capable of expressing himself would have a vehicle in which to travel and present that work" (Spiegelman 2007: 26). The operative mode, Mouly

10 Nihilism in the mainstream comics is discussed in Wright 2008.

points out, is experimental: "we're just interested in saying 'Don't' follow the usual rules, but play around, experiment and stretch things out'" (Spiegelman 2007: 27). Spiegelman serialized *Maus* in *RAW*, and in 1992 received the Pulitzer Prize for that text, around which time *RAW* came to and end. Both editors went on to *The New Yorker*, Spiegelman as a contributing editor and Mouly as Art Editor, a position she holds as of this writing (Spiegelman 2007: xx). The overriding thrust of their contribution has been to shift *The New Yorker*'s visual sensibility closer to *Arcade*'s and *RAW*'s. Through varying methods — countercultural and mainstream publication, experimental and authorial anthologizing — Speigelman's projects of the seventies through the early nineties are involved in naming comics as literary within the more-or-less mass media format of the popular magazine. From this observation comes a major point: comics has been defined as a sequential medium distinct from literature, but the most powerful statements of its authority in America — Spiegelman and Mouly's arrival at *The New Yorker*, Spiegelman's achievement of a special Pulitzer Prize for *Maus*, *Watchmen*'s election to *Time Magazine*'s list of the 100 most important novels since 1923, Alison Bechdel's National Book Critics Circle Award for *Fun Home*, Michael Chabon's 2001 Pulitzer for his novel of comics, *The Amazing Adventures of Kavalier and Clay*, and so forth — has occurred though an integration with literary culture.

Ironically, the most successful term emerging from the seventies for this literary authority, "the Graphic Novel," defines comics — whether they are serialized pamphlets, short stories, or extended narratives — as an independent medium of cultural authority. As a result, comics has risen in prominence strangely at odds with its history. We can see this by returning to *Watchmen* through Zack Synder's 2009 film adaptation, one made specifically in the face of Moore's explicit objections. In brief, after agreeing to have *Watchmen* filmed, Moore was dismayed by the adaptation of *From Hell*, and after a significant conflict during the production of the movie version of *The League of Extraordinary Gentlemen*, refused to be associated with either a *V for Vendetta* or a *Watchmen* movie. He recalls, "now, this was starting to feel a little bit to feel uneasy for me. Because I was realizing that, while I might have a very clear distinction in my mind as to the differences between the book and the film, the average cinema-goer is not even going to be aware that it was based upon a book. Or, if they are they're probably going to assume that the film is a pretty fair reflection of what was in the book" (Baker 2007: 13). Because DC owns the rights to all of Moore's work with it, he has had little recourse beyond insisting that his name be removed from the films and forwarding his royalties on to the illustrators, David Lloyd and Gibbons. Still, the advance trailers to the movie proclaim *Watchmen* "The most celebrated Graphic Novel of all time," and in this case Moore has suffered his worst fears: the book and the film have become conflated.[11] Damning author and director both, *New Yorker* film critic Anthony Lane writes:

> Amid these pompous grabs at horror, neither author nor director has much grasp of what genuine, unhyped suffering might be like, or what pity should attend it; they are too busy fussing over the fate of the human race — a sure sign of metaphysical vulgarity — to be bothered with lesser plights. In the end, with a gaping pit where New York used to be, most of the surviving Watchmen agree that the loss of the Eastern Seaboard was a small price to pay for global peace. Incoherent, overblown, and grimy with misogyny, *Watchmen* marks the final demolition of the comic strip, and it leaves you wondering: where did the comedy go? (Lane 2009)

Lane, fitting the role of a *New Yorker* critic, uses the review to articulate cultural authority, to separate art from genre fiction, that is, to separate sophisticated artwork from entertainment for the masses. Thus in asking, "where did the comedy go?," he asks not after generic distinction — ending with the expectation of marriage as it does, *Watchmen* is of course technically a comedy — but after a conviction that good art should not feature blue supermen hypothesizing about the existence of God from a seat on Mars. So, Lane defines *Watchmen* as belonging to a festering pool of anti-intellectual traits, one so effluent as to destroy the comic strip itself. Accordingly, Moore falls into metaphysical vulgarity, while Lane favors what he calls "masterwork[s], such as 'Persepolis' or 'Maus.'"

Vulgarity, or the lack thereof, can hardly be a principle of distinction for comics, and Lane's assessment rests uneasily next to what is actually printed in pages of *The New Yorker*, which recently featured perhaps one of the most vulgar metaphysicians — if not vulgar misogynists — in comics, Crumb, drawing the Book of Genesis (Crumb 2009). Crumb's significance as a major figure of late twentieth-century literature cannot be disputed, but his bibliography, featuring male characters decapitating females, endless fantasies of sexual exploitation, and a litany of reactionary tirades, is vulgar in the extreme. Vulgarity is part of the experimentation that allows art to move forward, and this as true for Moore and Gibbons as it is for Crumb, Spiegelman, Marjane Satrapi, and Burroughs. Lane demonstrates that the process of granting the authority of masterworks involves the alienation of one type of comics as genre fiction and the embrace of another, regardless of media and almost regardless of content.

By recognizing media, we can also recognize content. The graphic, or rather pornographic qualities of the Synder movie that Lane so objects to

11 <http://www.youtube.com/watch?v=dJmILsYp_Dw>. Viewed 7/12/09.

are fundamentally at odds with the medium of the book. For example, the sequence on page twenty-three is repeated twice in the movie. We first see it when we meet Dr. Manhattan, who is introduced as investigating his supersymmetrical theory and demonstrates his worldview by touching Laurie's forehead, initiating a fast montage of scenes that review her childhood and suggest the Comedian's looming importance to her life. This montage is replayed at greater length when Laurie and Dr. Manhattan talk on Mars. There, she requests "Do that thing you do," and he touches her once again. Instead of inhabiting Dr. Manhattan's viewpoint, then, Laurie has it thrust upon her, indeed, thrust into her. And so the movie imagines her a passive receptacle and, fittingly, the camera continually lingers over the actress, Malin Åkerman, as various men and supermen do that thing that they do to her. In the book, Laurie is the one character who transcends her viewpoint, who matures from a complaining and oversexualized heroine to a person capable of coming to a powerful realization about the past, of accomplishing time travel without a bank of televisions hidden in a frozen fortress, an atomic signature, or even Trak's IBM machine. This Laurie goes from being denied the possibility of reading Mason's memoir to being a proxy for the reader. In the movie, Laurie is not a reader at all but a recipient of feelings, sounds, and images.

To my view, these two renditions of Laurie epitomize the difference between the audience's role in the two media: books, whether authored by Burroughs, Moore, or Spiegelman present a physical experience of the imaginary in which the material object stands in for the fictional world it imagines and as such can be manipulated — written in, highlighted, folded, cut, and generally inhabited — by the reader. Films project their art on the screen in rush of sound and light, penetrating the viewer at twenty-four feet per second. The two media supply very different answers to the question "Who watches the watchmen?" For the book, the reader must bring the Watchmen to life. Without her, they remain dormant, nothing more than ink and paper; with her they become strangely conscious of their own fictional status. For the movie, it is the viewer who watches the Watchmen, whose chest pounds with the soundtrack, whose eyes dilate with the changes in light, and who leaves the theater knowing that the experience will be repeated in her absence. If there is misogyny in the Synder film, it lies in its rendition of Laurie as spectacle; if there is pornography, it is generated by the way the movie makes us watch this spectacle be penetrated over and over. Lane's assessment of *Watchmen* entirely overwrites media, imagining that one can be a valid substitute for the other. Accordingly, no one would watch the *Watchmen* at all.

The elision of media recalls the work of the third pillar of the 1986 trifecta, Frank Miller, whose recent efforts have been largely to translate comics to film. Prior to *The Dark Knight Returns*, Miller was one of the most experimental creators in mainstream comics. Beginning in 1978, he introduced deeply troubling themes into Marvel's lackluster *Daredevil* series and went on to bring Manga techniques to the American audience through his series for DC, *Ronin* (1983–84). *The Dark Knight Returns* powerfully unified his generic and visual experimentation within what had become a threadbare franchise. Where Spiegelman and Moore have resisted filmic adaptation, Miller has embraced it, first with the film version of his independent work, *Sincity*, made with Robert Rodriguez and Quentin Tarantino in 2005, then with Synder on the adaptation of *300* (2007), and most recently with his own interpretation of Will Eisner's *The Spirit* (2008). Miller is currently working on a sequel to *Sincity* and an adaptation of Raymond Chandler's *Trouble is My Business*. In this, he is part of the trend in mainstream comics publishing, which is increasingly moving into non-book media as a route to financial success. DC has long been owned by Warner Bros., and Marvel has recently been acquired by The Walt Disney Company. In both cases, these publishing houses have become, in a sense, research and development arms for their parent companies' more lucrative movie businesses. Correspondingly, the mainstream comics page has gravitated from the complex sense of sequencing and design we see in *Watchmen* to the use of "widescreen" paneling, the aesthetic complement to film.[12] Even much smaller mainstream publishers such as Image seem devoted to such a filmic notion of narrative storyboarding, as demonstrated by comics such as *Girls* by Joshua Luna and Jonathan Luna and *The Walking Dead* by Robert Kirkman, Charlie Adlard, and Cliff Rathburn. Further, various marketing techniques such as *Marvel Digital Comics Unlimited* attempt to circumvent book production and distribution entirely by providing "online versions of your favorite Marvel Comics created from the original files used to print them."[13] As in "Where You Belong," the part cannot be separated from the system, and so as comics develop into digital media and film, its semiotic constitution will be forced to change as well.

Change is intrinsic to literary form. In 1974, Burroughs observed,

> I think that the novelistic form is probably outmoded and that we may look forward perhaps to a future in which people do not read at all or read only illustrated books and magazines or some abbreviated form of reading matter. To compete with television and photo magazines writers will have to develop more precise techniques producing the same effect on the reader as a lurid action photo (Burroughs 1974: 27).

---

12 For the "Widescreen" format, see Salisbury 2000: 123.

13 <http://www.marvel.com/digitalcomics/>. Viewed 13 February 2009

Comics is one of these new techniques, and as such they afford us a way back into in the future of the book.

To this end, I submit three main conclusions:

1. *Literary History*: Current writing on comics treats its history as distinct from literary history. The implication of this argument is to divide one form of the literary book from another, as if to say that William S. Burroughs had never thought of the visual capacities of the book, that Art Spiegelman was ignorant of the trends in experimental writing when he took up *Maus*, that Alan Moore did not read carefully in postmodern fiction throughout his tenure with DC, and that Frank Miller had no sense of hardboiled prose as he revolutionized the mainstream superhero. The task ahead of literary and comics criticism alike is to elaborate the implications of the literary history of comics.

2. *Medium:* The claim that comics is an independent medium is largely a bid for the cultural authority of high art. The cost of this claim has been a sharp division between genre fiction and so-called masterworks, as well as the obfuscation of the multivalent nature of the book. All literary books combine sequence with figuration, particularly metonymic figuration, to create a powerful relationship between the reader and the imaginary statement contained within. They accomplish this by presenting a synthesis of rhetorical and material forms, which represent the intersection of individuals — writers and readers, illustrators and colorists, typesetters and publishers — with time. I term this symbolically laden object, *graphia*.

3. *Vulgarity:* By recognizing graphia as a historical mode of literary production that contains within it an approach to temporal sequence and history both, we can begin to think our way around a progressive understanding of media and into a vulgar metaphysics of twenty-first century narrative. Comics and graphic novels are the latest iteration of a long trajectory of expressive uses of the book format, every historical permutation of which — the vernacular manuscript, the printed book, the dramatic quarto, the serialized novel — appeared at first as in some way tawdry before taking its place as a legitimate cultural mode. Criticism, be it popular or academic, needs to recognize that all art involves the violation of nicety in pursuit of some new articulation of the human condition. The book is a vulgar medium and comic books are excitingly so.

References

Baetens, Jan (2008). "Graphic Novels: Literature Without Text?" In Kuskin 2008: 77–88.
Bernard, Mark and James Bucky Carter (2004). "Alan Moore and the Graphic Novel: Confronting the Fourth Dimension." *ImageTexT: Interdisciplinary Comics Studies* 1.2: http://www.english.ufl.edu//imagetext/archives/v1_2/carter/index.shtml. Viewed 7/19/09.
Baker, Bill (2005). *Alan Moore Spells it Out.* Milford, CT: Airwave Publishing.
– (2007). *Alan Moore's Exit Interview.* Milford, CT: Airwave Publishing.
Burroughs, William S. (1966). *The Soft Machine.* New York: Grove Press.
– (1997 [1962]). *The Ticket that Exploded.* New York: Grove Press, 1967.
– (1974). *The Job: Interviews with William S. Burroughs,* ed. Daniel Odier. New York: Grove Press.
– (1980 [1964]). *Nova Express.* In: *Three Novels by William S. Burroughs.* New York: Grove Press.
– (1981). *Cities of the Red Night.* New York: The Viking Press.
– (1995). *Call Me Burroughs.* Los Angles: Rhino.
– (1998). *The Best of William S. Burroughs.* New York: Giorno Poetry Systems Institute.
– (2001a). *Naked Lunch: The Restored Text.* 1959. Ed. James Grauerholz and Barry Miles. New York: Grove Press.
– (2001b). *Break Through in Grey Room.* Brussels: Sub Rosa.
– (2003). *Junky: The Definitive Text of "Junk."* 1953. Ed. and with an introduction by Oliver Harris. New York: Penguin.
Burroughs, William S. and Brion Gysin (1978). *The Third Mind.* New York: The Viking Press.
Burroughs, William S. and S. Clay Wilson (1975). "Fun City in Ba'dan." *Arcade: The Comics Revue* 4:11–13.
– (1989). *Tornado Alley.* Ann Arbor: Cherry Valley Editions.
Chute, Hillary and Marianne DeKoven (2008). "Introduction: Graphic Narrative." *Modern Fiction Studies* 52.4: 767–82.
Crumb, R. (2009). "The Book of Genesis." *The New Yorker,* June 8 & 15: 90–101.
Di Liddo, Annalisa (2009). *Alan Moore: Comics as Performance, Fiction as Scalpel.* Jackson, MS: University Press of Mississippi.
Damon, Samuel Foster and Morris Eaves (1988). *A Blake Dictionary: The Ideas and Symbols of William Blake.* Lebanon, NH: Brown.
Donahue, Don, Susan Goodrick, and Jay Lynch (1981). *The Apex Treasury of Underground Comics & The Best of Bijou Funnies.* New York and London: Omnibus Press.
Eisner, Will (2005 [1985]). *Comics and Sequential Art: Principles & Practice of the World's Most Popular Art Form.* Tamarac, FL: Poorhouse.
Estren, Mark James (1974). *A History of Underground Comics.* San Francisco: Straight Arrow Books.
Fox, Gardner, Mike Sekowsky, Bernard Sachs, Joe Giella, and Murphy Anderson (1992). "Starro the Conqueror!" *The Brave and the Bold* 28 (1960). Reprinted in *Justice League of America Archives.* Vol. 1. New York: DC Comics, 13–39.
Groensteen, Thierry (2007). *The System of Comics,* trans. Bart Beaty and Nick Nguyen. Jackson, MS: University Press of Mississippi.

Hayles, N. Katherine (1999). *How We Became Posthuman: Virtual Bodies in Cybernetics, Literature, and Informatics*. Chicago: University of Chicago Press.
Kukkonen, Karin (2008). "Beyond Language: Metaphor and Metonymy in Comics Storytelling." In Kuskin 2008: 88–98.
Kuskin, William, ed. (2008). *Graphia: Literary Criticism and the Graphic Novel*. Special issue of *ELN* 46.2.
Lane, Anthony (2009). "Dark Visions: '*Watchmen*' and '*Leave Her to Heaven*.'" *The New Yorker*, March 9, 2009:<http://www.newyorker.com/arts/critics/cinema/2009/03/09/090>.Viewed 5/10/09.
Loranger, Carol (1999). "'This Book Spill Off the Page in All Directions': What Is the Text of *Naked Lunch*?" *Postmodern Culture: An Electronic Journal of Interdisciplinary Culture* 10: <http://pmc.iath.virginia.edu/text-only/issue.999/10.1contents.html>. Viewed 7/14/09.
Lydenberg, Robin (1987). *Word Cultures: Radical Theory and Practice in William S. Burroughs' Fiction*. Urbana: University of Illinois Press.
McCloud, Scott (1994 [1993]). *Understanding Comics: The Invisible Art*. New York: HarperCollins.
Meskin, Aaron (2009). "Comics as Literature?" *British Journal of Aesthetics* 49.3: 219–39.
Moore, Alan (2007). *Alan Moore's Writing For Comics*. Rantoul, IL: Avatar Press.
Moore, Alan and Dave Gibbons (1986). *Watchmen*. New York: DC Comics.
– (2005). "The World." In: *Absolute Watchmen*. New York: DC Comics, 2005.
Murphy, Timothy S. (1997). *Wising Up the Marks: The Amodern William Burroughs*. Berkeley: University of California Press.
Nyberg, Amy Kiste (1998). *Seal of Approval: The History of the Comics Code*. Jackson, MS: University Press of Mississippi.
Rozanski, Chuck (2009). "From Porn to Pulitzer, Comics Appreciation at the University of Colorado." In: *Graphia: Exhibition Catalogue*, ed. William Kuskin. Boulder, CO, 7–8.
Salisbury, Mark (2000). *Artists on Comic Art*. London: Titan Books.
Spiegelman, Art (1975). "Day at the Circuits." *Arcade: The Comics Revue* 2: 44.
– (2007). *Conversations*, ed. Joseph Witek. Jackson, MS: University Press of Mississippi.
– (2008). *Breakdowns: Portrait of the Artist as a Young %@&*!* New York: Pantheon.
Spiegelman, Art and Bill Griffith (1975). "Editorial: An Introduction." *Arcade: The Comics Revue* 1: 4.
Versaci, Rocco (2007). *This Book Contains Graphic Language: Comics as Literature*. London: Continuum.
Wright, Bradford (2008). "From Social Consciousness to Cosmic Awareness: Superhero Comic Books and the Culture of Self-Interrogation, 1968–1974." In Kuskin 2008: 155–74.

Jason Mittell
(Middlebury College)

Previously On: Prime Time Serials and the Mechanics of Memory

In recent years, American television has embraced a model of narrative complexity that has proven to be both artistically innovative and financially lucrative. Dozens of series across genres, from comedies like *Seinfeld* and *Arrested Development* to dramas like *Buffy the Vampire Slayer* and *24*, have explored serialized forms and non-conventional storytelling strategies such as intertwined flashbacks and shifting narrative perspectives that had previously been quite rare within mainstream American television. Serialized television has emerged as a vibrant artistic form that many critics suggest rivals previous models of long-form narrative, such as 19th century novels.

Television's poetics of narrative complexity are wide ranging. Series embrace a balance between episodic and serial form, allowing for partial closure within episodes while maintaining broad narrative arcs across episodes and even seasons. Such programs also embrace more elaborate storytelling techniques, such as temporal play, shifting perspectives and focalization, repetition, and overt experimentation with genre and narrative norms. Many contemporary programs are more reflexive in their narration, embracing an operational aesthetic, encouraging viewers to pay attention to the level of narrative discourse as well as the storyworld. In all of these instances, narratively complex television programs both demand that viewers pay attention more closely than typical for the medium, and allow for viewers to experience more confusion in their process of narrative comprehension. In short, television has become more difficult to understand, requiring viewers to engage more fully as attentive viewers (see Mittell 2006).

In this essay, I want to explore how complex serials strategically trigger, confound, and play with viewers' memories, considering how television storytelling strategies fit with our understanding of the cognitive mechanics of memory and highlighting the poetic techniques that programs use to engage viewers and enable long-term comprehension. The television medium employs specific strategies distinct from other narrative media. For instance, cinematic narratives typically engage a viewer's short-term memory, cuing and obscuring moments from within the controlled unfolding of a two-hour feature film, while literature designs its stories to be consumed at the reader's own pace and control, allowing for an on-demand return to previous pages as needed. The typical model of television consumption, divided into weekly episodes and annual seasons, constrains producers interested in telling stories that transcend individual installments, as any viewer's memory of previous episodes is quite variable, with a significant number of viewers having missed numerous episodes altogether. These constraints have helped lead to a specific set of storytelling conventions and poetic possibilities that distinguish television as a narrative medium.

The Historical and Institutional Contexts of Television Storytelling

Before exploring television's mechanics of memory, it is important to understand the numerous reasons why it has taken 50 years for television to broadly adopt such complex poetic possibilities. The commercial television industry in the United States avoids risks in search of economic stability, embracing a strategy of imitation and formula that often results in a model of "least objectionable content." For decades, the commercial television industry was immensely profitable producing programming with minimal formal variety outside the conventional genre norms of sitcoms and procedural dramas. Serial narratives were primarily confined to the lowbrow genre of daytime soap operas, with more prestigious primetime offerings avoiding continuing storylines in lieu of episodic closure and limited continuity.

Economic strategies privileged the episodic form—in large part, serialized content posed problems for the production industry's cash cow, syndication. Reruns distributed by syndicators could be aired in any order, making complex continuing storylines an obstacle to the lucrative aftermarket. Additionally, network research departments believed that even the biggest hit series could be guaranteed a consistent carryover audience of no more than 1/3 from week-to-week, meaning that the majority of viewers would not be sufficiently aware of a series's backstory to follow continuing storylines. Coupled with the general risk-averse attitude of networks and the ongoing success of episodic programming, there was little economic rationale for television producers to undertake the risks necessary to embark on experiments in more serialized and complex storytelling.

These industrial conditions have changed over the last twenty years, with the much-reported erosion of broadcast networks' audience size, and increased competition from cable, satellite, online video, and other media. In the wake of decreased audience shares, the industry found itself in a situation where programming risks could be justified as an attempt to discover a new model of popular programming—audience shares that would once be considered fringe or cult now qualify as mainstream hits. Cable channels could find a lucrative dedicated audience by creating programming that demanded regular viewing, and in the case of HBO and Showtime, help justify monthly subscription fees. Additionally, new technologies of recording and playback, from DVDs to DVRs to online streaming, all allow viewers more opportunities to catch up on missed episodes. Thus the underlying contexts of television programming have transformed sufficiently to allow a mode of narrative complexity to flourish since the late 1990s (see Lotz: 2007).

As with any popular narrative mode, specific formal strategies have emerged to manage audience comprehension. These strategies have been formed through a mixture of industrial conventions and norms, and creative innovations that have shifted dominant practices. Even though the rise of cable and decline in network domination has resulted in greater risk-taking and innovation, there are still crucial assumptions that shape television storytelling. The industry still adheres to the view that viewers are rarely dedicated enough to consistently watch every episode in sequence. Thus producers are encouraged to develop strategies to fill-in narrative gaps and catch up erratic viewers. Additionally, the television industry is understandably reluctant to program a series whose narrative is so densely constructed that it is impossible for new viewers to leap in mid-series.

Along with this industrial conventional wisdom, viewers bring their own assumptions as to what they expect from narrative television. Even though other sites of evidence suggests that viewers are more likely to watch a series consistently than the industry assumes, most viewers still want to be able to miss an episode or start a series midway through a season without being alienated or confused. They also assume that there will be some means available to them to catch up on necessary backstory, whether within the show itself or through some external site. Finally, they come to complex narratives with the expectation that mysteries and enigmas created within a series will eventually be revealed, hopefully with a satisfying resolution.

Television's mechanisms of storytelling also provide some important constraints on how stories can be told. More than almost any other medium, commercial television has a highly-restrictive structured delivery system: weekly episodes of prescribed lengths, often with required breaks for advertisements. A given season will have a specific number of episodes, with variable scheduling for how long breaks between episodes might be — often producers cannot plan on precisely when a series will be aired or even in some extreme cases, in what order episodes might appear. Additionally, the series is consumed as it is still being produced, meaning that adjustments are often made midstream due to unexpected circumstances. Such adjustments can be due to casting constraints, as in an actor's illness, pregnancy or death, or feedback from networks, sponsors, or audience in reaction to an emerging storyline. Constraints like these make television storytelling distinct from nearly every other medium — a parallel would be if literature demanded the exact same word count for every chapter of every novel, regardless of genre, style or author.

Finally, a successful television series typically lacks a crucial element that has long been hailed as of supreme importance for a well-told story: an ending. Unlike nearly every other narrative medium, American commercial television operates on what might be termed the "infinite model" of storytelling — a series is deemed a success only as long as it keeps going. While other national television systems might end a successful series after a year or two, American series generally keep running as long as they are generating decent ratings. This becomes a significant issue for storytellers, who must design narrative worlds that are able to sustain themselves for years rather than closed narratives plans created for a specific run. Not surprisingly, this need to accommodate an infinite run privileges episodic content with little continuity and long-term story development, with recyclable characters and interchanging situations typical of police dramas and sitcoms.

Diegetic Techniques for Managing Memory

Despite all of these constraints and norms, American television has developed a new mode of narrative complexity that pushes back against many of these limitations. This serialized mode transcends individual genres, with a range of sitcoms, crime dramas, medical shows, and other forms embracing narrative complexity as a storytelling strategy. One of the specific challenges that such series have faced, with their emphasis on storyworld continuity and non-linear narration, is managing the memories of viewers. If the characters and events in the storyworld have internal coherence and continuity, then viewers need to follow along with the expansive narrative universe. When it concerns a series that is told over a period of months and years, this becomes a challenge for the mechanics of memory.

These challenges pull storytellers in a number of directions. Even though technologies and distribution systems have made it more possible to catch up on missed episodes, television producers still need to provide opportunities to fill in gaps for viewers who may have missed an episode or two. However, they cannot be so redundant as to bore or annoy diehard fans who watch every episode, or DVD viewers who might be watching an entire season in a marathon binge. Likewise on some complex shows like *Lost*, which tells its story of a mysterious island with an array of temporal leaps and misdirection, or *Battlestar Galactica*, a science fiction drama dependent on complex continuity across seasons, dedicated fans might fill in gaps between weekly episodes by reading online recaps and commentaries, keeping the events of previous weeks fresh in their minds. Thus writers need to balance between the needs of erratic and dedicated viewers.

Similarly, individual episodes need to manage the short-term memory of events that roll out over the course of the episode along with the longer term serialized recall from weeks, months, or even years beforehand. While the stereotype of the distracted television glance is less relevant today, especially concerning demanding and slow-paced narratives like *The Wire* or *Mad Men* that might take years to payoff long dormant story threads, producers still need to create programs for a domestic environment that is prone to split attention and multitasking viewers more than for other media. Over the course of an episode, television narratives embed minor redundancies that remind viewers of key story information, ranging from establishing visuals locating a scene's setting to subtle repetition of characters' names and relationships. The entire process of narration in a television series needs to constantly reinforce story information and remind viewers of what they need to know to comprehend the next event.

Television producers have always erred toward redundancy and repetition in their narrative strategies, a tendency that was established in earlier modes of serial narrative. Before the last two decades, the primary model of serial television in America was the daytime soap opera, which developed its own conventions and norms for managing memory. As Robert Allen has explored, soap operas embrace a poetics of redundancy — instead of treating repetition as a necessary evil, soaps raise it to an art form. Allen suggests that soap operas, which were designed both for dedicated fans as well as distracted and erratic viewers, derive their narrative pleasures less from the forward-moving plot of new events and developments, but more from the ripple effects of an event across the community of relationships within the drama (Allen 1985; see also Spence 2005).

The redundant narration of soap operas depends on a device that both facilitates viewer recall and the pleasures of watching character reactions to past events: *diegetic retelling*. Typically, a soap opera might portray a key event on-screen, although if it is a spectacle that would require a high-budget production like a car accident or disaster, it might occur off-screen. The event itself becomes less narratively important in its initial portrayal than in the chain of on-screen conversations about the event. Thus any single event might be retold through the dialogue-heavy conventions of the genre, as each character reacts to the news of hearing about the event and we witness the impact each moment of retelling has upon the characters and their web of relationships. Through this convention of recall, we are both repeatedly reminded of what happened with our attention focused on the characters and their emotional lives, making redundancy an active pleasure of the genre.

Soap operas use diegetic retelling following particular episodic structures. Typically an episode features between four and six separate storylines intercut throughout the hour, selecting between dozens of potential ongoing stories on a series. At the beginning of the episode, each storyline gets one scene to set up that day's conversation, typically with the characters talking about some recent event and revealing some new information about how that event impacts their relationship or situation. These initial scenes are highly focused on retelling, reminding and catching viewers up about every element in the scene — previous events, relationships, settings, and even character names. As the episode progresses, the process of retelling continues, especially to remind viewers as each scene cycles back from a commercial break, but advances the plot by highlighting the new story elements rippling out from past events. At end of the episode, each scene concludes with a moment of uncertainty to prompt a series of retellings when the next episode featuring that storyline airs. While a viewer closely focused on every episode may find the level of repetition frustrating, more erratic, casual, and distracted viewers learn to use the redundancy as both a means of following the plot and enjoying the relationship-driven storytelling.

Prime time serials are far less dependent on the dialogue-based practice of diegetic retelling as a core narrative pleasure than daytime soaps, but still frequently use this traditional technique. Characters call each other by name and reference their relationships more frequently than in everyday life, using dialogue as a way to keep crucial character information active in our minds. Often past events are retold to new characters both to update them on the status of a situation and to remind us of what we have already seen. For a typical instance, early in *Lost*'s fourth season episode "Cabin Fever," a scene shows mercenary leader Keamy arriving via helicopter on a freighter with an injured man. The ship's doctor asks, "What did this to him?" Keamy replies, "A black pillar of smoke threw him 50 feet in the air... ripped his guts out," retelling an event spectacularly portrayed two episodes earlier ("The Shape of Things to Come"). While anyone who saw the previous episode was unlikely to have forgotten the source of the injury, this diegetic retelling reminds us of the events via naturalistic dialogue and reinforces what we have already previously seen.

This example points to an important concept in the way that viewers make sense of ongoing serials. At this point in *Lost*'s run, a dedicated viewer will have watched 79 episodes over the course of four years, creating a vast array of narrative information to retain and recall. Even the most attentive and intent viewer could not possibly have all of that narrative information active in her operative working memory — most of the story information she has retained would be archived in long-term memory. When a character's dialogue uses diegetic retelling, the viewer activates that bit of story information into working memory, making it part of her immediate narrative comprehension.[1] While certainly some viewers might have been actively thinking about the smoke monster's attack from two weeks earlier when starting "Cabin Fever," this diegetic retelling ensures that everyone has this context active in working memory while watching the rest of the episode, as subsequent events build upon this past event to motivate Keamy's actions to find his betrayer and return to the island.

The use of dialog to recall previous events does not have to necessarily be motivated toward clarity; diegetic retelling can also work to purposefully create a sense of confusion or curiosity. As a series, *The Wire* tends to avoid redundancy, favoring a naturalistic mode of long-term storytelling in which viewers are often confused as to who is who and how it everything fits together. Eventually over the course of a season, the characters, roles, and systems become clear, making the process of discovery part of the show's narrative pleasure. However, some elements are left perpetually vague; for instance, Lieutenant Cedric Daniels is introduced in the first season as an upright, career-driven police officer. This perception is undercut when an FBI officer tells Detective McNulty that there's some dirt in Daniels's past, and that the police department covered it up. This information is never directly addressed or fully clarified in the first season, serving as backstory on the otherwise ethical Daniels. In the fourth season, Daniels is promoted up the ranks by the new mayor with possibilities of rising to Commissioner, prompting current Commissioner Burrell to mention to his confidants, "I happen to know he's less the saint than he pretends to be." This casual mention is the only direct reference to the scandal until

1 For an overview of the cognitive understanding of memory, see Roediger et. al. 2007; for an application of cognitive theories of memory to moving image storytelling, see Bordwell 2008.

the fifth season, when Daniels's still-vague past crimes prevent him from taking the Commissioner job. For *Wire* fans, the casual reference to the dirt on Daniels rewards our long-term memories from years before, but prompts the continued curiosity into the character's enigmatic past that is never fully revealed in detail.

Diegetic retelling typically uses dialogue as a means to activate past events into working memory, but more subtle cues can also serve a similar function. As television is both an audio and visual medium, *visual cues* like objects, setting, or shot composition can serve the function to activate long-term memories. For instance, in the third season *Battlestar Galactica* episode "Maelstrom," pilot Kara Thrace gives Admiral William Adama a figurine of a goddess to use as a masthead for his model ship; at the end of that episode, Adama destroys the model out of grief when Thrace's ship appears to be destroyed in a fatal crash. In the next season's episode "Six of One," Adama is shown rebuilding the model after Thrace has seemingly returned from the grave. Lingering shots of the figurine and ship activate memories of the earlier episode, adding resonance to these characters' relationship and the mysterious circumstances of Thrace's survival, but without the explicit expository function of dialog. Typically, visual cues are more subtle than dialog, functioning less to catch-up viewers who might have missed an episode than integrating more directly into a naturalistic style of moving image storytelling.

Managing Memory by Non-Naturalistic Narration

Producers of long-form stories constantly need to balance the needs of forward narrative momentum with the ability to keep the audience's memories activated for relevant story information from previous episodes. While diegetic strategies of dialog and visual cues are a primary means for activating viewer memories, many programs use non-naturalistic techniques to trigger recall. The use of voiceover is a common way to convey story information via a more self-conscious mode of narration. While many writers condemn voiceover as overly literary and a lazy tool for film and television, it can be used effectively in certain genres like detective shows, serving to both guide viewers within the narrative world and offer a distinctive personality to the storytelling.

The *film noir* infused teen drama *Veronica Mars* uses often sarcastic *first-person voiceover narration* by the titular character to both keep viewers on track with the complex story and convey the character's perspective on narrative events. For instance, in the first season episode "Silence of the Lamb," Veronica is helping her friend Mac grapple with the discovery that she was switched at birth with another baby. Veronica's voiceover narration intones, "I could tell Mac I know how she feels, but the truth is, I don't. When I had the opportunity to learn my paternity, I chose blissful ignorance with a side of gnawing doubt." This reference to Veronica's paternity refers to an event from two episodes earlier, as Veronica discovered that her mother had been unfaithful and she ordered a kit to test her father's DNA, but decided not to go through with the test. While Veronica's mysterious parentage does not become a significant plot point until later in the season, recalling this previous event helps viewers draw parallels between Mac and Veronica, and colors the way that Veronica and her father interact later in the episode.

Less commonly for television, voiceover narration can resemble the more literary model of third-person omniscient storytellers. Such narrators typically act only to frame a story, as in Rod Serling's opening and closing narration on the 1960s science-fiction anthology series *The Twilight Zone*, but some recent series have played with *third-person voiceover narration* as a self-conscious device. *Pushing Daisies*, a whimsical cross between fantasy romance and detective fiction, uses the voice of Jim Dale, recognizable as the reader of the *Harry Potter* audiobooks, as an omniscient narrator to both present new story information and remind us of past events. In episode seven, "Smell of Success," the narrator comments, "Chuck continued to keep the secret ingredient of her pies secret. Not even Olive Snook knew the baked secret she delivered contained homeopathic mood-enhancers meant to pry Chuck's aunts out of their funk." This voiceover reminds us of a plot development introduced four episodes earlier and that continued to run through the season; the reminder helps viewers remember both what is happening, and who knows what about the secret pie ingredient. Given *Pushing Daisies*' highly elaborate narrative mechanics and fanciful storyworld, the omniscient narrator's storybook style, reinforced by the intertextual link to *Harry Potter*, functions both to manage memories and promote a self-conscious playful tone.

An even more farcical use of third-person voiceover can be found in the farcical sitcom *Arrested Development*, with producer Ron Howard narrating the action about a dysfunctional wealthy family as if he is providing deadpan commentary within a nature documentary (see Thompson 2007). Howard's narration constantly fills in gaps and moves the story forward, allowing the fast-paced show to cover an astounding amount of storytelling ground in a half-hour. The narrator frequently provides a clarifying reference to a previous episode — in the second season episode, "The One Where They Build a House," aspiring actor Tobias appears with blue paint on his ear, leading Howard to clarify, "Tobias had recently auditioned as an understudy for the silent performance-art trio, the Blue

Man Group," an event that occurred in the previous episode. Howard's deadpan narration often serves to humorously undercut or comment on the character's action, providing narrative momentum, clarifying recall, and comedic density.

Arrested Development's narration highlights how moving image media rely on more than just language to convey meaning—often the narrator's comments are accompanied by images and scenes to further trigger memories and move the narrative forward. Following the comment on Tobias and the Blue Man Group, the scene shifts to a flashback of Tobias auditioning for the part. While this references an event that happened over the course of the previous episode, this scene was never shown, making it a flashback within the storyworld but adding new narrative information beyond just triggering recall. *Arrested Development* uses more than flashback scenes to retell past events, relying on a number of pseudo-documentary techniques for comedic effect. Later in the same episode, Michael and his son are talking about how he is no longer in charge of the family company. Howard's narration reminds us of another event from the previous episode: "In fact, since Michael's father escaped from prison, his brother G.O.B. had been made president." The visuals cut to a shot of a newspaper reporting both the prison escape (complete with still photo taken from the previous episode) and the leadership succession. The scene then shifts to a conversation between Michael and G.O.B., in which they recount the events that led to G.O.B.'s presidency and the accompanying criminal investigation, all framed with the running gag of Michael disingenuously saying, "I have no problem with that," which is even quoted in the newspaper. The effect of these narrative strategies is to combine a range of ways to prompt viewer recall while maintaining a humorous tone and self-conscious style.

Since narration is not necessarily verbal in moving image media like film and television, other techniques can be used to retell information aside from voiceover. Flashbacks are a more common technique than voiceover to incorporate previous events into an episode, and like voiceover, they can follow first or third-person focalization. A first-person *subjective flashback* is more common, presenting a character's memories as cued by suggestive close-ups, subjective visuals, and special effects. For instance, in the season four *Battlestar Galactica* episode, "Guess What's Coming To Dinner," Cylon leader Natalie tells a group of humans that being rescued by Kara Thrace was their destiny. Kara watches the speech as the image begins to blur and break-up, leading into a subjective flashback of Kara being told that she is the "harbinger of death" in the previous episode. While this was an important prophecy that viewers are likely to recall, the explicit flashback both activates the memory and highlights its importance to Kara in imagining her own role in the battle between humans and Cylons. Reinforcing this line by re-showing the scene via flashback makes it more prominent in the show's long-term mythology, which proves to be a central narrative concern in the show's final season. Such glimpses of character's memories via flashbacks are a common cue to trigger a viewer's own memories, promote empathy with a main character, and frame our comprehension of an upcoming set of events.

Flashbacks can be paired with voiceover narration as a way of visualizing a narrator's memories. *Veronica Mars* frequently uses this device, as we see bits from Veronica's memories and clues about a lengthy mystery, often that we witness multiple times throughout a season. Comedies can use a similar technique, such as on *My Name Is Earl*, where Earl will reference a minor character we've met previously, and narrate a flashback comprised of earlier appearances and footage. In these instances, the voiceover typically serves as a determining thread of knowledge, framing previous scenes and cueing the relevant memories of earlier events and relationships as needed to advance the ongoing story.

Flashbacks presented from a more objective third-person perspective, or what we might call *replays*, are more commonly used as a way to fill in backstory rather than triggering memories — series like *Lost*, *Jack and Bobby*, and *Boomtown* use atemporal storytelling to craft their complex narratives, but flashbacks are rarely used to trigger memories rather than present new narrative material on such programs. Flashbacks of previously-seen events that are not framed as character memories are quite uncommon. Crime shows like *C.S.I.* often use replays in the context of retelling the previously-seen crime scene, but present new narrative information in the retelling, making the flashback less about memory than gap-filling. Legal thriller *Damages* and hostage drama *The Nine* both use complex atemporal structures to narrate their core crime stories, portraying previous events repeatedly throughout the season and adding more information each time to string together a new storythread — again, this model of repetition is more about filling in gaps in multiple timelines rather than reminding us what we might have forgotten. Matt Hills discusses such objective flashbacks in the most recent version of the British science-fiction series *Doctor Who*, but suggests that they function more to invite new viewers into the complex narrative rather refresh the memories of long-term fans (Hills, 2009).[2]

---

2 One atypical example of a pure replay in a dramatic primetime serial was found in the sixth season *Lost* episode "Across the Sea," aired while this volume was in press. Taking place nearly entirely in a time period more than a thousand years before the show's narrative present, the episode ends with a character placing the dead bodies of his mother and

A more common place to see such replays is reality television. Subjective flashbacks are a rarity, but it is quite common for a reality show to replay earlier scenes and moments to refresh our memories of previous events. This technique is more consistent with the documentary style of reality television, as a subjective flashback would feel out-of-place, and the replays can be motivated as coming from the more omniscient documentary gaze. Reality television also uses more short-term replays, often returning from a commercial break by repeating the final few moments from the previous segment, or similarly starting a new episode with the final scene of the last. Scripted television sometimes adopts this technique between weeks as well, starting the new episode by replaying an earlier cliffhanger moment a bit to regain momentum and refresh viewers' memories.

The most common examples of objective replays triggering memories within American narrative television might be within comedies. One recent trend has been the rise of the cutaway aside as a comedic technique, commonly found in animated series like *Family Guy* or single-camera sitcoms like *Scrubs*. Such asides frequently cut from the main action to an often random vignette to offset or comment on whatever just happened in the story. These asides can be fantasy sequences, unknown moments from a character's past, or replays from past episodes. An example of the latter comes from "Kidney Now," a third season episode of the satirical showbiz comedy *30 Rock*. Tracy tells Kenneth that he never cries, which cuts away to a montage of six moments from previous episodes showing Tracy crying. The sequence is certainly functions as a comedic aside, but builds upon our memories of Tracy's frequent crying jags that counters Tracy's own statement. However, the paucity of relevant examples suggests that replays are a comparatively less utilized strategy to promote memory recall.

Prompting Recall Outside the Narrative Frame

Thus far, the strategies of triggering memories I have discussed all occur within the diegetic narration of serial television. However, television has also adopted a number of strategies outside of the core storytelling text to help manage memories. Most notably, most contemporary serials air

---

brother in a cave. The episode then replays selections from a first season episode, in which the show's main characters discover the bodies and speculate on their origins. The anomaly of this technique was highlighted by fan reactions to the replays, as most viewers bristled at the heavy-handed recall to an important mythological moment, suggesting that replays have little place within the poetics of primetime serials.

a one-to-two-minute *recap* before each episode to summarize key events "previously on" the series. These recaps are generally crafted by producers, choosing key moments that they believe vital to refresh viewers' memories for upcoming storylines and to enable new viewers to get on board with the series. While they are designed for the weekly original airings, recaps often do get included on DVDs, with some series offering the option of viewing each episode with or without recaps, while others leave them integrated into the core episode. The presence or absence of recaps can drastically change the way episodes are consumed and comprehended.

Most recaps highlight the most pertinent narrative information for the upcoming episode. For instance, the *Veronica Mars* episode "Silence of the Lamb," replays three brief scenes in the recap, drawing from three different episodes, ranging back over nine weeks. The scenes capture highly expository moments — first is a two-line exchange between Veronica's father and former sheriff Keith Mars and his successor Lamb, discussing the controversial murder case of Lily Kane, the basis of the main season-long arc. Next is the scene where Veronica and Mac meet, setting up Mac's role in this episode's primary plot. Finally, shots of Veronica investigating her mother's past are overlaid with a voice-over explaining the contested paternity, which sets up the secondary plot of this episode. In just 30 seconds, the show triggers which long-term plotlines need to be activated into working memory to comprehend this episode's developments. However, these clips would mean almost nothing to someone who had not seen most of the previous episodes, as the snippets are far too minimal to actually provide adequate exposition for new viewers. Just as notable is what the recap omits, with no reference to major characters Logan and Duncan — these characters do not appear in this episode, and thus can stay archived in long-term memory.

Recaps can serve more expository roles, especially early in a series run. The second episode of crime drama *Dexter* features a two-minute recap, culled exclusively from the 52-minute pilot. This recap functions as a true summary of the pilot, providing glimpses of each main character, highlighting the core narrative scenario of a serial killer working for the Miami Police Department, and establishing the ongoing arc of Dexter's ludic pursuit of another serial killer. While it might be a bit confusing, it would certainly be possible to watch the series without viewing the pilot, filling in narrative gaps solely from this recap and other internal redundancies. For viewers who had seen the pilot, the recap seems quite redundant, offering little to cue memories aside from character names — the core narrative situation of a serial killer working as a forensic investigator is sufficiently memorable as to not need refreshing, as simply thinking about the name of the show would likely activate that basic narrative memory.

The recap from *Dexter*'s first season finale is much more in keeping with the memory-refreshing role typically found later in a season. The 1:45 recap contains clips from many of the previous 11 episodes, and presents them in such quick succession that they would be incomprehensible to a new viewer. For ongoing viewers, however, the flashes of clues remind us of how far Dexter had gotten in his pursuit of the Ice Truck Killer, and the final shots of his sister in peril refreshes the cliffhanger from the previous episode. The recap also focuses on the stabbing of police office Angel from episode 10, which becomes a major plot point in the finale. More than anything, recaps like this one serve to filter the hours of story information that an ongoing viewer accrues, activating the most crucial bits of narrative into working memory while allowing other moments that will not become relevant in the upcoming episode to continue to reside in the archives of long-term memory.

Recaps can often trigger long dormant memories which might work to foreshadow upcoming narrative events. Often in complex narratives, a recap will remind viewers of a key mystery or enigma that has receded to the background in recent serialized episodes. In the first season of *Lost*, castaway Sayid is attacked and knocked unconscious while trying to use radio equipment to send a message off the island in the show's seventh episode, "The Moth." Sayid recovers in the following episode, but it is left uncertain as to who attacked him — the incident goes unmentioned for numerous episodes. In *Lost*'s 21st episode, "The Greater Good," the recap replays this scene that had first been seen five months earlier, suggesting (correctly) that this dormant question as to who attacked Sayid would finally be addressed. While different viewers might have varying investments on that particular mystery, *Lost* had introduced so many burning questions and enigmas over the months between these two episodes, it seems fair to say that without this recap, the mystery over Sayid's attack would be fairly unlikely to be active within most viewers' working memories. The recap plays the scene again to encourage viewers to remember this lingering question and trigger the narrative satisfaction of its forthcoming resolution.

Sometime, recaps can trigger memories beyond dormant questions, highlighting instead important character backstories or relationships. For instance, the recap before the fourth season *Battlestar Galactica* episode "Escape Velocity," includes a scene from the third season episode "Exodus (part II)" featuring the death of Ellen Tigh, wife of Colonel Sol Tigh. The gap between the original airdates of these episodes was over 18 months, marking this scene's presence in the recap as unusual — at the time I first saw it, I hypothesized that the inclusion of Ellen's death in the recap must mean that she'll reappear in some fashion in the episode. That prediction proved correct, as Sol Tigh begins to hallucinate visions of Ellen, a connection that proves to be even more significant in the series mythology later in the season. The recap effectively reminded me about Ellen, who had certainly receded from my active memory, but also made her reappearance more predictable than it would have been within the diegetic narrative without the recap. Viewers watching the series on DVD or DVR might choose to fast-forward through the recaps, which might make Ellen's reappearance prompt confusion or surprise, two reactions mitigated by her presence in the recap.

The strategies of recall prompted by recaps can run counter to one of the core narrative pleasures of most genres of storytelling: surprise. Within many complex long-term narratives, the deep mythology of the storyworld can be confusing and hard-to-follow without recaps to active working memories and remind us of deep-seated backstory. However, seeing a character or event in a recap can effectively "spoil" a surprise appearance or twist, undercutting the narrative effects that creators might have been hoping to produce. Clearly recaps need to balance between the dual demands of activating memories for comprehension and avoiding foreshadowing to allow for surprise to register for viewers without being confusing. Creators have devised a number of strategies for avoiding such recap spoilers.

One option is the use of diegetic flashbacks to serve as embedded recaps for viewers in the moment of the surprise itself. "Daybreak," the series finale of *Battlestar Galactica* offers a good (if convoluted) example. Five characters agree to use a complicated technological process that will share their memories with each other to facilitate a peace agreement between the warring Cylons and humans. Prior to the procedure, Tory mentions that they may discover things that are shameful in their pasts, a protest that another character brushes aside. During the procedure, we glimpse memories in the form of flashbacks of some key moments from each character. Among these events, we see Tory confronting Cally, the late wife of Galen, another character in the memory exchange. Galen starts to focus on these memories, and we see Tory's murder of Cally, prompting him to break from the procedure and strangle Tory. The flashbacks are to another season four episode, "The Ties That Bind," which had originally aired 11 months before "Daybreak."

Producer Ron Moore stated in his podcast that they intentionally "buried" the storyline of Cally's murder, waiting for the climactic moment to payoff Galen's revenge with high narrative stakes in the finale.[3] Notably,

3 <http://media.scifi.com/battlestar/downloads/podcast/mp3/421–423/bsg_ep421–423_FULL.mp3>

the recap for "Daybreak" contains no reference to Cally or the murder, allowing the viewer to experience the memory along with Galen's realization. While a dedicated viewer certainly could have recalled that Tory had murdered Cally without getting caught, it was far from active memory after 11 months and many subsequent plot machinations — viewers later watching the series on DVD would have a more compressed experience, and thus would be more likely to have the lingering plot point fresh within their minds. For me and some other viewers I spoke with, the revelation prompted a gradual surprising realization that Galen will witness his wife's murder and the shock of his reaction. Had the recap reminded us about the murder, we would have been better able to anticipate the result of the memory meld, defusing a moment of high drama. The effect of such revelations might be called *surprise memory*, or the moment of being surprised by story information that you already know, but don't have within working memory.

Surprise memory does not need to be triggered by a flashback. In the fourth season episode of *Lost*, "Cabin Fever," which notably aired without a "previously on *Lost*" recap, castaway Claire awakens in the jungle to discover that her infant son is not with her. She looks around for him, and we see Christian Shephard holding him. Claire looks at him with confusion and says, "Dad?" right before we cut to commercial. It had been revealed via off-island flashback that Christian, who was introduced as main character Jack's father in the first season, was also Claire's father in the third season episode "Par Avion," but that relationship had not been actively referenced for over 10 months. While it is surprising enough to see Christian in the woods (especially given that he is dead and previously had only appeared on the island as a mysterious apparition for Jack!), the average viewer would not likely have his identity as Claire's father in working memory until she calls him Dad, prompting this satisfying moment of surprise memory.

The practice of surprise memory highlights the importance of working memory for storytelling practice. When a long-term viewer has accrued a large amount of story information, a storyteller can guide emotional reactions based on what is in working memory — a show might highlight particular relationships and connections within working memory, or prompt surprise or suspense via elements buried in long-term memory. The feeling of being surprised through the act of remembering is quite pleasurable, rewarding the long-term viewer's knowledge base while provoking the flood of recognition stemming from the activation of such memories. Such pleasures are hard to imagine working in non-serialized formats, as the shorter-term forms of cinema or novels do not allow sufficient time over the course of narrative consumption to enable the process of archiving, forgetting, and reactivation needed to create surprise memory.

One additional source of memory within television episodes can be the *credit sequence*. While such sequences vary greatly, from just a brief title card as on *Lost* or *Breaking Bad*, to a 2-minute sequence as on *Deadwood* or *Veronica Mars*. Some title sequences use footage outside the narrative, as with Tony's drive from New York to his house on the gangster drama *The Sopranos*, with the sequence working to emphasize the setting and milieu of the show, or *Dexter*'s visually stylized images of the title character preparing to go to work, highlighting the theme of finding the gruesome within the mundane. Many longer title sequences include images from the series itself, which for both episodic and serialized shows can evoke fond character moments, as with sitcom *Friends* or teen horror drama *Buffy the Vampire Slayer*.

One series whose credit sequence adds to mechanics of memory is *The Wire*. Each season offers a new montage of images of Baltimore and from narrative moments of the series, most of which have little explicit resonance within story. But some images do trigger particular memories. For instance, season four's credits includes a brief close-up of an unidentified man putting a lollypop into his pocket. For the first four episodes, this image bears no real meaning, and seems out of place next to images of criminals, cops, and kids on the street. In the season's fourth episode, "Refugees," we see the image in context, as crime boss Marlo pickpockets the lollypop in an act of petty crime aimed to openly mock a security guard, who is later killed for daring to confront Marlo about shoplifting. For the rest of the season, this repeated image in the credits serves as a reminder of Marlo's arrogance and cold-blooded lust for power, highlighting how he might do anything to climb the ranks of Baltimore's drug game and build his reputation. Through this repetition and constant reminder, we keep this minor action in working memory, consistently shading Marlo's character.

The process of consuming television narratives plays out in a broader context than the television text itself. The television industry has devised a number of extra-textual means of helping manage viewer memory. One long-standing tradition that has been in decline is the *rerun*—for decades, networks typically played each episode of a season twice throughout the year, filling in off-times with earlier episodes. These network reruns have become less common in the 2000s, especially with DVD, DVR, and online video as methods for viewers to rewatch or catch-up on missed episodes. For instance, *Lost* aired with reruns over the summer and during breaks from new episodes in its first two seasons, but ABC ceased this practice in later seasons. Instead, *Lost* and other network shows have taken a page from cable channels, showing the same episode multiple times throughout the week of its first run, a scheduling practice that allows viewers to refresh their memories or take a closer look at an episode during the week's gap, or catch-up on missed material.

Lost has take advantage of these multiple airings by offering what they call "enhanced versions" of episodes after the initial airing — these versions add caption annotations to the action, clarifying references and previous events. For instance, in "Something Nice Back Home" when Claire encounters Christian, the captions read: "Christian Shepard is also Claire's father, making Jack and Claire half-brother and sister, though neither one of them know it." Such comments certainly help refresh memories for viewers, but most diehard fans report dissatisfaction with the "enhanced" experience for being too obvious, literal, or trivial in its annotations.

More commonly, serialized programs have created stand-alone texts designed to refresh memories and initiate new viewers. *Lost* has aired twelve hour-long *compilation shows* over the course of its first five seasons, with each show replaying key moments from the series along with voice-over narration retelling the narrative. Similar recap compilation shows have been used by *Battlestar Galactica* and *The Wire*, among others, often airing before the start of a new season to refresh viewer memories and invite new viewers. Compilation shows, like recaps, are quite strategic in their summaries, selecting plot threads with continued relevancy while ignoring storylines that have been resolved and made dormant within the ongoing narrative.

The rise of online video has enabled a number of other strategies for recapping. Some networks, channels, and programs have created "minisodes" briefly summing up previous episodes, such as NBC's online-only "2 Minute Replays" or *Rescue Me*'s "3 Minute Replays" that can be seen both online and on cable channel FX. Such replays probably function more to allow viewers who missed episodes to fill gaps, but they could also serve as memory refreshers like pre-show recaps; however, such replays are more designed to retell the entire episode rather than strategically present key story information for the upcoming episode.

More notably, a trend emerged online in 2007 with the popular YouTube video "The Seven Minute *Sopranos*."[4] A highly rapid recap of the previous five and a half seasons in advance of the final episodes, the humorous but affectionate fan-created video garnered over a million views and successfully promoted the final season. Producers took note of the success, and enlisted marketers to create similarly glib online recaps, such as "*Lost* in 8:15" and "What the frak is going on?" for *Battlestar Galactica*. These humorous recaps are designed for long-term fans as affectionate parodies,

---

4 <http://www.youtube.com/watch?v=Tz_Ees_-kE4>

but they also function to effectively remind viewers of key events and highlight patterns and repetitions across the series, such as the numerous times that Carmela Soprano "gets pissed" at her husband Tony, captured by the repeated visual of her throwing his luggage at him down the stairs.

Online recaps can be written as well presented as edited video. Network websites typically provide *episode summaries* for many series, but fan-created sites can serve as encyclopedic repositories of information for a complex long-form narrative. The fan-generated wiki Lostpedia is best known, but nearly every television series has a wiki where fans compile summaries and catalog events and characters, as well as using broader platforms such as Wikipedia and IMDB. The effect of this array of online media is that nearly any question a fan might have about a serialized television program can be answered by a quick Google search or perusing the show's most active fansites, making these long-form storyworlds effectively searchable and highly documented (see Mittell 2009).

Memory of Form

While the primary aspect of narrative memory involves the events and characters within the storyworld, television fictions also rely on and play with viewer memory for how stories are told. As I have discussed elsewhere, narratively complex television plays with storytelling form in a range of ways, prompting an "operational aesthetic" in which viewers are simultaneously concerned with the storyworld and its telling, or in narratological terms, both story and discourse (Mittell 2006). For viewers attending to the storytelling patterns that a series uses to convey its narrative world, *formal memory* helps frame the intrinsic norms that a series follows, and establishes storytelling expectations that can be relied upon or thwarted by creators.

One facet of formal memory involves the use of stylistic cues. While television has been much more aesthetically adventurous concerning narrative than visual style, some series do use particular stylistic strategies as part of a show's long-term reservoir of memory. *Battlestar Galactica* offers one such usage in the third season — for the first time in the series, we are taken inside a Cylon basestar as human Gaius Baltar is taken into custody by the Cylons. The scenes inside the basestar are edited with layered dissolves between shots, creating a dreamy and unreal quality to the setting. Across numerous episodes, the use of this formal pattern triggers memories of the setting and its previous events, serving as a means to create both a distinct sense of place and reinforce longer narrative arcs about the Cylon's home.

A prime example of an intrinsic storytelling norm being used to play with viewer memories and expectations is *Lost*'s use of flashbacks. Over the first three seasons, nearly every episode features a series of flashbacks focused on a single character (or couple, in the case of Sun and Jin), offering glimpses into lives before arriving on the island. These flashbacks are cued by a number of formal norms: typically starting with a close-up of the key character, followed by a "whooosh" sound and a straight-cut to the flashback. While these are not framed as character memories explicitly, they function as subjective narrative, providing story information that only one character on the island knows. As David Bordwell explores for film narration, learned intrinsic norms or schemas of a text help viewers make hypothesis, fill-in gaps, and anticipate actions, drawing upon earlier experiences to make sense of an ongoing narrative (Bordwell 1985). For an ongoing serial, intrinsic norms are more long-term, requiring active engagement with memory. Thus when *Lost* viewers see and hear these cues, we draw upon our formal memories to comprehend the upcoming sequence as a flashback.

In "Through the Looking Glass," the third season finale, *Lost* strategically plays with our memories to invite viewers to make a faulty assumption and prompt a spectacular surprise. The episode cues its off-island storyline as a flashback for the heroic character Jack, portraying him as drug-addled and despondent in Los Angeles. The formal devices used to present these sequences follow the norms we expect for flashbacks, leading viewers to assume that this is set in Jack's pre-island past by activating the well-established formal memories of how *Lost* tells its stories. But in the episode's final scene, we see Jack converse with fellow crash-survivor Kate about possibly returning to the island, establishing that what we've been seeing was actually a flash-forward. The only reason why this "narrative special effect" (Mittell 2006) works is because of our activated memories of the show's intrinsic norms, established over dozens of episodes throughout three seasons, highlighting the important role that formal memory plays within serial narrative.

Clearly, prime time serials use a range of narrative strategies to trigger and play with viewer memories. The significance of this catalog of poetic techniques is to highlight the importance of underlying cognitive processes in the seemingly simple act of narrative comprehension. Managing a multi-year narrative universe is difficult enough for television writers, but they also face significant challenges to ensure that viewers can follow the action without falling into either confusion or boredom from redundancy. As serialized television has evolved into a robust and unique art form over the past decade, producing some of this century's most compelling stories regardless of medium, it is vital that we recognize television's unique narrative techniques and highlight the innovative strategies it employs that help make it a distinctive and aesthetically valid medium. If we want to understand the potential ways that long-form narratives can be constructed and consumed, we need to remember how television has offered compelling solutions for mastering the mechanics of memory.

References

Allen, Robert C. (1985). *Speaking of Soap Operas.* Chapel Hill: University of North Carolina Press.

Bordwell, David (1985). *Narration in the Fiction Film.* Madison: University of Wisconsin Press.

– (2008). "Cognition and Comprehension: Viewing and Forgetting in *Mildred Pierce.*" In: D. Bordwell. *Poetics of Cinema.* New York: Routledge, 135–150.

Hills, Matt (2009). "Absent Epic, Implied Story Arcs, and Variation on a Narrative Theme: Doctor Who (2005–2008) as Cult/Mainstream Television." In: *Third Person: Authoring and Exploring Vast Narratives,* ed. Pat Harrigan and Noah Wardrip-Fruin. Cambridge: MIT Press, 333–342.

Lotz, Amanda D. (2007). *The Television Will Be Revolutionized.* New York: New York University Press.

Mittell, Jason (2006). "Narrative Complexity in Contemporary American Television." *The Velvet Light Trap* 58: 29–40.

– (2009)."Sites of Participation: Wiki Fandom and the Case of Lostpedia." *Transformative Works and Cultures* 3, http://journal.transformativeworks.org, http://journal.transformationworks.org/index.php/twc/article/view/118/117.

Roediger, Henry L., Dudai, Yadin and Fitzpatrick, Susan M., eds. (2007). *Science of Memory: Concepts.* Oxford: Oxford University Press.

Spence, Louise (2005). *Watching Daytime Soap Operas: The Power of Pleasure.* Middletown, CT: Wesleyan University Press.

Thompson, Ethan (2007). "Comedy Verité? The Observational Documentary Meets the Televisual Sitcom." *The Velvet Light Trap* 60: 63–72.

Paul Cobley
(London Metropolitan University)

The Paranoid Style in Narrative: The Anxiety of Storytelling After 9/11

"Catastrophe or the fear of catastrophe is most likely to elicit the syndrome of paranoid rhetoric"
(Hofstadter 1964: 39)

In a classic essay of political science, Richard Hofstadter describes paranoia in politics as an oratorial style which relies on the notion of a conspiracy against "a nation, a culture, a way of life" (1964: 4). He takes examples from a 1951 speech of Senator Joseph McCarthy, an 1895 statement of the Populist Party, a Texas newspaper article on Catholicism from 1855 and a 1795 Massachusetts sermon on the threat to Christianity that resides in Europe (7–10). Because the paranoid style is "above all, a way of seeing the world and of expressing oneself" (4), it is the place where the paranoid theme of conspiracy meets a mode of representation. It is not just a statement about conspiracy but an enunciation in a conspiratorial vein.

The realm of fictional narrative presents specific difficulties where such a style is concerned. Firstly, there is the issue of presenting a conspiracy within a narrative, as with, say *The Maltese Falcon* (1941), in which conspiracy makes up the subject matter of the story but the events surrounding it are narrated largely in a 'neutral' style that reveals the conspiracy bit by bit. On the other hand, and arguably characteristic of most 'paranoid' narratives, especially films, the conspiracy is narrated in an 'ambiguous' style. The early films directed in the West by Roman Polanski, for example, show a 'conspiracy' from the point of view of a neurotic young woman (*Repulsion*, 1966), through the eyes of an insecure expectant mother (*Rosemary's Baby*, 1968), in the twisted vision of an alienated exile in Paris (*The Tenant*, 1976) and even, as unanticipated in its full depth by a man who thinks he's seen life (*Chinatown*, 1974). A conspiracy is shown – but the audience is not necessarily sure that there really was a conspiracy in the way it was seen by the protagonist.

Traditionally, the presentation of conspiracies in fiction has been in the service of *suspense*. In 'neutral' narrations, protagonists and audiences are not always fully apprised of a conspiracy's co-ordinates. In 'ambiguous' narrations, on the other hand, the protagonist is usually convinced of the existence and details of a conspiracy, but the audience might be left wondering whether the protagonist is deluded or partial in some way. Neutral narrations, particularly in the thriller genre, present unbelievers or innocents that find themselves abroad in threatening circumstances whose hidden architects and whose chains of reasoning they cannot grasp. In general – Hitchcock's films are a good example – those presenting events, along with the reader of the narrative, know more than the protagonist. Equally, in ambiguous narrations, there is suspense regarding whether the protagonist will come to his/her senses or reveal a real conspiracy (e.g. *Klute*, 1969; *The Parallax View*, 1974; *Charlie*, 1984; *The X Files*, 1993, etc.).

Some film narratives promote suspense by showing a great deal of the conspiracy that besets protagonists, for example, *The Manchurian Candidate* (1962), *The Taking of Pelham 123* (1975) or *JFK* (1991). Others show relatively little of the conspiracy in the early parts of the narrative: *North by Northwest* (1959), for example, or *Twin Peaks* (1990).

Yet, while the device of suspense has obviously been instrumentally employed in narratives (*pace* Auerbach 1968) since Homer, there have been, equally obviously, times in history when narratives have presented conspiracies that do not simply provoke interest in how they will be resolved. Clearly, there have been numerous instances when readers and producers of narrative may have found the notion of hidden conspiracies very credible in their fabric, leading to the conclusion that some degree of paranoia is sensible both for the protagonist and, by extension, for any citizen of that society. To some extent, this has been the case for the duration of the existence of the thriller narrative. Yet, there are some salient periods where the fear of conspiracy has been seen as a credible reaction: in the US in the 1970s this was arguably so (see Cobley 2000) and in the post-9/11 period, with a different complexion, it is also the case. In such circumstances, the extra-textual phenomenon of 'anxiety' is more appropriate to thinking through the process than the textual trope of 'suspense' (see Cobley 2009).

Suspense, of course, does not disappear within anxiety. In films based on the stories of true conspiracies, even a small amount of the conspiracy shown in such narratives is sufficient to generate a great deal of suspense, despite the fact that the audience will know something about the conspiracy, particularly, if it was recent. Examples might include *Serpico* (1976), *All the President's Men* (1976) and *United 93* (2006). The present essay, as it proceeds, will expand on the issue of suspense. It focuses more keenly, however, on the way that *narration* of conspiracies takes place after 9/11, the style that is used to portray contemporary conspiracies. 'Conspiracy', then, is not simply a matter of a narrative's content – what the story is about - but, also, and importantly, a matter of the *style* – the narrative devices – by which a narrative is presented.

Since it will be argued that the post-9/11 paranoid style is characterized by the weaving of contemporary surveillance techniques into narration, some initial elaboration is therefore necessary on the connections and distinctions between a surveillance *theme* and the paranoid *style* of the period. Clearly, there are audio-visual narratives which have a surveillance theme but which have not adopted what is here identified as a paranoid style of narration. *Panic Room* (2002) is an example of a film with a surveillance *theme* but in which, as Kammerer (2004: 472) points out, "there is not a single shot from the point of view of a surveillance camera, in the typical blurred, grainy 'video look'". Conversely, there are also films from the pre–9/11 period with surveillance themes which sometimes show views as if from the contemporary surveillance equipment that is featured in the narrative: for example, *Rear Window* (1955; cameras), *Blow Up* (1966, cameras), *The Anderson Tapes* (1971, CCTV). Such films have their own, historically located, paranoid style. Yet, what characterizes the post-9/11 paranoid style as discussed in the present essay are most of the following:

- a surveillance theme;
- a narration which shows surveillance techniques;
- a narration which frequently incorporates surveillance technology (grainy CCTV footage, computer read-outs, etc.) without necessarily including other items extraneous to the technology in the frame;
- a narration which weaves elements of the technology of surveillance unseen by the protagonists into the storytelling (for example, satellite movements, interior views of machines, light coursing down a cable); and
- a narration that sometimes edits in news or (seemingly) amateur footage of events.

The proximity of the surveillance *theme* and the *style* is close. This is because, despite the fact that surveillance technology is part of the fabric of 'reality TV' programmes such as *Big Brother,* it is not really conceivable that the post-9/11 style of fictional narratives could be employed in a narrative that did not implicate surveillance. In the instance of *Big Brother,* what is viewed is not strictly a constructed narrative nor is the surveillance part of a covert conspiracy.

Paranoia, of course, suggests delusion, unjustified obsession. By this criterion, a surveillance theme need not necessarily involve a 'paranoid' style, particularly if it has been widely accepted that the West is now a 'surveillance society'. So, can a surveillance theme be treated in a calm, objective manner? As noted above, *Panic Room* eschews the paranoid style as, to a great degree, does *The End of Violence* (1997). Yet, the majority of post-9/11 audio-visual narratives with a surveillance theme have embraced the paranoid style. As such, there is a suggestion in this development that—among other things—there is considerable unease and anxiety about, rather than comfort with, the growth of the surveillance society. Surveillance and paranoia, in post-9/11 films at least, are therefore inextricable.

In considering audio-visual narratives, however, a further issue must be broached. This arises from the long tradition of work in both film and photography studies—as well as in those studies, across fields, of ocular devices as instruments of 'discipline'—suggesting that the camera and even the eye are inherently surveillance devices. If surveillance and paranoia have a close relationship, the logical trajectory of this tradition is that all movies—and all looking—are examples of paranoid style. In the course of the discussion, this essay will be making no conclusions of this sort. Instead, it will be argued that while the paranoid style can be characterized by its narratorial devices, in its purposes it is resolutely and historically specific. Nevertheless, this essay will have cause to return to the matter of panopticism and the 'denigration of vision' at greater length later.

Introducing the paranoid style

Where the style of conspiracy films from *noir* to the 1980s heavily relied on different levels of dark and light to convey mood in narration, many post-9/11 narratives have been dominated by very rapid editing and the incorporation of surveillance techniques, surveillance and/or news footage into narration. That is, in an age when surveillance has expanded to such an extent for the West to be dubbed a 'surveillance society', thriller narratives in particular have embraced the kind of visions that surveillance might provide. The chief reason for doing this is to do with the genre's co-ordinates. That is, the thriller sustains itself by adopting modes of narration which are geared to produce the most credible depiction according to a nebulous body of public opinion. The thriller's narration has largely conformed to a regime of verisimilitude that is 'doxalogical' rather than a strict correlation with the 'real' (see Cobley 1997). In turn, thriller narratives have been particularly pointed and prescient at times when a paranoid disposition in respect of public life might be likely among citizens of the West.

Paranoia, in general, is often questioned and dismissed as a worldview because it can be delusional. Yet, at the beginning of the twenty-first century, three book-length academic studies suggested that the paranoia supposedly fostered in narrative representations should not be depredated or dismissed. Pratt (2001: 2) argues that many American 'political' films are "unconscious reflections of state-supported repression of movements for human emancipation, or the belief among significant sectors of the public that their lives are no longer under their control". Melley (2000), concentrating chiefly on print fiction, contends that seeing conspiracies is, on the one hand, a means of dealing with the complexity of late modern life and, on the other, that it is a vision of manipulation amidst a crisis of agency in which the very self of the human is under threat (realistically or unrealistically). Cobley (2000), focusing on genre narrative in print and audio-visual media during the 1970s, holds that there were a number of firm extra-textual grounds beyond mere historical events during the period which would encourage readers to take the conspiratorial vision of contemporary fictions very seriously.

Each of these three studies also imply, without fully delineating it, a 'paranoid style' in the narratives they analyse. All mention, without expanding at length, arguments about surveillance developing at the time that they were written. And, each study appeared before 11th September 2001. This last point, unsurprisingly, is crucial. Not only has 9/11 re-drawn much of geo-politics, it has also re-drawn the grounds of representation. After 9/11, issues surrounding surveillance were thrust forward, along with the burgeoning of a relatively new academic field of 'surveillance studies'. Surveillance technologies post-9/11 were to become synonymous with, and allow here the positing of, a paranoid style in (audio-visual) narrative.

"Smile for the FBI"

As is often the case with popular narrative, the post-9/11 paranoid style discussed in this essay does not have a straightforward lineage. Indeed, the key narrative which can be said to embody or prefigure it comprehensively is from 1998: *Enemy of the State*, directed by Tony Scott and written by David Marconi. In turn, this film pays homage to various other, earlier paranoid narratives or surveillance thrillers. Yet, in terms of its paranoid style and some of its themes, *Enemy of the State* looks forward. Apart from the fact that it shows characters watching newscasts rather than incorporates newscasts into the narration, it exemplifies all the components of the paranoid style itemized earlier. More specifically, firstly, it is suffused with surveillance: it is *about* surveillance and the narrative presentation is dominated by attempts to ape (in a stylized way) surveillance devices. It is concerned with two plots regarding surveillance tapes — not so much parallel plots, but neither is the 'Pintero' strand of the narrative merely subordinate since it precipitates the Mexican standoff at the climax of the film. Secondly, the narrative puts surveillance at the centre of daily life rather than just in the shadowy corners inhabited by espionage operations. Thirdly, and connected with everyday life, it is informed by an apparently simple 'dialectic of watching' in which the watchers are sometimes watched and/or hoisted on their own petards. As such, it implies that surveillance is not so much bad or good, but, rather, the site of hegemonic struggle. Further evidence of the narrative's far-from-naïve presentation is the way that, through its casting and through references in the narrative, it pays homage to other surveillance thrillers.

On the basis of a plot summary, *Enemy of the State* does seem like a routine thriller. On the eve of the vote on the Telecommunications and Privacy Act (giving unlimited power to the government to spy on citizens), an opponent of the Act, Congressman Philip Hammersley (Jason Robards), is murdered on the banks of a lake by the henchmen of National Security Agency executive, Thomas Reynolds (Jon Voight). It transpires, however, that this act, committed by the vanguard of government surveillance, is captured on film by an amateur ornithologist, Daniel Zavitz (Jason Lee) who passes it to his old Georgetown classmate, labour lawyer Robert Clayton Dean (Will Smith), whom he bumps into while trying to escape the NSA. As a result, Dean himself, a Hitchcockian innocent, is now pursued by the NSA villains who also burgle his home and employ smear tactics on his work and private life. So far, this might be considered standard thriller fare. The film uses on-screen time/date/location captions tapped out as if by a teleprinter, already a characteristic of many thrillers before 1998. Yet, it is worth devoting some time to both the narration (incorporating surveillance methods) and the narrative (the surveillance theme) of this film in light of developments in narration post-9/11.

As the action begins, the surveillance style of narration is ramped up, with shots of a satellite in orbit preceding fine clarity overhead shots of buildings with humans moving between them. Dean's house and clothes are bugged and the numerous tracking devices in his home and his garments are mirrored in the narration from the side of the group of nerdy white surveillance technicians (Jack Black et al). In addition to the satellite shots, shown at increasing points of zoom, the protagonists and main locations are presented as if through CCTV surveillance cameras; numerous sequences are shot through a blue filter to give this effect and the colour of the exterior sequences in particular is washed out. Phone calls are sometimes visualized as light coursing through a fibre. Computer monitors at NSA headquarters appear in full screen to monitor movements. Much of the sound in the film is 'overheard', as if through special electronic devices, and both sound and vision are frequently subject to minor distortion (e. g. white noise or picture interference). In short, this saturation of the narration with surveillance or quasi-surveillance devices was to become the paranoid style in post-9/11 fiction. It is a simple point, yet it has significant ramifications.

The film, in fact, has an early, rapidly edited, sequence which serves to effect the move from surveillance depicted *in* the narrative to surveillance *as* the narration. It is the sequence where the NSA discovers that Zavitz knows the import of the video he has in his possession. The sequence of shots (with some of the dialogue omitted here), is as follows:

1. Washed out, blue filter overhead view of satellite station.
2. KENT ISLAND INTERCEPT STATION (typed out on screen)
3. Ground level, blue filter, speeded up pan of satellite dishes.
4. Interior shot of Fiedler (Jack Black) at console, speaking into phone.
5. Close-up of Fiedler
6. Shot of Hicks (Loren Dean) walking round NSA control room (low light, bright computer monitors).
7. Close-up of Fiedler.
8. Interior shot of Hicks in his office.
9. NSA DEBRIEFING ROOM 1453 hrs (typed out on screen).
10. Two shot of Krug (Jake Busey) and Jones (Scott Caan), two ex-Marines seconded to the NSA whose record Hicks discusses.
11. New two shot as Bingham (Ian Hart) enters the scene.
12. Exterior street scene, three-storey building at rear, traffic noise on soundtrack.
13. Shot of window on top floor of building.
14. Mid-shot of Zavitz at computer.
15. Shot of computer monitor (film of ducks)
16. Then full screen (blue filter) of the film of the ducks.
17. Zavitz, mid-shot.
18. Shot of TV in the room, showing news of Congressman Hammersley's Mercedes being removed from the lake.
19. Computer – Hammersley throwing ball to dog near the same lake.
20. Zavitz sits up.
21. Close-up of finger typing, bleep as each key hit.
22. Computer screen, picture zooms.
23. Sequence on computer showing Hammersley's murder.
24. Extreme close-up on Zavitz' eyes.

25. Sounds of typing.
26. Zoom on replayed murder scene.
27. Bleep. Closer again. Replayed.
28. Bleep. Closer again. Replayed.
29. Close-up on Zavitz' face. "Fuck a duck. Holy shit".
30. Hammersley being bundled into car.
31. Zavitz smiling wryly. Calls Blum on mobile phone.
32. Interior shot of second-hand bookstore where Blum is in silhouette.

The sequence then cuts back and forth from Blum to Zavitz as they discuss the film the latter has, with Zavitz getting the computer screen to zoom on Reynolds, "Some anal retentive with what looks like a serious vitamin B deficiency".

As Zavitz tells Blum how he got the tape, there are close-ups of Hicks and Fiedler as they listen to his words on the soundtrack.

1. Shot of fluctuating graphic read-out of Zavitz' words.
2. Two shot, Fiedler and Hicks. Fiedler picks up his phone.
3. Shot of Hicks rubbing face worriedly.
4. Shot of Reynolds in office, switching land line to mobile phone. "Fiedler, is this line secure?".
5. Shot of Fiedler confirming and giving details of Blum's anti-war background.
6. Shot of Reynolds demanding tap on Blum and asking for a dedicated satellite.
7. Fiedler: "It's already done".

The sequence is still dominated by the narrative of people interacting. Yet, more subtly than might be expected, through zooms, close-ups, graphic read-outs and devices such as the blue filter, the narrative of surveillance becomes itself a surveillance using the same technology. This sequence suggests, at first, the NSA surveillance operation in action; however, by the time it is over, there is the suggestion that surveillance is almost everywhere and that it is the way to see — and narrate — things today.

If *Enemy* is compared with some of the classic surveillance thrillers from previous decades, it is distinguished by the way it so thoroughly implicates surveillance in everyday life. Whereas, say, *No Way Out* (1987) is rooted in Pentagon and Washington politics, *Three Days of the Condor* (1975) is concerned with splinter groups from the CIA, and *The Conversation* (1974) largely inhabits the murky world of industrial espionage, *Enemy* brings surveillance to the centre of domestic life. The depiction of Dean's family life is crucial in the narrative: his wife, Carla (Regina King), is suspicious of the Surveillance Act and is suspicious about the relationship of Dean and his liaison, ex-girlfriend, Rachael Banks (Lisa Bonet); Dean's son, Eric (Jascha Washington), makes off with Zavitz' video when it enters the house; the Dean home is invaded, violated and bugged thoroughly by the NSA. When Dean is first realizing the extent to which his life is being taken apart through NSA surveillance, it is not so much at the moment he is smeared and suspended from his job, or when his wife expels him from the house believing him to be having an affair with Rachael, but when he finds that his credit cards no longer work. The paranoid style of the narrative — by this time in the film showing the argument of Carla and Robert Dean through the surveillance cameras of the NSA vehicle parked nearby and with Van (Bodhi Elfman) watching and commenting — gives the impression that no movement goes unnoticed, no financial transaction goes unregistered, no phone call ever fails to be overheard or logged and that all surveillance devices in the public domain — from 'private' CCTV cameras to automatic cash tellers and electronic point of sale (EPOS) monitors — are linked. The 'Making of' featurette available with the 2006 DVD extended cut of *Enemy* seeks to demonstrate that many of the linked surveillance technologies depicted in the film were available to some agencies in 1998.

Given the way in which surveillance is shown to be omnipresent in daily life, Dean's only chance of redemption in the narrative is to somehow go beyond the bounds of the quotidian. Before Rachael is murdered, he is put in contact with Brill (Gene Hackman), a shadowy figure outside law and society who has previously supplied her with information to leak to lawyers like Dean. Brill is a typical outsider, hard-bitten, bereft of family ties, a little like Quint from *Jaws* (1975): alone but sometimes operating in the interstices of society. As it transpires, his identity is fluid: 'Brill' has already been impersonated by someone in the pay of the NSA (Gabriel Byrne) and Hackman's character is revealed to be an ex-NSA operative named 'Edward Lyle' who originally ran special ops but then went missing in the late 1970s. The face of the agent shown on the NSA's archive screen is that of Hackman in the character of Harry Caul from the 1974 surveillance classic, *The Conversation*. The links between the two characters are obvious, although the moral uncertainty of Caul has been replaced by the anti-establishment grit of Brill. It is he who will be Dean's redeemer, helping him to regain the identity that surveillance has taken away, but able to do so because he has relinquished his own 'identity' for a life underground.

The ubiquitous surveillance that marks the paranoid style of *Enemy* might suggest, rather complacently, that surveillance is an unavoidable fact of life or, more in the spirit of reform, that surveillance is insidiously pervasive. The strapline in publicity for the film — "It's not paranoia if they're really after you" — tends to suggest a reformist reading. Lyon

(2007: 147–8), on the other hand, seems to feel that the paranoid style in the film demonstrates too readily a belief in the efficacy of technology. Yet, at the same time, Lyon's own work on surveillance (1994, 2001, 2003) suggests the ambiguities in the continuum of 'care' and 'control' as well as 'resistance' in contemporary surveillance that the narrative arguably begins to articulate. For Pratt (2001: 243), "*Enemy of the State* is high-tech Orwell for the twenty-first century"; for Lyon (2007: 147), the film lacks depth and concern about the nuances of technology. But attention to the narrative shows that the film is a little bit more sophisticated than both of these assertions allow. The film does not show an omnipotent 'surveillance society': instead there is personal and structural conflict within the use of surveillance itself. This is evident not just in Admiral Shaffer's (Dan Butler) threat of prison to whoever (i. e. Reynolds) had the "unilateral wet dream" of inventing and planting maverick bugs, but also in the Mexican standoff of the NSA with Pintero's mobsters, a theme that recalls Babe's pitting of a CIA splinter group against the neighbourhood feral Hispanic youths in the classic paranoid thriller *Marathon Man* (1976; see Cobley 2000: 158).

Surveillance is shown as the battleground of conflicting interests and this is built into the narrative from the start. Arch-surveillor, Reynolds, is caught on camera by the vaguely counter-cultural Zavitz; Pintero is being watched by the Feds and, as one of his men escorts Dean from the premises, instructs him to look up and "Smile for the FBI" — the Feds later find themselves in conflict when the NSA turn up with a captive Brill in police uniform; the Telecommunications and Privacy Act's political pimp, conservative Congressman Sam Albert (Stuart Wilson), is filmed having sex with his secretary as a result of the planting in his room by Brill of a device stolen from the NSA. The watchers can easily become the watched. As Brill puts it to Dean,

> Well, if they're big and you're small, then you're mobile and they're slow. You're hidden and they're exposed. You only fight battles you know you can win. That's the way the Vietcong did it. You capture their weapons and you use them against them the next time.

In the denouement of the narrative, Brill and Dean do just this and, while Dean's 'identity' is restored, Brill escapes from society once more. In the final Dean household scene, the family are watching a television newscast in which Congressman Albert concedes that while enemies have to be monitored, so too do their monitors. Carla Dean, the surveillance critic, asks "Well, who's gonna monitor the monitors of the monitors?" This dilemma of surveillance and power is perhaps answered when she puts Eric to bed and the television transmission is interrupted by a picture on the screen, observed by Dean, of himself at that moment, under surveillance, followed by footage of a beach with 'Wish you were here?' written in the sand, evidently by Brill. That the *narration* is so filled with surveillance techniques means that this sequence in the narrative is that much easier for the audience to take.

Enemy is a thriller and, as a genre text, tries to reproduce the expectations of previous texts. Yet, in its paranoid style, it does not lack self-consciousness. The casting alone speaks for itself in its reference to previous paranoid classics: Hackman (referencing *The Conversation*), Byrne (*Defence of the Realm* [1985], *The End of Violence* [1997]), Voight (*The Odessa File* [1974], *Mission Impossible* [1996]), Robards (as Ben Bradlee in *All the President's Men* [1976]). In the watchers/watched theme, there is a wealth of resonances with other surveillance films such as *Rear Window*, *Blow Up*, *Blow Out* (1981) and even *Peeping Tom* (1960), and with other thrillers such as *Marathon Man* (1976, particularly the night chase with Dean in a dressing gown) and TV series such as *The Prisoner* (1967). In this lineage, the film does not profess to present a dystopian vision of surveillance (cf. Marks 2005); nor does it seem to present "surveillance as a means of predicting, pre-empting and preventing undesirable behaviour" (Lyon 2007: 149) in the apparent manner of the futuristic movie *Minority Report* (2002). Rather, in respect of the specific verisimilitude of the thriller — that is, the attempt to reach high levels of 'realism' and credibility — *Enemy* offers an image of what surveillance *is* now in the popular imagination, reinforced by the high tech narration that apes surveillance devices. The post-9/11 paranoid style shows how people can be *subject to* surveillance and, in so doing, has the potential for differing consequences.

24 and the paranoid style

The marrying of thriller verisimilitude and the surveillant outlook is taken to considerable lengths in the 'real-time' American TV series, *24* (2001). Along with the UK series, *Spooks* (2002), *24* has run for 8 seasons and maintained topical storylines. Also like *Spooks* (see below), it has narrated in a paranoid style. It is easily assumed that the way that *24* is narrated, with location/time captions and split screens, chiefly services the events of the series taking place in 24 hours, narrated over 24 episodes, each tracked by an intermittent on-screen clock (although, because of the demands of commercial breaks on US television, each episode only lasts about 45 minutes). The first season, broadcast in November 2001, features the work of Jack Bauer (Kiefer Sutherland) and a Los Angeles-based government Counter Terrorism Unit (CTU). From 12:00 AM on the day of the California presidential primary CTU agent Jack Bauer is embroiled in two plots in which he has to prevent an assassination attempt on Senator David Palmer (Dennis Haysbert) whilst also dealing with his recalcitrant teenage daughter who, along with his wife, then become targets of the assassins. Ultimately, it becomes evident that Bauer and Palmer are both the targets of retribution for their involvement with a covert US mission in the Balkans.

The narration is fast throughout, deftly tangling the lives of Palmer and Bauer. The speed of narration, however, and the repeated use of split screen along with the captions tracking time do not serve the plot and suspense in the traditional fashion. Suspense, here, is not simply a matter of the withholding and release of textual information by narrative agencies. Instead, there is an apparent attempt to show as much as possible at once. Split screens and, in this case, the inculcation of surveillance devices, are part of what Linda Williams (1991), in her study of hard-core pornography, has called a "frenzy of the visible", an attempt to offer through machinery the comprehensive vision that might be desired but not delivered by the naked eye (cf. Comolli 1980). Put another way, it is the meeting of vision with a will to knowledge and the promise of (potentially) realizing the aims of that meeting through technology.

Consider the opening sequence of the very first episode — an initial caption and voice-over reveals that the "Events occur in real time"; then:

1. An aerial panning shot of the Petronas Towers (at that time, the tallest buildings in the world, under construction), Kuala Lumpur.
2. Caption:
   KUALA LUMPUR
   Local Time
   4:08:29 PM (last digits moving to 30, 31)
3. The screen splits into two to add to the towers a street level shot teeming with people.
   At street level, one male figure is moving suspiciously.
4. The towers and street scene are now replaced by the street scene and the man looking back and forth at different angles for each shot.
5. Full screen: the man enters a private building.
6. As he opens a laptop the screen splits into two with different angled shots of him looking at the monitor.
   The sound of a phone being dialed is heard on the soundtrack.
7. Full screen: he picks up a mobile device.
   Male voice on mobile device says "Identify"
   "Victor Roebner. Permission to transmit"
   "Log in"

8. Split screen shot of a satellite orbiting earth.
9. Split screen of Roebner's profile in darkness and laptop monitor showing "downloading encrypted file".
10. Full screen pan of Roebner and computer.
11. Split screen with mid-shot and close-up.
12. Aerial shot of helicopter flying over city at night.
13. LOS ANGELES
    12:02:13 AM (last digits moving to 14, 15)
14. Interior full screen shot of party, people mingling. Phone ringing.
15. Screen splits into two: mid-shot of party/close-up on Richard Walsh (Michael O'Neill).
    (To party guests) "Excuse me a moment . . . (to phone) This is Walsh"
16. Third split on screen showing profile of man with phone in a dark office:
    "We just heard from Roebner. He confirmed there'd be an attempt today".
    Walsh: "Have you found out who the target is?"
    "Senator David Palmer".
17. Full screen: close-up on Walsh, alarmed.
18. Mobile interior shot, hand-held camera, of woman carrying hot drinks on a tray from one room to another.
19. SENATOR DAVID PALMER
    CAMPAIGN HEADQUARTERS
    12:02:45 AM (last digits moving to 46, 47)
20. Arrives at balcony where Palmer is discussing documents with others. Scene continues for about 30 seconds.
21. Full screen exterior establishing shot of modest private residence.
22. 12:03:25 PM (last digits moving to 26, 37)
23. Interior, mid-shot of Jack Bauer talking.
24. Two-shot of Bauer and daughter, Kim Bauer (Elisha Cuthbert)

There follows a longer scene with the Bauer family, including Teri Bauer (Lesley Hope). But when Bauer is urgently summoned to his office, the screen splits again as he calls his daughter's ex-boyfriend and the conversation is observed. This is followed by Bauer calling home (split screen again) and then aerial shots of Bauer's movement through the city.

The opening shot of the two towers under construction is probably not coincidental in light of the two towers destroyed barely two months before the broadcast of this episode. The main point, however, is that the sequence sets in motion the promise of showing the viewer everything immediately: international satellite communications; the links between characters separated by distance and time; their locations (e.g. CTU control room — low light, bright computer monitors — as opposed to home or street); in real time; and with a heightened sense of simultaneity engendered by the fact that the screen is filled — at once — with events and characters that are in different places. Of course, narrative in general has always held such a promise; yet it has not done so with such pace, insistence and exposure of the machinery of surveillance.

"Let me amaze you with the vulnerability of the modern world"

Arguably extending *24*'s paranoid style, the spy drama *Spooks* was premiered on BBC in May 2002 (in the US later as *MI–5*). Its eighth series ran in the Autumn of 2009. It followed the fortunes of four young, attractive, clean-cut, middle-class MI5 agents, one of whom was, in an unexpected, violent and controversial scene which also upset the usual expectations of narrativity, murdered in the second episode. In the present context, the series is a notable contribution to the paranoid style with its technological trappings. Conversely, films directly depicting the events of 9/11 have been careful to seem fairly low-key and focused in their narration: *United 93* (2006), the narrative of the flight that was forced to crash in Pennsylvania, features an opening titles shot of New York from a surveillance helicopter and extensive views of air traffic control monitors, but none of these become part of the narration; *World Trade Center* (2006) is concerned with the fate of some Port Authority police officers and their families on 11th September 2001 and, despite showing people looking at news reports (and even showing, at one point, a satellite), eschews surveillance technology as a means of telling the story. Whereas *Enemy of the State* is absolutely suffused with surveillance in its narrative and narration and *24* supplements surveillance with liberal use of split screen, *Spooks* uses every available device to attempt to provide a vision of contemporaneity. It consistently features rapid edits of surveillance footage, poorly shot footage ('citizen journalism'?), hand-held camera narration, news footage (and newscasts), surveillance photographs and shots of (fictional) official files, as well as slow motion and computer technology woven into the narration plus similar split screen techniques as *24* and location captions arriving on screen as if in a blast of interference.

In the first series, episode 4 is a good example of this full-blown paranoid style in action. Zoe (Keeley Hawes) and Danny (David Oyelowo) are in a room surveying 'crowd activity status' on the eve of a visit to Britain of President George W. Bush. With camera and binoculars they are spying on an anti-globalisation demonstration and constantly checking pictures of the demonstrators against their computer files. Repeatedly, there are point-of-view shots through their binoculars. One of the demonstrators then looks back: at the spies and at the audience. It transpires that he is a much-respected MI5 officer, Peter Salter (Anthony Head), run by Tom (Matthew Macfadyen), who seems to be working undercover even though he has not informed the rest of the team. It transpires that he is on the trail of a notorious anarchist, Istvan Vogel (Jules Werner), whom the head of the Counter-Terrorism Department, Harry Pearce (Peter Firth), later discusses as grainy hand-held (news?) footage of riots crosses the screen. At a subsequent meeting with MI6 chief, Jools Siviter (Hugh Laurie), it is revealed that MI6 have Salter under surveillance and the audience can later see – and hear – Salter having sex with Andrea Chambers (Bronwen Davies), a rich and previously aimless 25-year old anarchist. The audience can also see how Salter reveals to her he has a 'dead ground map' showing every security installation in the country; he then begins to tear the apartment to pieces, pulling numerous bugging devices from it. He and Chambers then retreat to a bed and breakfast accommodation in Camden. Here, they are watched from outside their residence by Zoe and Danny, once more, who are holed up in a car doing old-fashion non-technologically-enhanced surveillance. In a replay of a scene from *Enemy of the State*, Danny and Zoe are then apprehended by the police who have received a tip-off regarding anti-social behaviour. Salter and Chambers make their getaway in a car delivered by Horst (Jukka Hiltunen) —as the latter interrogates Salter and Chambers drives, the screen is split into three: the view of the road; Salter being searched; Chambers' eyes in the rear-view mirror. When he eventually meets Vogel, in addition to the dead ground map, Salter also offers them access to the air traffic control mainframe and the group breaks into the Geography department of (the fictional) Medway University where access is located. The break-in and hacking is narrated through a three-way screen split, CCTV footage and computer imagery.

When Tom brings in Salter to debrief him and to determine whether he has 'gone over', Pearce and Siviter are watching the interrogation through cameras in the Thames House headquarters of the Counter Terrorism Department of MI5 (low light, bright computer monitors). As they suspected he would, Salter reveals his treachery to Tom and the others. He then asks to go to the toilet. Tom, of course, accompanies him and keeps the door open to watch and the conversation going as Salter urinates. However, Salter then punches Tom in the throat, rendering him semi-conscious and immobile, before taking Tom's belt and hanging himself with it from the door frame.

It should be said that while this episode features the rapid cutting characteristic of *Spooks*, it is by no means as saturated with the split-screen and surveillance-style narration of many other episodes. However, the way that it implements the narration in connection with the theme of surveillance in the narrative is notable. As with *Enemy of the State*, there is the matter of the watcher dealing with someone who is knowingly watched and responds. There is the clash of surveillance regimes: at the beginning, it is not certain that Salter has been cleared because Tom is on leave, injured; Salter is being run by Tom, but it seems that Harry Pearce is also running him counter to Tom's aims; then the surveillance of MI6 undermines the operation of MI5. (In *Enemy*, it is the traditional rivalries of the FBI, the NSA and the police which are highlighted). The split in loyalties that this episode dramatizes, is not dissimilar, too, from that at the beginning of *24* where Bauer is torn between the fate of his daughter and the fate of Palmer.

The 'pacy direction' (see 'The Look of *Spooks*' 2002) often attributed to first director, Bharat Nalluri, and the paranoid style of *Spooks* — particularly the rapid weaving of news and surveillance footage — serves specific purposes of verisimilitude. If anything is remarkable about *Spooks* it is the way in which its quick production and its canny writers provide stories that seem to be almost fully in consonance with the news headlines. These range from a dangerous international financier who threatens to bankrupt the UK (Series 7, Episode 5 broadcast in Autumn 2008) to an undercover operation in an extremist mosque in which a peace-seeking Algerian Muslim averts large scale bloodshed (Series 2, Episode 2 broadcast June 2003), the latter being one of a number of *Spooks* storylines that sparked controversy (see The Secret State 2003). In combination with the will to knowledge and the will to see in the paranoid style of the series, it has been argued elsewhere (Cobley 2009) that what is at stake is not so much the mechanism of suspense as the generation of anxiety. That is, audience anxiety is likely to derive from the frenetic depiction of a world that embodies the same kind of threats that might be felt to be experienced in the post-9/11 West while also heightening them through the technologies of vision. That 'realistic' fiction involves depiction of worlds that seem like 'our own, but more so', is an old, and even hackneyed, idea. Yet, where the matter of surveillance in contemporary thrillers is concerned, it will have political consequences.

Conclusion

Although there were signs of it taking place before 9/11, the narration of thrillers has changed. Specifically, the paranoid style points to greater awareness about the general phenomenon — if not the causes or consequences — of surveillance. The traditional espionage narrative depicted a world of spies whose operations uncovered conspiracies, often in the very heart of some instance of everyday life. As Ralph Harper recognized a long time ago (1969), the world of the thriller is a special world for protagonist and reader, a world of existential insecurity. Yet, the relatively local insecurity experienced by Greene's or Le Carré's protagonists — or even in *The Parallax View* (1975) or *All the President's Men* (1976) or *Edge of Darkness* (1986) — is as nothing compared with the threat of insecurity from widespread contemporary surveillance. The protrusion of surveillance into seemingly every sphere of contemporary Western life has the potential to create paranoia and anxiety however much citizens do not think twice about the need for, say, PIN numbers or medical records, or however much they celebrate interactivity in media (cf. Andrejevic 2007). Put another way, the present provides fertile ground for audio-visual thriller narratives since all of everyday life has become the domain of conspiracy; and for everyone, not only spies.

Notwithstanding the efforts of Frederick Forsyth and Alex Berenson, there have been few prominent post-9/11 print thrillers dealing with widespread surveillance and espionage activities directly resulting from the attack on the World Trade Center or the subsequent 'war on terror' (cf. Weinman 2007). Indeed, the best, most tautly written of these, is *The 9/11 Commission Report* (2004). It is on film and television where the drama has largely been played out in thrillers, including numerous examples such as the *Bourne* trilogy (2002, 2004, 2007), *Caché* (2005), *Déjà Vu* (2006) and *Body of Lies* (2008) which cannot be discussed here for reasons of space. Clearly, the post-9/11 surveillance regime is implicated in the fact that audio-visual narratives of espionage are currently dominant over print and those aspects of the narratives which allow the 'frenzy of the visible' are more suited to representation than, say, the storing of data in computers about consumption patterns. Surveillance will thus have specific *visual* and 'visualisable' co-ordinates in the contemporary thriller narrative.

As with Harper's (2008: 24) suggestion that "a more nuanced view of the paranoid position and of conspiratorial narratives could enrich surveillance studies", it is also important to understand the paranoid style, the frenzy of the visible associated with surveillance in post-9/11 thrillers, as subject to specific contexts and potential readings. Both *Spooks* and *24* suggest that surveillance works to a certain extent; in later series of *Spooks*, for example, the computer nerd/technological genius, Malcolm Wynn-Jones (Hugh Simon) appears to have every CCTV camera at his disposal and access to almost every computer in the world. Yet, villains are still a threat in both television series; furthermore, surveillance cannot always be used successfully against either criminals or law abiding citizens to find out what they do or think. When surveillance techniques and technology are woven into narration to form a paranoid style, they will doubtless embody this ambiguity. Indeed, as the study of narrative as representation holds, even the frenzy of the visible associated with the paranoid style in audio-visual narrative can only create the merest feeling of total surveillance. It must bracket out the mundane quotidian acts of surveillance in people's lives simply because they are too boring to narrate.

The difficult task that remains for the analyst of narrative or the commentator on the post-9/11 thriller is to sort out the differing consequences of the paranoid style. The omnipresence of surveillance in *Enemy*, *24* and *Spooks* could be a demonstration of a nuanced form of paranoia which rightly foregrounds the hidden surveillance measures employed in the maintenance of a semblance of 'normality' in everyday life and which is used to protect the powerful and to expose the weak. Arguably, this is one rationale for the paranoid style in *Enemy*. Alternatively, the weaving of surveillance techniques into the fabric of narration — as well as the events of the narrative — might suggest not just the omnipresence of surveillance but also its omnipotence, despite the fact that surveillance systems are "far from foolproof" (Lyon 2003: 9). One might see this also in some subsequent developments of *24*. A third position on the issue is that the ubiquity of surveillance techniques in narration carries the danger of 'softening' people up for more surveillance. Laidler (2008: 37) investigated fingerprinting of children as young as three years old in UK schools, concluding that, at the very least, such processes of surveillance could have the effect of encouraging people to routinely expect more.

Related to this third position is an even more paranoid position on surveillance, although its adherents would claim that it is 'critical', is not deluded and does not entail a conscious conspiracy. Here, then, this essay revisits the tradition of 'anti-ocularcentrism' or the 'denigration of vision' (Jay 1993). This strain of thought takes a number of forms. One is where the camera — and its implementation in Hollywood movies in particular — is taken to be voyeuristic or instituting a 'male gaze' (the over-cited source for this reduction is Mulvey 1975). Another form relates to Foucault's positing of vision as having the tendency to enact 'disciplinary' surveillance. The idea is derived from Jeremy Bentham's unrealized plans, from 1785 onwards, for an ideal prison — the Panopticon — where prisoners would be under constant surveillance and punishment would be a spectacle. For Foucault, Bentham's projections serve as an exemplar of the way that power is inscribed in civil practices of seeing and overseeing. However, others have subsequently applied Panopticism to cultural artifacts with a scatter-gun approach. This is perhaps to be expected in respect of audio-visual texts. Yet, the over-eagerness to apply the Panopticon idea has been demonstrated in other areas of narrative, as well.

Some time ago, and with special reference to a number of broadly New Historicists drunk on Foucault, Dorrit Cohn pointed out the pitfalls of not investigating the full potential inherent in narrative devices (see Cohn 1995a, 1995b; Bender 1995; Seltzer 1995). Specifically, she argued that book-length monographs on the novel by Miller, Bender and Seltzer were guilty of forcing a univalently predetermined meaning on narrative form, especially taking 'free indirect style' to be a key part of the equipment of a "novelistic panopticon" (Miller 1988: 32). Cohn's argument, although concerned with the novel, is richly illustrative for the present focus on the post-9/11 paranoid style of narration. She observes, with reference to free indirect style, that

> a novel bent on transmitting the most decisive values may rely on figural focalization, just as a novel intended to present normative ambiguities may be focalized by an eloquent narrator. I would maintain that this potential reversal of the mode-meaning correspondence vastly complicates the interpretive task (1995a 16).

Free indirect style, then, a form of focalization, can serve a stable, conservative purpose just as it might serve an ambiguous, potentially disruptive purpose when employed in narration. As a narratologist well versed in the varied uses of narrative devices, Cohn is wary of the way that some cultural historians might simply identify a narrative device and put a unitary complexion on it. Yet, as a semiotician interested in narrative, I would go further than Cohn. As I have argued previously in relation to focalization in the novels of Leonard and Higgins (Cobley 2000: 78–99), so I would also argue here in relation to narration and the paranoid style in audio-visual narratives. The signs in narration — be they free indirect discourse or the aping of surveillance in the paranoid style — will operate for readers in a context. Particularly in genre texts, and particularly where the genre in question is the thriller, the signs will be in the service of that genre's specific regime of verisimilitude. As such, readers will be bringing expectations to the text which are derived from the doxa or public opinion regarding what is credible at that moment. The political complexion of the paranoid style is therefore variable, dependent on the expectations that are brought to the genre from the contemporary climate and previous experience of the genre.

Furthermore, this variable position is built not just on the possibility of taking something 'bad' — surveillance — and demonstrating that surveillance techniques can be used to show that the suspicion of surveillance is actually 'good'. While surveillance of the population in the West in the post-9/11 period has undoubtedly involved infringements of civil liberties, it is somewhat of a leap to suggest that all vision is oppressive. Echoing the idea that surveillance *technologies* are far from foolproof is the observation that the human *eye*, too, is by no means all-seeing. Indeed, undermining the entire argument about ocularcentrism and anti-ocularcentrism, one interdisciplinary semiotician used narrative texts to suggest that the vision of the human species takes place through the limited aperture of "Captain Nemo's porthole" or "Sherlock Holmes' windows" (Sebeok 1981; see also Cobley, in press). In this scenario, the relative poverty of vision at the current stage of human development indicates that there is some way to go before the Big Brother of *Nineteen Eighty-Four* or the pre-cogs of *Minority Report* can anticipate acts of resistance.

Nevertheless, there are some more local matters arising from the paranoid style. As Dandeker (2007: 50), Lyon (2003) and others note, much surveillance, from that carried out on consumers to that enacted in the name of the 'war on terror', is in the service of identifying and constituting groups. "To think of surveillance as primarily endangering personal spaces of freedom is highly individualistic" writes Lyon (2003: 151). The paranoid style in such an individualist form as contemporary narrative could easily contribute to the impression that surveillance controls or protects personal levels of freedom. Another point made by surveillance theorists is that restricting some kinds of surveillance will lead to an upsurge of others (Marx 2007). This, again, translates directly into the issue of film narrative where visual technologies of all kinds are believed to be ocularcentric and potentially oppressive (see Heath and de Lauretis 1980). Surveillance in narratives, the argument goes, bolsters surveillance in the real world. Whether viewers of audio-visual narratives are/become/have a disposition to develop into voyeurs or whether they become more accepting of the potential infringement of rights entailed by surveillance has not yet been proved, however.

Yet, still, two issues remain. The first concerns outright resistance to surveillance, on which there is now a considerable literature (see Lyon 2003: 142–166; 2007: 159–178). Clearly, this rests on the contradictions and conflicts that are inherent in contemporary surveillance. In *Enemy*, these are dramatized by the bitter rivalry between different agencies of surveillance which play a part in the final Mexican standoff. It seems to demonstrate that there is no Big Brother, no unified surveillance agency even within government. In a sense, the paranoid style of the film is vitiated by these conflicts since they demonstrate that no surveillance system is any more foolproof than its operators. Of course, the film retains an individualized notion of surveillance in relation to persecuted and persecutors, so the possibility of surveillance machines producing results irrespective of their agents is incidental even while it is actually crucial to the plot (e. g. Zavitz's camera). In the *Spooks* episode analysed above, there is a slightly more ironic take on the matters of surveillance, power and resistance. At the end of the episode, scripted by the distinguished left-wing playwright Howard Brenton, MI5 discover that Salter's 'resistance', a far more effective plan than the anarchists' attempt to merely cause the cancellation of the Bush visit to Buckingham Palace, involves causing aerial havoc by changing the contours of the landscape (lowering mountains) represented on the air traffic control computers. As Danny and Tom work this out and frantically try to sound an alert, it is announced on the news that air traffic control computers have 'gone down' and that Bush's plane has simply been diverted to Paris. The whole paraphernalia of surveillance on both sides has been shown to be redundant.

Both of these examples in respect of resistance are connected to a second point to do with interpretation, for which I will introduce a relatively innocuous personal experience. Living in an area of the UK with some of the hardest and undrinkable water, I tend, like my neighbours, to buy a great deal of bottled water. Indeed, my local superstore records the highest number of bottled water purchases of any of its branches. However, the majority of that bottled water is 'still' rather than 'sparkling'/'carbonated' and, seeing on their EPOS returns the huge per centage of still water against sparkling that was being sold, the superstore decided to cease retailing sparkling water. It was only when the head office realized months later that the amounts of bottled water in general being sold in the store were also huge compared to stores in other regions (despite a massively disproportionate ratio of still to sparkling water sales) that the superstore resumed its sale of sparkling water. It is not known how many such acts of misinterpretation of surveillance data take place every day. Nevertheless, it throws into relief the point, once more, that surveillance is not foolproof.

No doubt the paranoid style will continue to be *de rigeur* in some depictions of the surveillance society. It seems fitting and stylistically contemporary. What the paranoid style entails will depend on the contemporary climate of anxiety outside the bounds of the text, as well as the informed way in which narratives using the paranoid style depict the sometimes glaring contradictions of surveillance. There are dangers inherent in the growth of surveillance in the contemporary West and, similarly, there are dangers in the naturalization of the paranoid style. Yet, compared with the dangers of papering over the excessive surveillance experienced in the present, the danger of representation is one that consumers of thriller narratives will have to face.

References

Andrejevic, Mark (2007). *iSpy: Surveillance and Power in the Interactive Era.* Lawrence: University Press of Kansas.

Auerbach, Erich (1968). "Odysseus' scar." In: *Mimesis: The Representation of Reality in Western Literature.* Princeton: Princeton University Press.

Bender, John (1995). "Making the world safe for narratology: a reply to Dorrit Cohn." *New Literary History* 1995, 26.1: 29–33.

Cobley, Paul (1997). "The specific regime of verisimilitude in the thriller." In: I. Rauch and G. Carr (eds.). *Synthesis in Diversity: Proceedings of the 5th Congress of the IASS.* Berlin: Mouton de Gruyter.

– (2000). *The American Thriller: Generic Innovation and Social Change in the 1970s.* London: Palgrave.

– (2009). "'It's a fine line between safety and terror': crime and anxiety re-drawn in *Spooks*." *Film International* 7 (2): 36–45.

– (in press). "Sebeok's panopticon." In: Paul Cobley, John Deely, Kalevi Kull and Susan Petrilli (eds.) *Semiotics Continues to Astonish: The Intellectual Legacy of Thomas A. Sebeok.* Berlin-New York: de Gruyter.

Cohn, Dorrit (1995a). "Optics and power in the novel." *New Literary History* 1995, 26.1: 3–20.

– (1995b). "Reply to John Bender and Mark Seltzer." *New Literary History* 1995, 26.1: 35–7.

Comolli, Jean-Louis (1980). "Machines of the visible." In: Stephen Heath and Teresa de Lauretis (eds.). *The Cinematic Apparatus*, London: Macmillan, 121–142.

Dandeker, Christopher (2007). 'Surveillance: basic concepts and dimensions.' In: Sean P. Hier and Josh Greenberg (eds.). *The Surveillance Studies Reader*, Maidenhead: Open University Press, 39–51.

Final Report of the National Commission on Terrorist Attacks on the United States (2004). *The 9/11 Commission Report.* New York and London: Norton.

Foucault, Michel (1977). *Discipline and Punish: The Birth of the Prison*, trans. A. Sheridan. Harmondsworth: Penguin.

Harper, David (2008). "The politics of paranoia: paranoid positioning and conspiratorial narratives in the surveillance society." *Surveillance and Society* 5 (1): 1–32.

Harper, Ralph (1969). *The World of the Thriller.* Baltimore and London: The Johns Hopkins University Press.

Heath, Stephen and de Lauretis, Teresa, eds. (1980). *The Cinematic Apparatus.* London: Macmillan, 121–142.

Hofstadter, Richard (1964). "The paranoid style in American politics." In: *The Paranoid Style in American Politics and Other Essays.* New York: Vintage, 3–40.

Jay, Martin (1993). *Downcast Eyes: The Denigration of Vision in Twentieth-Century French Thought.* Berkeley: University of California Press.

Kammerer, Dietmar (2004). "Video surveillance in Hollywood movies." *Surveillance and Society* 2 (2/3): 464–473.

Laidler, Keith (2008). *Surveillance Unlimited: How We've Become the Most Watched People on Earth.* Cambridge: Icon.
'Look of *Spooks*, The' (2002). Disc 2 'extra' on *Spooks* Season One DVD, London: Kudos Productions, distributed and licensed by the BBC.
Lyon, David (1994). *The Electronic Eye: The Rise of Surveillance Society.* Cambridge: Polity Press.
– (2001). *Surveillance Society: Monitoring Everyday Life.* Buckingham: Open University Press.
– (2003). *Surveillance After September 11.* Cambridge: Polity Press.
– (2007). *Surveillance Studies: An Overview.* Cambridge: Polity Press.
Marks, Peter (2005). "Imagining surveillance: utopian visions and surveillance studies." *Surveillance and Society* 3 (2/3): 222–239.
Marx, Gary T. (2007). "What's new about the 'new surveillance'? Classifying for change and continuity." In: Sean P. Hier and Josh Greenberg (eds.). *The Surveillance Studies Reader.* Maidenhead: Open University Press, 83–94.
Melley, Timothy (2000). *Empire of Conspiracy: The Culture of Paranoia in Postwar America.* Ithaca and London: Cornell University Press.
Miller, D. A. (1988). *The Novel and the Police.* Berkeley: University of California Press.
Mulvey, Laura (1975). "Visual pleasure and narrative cinema." *Screen* 16 (3): 6–18.
Pratt, Ray (2001). *Projecting Paranoia: Conspiratorial Visions in American Film.* Lawrence: University Press of Kansas.
Sebeok, Thomas A. (1981). "Captain Nemo's porthole." In: *The Play of Musement.* Bloomington: Indiana University Press.
Secret State, The (2003). http://www.salaam.co.uk/themeofthemonth/january03_index.php?l=42%82%22=0 (accessed 02.01.09)
Seltzer, Mark (1995). "The graphic unconscious: a response." *New Literary History* 26 (1): 21–28.
Weinman, Sarah (2007). "Post–9/11 thrillers." *Los Angeles Times* 2007, 10 June.
Williams, Linda (1991). *Hard Core: Power, Pleasure and the Frenzy of the Visible.* London: HarperCollins.

Samuel Ben Israel
(University of Southern Denmark)

Inter-Action Movies: Multi-Protagonist Films and Relationism

1. Introduction

The past 15–20 years have witnessed a pronounced proliferation of films within so-called art or independent cinema that do not focus on a single main character.[1] Consequently, we may refer to these films as 'multi-protagonist films'. To many, the quintessential multi-protagonist film would probably be Robert Altman's *Short Cuts* (USA 1993) or Paul Thomas Anderson's *Magnolia* (USA 1999) — two of the best known examples in recent American cinema. To some, it might be Mike Leigh's British film *Secrets & Lies* (1996) or even his earlier *Life Is Sweet* (1990). Several French films could also be considered, among them Robert Guédiguian's *The Town Is Quiet* (*La Ville est tranquille*, 2000) and Austrian director Michael Haneke's *Code Unknown* (*Code inconnu*, 2000), as well as the bulk of the Danish Dogme films, notably Lars von Trier's *The Idiots* (*Idioterne*, 1998) and Lone Scherfig's *Italian for Beginners* (*Italiensk for begyndere*, 2000). In Eastern Asian cinema we find films such as Hong Sang-soo's *The Day a Pig Fell into the Well* (*Daijiga umule pajinnal*, South Korea 1996) and Edward Yang's *Yi Yi: A One and a Two* (*Yi yi*, Taiwan 2000), while the Middle East is represented by, e. g., Iranian films such as Jafar Panahi's *The Circle* (*Dayereh*, 2000) and Abbas Kiarostami's *Ten* (2002). Last, but not least, Latin America can exhibit, e. g., Alejandro González Iñarritu's *Love's a Bitch* (*Amores perros*, Mexico 2000) and Fernando Meirelles and Kátia Lund's *City of God* (*Cidade de Deus*, Brazil 2002).

The main point with this short — but hopefully illustrative — list is that non-individualist character constellations are not confined to the so-

1 We can, of course, find examples of such organizational patterns almost since the inception of narrative cinema — as well as in other media, especially literature (see e. g. Altman 2008 and Garrett 1980) —, but my overall point is that there has never been such an abundance of multi-protagonist films, as at the present juncture.

called 'American smart film' (see Sconce 2002) or even to contemporary European (realist) art cinema, although here they "amass to such a degree in the 90s that you now can characterize them as a cultural phenomenon" (Tröhler 2001: 1),[2] but that multi-protagonist films are present in almost every film culture in the world and in the oeuvres of a range of diverse directors.[3] In spite of this, scholarly work remains relatively scarce. Multi-protagonist films have received some attention, but this has generally been focused on the 'thematic' aspects of particular films or — in an implied auteurist approach — on the directors who routinely employ the format; typically the narrative aspect of the films is only dealt with superficially or not at all (see e. g. Demory 1999, Evans 2006, Jerslev 2002, Langkjær 1999, Lippit 2004, Walters 2004, and Wayne 2002).[4] If we grant that any substantial analytical and interpretational activity presupposes aesthetic analysis and by extension analysis of the narrative 'architecture', this constitutes a problem. Not grounding our statements of what films 'mean' — ideologically, philosophically, psychologically, etc. — in a thorough analysis of their composition (and style), i. e. in the concrete films themselves, undermines the otherwise valuable insights that our analyses might present and we are often left with mere external 'applications' of theory and/or philosophy; no matter how profound this may seem, it only scratches the surface.

1.a. The Emergence of a Field of Research and a Problem

Fortunately, certain scholars have begun to approach multi-protagonist films as narratives, e. g., following Margrit Tröhler's *Gründer*-article "Les films à protagonistes multiples et la logique des possible" (2000).[5] A com-

---

2 Translations from German and the Scandinavian languages are by the author.

3 The methodological lesson I believe we can draw from this, is that neither 'national cinema' nor auteurism constitute the appropriate overall frame within which we should approach these films. Instead, it seems to confirm that non-mainstream cinema is indeed transnational (cf. Bordwell 1985).

4 A particularly striking example is the way Jerslev uses *Happiness* (Solondz, USA 1998) and *Magnolia* to illustrate 'hysteric realism'. The narrative aspect of her two examples — indisputably multi-protagonist films — is only mentioned at the very end of the article and then only in a single sentence: "The two films have the flickering narration in common, the concrete, non-hierarchical editing between a number of persons that are tightly or loosely connected to each other, a textual form that rests on the principle of juxtaposition" (Jerslev 2002: 95).

5 The article is a presentation of selected findings in her *Habilitationsschrift Plurale Figurenkonstellationen im Spielfilm* (Tröhler 2001), which has subsequently been published as *Offene Welten ohne Helden* (Tröhler 2007).

mon point among these scholars is that these recent films — in eschewing the individualistic, plot-driven, and causally coherent narrative organization of classical film narratives — tend to be narratively polyphonic, situational, more or less externalist, and have their main emphasis on character relations (Azcona 2005a and 2005b, Man 2005, and Tröhler 2007). In this vein Maria del Mar Azcona, for instance, enumerates some characteristics of contemporary multi-protagonist films:

> [...] the depiction of goal-bereft characters, the use of open endings, the substitution of serendipity for cause-and-effect and the emphasis on the relationships between the different characters to the detriment of tight lines of action [...] (2005b: unpaginated)

The last item on her list is, in my opinion, of central importance to the understanding of multi-protagonist films. Azcona thus also asserts that since multi-protagonist films "highlight a multiplicity of characters and plot-lines, they seem to be one of the ideal grounds to explore the relationships among the different characters" (ibid.). For my part, I would articulate this assessment more strongly: it is not just the case that they *seem to be the ideal grounds* to explore character relations, but this is what *mainly happens* in a great deal of these films, due to these and other compositional patterns[6]; we might say that in general the narrative emphasis is shifted away from the — sometimes conflicting — goal achievement of individuals to the portrayal of characters' interaction in social situations.

Another common point in the emerging research on multi-protagonist films is that they often include a tendency towards social commentary or critique and what Tröhler calls 'expressive ethnographic realism' (2005). In fact, another assumption — to some extent — shared by scholars of the field is that multi-protagonist films portray contemporary life and society in a 'more realistic' way than classically narrated films (see also Smith 1999). While I am personally sympathetic to this view, I find it — just as other claims invoking 'realism' — a very thorny issue indeed, and I therefore prefer to speak of the films' representation of social reality, a representation we can — broadly speaking — call 'ideological'. This means that the question of whether a certain depiction of society and social life is more or less realistic is shifted towards the values, norms, etc. implied by this depiction. Here, I will focus on a certain aspect, namely the way man (in a general or 'anthropological' sense of the word) is represented in multi-protagonist films, because — and this is one of my main conten-

6 I do not believe that Azcona and I are actually in disagreement on this point, and therefore it should be noted that the context of the above statement is influenced by reflections on the internal renewal of the romantic comedy as a genre.

tions — it is central to the social critique I and other scholars have found in the films.

To bridge these two points — multi-protagonist films' emphasis on relations and their ideological representation of man — I take my theoretical point of departure not from film studies or narrative theory proper, but from the metatheory of social psychology, most importantly from the distinction by the Swedish sociologist and philosopher Joachim Israel between the intrapsychic and the relationist perspective. Wherein the former perspective, the 'behavior' of people in everyday praxis is regarded "as expressions of internal factors, embedded in what you might call their personality structure" (J. Israel 1999: 11), in the latter perspective, emphasis is on the "analysis of peoples' social relations and the situations in which they act" (ibid, 12). This distinction is not just a descriptive one, since J. Israel clearly champions the latter, e. g. for normative or ideological reasons.

In my view, these two perspectives or types of description within social psychology broadly correspond to the classical mode of narration and the kind of alternative, relationally oriented narrative mode that we find in, e. g., multi-protagonist films. The point is that multi-protagonist films not only diverge from classical narration in various ways, but that, on the whole, in these deviations another kind of narration emerges, a relational narration that — just as the corresponding relationist perspective — is an ideological negation of the dominant notion of man in Western societies and culture, which finds its ultimate expression in classically narrated films. This does not imply any kind of 'direct influence' or inspiration. Instead, we are dealing with two modern, but different and opposing, conceptions of man, which we can find both within the social sciences, everyday praxis, and narratives.

1.b. Overview of the Chapter

To properly situate the social critique that may or might be found in multi-protagonist films I will first briefly outline the relationist critique of the intrapsychic perspective. I will also discuss how, e. g. methodological and theoretical, notions of man can be said to be ideological and — contextualizing J. Israel's distinction with the use of his own concept 'stipulations' (see 1972a and 1972b) — argue that this is not just a theoretical matter, but is also significant in everyday or so-called 'pre-scientific' praxis, e. g. filmmaking. I will then conclude the first section by illustrating the general correspondence between the intrapsychic perspective and the classical mode of narration. In the following section I will deal with some common critical responses to multi-protagonist films in order to arrive at a tentative explanation of the relative scholarly neglect of their narrative aspect, which I believe is a consequence of some of the widespread conceptions habitually used to make sense of narratives. Finally, in the third and main section I will try to show how the narration of multi-protagonist films is related to the three dimensions of the relationist perspective.

2. Reification, Ideology, and the Classical Mode of Narration

The term 'relationism' can designate positions in all metatheoretical areas, i. e. ontology, epistemology, and methodology (cf. Emirbayer 1997 and Ritzer and Gindoff 1992 and 1994), but in what follows I will focus on the latter within social psychology and take the two former — comprising my overall approach — largely for granted. On the other hand, this general (especially ontological) relationism necessarily implies that the (methodological) relationist perspective cannot simply be regarded as something in itself, i. e. abstractly, but that it must also be considered in relation to what it negates — that is: concretely (cf. Israel 1979).[7] The relationist perspective can thus be regarded as critical of the dominant intrapsychic perspective.

2.a. The Relationist Critique of the Intrapsychic Perspective

There are several reasons why the relationist perspective negates the intrapsychic perspective — of which both psychoanalysis and, more recently, cognitivism, e. g. within film studies, are influential expressions. According to J. Israel (1999), it is not just its internalist aspect — perpetuating Cartesian dualism only to exchange the 'outdated' notion of 'soul' with such concepts as 'psyche', 'consciousness', or 'mind' — that is problematic, but also the methodological individualism, causalism, and strong naturalistic and/or mechanistic bias that is associated with it in a historically concrete sense. A further important methodological problem is that the assumption of an internal psychological structure as a driving or motivating force, causing human action, "tends to lead to circular reasoning" (ibid.: 104); since an internal structure and driving forces are perceived to be the cause of human action, non-observable phenomena are taken to be the cause of

7 This point is, of course, also relevant in relation to alternative films and filmmaking.

observable ones. But the former can only be inferred from the latter, for which they are already, as causes, assumed to be sufficient conditions. Or, to put it differently: the assumption of internal causes begs the question, since the only proof of their existence is their purported effects, and this corresponds to putting the explanatory cart before the horse.

From a normative standpoint, the problem pertaining to the intrapsychic perspective is not so much a matter of logical fallacy, but rather of the "*reifying effect*", whereby man is viewed as a passive "object, as a plaything of [...] internal [...] uncontrollable forces" (ibid). The concept of 'reification', i. e. "the tendency to transform Man into an object" (J. Israel 1972b: 161), is central to J. Israel's social critique — itself an integrated part of his overall theoretical project. This critique, being generally Hegelian-Marxist, also draws on ethics and is inspired by Martin Buber's philosophy of dialogue and his distinction between 'I-Thou' and 'I-it' (see Buber 2004 and J. Israel 1992). These two so-called 'word-pairs' refer to basic types of interpersonal relations — subject-subject and subject-object — as well as to approaches or modes of action, being dialogical, non-finalizing, and communicative or monological, reifying, and strategic. The process of reification — relating to the 'utterance' of the word-pair 'I-it' — occurs on "both on a societal and a theoretical level" (J. Israel 1972b: 161), when man is either *treated* or *perceived* as an object. The latter kind I have already touched upon above, leaving us with reification in the practical sense, i. e. the transformation of man "into a commodity-like object" (Israel and Hermansson 1996: 84) in capitalist societies. But, this can also occur on a social or interpersonal level, when "I perceive the "Thou" as an object or make it into one, e. g. as means to my ends" (J. Israel 1992: 81). The point is that these different 'levels' of reification seem to be related. If we think of or perceive others as objects, we are likely to treat them as such as well and vice versa, and this, again, is related to the societal framing of our actions. Although not all relationist critiques of the intrapsychic perspective are couched in the same language or draw on Buber, we do find similar concerns among, e. g., clinical psychologists — traditionally the main proponents of individualist, internalist approaches — committed to more relational approaches (cf. Mitchell 1988, Robb 2006, and Stolorow and Atwood 1992); this would seem to prove that relationism and its attendant critique is not restricted to a few social thinkers, but is a broader tendency in Western thought and beyond.

2.b. Sketch of a Theory of Ideology

Social scientists (and, I would like to add, humanities scholars) are, according to J. Israel, not just faced with theoretical choices, but also with metatheoretical ones — although they may not always acknowledge them explicitly. Among these are choices of so-called stipulations, i. e. "normative assumptions about the character of the objects that are studied" (J. Israel 1972a: 21). They are normative by virtue of their "regulative function" (J. Israel 1972b: 125) within the social sciences (and, again, the humanities), since they "determine the content of [...] theories and, together with formal methodological rules, influence the procedures of [...] research" (ibid.). Furthermore they are "normative in the sense that they can be chosen from — and replaced by — alternative stipulations" (J. Israel 1972a: 33) and that the choice "of stipulative system is influenced [...] by values" (ibid.). This last point is important, as J. Israel generally rejects "the dogmatic belief in a 'value-free science'" (1972b: 182). He thus asserts that social theories always include "either openly stated or smuggled-in values" (Israel and Hermansson 1996: 8). Since the concept was originally developed in relation to the social sciences, J. Israel distinguishes between three types of stipulations: 1) notions or assumptions about the 'nature' of man, 2) the 'nature' of society, and 3) the relation between man and society. Due to my stated focus, it is stipulations of the first type that are of interest here.

The reason why these apparently lofty considerations are relevant in the present context is that stipulations are not just restricted to the praxis of the social sciences (or humanities), but are also significant in the "prescientific" (J. Israel 1972a: 27) praxis of everyday life. They influence our ways of relating to others, and since "we have certain conceptions about other people, we act in such a way that they in return are forced to act in keeping with our expectations" (J. Israel 1985: 21). This means that stipulations in both a scientific and an everyday context often "function as self-fulfilling prophecies" (J. Israel 1972b: 124), which "confers upon them not only the status of empirical statements but of *verified* empirical statements" (ibid.) — especially when they correspond to dominant ideological notions, which tend towards 'common-sense' status. Taking this and their normative character — in all of the abovementioned senses — into account, I believe that stipulations, i. e. in a stipulative system, can fruitfully be used to clarify the concept of 'ideology', "perhaps one of the most equivocal and elusive [...] one can find in the social sciences" (Larrain 1979: 13).

As a concept 'ideology' can thus be used in both a 'negative' and a 'positive' sense. In traditional ideology critique, the negative sense is dominant and ideology is viewed as 'false consciousness' or a "necessary deception" (ibid) by which the ruling class legitimizes the hegemonic societal order. In the positive sense we speak of ideolog*ies* or *Weltanschaungen*, i. e. the views, values, approaches, etc. of classes, groups, and individuals that must be viewed in connection with their social position as well as their life situation and conditions. In my opinion, the negative sense it not viable because of the risk of overlooking our own normative point of departure, while the positive one forces us to approach it reflexively. The consequence is not relativism, but a demand that we explicitly state our views and values, e. g. our chosen stipulations. Another important point, which I can only touch upon presently, is that ideology cannot be regarded as something in itself (except maybe analytically), but that we — from a relationist perspective in the ontological sense — necessarily have to understand ideology as part of the praxis-ideology relation of mutual production and legitimization (see S. B. Israel 2004).

From the above, it follows that filmmaking, as a particular mode of (everyday or, maybe rather, 'pre-scientific') praxis, is ideological in the sense that stipulations also play a part in this context — not only of the three mentioned, general types, but also stipulations specific to cultural production, e. g. about the product or artwork, its composition, and its social function, as well as about the audience and the relation between product/artwork and audience. Hence, I will treat the composition of film narratives as analogous to social theories, being radically different modes of description of man and of human action and interaction, on different levels of abstraction — either abstract and conceptual or concrete and related to narrative matters, such as organizational principles, — but nonetheless sharing this as a central concern; or even more simply: if there are different ways of conceiving man in theory, why should there not be in film narratives? If we assume that stipulations influence the way films are narratively constructed and that the representation of man in films is not just a matter of the films' 'surface representation' (i. e. what they are about and who occupies the different 'roles' in a specific sense), but also, and maybe even more significantly, a question of how characters are constituted through the narrative organization, this implies that the way humans — or rather: characters and their functions, motivations (or lack thereof), etc. — are construed in films, is ideological.

2.c. The Intrapsychic Classical Mode of Narration

In a manner similar to the intrapsychic perspective, classical narration (see e. g. Bordwell 1985) — still the culturally and commercially dominant mode of narration (cf. Bordwell 2006) — proceeds from the *single* individual and, just as in the intrapsychic perspective, "internal structure and [...] driving forces" (J. Israel 1999: 77) are regarded as the cause of "external, observable psychological phenomena" (ibid.), i. e. human or character action; or as David Bordwell puts it:

> The classical Hollywood film presents psychologically defined individuals who struggle to solve a clear-cut problem or to attain specific goals [...] The principal causal agency is thus the character, a discriminated individual endowed with a consistent batch of evident traits, qualities, and behaviors [...] The most "specified" character is usually the protagonist, who becomes the principal causal agent [...] (1985: 157)

Along these lines, the narrative of the classical film centers on the project of the protagonist, the conflict with the antagonist — which, taken together, make up the so-called 'plot' — and the resolution of this conflict. It is thus individualistic and goal-oriented — both towards the fulfillment of the project of the main character or 'hero' and towards the causal and ethical closure of the narrative; following the ordered progression — one event leading to the next — of the narrative, all (or nearly all) loose ends are tied, and the hero gets his reward, while the villain gets his due punishment.

Classical characters are equally goal-oriented and are in addition psychologically motivated towards these goals; in fact, this motivation may be regarded as the actual causal 'motor' of the classical film narrative. They are furthermore characterized as relatively stable structures of psychological traits, and their so-called 'development' consists primarily in the reversal to their "true character" (L. Israel 1991: 131; cf. Thompson 1999) from egocentric attitudes, perverse psychological states, etc. Consider, for instance, the character of the hardnosed, rogue hero, who is forced to choose between personal gratification and doing what is 'right', a dilemma that only becomes pertinent because he is (of course) essentially 'good'. Of course, the classical conception of motivation has been updated to include both the (traditional) 'want', i. e. some desired object (in some cases: another person), and the 'need' of the main character, i. e. his psychological fulfillment.[8] These two types of motivation — the outwardly object-oriented and the inwardly psyche-oriented — could also be seen to underlie the distinction *within* classical narration between (traditional) plot-driven and (more recent) character-driven narratives, i. e. a question of whether psychology and psychological 'development' is subservient to 'plot' or vice versa.

---

8 That I use the male personal pronoun here is not entirely accidental, but also reflects the oft stated case that heroes in classical films tend to be male.

The double motivational structure, which is considered to be a deepening of the classical film character (cf. Bordwell 2006), hints at a further characteristic of the classical mode of narration, namely the distribution of characters in a strict hierarchy of narrative functions, i. e. main and auxiliary characters, since generally only the main characters are endowed with it. This functional hierarchy is expressed by and is connected to the narrative's anchoring in the protagonist's project, the mentioned degree of 'sophistication' in characterization (also a matter of the sheer number of traits a character is endowed with and their possible conflicting 'nature'), and the distribution of 'focus' and 'perspective' — all analytically different, but compositionally related, aspects.

All this implies a certain 'narrative economy', expressed in a tight composition — e. g. exclusion of "*causally* unimportant periods of time" (Bordwell 1985: 160; my emphasis) that do not bring the action towards its goal. Besides this, and apart from centering the narrative on one or two main characters, the central status of the project-conflict structure (the 'plot') and motivation, as well as the anchoring of characterization in internal psychological structures, implies that the amount of *dramatis personae* has to be restricted (cf. Smith 1999). The available narrative time (typically 90–120 minutes) does not allow a superfluity of central fictional persons, as it is assumed that motivation and traits would become unclear. Exposition is, furthermore, generally seen as a compositional element that must be completed before the action proper, i. e. project and conflict, can commence. All this is expressed in connection with literary adaptations, where persons in the source are omitted or 'written together' in relation to their narrative function.

Composition and, especially, characterization in the classical mode of narration are expressions of the intrapsychic perspective and thereby of the dominant stipulations about 'human nature' in our society. And just as these psychologizing notions are reifying in theory, society, and everyday social praxis, this is also the case in the institutional praxis of filmmaking and the communicative praxis of narrative film. Classically narrated films are thus as much a product as a perpetuation of ideological, reifying tendencies in Western societies; although they may in some cases be superficially critical of 'the powers that be', they can never get to the heart of the matter, at least not from a relationist point of view.

3. Narratological Concepts and Multi-Protagonist Films

During the Cannes Film Festival in 2003, where *Elephant* (USA 2003) — yet another recent multi-protagonist film — won the *Palme d'Or*, the coming winner received a certain amount of critical flak. Reviewers especially criticized the film for its "descriptive distance" (Skotte 2003: 1) to its serious theme (high-school shootings) and to the characters, for not delving "deeply into the problem and the soul of the individual" (ibid.). The film's director, Gus Van Sant, had the following comments to the criticism:

> [...]the reviewers wanted good answers and drama. They asked: Why is the film so irritatingly non-dramatic? They almost asked me to make a film that could have been made in the 1950s. I could just as well ask: Why are the reviews so terribly old-fashioned? (quoted in ibid.).

It is not all that uncommon for reviews of alternatively narrated films to rebuke them for, e. g., not motivating and characterizing (i. e. psychologically 'grounding') their characters properly. This, in effect, is considered to impede the viewers' 'emotional engagement' with the characters and the film as a whole, which is considered to be a serious defect, since the arousal of various feelings is putatively the goal of *all* art.[9] The case in point being that some reviewers — mistakenly — judge alternatively narrated films using classical narration as a yardstick or measure, and that these films therefore are perceived as deficient, when *expected* compositional element are missing.[10] But, lack of psychological motivation need not be a flaw; Gus Van Sant, for instance, defended his film on the following grounds:

> I have been meaning to create a pure portrait of an event. [...] As a viewer, you just observe the events and have to make the associations yourself [...] We show the event as it played out. We do not show the *causes*. (quoted in ibid.; my emphasis)

3.a. The Concepts of 'Character' and 'Story'

A somewhat similar, but less judgmental, approach — probably the more common one among scholars — applies handed-down, taken-for-granted critical concepts and criteria to the understanding of alternatively narrated

---

9 At least according to the aesthetics of such seemingly disparate figures as Hitchcock and Disney, who nonetheless both — in their own different ways — can be regarded as contributing to the development and perfection of the classical mode of narration.

10 Of course, there are (a lot of) 'bad' classical films that simply do not meet the standards of their mode of narration, but these are not the issue here.

films, whereby significant narrative aspects are simply overlooked. Especially the concept of 'character' and more specifically the notion of a *main* character tend to generate a kind of cookie-cutter criticism in the case of multi-protagonist films that is not sensitive to the implications of the films' concrete composition, producing instead what Garrett (1980) calls 'monocentric reconstructions'. An example of the latter is Tim Walters' otherwise informed analysis of *The Idiots*. He rightly, in my opinion, stresses that the film "may be the most fully developed and compelling expression of Dogme ideology" (Walters 2004: 40), i. e. "not only 'anti-bourgeois *cinema*' but also 'anti-bourgeois'" (ibid, 43; my emphasis). Therefore he also poses the following critical question to the otherwise critically acclaimed *The Celebration* (*Festen*, Thomas Vinterberg, Denmark 1998) and *Mifune* (*Mifunes sidste sang*, Søren Kragh-Jacobsen, Denmark 1999):

> If they are so interested in challenging the implicit or built-in ideology of cinema, must they not also make that apparent by constructing radical narratives, for instance? (ibid.)

Where he seemingly misses the point in his demonstration of the 'radicalness' of the narrative of *The Idiots*, which he considers "inelegantly spare and lumpy, with a digressive and spontaneous rhythm orchestrated around the group's various diversions and pastimes" (ibid, 45), is in the contention that its, albeit, "nominal story [...] revolves around Karen" (ibid). If the narrative of *The Idiots* is so 'radical' that the film, according to Walters, almost amounts to the only true Dogme film, why does it necessarily have to include a main character, so typical of the traditional, 'bourgeois' narrative? Of course, it is true that the film begins and ends with focus on Karen (Bodil Jørgensen) and her situation (dealing with the loss of a child in a seemingly uncaring environment), but in other parts of the film she either 'acts' only as a kind of observer or recedes entirely into the background, while other members of the *spasser* collective 'take center stage', e. g. Jeppe (Nikolaj Lie Kaas) as well as Axel (Knud Romer Jørgensen) and Katrine (Anne-Grethe Bjarup Riis) and their ongoing 'lovers' quarrel'. In fact, is it not more fruitful to regard *The Idiots* as an ensemble film and Karen as — what Tröhler (2007) calls — an *Alibihauptperson*, a 'pretext main character'?[11]

11 For Tröhler these 'pretext main characters' can have 'symbolic' significance in relation to the "overall theme" (Tröhler 2007: 53) — in the case of *The Idiots*: spassing as revolt against petty-bourgeois norms — and function narratively as that which sets "the *structural* frame" (ibid). On the other hand, they "are neither as bearers of action nor as instance of narration, neither in their screen presence nor as emotionally engaging figures determinative" (ibid, 54).

In general, traditional conceptions of character are problematic in relation to multi-protagonist films, whether understood according to Chatman as a "paradigm of traits" (1978: 126) or in the Greimasian sense as a mere actant. The former because it reduces all *and even radically different* types or ways of constituting character through narratives with divergent organizational principles to a psychologizing model or understanding of man without considering the possibility of alternatives or, to use Tröhler's (2007) terms, different '*Figurenkonzeptionen*', and the latter because it merely equates character with narrative function or placeholder in a relatively restricted understanding of narratives that more or less coincides with the conception of the so-called 'plot' in classical narration; other approaches to the concept of character might be more fitting.

Similar points could be made in relation to the concept of 'story' and again specifically concerning the notion of 'minimal story'. Bordwell, for instance, describes his concept of 'fabula', as a "chronological cause-and-effect chain of events occurring within a given duration and in a spatial field" (1985: 49). Although this may seem unproblematic at first glance, especially his emphasis on the causal nature of the fabula should make us wonder, whether this, in fact, is a description of a specific ontology represented in classically narrated films, but not necessarily in alternatively narrated art cinema. Likewise, Chatman's in some respects parallel concept of 'story' is peopled by characters in the abovementioned sense that could also be said to represent a certain conception of man found mainly in classical narration.

Turning to the concept of 'minimal story', this is often understood as a structure consisting of three elements: a state, an event, and, a second (changed) state following from the event. As Rimmon-Kenan points out this notion "requires three principles of organization: (1) temporal succession; (2) causality; (3) inversion" (2002: 18). We also know this model from classical narration, where an initial state of harmony is disrupted, typically by the actions of the antagonist, and thus has to 'set right', typically by the actions of the protagonist/hero: the traditional structure of harmony→disruption→restored harmony. Rimmon-Kenan also argues, though, that "temporal succession is sufficient as a *minimal* requirement for a group of events to form a story" (ibid, 18 f.), partly because the implications of the other requirement are counter-intuitive: "If [...] we posit causality and closure [...] as obligatory criteria, many groups of events which we intuitively recognize as stories would have to be excluded from this category" (ibid, 19).[12]

12 In his attempt to redirect narrative theory, Altman (2008) makes several points similar to mine in his criticism of 'the traditional understanding of narrative'.

Some of these problems with the concept of 'story' are connected to its derivation in the concept of 'content' in the traditional distinction between content and form, which of course can be found in varying guises throughout communication theory, semiotics, etc. In spite of common riders that content is never independent of form, the distinction in itself seems to imply a tendency towards the privileging of content over form, i. e. a notion that content comes before form, whereby it acquires a status akin to Platonic ideas — evident in statements such as: 'The same story can be told in different ways'. While there are strong methodological reasons to uphold the concept of 'story', especially in relation to the problem of temporal order in concrete narrative texts, there are, in my opinion, equally great problems with the concept, centrally the insensitivity to the specific representations produced by the concrete composition of narratives. I would thus like to reverse the picture, and privilege form over content by speaking of specific narratives and the representations or represented 'worlds' produced through their composition rather than of story and discourse or fabula and syuzhet.[13] Or, to put it more succintly: you cannot say the same thing with different means, since what you say is influenced by the way you say it.

4. Multi-Protagonist Films and the Dimensions of Relationism

Although Tröhler makes an important distinction, regarding non-individualist character constellations that emerge so forcefully in the 90s, between ensemble and mosaic films, i. e. films that either revolve around groups with distinguishable characters or create network-like configurations of single characters, pairs, or small groups (2000, 2001 and 2007), in what follows I will concentrate on some general characteristics that I believe can be observed in both types. Furthermore, I believe that these general characteristics correspond to basic tenets or dimensions of the relationist perspective: the interpersonal, the situational, and the pragmatic

13 That I do not include spectatorial activity in this description is not to argue for a return to a notion of the autonomy of the text found in New Criticism or early structuralism, but is simply a matter of delimitation. First of all, I do not believe, I have anything satisfactorily consistent to say about the relation between film and spectator on the grounds of a relationist approach at the moment. Therefore I do not wish to champion multi-protagonist films for activating the viewer more than classical films, in the manner of Gus Van Sant in the above quotation. Note, though, that results from preliminary empirical audience studies (Azcona 2005a) seem to point in that direction.

or action-oriented, the result being a non-reifying conception of man that, I will claim, has ideological as well as profound ethical implications.

4.a. The Interpersonal

In the section before last I focused on relationism's negation of the intrapsychic perspective in relation to its tendencies towards circular reasoning and reification and only mentioned other problematic aspects in passing. But relationism also centrally negates the individualism integral to the intrapsychic perspective, because human beings are never "socially isolated atoms" (J. Israel 1999: 81), but always and necessarily take part in interactions and relations with others. As an example of this view, J. Israel thus refers to George Herbert Mead, who reversed the traditional notion of the self as "a precondition for [...] interaction with others" (ibid, 128), and, instead, argued that it is socially and intersubjectively constituted; that it "grows out of social interaction" (ibid).

While this strong version of relationism may not be immediately apparent in all multi-protagonist films, the fact that they present a multitude of narratively equal and more or less interrelated characters is clearly a negation of the individualism found in classical narration and highlights the social 'space' between the characters. This would seem to entail that non-individualist character constellations are indeed relational, at least to a degree, and that character relations cease to be merely attributive of individual characters (i. e. expressions of their 'personality'), functionally motivated by the plot (i. e. means to goal achievement), or a thematic concern, as they would be in classical narration. That the narrative emphasis of multi-protagonist films on character relations is a matter of narrative organization and not only thematically significant is also underscored by the absence of traditional 'plots', i. e. project-conflict structures.

The relational character of multi-protagonist films is, of course, also related to, what could be regarded as their most 'basic' characteristic, their "polyfocalised narrative stance" (Tröhler 2005: unpaginated) which seemingly determines them as multi-protagonist films. Apart from having implications for the narrative economy, e. g. making it extremely difficult to incorporate 'plot' and closure, it is also related to the breakdown or loosening of the classical films' functional hierarchy. The alternative is a more 'fluid' distribution of 'focus' and 'perspective', which gives the characters equal status, and can manifest itself both 'globally' and 'locally' in the narrative.

Changes or shifts in focus not only occur *between* different parts of a mosaic film, where they can be indicated by 'chapter headings', as in

Things You Can Tell Just by Looking at Her (Rodrigo García, USA 2000), or stylistic markers, as the different color and textural schemes of the three locations (the East Coast, Mexico and Southern California) with their, at least, six protagonist in *Traffic* (Steven Soderbergh, USA 2000), but also *within* individual scenes. In *Code Unknown* a scene takes place in a restaurant, where Anne (Juliette Binoche) in the company of some friends is celebrating the safe return from Kosovo of her boyfriend Georges (Thierry Neuvic), who is a news photographer. In the course of the scene, focus shifts by a repositioning of the camera — each scene in the film consists of only one shot — to Amadou (Ona Lu Yenke), a young West African immigrant, who is out on a date with a French girl at the same restaurant.

Another example from this film is the return to the family farm of Georges' younger brother Jean (Alexandre Hamidi) after the scuffle in a Paris street with Amadou in the film's opening scene. The scene's situational premise is that Jean has already at the very beginning of the film stated his frustration at the fate of having to take over the farm. When he enters, his father (Sepp Bierbichler) is already seated at the dinner table, eating, and they hardly exchange glances or words. There is seemingly no warmth in the father's actions, when he hands Jean a plate of cooked beets and a spoon, and Jean frustration seems quite understandable; this is what he is trying to escape from, when he at the very beginning of the film asks Anne, if he can stay with her and Georges in Paris. But again the focus shifts: the father gets up from the table, while Jean is still eating, and goes to the bathroom, where he sits down and sighs. He flushes the toilet, without having used it, and apparently (his face is turned away from the camera) begins sobbing silently. Suddenly, the father's 'perspective' is clear; the situation is as frustrating to him as it is to Jean. The point is that the two characters are put on equal footing — the narrative becomes polyphonic instead of individualistic — and the focus is now not just on Jean's frustration at his fate, but on their mutual relation; the question is no longer: 'What will happen to *Jean*?', or: 'What is *he* going to do?', but: 'What will happen to *them*?', or: 'How will *they* manage?' In the course of the scene, the situational premise thus changes from being centered on Jean and his problem to the relationship between father and son.

Of course, these shifts of 'perspective' within scenes are probably even more common in ensemble films, where the focus can shift between the different members of the group, whose interrelatedness — as a family, coworkers, etc — is already in place; it is what defines them as a group. Development in ensemble films can also be regarded as a relational rather than an individual matter; it is not the individual characters that evolve, but their relations. This is clear in several of Mike Leigh's films, especially *Life Is Sweet* and *Secrets & Lies*, which both thematize how the lack of communication and empathizing can damage relations, and that redemption or resolution is only possible through a communicative process, i. e. in a social setting. This theme is, of course, not uncommon in classically narrated, character-driven dramas, where the main character strives to achieve recognition, empathy, or the like from some significant other, e. g. a parent, lover, etc. One of the distinguishing marks of these films in relation to the two mentioned ones — as well as other ensemble films — is that the traditional functional hierarchy is still in place; they still revolve around the project of a single protagonist, but in these cases the desired object is not a 'thing', but another person, upon whom a thing-like status is conferred, i. e. who is reified.

The point is that in ensemble films the problem of relational estrangement is not just a thematic matter, but emerges from and is reinforced by the relational character of the narrative, i. e. the operative distinction here is one between thematic and narrative emphasis. In *Life Is Sweet*, the central relational issue — the petty conflicts between the daughter Nicola (Jane Horrocks) and, more or less, the rest of the family, but especially the mother Wendy (Alison Steadman) — and its development, is captured in two significant scenes of the family gathered in the living room of their home.

The first scene — early in the film and about three minutes long — is comprised of 71 shots (i.e. an average shot length of about 2.5 seconds), ranging from medium shots to medium close-ups, and mainly of only one character at a time; only four shots show more than one person, one of which is a travelling shot, while one shot shows only décor.[14] In most of the shots, the character shown also speaks, while other characters may be heard on the soundtrack; only in twelve shots the character shown does not speak, but is either the subject of or reacting to the dialogue. The reason why I point this out is that the scene's visual style — shot and edited more or less as a conventional dialogue scene — is actually not typical of Leigh's films, where scenes are generally done in long takes, featuring more than one person in the shot. The visual style thus becomes significant in underscoring the problematic interpersonal relations of the family, evident in the conflict-laden dialogue and also reinforced by Nicola's spatial position vis-à-vis the other members of the family.

The second scene — towards the end of the film and about one minute long — consists of only two shots, one of which is a typical Leighian shot, a static long to medium long shot lasting roughly 40 seconds, showing all four members of the family simultaneously. The visual style, as well as

14 All figures are based on timing of the Cinema Club edition DVD.

both the dialogue, which is much more considerate and warm, compared to the first scene, and the spatial configuration of the characters, stresses the beginning easing of conflicts in the family; they have begun to communicate and take care of each other. Interestingly, though, the film ends without complete closure, but just on a hopeful note. Another significant difference from the first scene is the much more distanced and at the same time collective focus that is achieved through the framing and the shot length, whereas in the first scene the focus continually shifts between the characters due to the framing and editing.

4.b. The Situational

Because of the sheer complexity of human action and interaction, J. Israel seriously doubts "the necessity or even the possibility of using causal explanations in this context" (1999: 77) — although this is commonly done, both within the social sciences and in everyday or 'pre-scientific' praxis, e. g. filmmaking. In, for instance, an interpersonal conflict it is "hardly meaningful to ask who started it, caused the conflict, or who is to blame" (ibid, 78), since the parties to a conflict are in a "reciprocal relation of influence" (ibid). Human relations are mutually interactional and therefore action, so the relationist argument goes, cannot be understood in an one-sidedly, deterministically causal manner. Thus, in a social scientific context (and why not also in humanistic and everyday ones?) we cannot take refuge in causal explanations and we will therefore have to settle for interpreting observable phenomena, e. g. in conflicts it is more feasible to "indicate reasons as to how [...] interactions began and how they elapsed. Such reasons are situational interpretations" (ibid).

This brings us to the next central dimension of the relationist perspective: the concept of 'situation'. J. Israel — inspired by, among others, John Dewey — points out that action, and thereby interaction, cannot be separated from the situations in which actors find themselves; it would simply be logically inconsistent to speak of action without somebody acting, and of action and actors not being situated in time, space, and a social setting. The situation thus frames action and interaction, and as a concept it refers "to the social and physical space in which the action occurs, the time at which it occurs, the expectations that exist and how the person reacts to these expectations, the social position or status she has when she acts and the position and status of the one towards whom the action is directed" (ibid, 71). This holistic or multi-dimensional situational dimension of relationism can be further understood as the negation of the causalist determinism common in the intrapsychic perspective.

The situational dimension can be found in multi-protagonist films on both the 'global' and the 'local' level. On the global level, the narrative as a whole, the situational dimension manifests itself in the typically episodic composition of multi-protagonist films, thereby eschewing traditional 'plots' as well as downplaying causality and closure. Of course, mosaic films are often the most explicitly episodic, since their composition is marked by the interweaving of different 'story threads' (Smith 1999), and the transition from one 'thread' to another does not necessarily imply that the action is picked up where it was previously left off. Instead, the different loosely connected scenes acquire a certain independence from the over-all narrative flow. They are and present, so to speak, small relational interaction games or plays.

If we turn to the ensemble film, I will again draw on *Life Is Sweet* for examples. Although we might consider the conflict — actually petty bickering — between Nicola and the rest of the family as the central relational issue, as I have done, considerable parts of the film only touch on this problem tangentially. I think here specifically of the two rather long sequences, where other matters are more prominent, the first concerning Andy (Jim Broadbent), the father of the family, buying a dilapidated snack van from the unemployed (and probably petty criminal) Patsy (Stephen Rea), and the second treating the ill-considered opening of a restaurant — symbolically named The Regret Rien — by Aubrey (Timothy Spall), a friend of the family. Depending on how we segment the film and which scenes we include, these two sequences last from about 35 minutes to a little over 40 minutes. If we also include the sequence, following the one about the snack van, where Aubrey shows his restaurant to Andy and Wendy, a couple of days before the opening, we can add almost 10 more minutes to matters that do not directly concern the relationships in the family.

Albeit this kind of quantitative measurement of time does not necessarily tell us a anything about the film's narrative, the fact that close to almost half of the film concerns other issues than what we might — with some right — consider the central one, is rather telling. Furthermore, both the buying of the van and the opening of the restaurant can be considered as fairly independent episodes that are not developed to any certain degree of conclusiveness. Andy's stated plans to renovate the van so he can quit his day job as the head chef at an unspecified restaurant or industrial kitchen are never realized, i. e. it is not a story of Andy's heroic attempt 'to break out of the rat race'; the matter pretty much just fizzles out. The same is also true of Aubrey's restaurant project, although this seemingly flounders with his passing out drunk and half-naked on the night of the opening. But again, Aubrey's misfortune has absolutely no bearing on the life of the family; it is, in effect, an independent episode. This is also underscored by the strange love affair that develops between Aubrey and his underling Paula (Moya Brady) before and during the restaurant opening sequence. The love affair, which is heavily marked by the social hierarchy, i. e. a relation between a dominating and a dominated position, in which Aubrey and Paula find themselves, is thus an example of one of the aforementioned relation games. This is also the case with the buying of the snack van, since it becomes the background for an ongoing 'negotiation' between Andy and Wendy about the prudence of the matter.

The situational dimension is also apparent in the central issue itself, since the roots of this remain undisclosed; it is not grounded causally. What remains is the here-and-now of the conflict, which mainly centers on dysfunctional communication in the form of bickering and inconsiderate jokes. The message seems to be that in order to deal with this kind of problem we have to communicate and be open and unprejudiced — in short: dialogic — towards others, which in fact is what Wendy tries to do towards the end of the film. This in turn opens up to a process of reintegrating Nicola into the family.

Another way the situational can be observed in many multi-protagonist films of both types is the way mundane, everyday activities are dealt with at the local level, i. e. in the single scene. Not infrequently these undramatic events are given time to unfold, much the same way as the often cited (and celebrated) scene from the neorealist classic *Umberto D.* (Vittorio De Sica, Italy 1952), portraying the morning chores of the maid Maria (Maria-Pia Casilio). And again, the sequential arrangement of such scenes is part of what constitutes the episodic composition of the narrative as a whole.

4.c. The Pragmatic

The final dimension of relationism, the pragmatic or action-oriented, negates the internalism of the intrapsychic perspective, i. e. the view that internal mental or psychological states and structures are primary to the understanding (or rather: explanation) of man and human action, e. g. as motivational causes, — a problem I have already touched on previously. Instead, relationism takes its point of departure in action itself as situated, meaningful, and intentional. To support this view, J. Israel draws — among other sources — on the theory of action formulated by the Finnish philosopher Georg Henrik von Wright. In his model, action consists of certain necessary elements, two of which are situation and intentionality. Leaving situation aside, since I have already dealt with this above, I will now turn to the concept of 'intention'. J. Israel points to two aspects of von Wright's conception of intentionality, being important from a relationist point of view. First of all, "von Wright decidedly rejects the thought that actions are caused by mental attitudes. Consequently he also rejects the thought that intentions could be mental processes or states" (J. Israel 1999: 29). This also means that the "intention is neither something "behind" or "outside" an action, as it would be misleading to claim that you could be able to locate the intention to a specific part of the action" (ibid). Instead, as stated earlier, we have to confine ourselves to ascribing reasons, being an integral part of 'situational interpretations', or as J. Israel also puts it: intentionality, so to speak, has "its place in a *narrative* about the actor" (ibid, my emphasis). In fact it is the action itself, which we can describe as being intentional.

From this, and from J. Israel's argument that the so-called 'retroduction' from (observable) actions to a (non-observable) personality or 'traits' is in fact circular, it follows that it is action itself, which we must perceive and describe as 'honest'/'deceitful', 'brave'/'cowardly', 'good'/'evil', etc., and this depends on the concrete social situation, as well as on the societal and cultural circumstances: "We can choose a number of so-called traits and always find that what it in fact is about is *mode of action*" (J. Israel 1985: 33). This does not mean that J. Israel rejects psychology completely:

> [...] for logical reasons we also have to use a psychological-mentalist language. We cannot actually do without concepts such as "think", "experience", "perceive", "feel", "dream", and so on when we describe man. The fact that we use the language game of [...] psychology constitutes neither necessary nor sufficient conditions for a claim that we *own* [...] a soul [...] (1999: 19)

The important point being — and here J. Israel draws on Roy Schafer — that we have to develop a language of action, with all that this implies, instead of the traditional language of traits or structures; in practical terms this means that we, e. g., have to use verbs and not nouns, when we describe psychological matters, at least if we want to avoid reification.

Due to the formal characteristics of the multi-protagonist film, especially the emphasis on character interaction, the polyphonic focus, and the episodic composition, I believe that it can be viewed as the cinematic equivalent of such a language of action. In this regard, Tröhler speaks of an "*external* focalization *on* the characters" (2007: 65) at work in multi-protagonist films, and conclude that "actions, speech acts, emotional expressions and gestures flow together and can only be understood *relationally*" (ibid, 274).[15]

---

15 Azcona makes a similar point regarding the issue of reception: "Through a heavy reliance on external focalization and the absence of other devices that could help spectators to probe

This external focalization is also underscored by the relative absence of traditional subjectivity, i. e. flashbacks motivated by memory, point-of-view shots, stylistic markers such as blurred images to signify dizziness or fadeouts to signify loss of consciousness, etc. An interesting example here can be observed in Denys Arcand's *The Barbarian Invasions* (*Les Invasions barbares*, Canada 2003). As the cancer-stricken Rémy (Rémy Girard) recounts his passage into sexual maturity as a series of 'love affairs' — he actually just talks about adolescent masturbation — with a number of beautiful actresses and other female public figures, his tale is intercut with film excerpts and archival footage. The effect, due to the marked stylistic differences, e. g. black and white instead of color, is not one of his subjective memories, but of extradiegetic inserts.

5. Concluding Remarks

In this chapter, I have tried to show what it means to claim that multi-protagonist films are relational, and not only in a thematic sense. This claim is not just my own, but one around which there is a certain agreement in the still relatively small research community. Of course, consensus is not verification that a claim is true — is there ever any? But, I believe, there is a certain strength and fruitfulness to the claim because it is based on, what we might call, a methodological 'sensibility', an openness towards letting the specific films challenge our taken-for-granted concepts and notions of narrative — while at the same time taking care not to overstress their critical or analytical potential. It is not that narratology has hitherto been wrong; I believe, for instance, that Bordwell's description of the classical mode of narration is very accurate. But, we do seem to live in times where different new forms and developments within older forms of narrative demand that we develop, supplement and revise our theories.

I also believe that these new forms of and approaches to narrative, and especially those that seem to 'break the rules', cannot just be regarded as something in themselves. We may see them as internal 'evolutionary' developments of the respective art forms, or as necessary responses to an increasing level of audience sophistication. We can also regard them as just one element in broader sociocultural tendencies that they either reflect or midwife, e. g. 'postmodernity'. None of these explanations are in my view sufficient — they cannot, for instance, explain the continuous

into the characters' minds [...] spectators are faced with opaque characters [...]" (2005a: 16).

cultural and commercial dominance of relatively traditional approaches to storytelling (cf. Bordwell 2006 and Thompson 1999). They might all 'be on to' a part of the picture, but not all of it. 'Rule-breaking' implies that there are rules to be broken, and this is a very important sense in which alternatives — also a relational notion — cannot just be conceived abstractly as something in themselves. A part of the truth may also be that we have to conceive them as — more or less intentional — negations of the dominant, the mainstream; i. e. as critical responses to the praxis and ideology of contemporary society, its values and morals. In the case of multi-protagonist films the brunt of the critique would seem to be towards reifying tendencies at different levels, but especially at the interpersonal one, and it probably does not get any more ethical than that.

Does this mean that multi-protagonist films always express a relationist critique? It might not, but I have tried to keep my description in this chapter at a certain level of generality by drawing on numerous films for examples. Of course, there are always perspectives for further research, and one that I find very important are the tendencies towards 'Hollywoodization' of multi-protagonist films, i. e. attempts to make them conform to classical storytelling principles.

References

Altman, Rick (2008). *A Theory of Narrative*. New York: Columbia University Press.

Azcona, María del Mar (2005a). "Making Sense of a Multi-Protagonist Film: Audience Response Research and Robert Altman's *Short Cuts* (1993)." *Miscelánea* 32: 11–22.

– (2005b). "A New Syntax for the Same Old Story?: Multi-Protagonist Romantic Comedies Today." Paper presented at the Society for Cinema and Media Studies Conference. London: March 31-April 3, 2005.

Bordwell, David (1985). *Narration in the Fiction Film*. Madison: The University of Wisconsin Press.

Bordwell, David (2006). *The Way Hollywood Tells It. Story and Style in Modern Movies*. Berkeley: University of California Press.

Buber, Martin (2004). *I and Thou*. 2nd ed. Trans. Ronald Gregor Smith. London: Continuum.

Chatman, Seymour (1978). *Story and Discourse. Narrative Structure in Fiction and Film*. Ithaca: Cornell University Press.

Demory, Pamela (1999). "'It's about Seeing…' — Representations of the Female Body in Robert Altman's *Short Cuts* and Raymond Carver's Stories." *Pacific Coast Philology* 34.1: 96–105.

Emirbayer, Mustafa (1997). "Manifesto for a Relational Sociology." *American Journal of Sociology* 103.2: 281–317.

Evans, Jo (2006). "*Piedras* and the Fetish: 'Don't Look Now'." *Studies in Hispanic Cinema* 2.2: 69–82.
Garrett, Peter K. (1980). *The Victorian Multiplot Novel. Studies in Dialogical Form.* New Haven: Yale University Press.
Israel, Joachim (1972a). *Om kunsten at løfte sig op ved hårene og beholde barnet i badevandet. Kritiske betragtninger over samfundsvidenskabernes videnskabsteori.* Copenhagen: Gyldendal.
– (1972b). "Stipulations and Construction in the Social Sciences." In: Israel, Joachim and Henri Tajfel (eds.). *The Context of Social Psychology. A Critical Assessment.* London: Academic Press, 123–211.
– (1979). *The Language of Dialectics and the Dialectics of Language.* Copenhagen: Munksgaard.
– (1985). *Sociologi. Indføring i samfundsstudiet.* 2nd ed. Copenhagen: Gyldendal.
– (1992). *Martin Buber. Dialogfilosof och zionist.* Stockholm: Natur och Kultur.
– (1999). *Handling och samspel. Ett socialpsykologiskt perspektiv.* Lund: Studentlitteratur.
Israel, Joachim, and Hans-Erik Hermansson (1996). *Det nya klassamhället.* Stockholm: Ordfront.
Israel, Lena (1991). *Filmdramaturgi och vardagstänkande. En kunskapssociologisk studie.* Gothenburg: Daidalos.
Israel, Samuel Ben (2004). *Samspillefilm. Den relationelle fortællemåde i et relationistisk perspektiv.* Cand.Mag. thesis. Copenhagen: University of Copenhagen.
Jerslev, Anne (2002). "Realismeformer i Todd Solondz' *Happiness* og Paul Thomas Andersons *Magnolia.*" *K&K* 30.93: 72–96.
Langkjær, Birger (1999). "Fiktioner og virkelighed i Lars von Triers *Idioterne.*" *Kosmorama* 45.224: 107–120.
Larrain, Jorge (1979). *The Concept of Ideology.* London: Hutchinson.
Lippit, Akira Mizuta (2004). "Hong Sangsoo's Lines of Inquiry, Communication, Defense, and Escape." *Film Quarterly* 57.4: 22–30.
Man, Glenn (2005). "The Multi-Protagonist Film and the Aesthetics of Intersection." Paper presented at the Society for Cinema and Media Studies Conference. London: March 31-April 3, 2005.
Mitchell, Stephen A. (1988). *Relational Concepts in Psychoanalysis. An Integration.* Cambridge: Harvard University Press.
Rimmon-Kenan, Shlomith (2002). *Narrative Fiction. Contemporary Poetics.* 2nd ed. London: Routledge.
Ritzer, George, and Pamela Gindoff (1992). "Methodological Relationism: Lessons for and from Social Psychology." *Social Psychology Quarterly* 55.2: 128–140.
– (1994)."Agency-Structure, Micro-Macro, Individualism-Holism-Relationism: A Metatheoretical Explanation of Theoretical Convergence between the United States and Europe." In: Sztompka, Piotr (ed.). *Agency and Structure. Reorienting Social Theory.* Yverdon: Gordon and Breach, 3–23.
Robb, Christina (2006). *This Changes Everything. The Relational Revolution in Psychology.* New York: Farrar, Straus and Giroux.
Sconce, Jeffrey (2002). "Irony, Nihilism and the New American 'Smart' Film." *Screen* 43.4: 349–369.
Skotte, Kim (2003). "*Elephant*-orden i Cannes." *Politiken* May 30, sec. 2, 1.
Smith, Evan (1999). "Thread Structure: Rewriting the Hollywood Formula." *Journal of Film and Video* 51.3–4: 88–96.

Stolorow, Robert D., and George E. Atwood (1992). *Contexts of Being. The Intersubjective Foundations of Psychological Life.* Hillsdale: The Analytic Press.
Thompson, Kristin (1999). *Storytelling in the New Holly. Understanding Classical Narrative Technique.* Cambridge: Harvard University Press.
Tröhler, Margrit (2000). "Les films à protagonistes multiples et la logique des possible." *Iris* 29: 85–102.
– (2001). *Plurale Figurenkonstellationen im Spielfilm.* Habilitationsschift. Zurich: University of Zurich.
– (2005). "Multiple Protagonist Films as a Vernacular Cultural Practice." Paper presented at: Society for Cinema and Media Studies Conference. London: March 31-April 3, 2005.
– (2007). *Offene Welten ohne Helden. Plurale Figurenkonstellationen im Film.* Marburg: Schüren.
Walters, Tim (2004). "Reconsidering *The Idiots*: Dogme95, Lars von Trier, and the Cinema of Subversion?" *Velvet Light Trap* 53: 40–54.
Wayne, Mike (2002). "A Violent Peace: Robert Guédiguian's *La Ville est tranquille.*" *Historical Materialism* 10.2: 219–227.

Per Krogh Hansen
(University of Southern Denmark)

All Talking! All Singing! All Dancing! Prolegomena: On Film Musicals and Narrative[1]

Anything goes

Its technical and narrational complexity taken into consideration, it does seem rather strange that the musical genre hasn't received more narratologically oriented critical attention. The genre's demand for multimodal expression and eclectic complexity brings together diverse elements from both pop-culture and fine arts — from tin-pan alley to opera; from stand-up comedy to performance theatre — and many of the film industry's most important technical innovations are closely connected to the establishment of the genre: sound film itself,[2] special visual effects of numerous sorts,[3] etc. The film musical has been (and still is) a testing ground for techniques of filmmaking in nearly all aspects — technically, cinematically, choreographically. Taking upon itself a declared artificiality — not of necessity, but by virtue — the film musical is an art form where anything goes.

Considering the possibilities the 'anything goes'-philosophy gives, it can seem rather disappointing to encounter the stories of the musicals, especially from the classical Hollywood period. Rick Altman has shown how the recurring narrative scheme for these films is formed as what he

1 This article is a slightly revised version of "Prolegomena. On Film Musicals and Narrative." In Per Krogh Hansen (ed.). *Borderliners. Searching the Boundaries of Narrativity and Narratology/Afsøgning af narrativitetens og narratologiens grænser*. Holte 2009, 263–278.

2 The first feature-length movie originally presented as a talkie was the *The Jazz Singer*, released in October 1927 and not considered a 'genuine' musical even though one of its main attractions was Al Jolsson singing and performing. *Lights of New York* from 1928, the first Warner Brothers all-talking feature, included a nightclub scene, and the 1929-succes of *The Broadway Melody* — the first 'real' musical — formulated the agenda for the following years' movie production in Hollywood.

3 In a straight line from the groundbreaking use of zoom, slow motion, tilt, edited musical act, etc., in Mamoulian's *Love me Tonight* (1932) to the spectacularities of Luhrmann's *Moulin Rouge* (2001).

labels a 'dual-focus narrative'. Instead of a chronological order, they take the dual-construction around the two principal characters as the point of departure (Altman 1987: 16 ff), and Altman shows how they most often are constructed around a very explicit parallelization of opposites (male/female, adult/child, rich/poor, etc.). Hereby they make dialectical or symmetrical patterns possible, which, in the end, are transgressed by the unity of marriage.

But in general the conviction of the musical-creators and performers seems to have been that the story is only there as an excuse; as a loose frame for the artistry and imagery of the show. The genre has therefore also been labelled 'the show film' (Ulrichsen and Stegelmann 1958). Building on romantic and comic schemata, very little is done to give the characters profile or complexity or to make the plot coherent. The plot's only purpose is to bring us to the next show act, and the characters often disappear behind the actor realizing their existence — we are likely to see Gene Kelly instead of Don Lockwood in *Singin' in the Rain* (1952) and Fred Astaire instead of Tom Bowen in *Royal Wedding* (1951). Well-formed and well-functioning narratives with something essential to say beyond the trivial love-stories has hardly, give and take a few deviant examples, ever been an issue for the classic musical.[4]

Narrative impossibilities?

Yet from a narratological point of view, it should be interesting to examine the musical genre's handling of plot, narrativity and realism. It is a constitutive trait for the genre that it incorporates both narrative and non-narrative strategies, insofar as it implements a plot consisting of progression, conflict and transformation, and musical-acts functioning in accordance with strategies we consider lyrical or poetical, since they suspend the chronological story-time and introduce another mode for the expression of emotions, character traits or situations.

4 This is not to be confused with the often raised accusation of the classic musical with being escapist. As shown in a number of different studies, the musical addresses a wide amount of central issues and conflicts in the American interwar-period. See for example Dyer 2002 for a study which shows how the musical's focus on abundance, energy, intensity, transparency and community functions as illustrations of the utopian solutions offered by capitalism itself to the social tensions or inadequacies in society — scarcity, exhaustion, dreariness, manipulation and fragmentation. Another interesting study in the same direction is made by Mark Roth, who shows how the early Warner musicals (*42nd Street*, *Footlight Parade*, *Golddiggers of '33*, etc.) can be read as thematizing the spirit of the New Deal in the 30's (Roth 1981).

In general, there is no problem in integrating narrative into song and dance. Ballet and opera (but also e.g. epic poetry) are obvious examples. But when it comes to the musical, the case is different. First of all, the musical rarely lets the song- and dance-act have a direct narrative function. Exceptions are found in the 'ballet sequences', for instance in *Oklahoma!* (1955), *An American in Paris* (1951) and *Singin' in the Rain* (1951), where — at least in the two first mentioned musicals — the stories are summed up in long dance-acts, reflecting without words the story of the film as such.[5] But in most cases the acts are rather redundant when it comes to their function in the storyline. Secondly, the musical (and especially the classical Hollywood format) is very persistent in demanding both a realistic (mimetic or representational) framing of the story and a nonrealistic (spectacular or non-representational) implementation of the song- and dance-acts — and an integration of the two modes. The modus operandi of the musical is therefore a rather complex, not to say paradoxical, constellation built of two incommensurable textual structures: on the one hand, the narrative structure, with progression, causality, conflict, etc.; on the other hand, the musical acts' lyrical structure, most often taking the form of time-loops, breaking up the narrative structure and putting the story's progression on standby for a moment, establishing a non-temporal room, where an emotion, a situation or the like, is unfolded — not as progression, but as a state of mind, a condition. Illustrated by the structuralist distinction between the syntagmatic and the paradigmatic structural principles of language[6], the narrative's syntagmatic linking of events is contrasted by the musical acts' paradigmatic function. The latter develops, explores or (perhaps most often) doubles one of the parts of the syntagma and thereby functions metaphorically (in opposition to the narrative's general metonymic principle for linkage) by commenting on the story and the characters (as the choir in Greek tragedy), or by giving room to dwell on an expression of feelings and emotions towards a situation, another character or oneself.

Because of this fundamental difference, the transition between 'narrative mode' and the non-narrative 'musical mode' is essential and worth studying. First of all, since the musical genre's main characteristic is its grounding in two incommensurable textual *and* cognitive procedures, we

---

5 In *Singin' in the Rain*, the ballet sequence does not have the same mise-en-abyme function. "Broadway Melody Ballet", as the number is called, is presented as a retelling of the story of the protagonist — "the story of a young hoofer who comes to New York", as it is said in the film, but in the form of a suggested (but for the movie spectator visualized) show-act without any significant relevance in the plot of the movie.

6 As formulated e.g. by Roman Jakobson in his analyzis of aphasia (Jakobson 1956).

might learn important lessons not only about the musical, but also about narrative by observing how the musical tries to transgress this in principle non-transgressional border. Secondly, if we apply a more general fiction-theoretical approach, the musical's non-representational mode should also have our attention. Related to — or perhaps the basis for — the musical's dual mode is the rather peculiar logic of the musical universe where people are allowed to dance and sing (either solo or jointly) whenever they find it necessary or appropriate. This, of course, makes the universe of the musical genre non-identical with that of our real world, but also distinct from most other genres based on the conception of realism. We can compare this to one of the musical's most important successors due to the work on timing, rhythm and choreography: the action movie, where the rage, violence and action most often will be highly exaggerated, is, at least in principle, integrateable with a real world model. To express it more straightforwardly: people do beat up each other and participate in car chases in our real world — but they do not start singing publicly and of inner necessity when they fall in love or their hearts are broken. Here the musical explicitly marks its artificiality — even though the story most often belongs to a recognizable world and is set in a modern interior fairly close to the spectator's world. Film musicals are in this respect packed with absurdities or — to use Rubin's concept — "impossible" (Rubin 1993: 37–44). Rubin mentions two people that were hitherto strangers to each other suddenly bursting into a duet in *Show Boat* (1936), Astaire's and Rogers' brilliant dance on roller skates in *Shall We Dance* (1937), defying their explicitly expressed lack of skills on roller skates, etc. The list can be extended ad libitum, since every film contains several more or less sophisticated examples, a task that shall not be pursued here. But how the genre manages to integrate this marked fictionality into the realistic diegesis, and what it means for the reader's empathy, etc., are problems of great interest which do need more systematic studies as a kind of complimentary consideration to Roland Barthes' theory of 'the reality effect', whether it should be called 'the musical' — or 'the fictional effect' if we want to include other genres as well. Verse drama, opera, theatrical musicals, etc. might very well be included in such a survey (which very well might take on a diachronical perspective also), insofar as they often often rely on a contradiction of and cooperation between fictional and realistic codes.

Integral solutions

The challenge of the musical as genre and art-form is therefore to be considered as a double integral task. On one hand, the non-realistic musical acts are to be integrated in the mimetic-realistic framework of the diegesis. On the other hand, the musical acts considered as paradigmatic textual units are to be integrated in the syntagma of the narrative. John Mueller has outlined some central categories for the relation between plot and musical acts depending on the relevance of the act in the storyline:

1. *Numbers which are completely irrelevant to the plot.* In film musicals this category is most often seen in the form of show- or nightclub-acts watched by the major characters along with the diegetic audience. As Mueller notes, this is the way ballet traditionally is integrated into opera, and jazz music into gangster movies, and if it is the only way musical numbers are incorporated into the film, the result is seldom considered a musical.
2. *Numbers which contribute to the spirit or the theme.* In general, the use of background music (also in non-musicals) has this function by introducing leitmotifs, emotions, etc. In musicals many numbers have a similar function, insofar as what at first hand may look disparate and non-integrated serves as indirect elaborations of the theme. Here, the number is related to the plot in the form of a metaphor. An example is "Rich Man's Frug" — one of Bob Fosse's most famous choreographies — from *Sweet Charity* (1969). This number is formed as a show in a nightclub which the protagonist Charity Hope Valentine visits and in this respect fits the first category mentioned. But at the same time it is obvious that the stylized choreography thematizes the relation between man and woman, which is a central theme in the musical.
3. *Numbers whose existence is relevant to the plot, but whose content is not.* This applies to musicals of the backstage-genre, where the plot is concerned with musical-performers; for this reason, singing and dancing will take place in the diegesis, but not with any necessary relevance as regards content. Busby Berkeley's large-scale choreographies in the Warner Bros musicals from the 1930's may be considered as examples of this.
4. *Numbers which enrich the plot, but do not advance it.* Love duets or characters singing out their present emotional situation are in this category. In the terminology suggested above this sort of act is genuinely paradigmatic. The aforementioned ballet-sections, which themselves are syntagmatically formed (as mini-narratives), also belong to this category.

5. *Numbers which advance the plot, but not by their content.* Classical examples are audition acts where a young dancer gets a job, thereby making them a part of the plot. The contents are of very little importance in these acts, except for the fact that they are well done.
6. *Numbers which advance the plot by their content.* During the number something happens which changes the character and/or the situation. These numbers are considered 'truly integrated' insofar as the plot would not be intact if the number was left out or exchanged with another number (Mueller 1984).

On a general level, the musical has answered the integrative challenge by, broadly speaking, three different strategies: by assimilation, differentiation, or conceptualization. These strategies will often be intermingled, but with preference for one of them. It is also here we find the key to subgenres such as the integrated musical, the backstage musical and the concept musical.

The assimilating strategy is the basis for what is referred to as 'the integrated musical', a musical in which the book, lyrics, and score all grow from a central idea and all contribute to the story line[7], and in which the singing and dancing is integrated into the diegetic universe. The Fred Astaire and Ginger Rogers RKO musicals from the 30's are early examples, even though the fact that the roles they play often are those of actors or dancers pulls in the direction of the differential strategy. More genuine in this respect are musicals like e.g. *Oklahoma!*, *An American in Paris* or *Hair*—the first taking place among cowboys and settlers in a village in Oklahoma; the second among artists and aristocrats in Paris and the third among hippies in New York—where there, so to say, is no excuse for the characters to dance and sing in the diegetic universe they inhabit. Quite the opposite, it is a distinctive feature of this universe that people dance and sing, that music comes out of nowhere, eventually crossing the border from being an extradiegetic leitmotif to becoming a diegetic issue for the characters to express themselves through.

Thereby it is also hinted that a common strategy for the musical to integrate the song and dance acts in the diegesis is by establishing a separate space for them to take place in or to let them depend on character traits or qualities. This is what we will refer to as the differentiating strategy, and it is the basis for the subgenre referred to as the 'backstage musical', where

7 Kern and Hammerstein's Broadway-success *Show Boat* (1925) is considered the first example in this respect.

the story takes place in a theatre- or show-business environment.[8] Here there are plenty of opportunities to give the song and dance sequences a natural place in both one aspect and the other. Lloyd Bacons *42nd street* (1933) is prototypical: all song and dance acts belong either to the rehearsals or the final premiere of the show the crew is putting together. In this way, the musical cheats out of addressing its own problem: by letting the plot be constructed around the problems the crew has with the production of the show, we are only indirectly engaged with the integral problem being constitutive for the genre. Thus the backstage musical gives way to an integration of the song and dance acts by framing. It deliberately disintegrates or differentiates the acts from the main story into a secondary story which, on the other hand, is postulated to fulfil the musical's task of integrating the two different modes; that is, doing what the main story only does indirectly.

Graduated integration

This is also the case for most of the song and dance acts in Stanley Donen's *Royal Wedding* (1951). Here, the principal characters are a dancing brother and sister who visit London with their act. The major part of the musical numbers take place on stage and during rehearsals. But two numbers differ radically from this scheme and exemplify two of the musical genre's most important modes of integration.

In the first, the male principal character Tom Bowen (Astaire) is returning to his hotel room longing for the woman he is falling in love with. As he enters his room, the background music becomes stronger and is at last supplied with a singing voice (probably Astaire's) which as a sort of voice-over narrator comments on Tom's emotional situation. Shortly after, Tom takes over the melody and sings and dances out his longing—including the surprising effect of dancing on the wall and ceiling—before returning to the initial position, which (considered in the light of the violation of our normal physical laws) gives the whole sequence an expression of daydream or mental escapism. The frame (the identical positions in the beginning and the end of the act) and the rather unusual dance lets the spectator understand the scene as an expression of Tom's mental

8 The backstage solution is of course not the only one. Lars von Trier finds another in his *Dancer in the Dark* (2002), when he is letting nearly all musical acts take place in the mental space of the protagonist Selma.

Figure 1: *Royal Wedding (1951)*

condition, i.e. as a shift of diegetic level, which leaves the realistic mode of the story intact.

But the shift between the two spaces is established gradually as Tom Bowen loosely synchronizes his movements to the background music: the closing of the door, the placing of the picture, etc., is not perfectly in time, but takes form as an increasing preparation for the moment where he, sitting in the chair, stylizes his hand- and head-movement taking on the body language of the dancer. So while the background music first functions as a leitmotif, characterizing the mental state of the protagonist, it is secondly given the function of actually *being* his mental state. This state is, on the other hand, of plot importance. While the scene (and music) was first characterized by longing and melancholy, it changes entirely when the protagonist steps into the musical mode and takes over the voice. From this point on the song is joyful, energetic and vital, symbolizing how the melancholy is a result of Tom being grounded in a physical world, but that the real feeling hiding below is love. And as soon as he lets go of the physical world and the longing this causes him to have, he can enjoy the real feeling. One might be tempted to see this dance scene as a metaphor for the emotional state of Tom Bowen, due to the fact that we shift (though gradually) to another diegetic level. But it would be more correct to claim that the scene has the function of metonymy, insofar as the dance doesn't take on any other expression than what it is — a dance expressing the feelings of our protagonist according to an *effectus pro causa* principle, and we might consider this an example of quoted interior monologue being supported by the visuals.

The scene belongs to the sixth of Mueller's categories since the number advances the plot due to its content (Tom Bowen is closer to his true feelings after the scene), and it illustrates how carefully integration can be made without letting go of the differentiating strategy. The dualism between the music world and the realistic diegetic world is intact, but the demarcation line between them is blurred so that the shift between them is effectuated gradually, but radically nonetheless: the background music becomes first leitmotif and then an integrated part of the scene; that is a means for Tom's vocal expression of a quoted interior monologue. The voice-over narration is taken over by Tom, indicating that his bodily presence has left the first diegetic level in favour of another — that of his interior monologue, which in itself belongs to the same diegetic level as the main action. The bodily movement pattern changes from neutral to marked as Tom slips into the stylized movements of the dancer-attitude. And finally, the law of gravitation is suspended during the dance act — gradually and surprisingly — before the music comes to an end and leaves both Tom and the spectator back where we physically started, but mentally in another state; a state where Tom is more certain about his feelings, and where the spectator knows that Tom is closer to his loved one than before.

Metaleptic integration

The second song- and dance-act placed outside the theatrical-frame of the story in *Royal Wedding* does not give us a frame for naturalization as was the case with the scene just commented upon: near the end of the movie, on the day of the wedding referred to in its title, we follow Tom and Ellen's promoter on his way to their home. The scene opens with a close-up of church bells ringing, initiating a song to be sung by the promoter and the people he is passing — shoppers, the doorman at the hotel, the elevator attendant. In this scene, the assimilative strategy is used: the singing takes place explicitly in the diegetic universe and is not motivated as a rehearsal of an act or a shift of the diegetic level.

But furthermore, the scene is cut in accordance with the song, causing major ellipses in the visuals. We see the promoter walk into the hotel and out of the elevator within two bars, singing respectively with the doorman and the elevator attendant, while the walk through the hotel's hall and the ride in the elevator is left out — not just as a normal omission of nonessential acts, but more radically: the structure imposed by the music does not leave any room for these scenes, and the result is perhaps closer to what Genette has called metalepsis[9] than to ellipsis. In any case, the central point is that the scene subordinates the characters, space and time to the music. It lets the events take place on the premises of the music and not — as it is the case in all other scenes in *Royal Wedding* — the other way around, by subordinating the song- and dance-acts to the diegesis.

But even though the cutting establishes discontinuity comparable to the jump-cut, it maintains continuity at the integrated musical level by way of the singing. Compared to the assimilative strategy in the scene formerly commented upon, where all discursive levels were integrated, but on the basis of a differentiating strategy where the number was presented as a dream- or mental scene, this number makes the opposite move. From the sound of the church bells, the musical level is entirely integrated in the diegetic universe, but the metaleptic editing disintegrates the two levels, pointing out the illusory nature of the scene. In that sense both scenes disrupt the full integration: the first by letting the spectator watch the dance scene taking place at another diegetic level, the second by highlighting the artificiality of the scene through the editing.

Integrating the spectator by disintegrating the show-act

This element of letting discontinuity be a highlighted issue in a genre that has contributed remarkably to the development of cinematographic continuity (Hollywood style) is by no means a single occurrence. Quite the contrary, it seems reasonable to claim that disruption of full integration is a recurring strategy. In spite of the rather consistent maintenance of the realistic mode in the backstage musical, it is often broken down in other ways. One is by letting the lyrics of the songs sung on-stage in

9 The act of narrating itself provides a link between two domains that are normally distinct from one another. Metalepsis forces disparate levels together by letting the narrators or the narratees enter the domain of the characters or vice versa. Usually, metalepsis is marked explicitly, but when it dispenses with the diegetic relay, it undermines the distinction between the two narrative levels and, more generally, destabilises the operability of representation as such. See Genette 1980: 237f.

the production the characters are setting up serve as indirect comments on the general plot of or situation in the story. Another, and more radical, disruption of the realistic mode, is the transgressive character of the show-acts as seen in e.g. Busby Berkeley's choreographies for the Warner Bros. musicals of the 30's — the formerly mentioned *42nd Street*, *Gold Diggers of 1933* (1934), *Dames* (1933), etc. As discussed by Rubin in his book on Berkeley, the Warner musicals for which Berkeley supplied the choreography differ radically from e.g. the integrated RKO musicals with Fred Astaire and Ginger Rogers.[10] The Warner musical's structure is better described as aggregational rather than integrational, insofar as it pushes the major routines towards the end of the movie and doesn't give them any significant thematic relation to the plot. These spectacular routines always take the form of the premiere or a performance of the show that the troupe or the protagonists of the films are engaged in. To begin with, the show is played on stage and the film spectator is observing the show from the position of the theatre audience. But as the choreography develops, it transgresses the frame of the theatre by expanding the scene considerably, giving room for more dancers and a much larger choreography than the theatre scene allows, and by performing dance routines and making camerawork not intended for or visible to the intradiegetic spectator of the theatre, but only to the movie spectator. In the end of *42nd Street*, we find this performed through a tracking shot in between the legs of the chorus girls, closing up on two central characters looking directly into the camera and out on the movie spectator, and thereby breaking down the diegesis and changing the communicative axis from that between the characters and the diegetic audience in the theatre to that between the actors and the movie spectator. In that sense, it is as if integration finally is effectuated — not by giving the show-act a proper position in the narrative syntagma, but by transgressing the borders of fictionality: at first by disrupting the verisimilitude of the theatre; secondly by addressing the spectator directly.

10 See Rubin 1993: 98f. Berkeley has been quoted for saying that he hardly knew who did the directing of the movies he choreographed.

Figure 2: The illusion of the on-stage dance routine in *42nd Street* is disintegrated by choreographies not being visible for the diegetic audience—in the top-shot in the second frame and the direct gaze into the camera in the fourth frame

Integration through conceptualization

But if the large-scale choreographies of Berkeley might not have any direct thematic relevance to the plot, they do at another level quite often serve as comments on the themes of the narratives they are included in. Numbers like "We're in the money" and "Remember my forgotten man" from *Golddiggers of 1933* comment on Depression-era poverty and losses due to warfare — not directly in relation to the progress of the plot, but at a more general, paradigmatic or 'metaphorical' level, we might say with reference to Jakobson above.

This means of integration, where the musical act comments on a core theme or issue for the musical, is the founding principle for what has been called the concept musical. Ethan Mordden has defined this as "a presentational rather than strictly narrative work that employs out-of-story elements to comment upon and at times take part in the action, utilizing avant-garde techniques to defy unities of time, place and action."[11] Gerald Mast argues that it would be better to speak of the 'modernist' musical instead of the concept musical:

> Like the modernist move toward self-consciousness in every twentieth-century art, the concept musical explored itself – its forms, its traditions, its variants, its conventions of credibility and style. Songs became less psychological expressions of specific characters than metaphoric comments on personal belief, social custom, or musical tradition. 'Modernist musical' or 'musical metaphor' describes the new concept better than 'concept musical', which simply changed concepts to fit the new cultural times (Mast 1987: p. 320f).

I will not enter this discussion of sub-genre labelling here, but instead just focus on the ways in which the integrative tasks are being fulfilled.

Prominent stage examples of the concept/modernist musical are *Company* (1970) written by George Furth and music and lyrics by Stephen Sondheim; Bob Fosse's important Broadway works *Pippin* (1972) and *Dancin'* (1978), and Kirkwood and Dante's *A Chorus Line* (1975). The latter, which in 1985 was adapted into a movie by Richard Attenborough, can very well serve as illustration: the musical is set on the bare stage of a Broadway theatre during an audition for chorus line members of a musical. During the play we are presented with the lives and careers of the dancers and the choreographer, as they present themselves during the audition. At the end of the play, a group is given the job – but the selection made by the choreographer is to a certain extent random. In that sense, if one expects a motivated outcome of the narrative progression of the play, one will be disappointed. There is hardly any plot in *A Chorus Line* and no motivation for the selection at the end of the audition. Instead, all acts focus on the conception of a dancer's life and showing different aspects hereof.

The same structure is found in other movie musicals. In Milos Forman's adaptation of *Hair*, the songs, thematizing hippie culture and the youth revolt of the late sixties, are rather randomly spread out over the film and only loosely integrated into the plot of Claude's draft for the Vietnam War and Berger's attempt to make him refuse. In Bob Fosse's *Cabaret* (1972) all but one of the musical acts (commenting indirectly on different interwar issues like the growing pogroms, capitalism, etc.)

---

11 Mordden 2003. Here according to John Kenrick. *History of The Musical Stage. 1970s II: Concept Musicals*. http://www.musicals101.com/1970bway2.htm, 1996–2003, latest visit: June 20 2008.

are confined to the stage of the cabaret and not attached to the general time-progression of the movie. But at the same time there are 'hooks' from the diegesis into the musical acts of the cabaret. When Brian for instance begins to show more than just friendly feelings towards Sally after her persevering advance, the song "Maybe this time" is crosscut into sequence depicting the developing relationship; when Sally runs into the rich soon-to-be-friend Maximilian von Heune, the show number "Money, Money" is performed; and when the Kit-Kat club's bouncer is being beaten up by Nazis in the backyard, "Slap Happy" is performed on stage, just to mention a few examples. Attenborough's *Oh! What a Lovely War* (1969) follows a similar model for the songs of the movie (being original soldier songs from The Great War); here the effect of the inclusion is more of a mosaic-picture than of a progressive narrative order.

The integrative strategy of the concept musical is based on a decimation of the narrative and therefore moves in the direction of the paradigmatic axis of Jakobson's model,[12] toning down the syntagmatic and metonymic aspect in favour of the metaphoric. Even though this, of course, is a prominent feature of the subgenre of the concept musical, it is not exclusive. We might rather say that it is a common feature for the genre in general.

Perspectives

But even though it is possible to map out a group of common functions for how the musical is making these integrative movements, it should not be neglected that it is a very wide genre we here are approaching, and that it changes historically. Risking the accusation of historical teleological thinking, one could claim that the musical from around 1960 enters a more 'serious' mode, where the artistry from the former period is changed into art. *West Side Story* (1961) implements tragedy in its depiction of gang wars and racism in New York, borrowing the plot from Shakespeare's *Romeo and Juliet*, and brings the integrative task to new horizons in both the musical score and the choreography. Bob Fosse, being one of the radical renewers of the Broadway-musical, puts focus on Nazism in *Cabaret* and the pains of the dying artist in *All that Jazz* (1979). Jean-Luc Godard

12 Yet, it is also obvious that in all three examples narrative is present in a different way: through the respective wars being part of the setting for these musicals. One can argue that to at least *Hair* and *Cabaret* (but partly also to *Oh! What a Lovely War*) a fundamental theme is the emancipation of man and therefore an attempt to be free of society's and history's historical progression. No need to say that in all three cases this attempt fails.

explores and decomposes the genre in *Une femme est une femme* (1961), and several of the New Hollywood Cinema's major directors engages with it up during the 70's and the 80's: Scorsese (*New York, New York*, 1977), Coppola (*One from the Heart*, 1982) and Forman (*Hair*).

It seems almost impossible to suggest a general model by which we can describe the solutions for the double integrative task performed by the musicals. At a general level, we can begin by defining two overall strategies: one where the diegesis' realism is subordinated to the musical mode (this was what we examined in the elliptic cut scene from *Royal Wedding*, above), and another where the musical universe is subordinated to the diegesis' realism (as in the scene where Astaire entered a mental space and danced at the ceiling in the same movie). These two different strategies, can be considered as paradigmatic for how the genre in general handles the integration, and will in many cases — as in *Royal Wedding* — co-exist in the same movie. The aggregational solution we touched upon in relation to the Warner Brothers' musicals from the 30's where the large-scale productions to a wide extent were pushed to the end of the film, is another way of including both strategies: realism dominates in the first part of the movie; the musical mode in Berkeley's productions.

One might claim that one of the differences marked by the modern musical is that it to a wider extent more exclusively follows only one of these strategies. In Fosse's later works like *Cabaret* and *All That Jazz*, realism dominates insofar as all acts are in accordance with our real world understanding — they are motivated, staged, rehearsed, hallucinated or dreamt. By contrast, the examples of *West Side Story*, *Hair*, and in its own peculiar way *One from the Heart* lets the musical mode dominate universally and hardly ever gives the spectator an excuse to 'naturalize' the singing and dancing in relation to his or her real world model.

This tendency of giving almost exclusive priority to one strategy or the other is, of course, not only a matter of style and manners, but can be developed more substantially. Musical has to a large extent always been self reflecting insofar as the staging of musicals has been common subject matter for the shows themselves. But several of the modern musicals not only thematize the making of musical, but more radically explore its possibilities, not only as a genre but as a mode of expression and understanding, and also with respect to the strategies in question here. Baz Luhrmann, for example, follows the latter discussed solution when he in *Moulin Rouge* (2001) 'musicalizes' the story world entirely. Here there is no realistic frame to be broken when the music plays and the dancers dance. Instead, everything is taking place on the conditions of the musical — the story world is staged as a set piece, and characters are transferred from one room to another in accordance with the music's demands, transcending physical laws and logic. Quite the opposite, Lars von Trier's *Dancer in the Dark* (2002) follows the other model by letting all the musical acts — with one exception: the closing a cappella — be placed in the mental space of the protagonist Selma, thereby leaving the story-world's realistic mode intact. In this way, von Trier, on the one hand, explores the escapist accusations the genre has been met with, and on the other, builds up a strong momentum to the final diegetic a cappella song. Where the musical acts have had an escapist function in the rest of the film, the 'real' and the 'imagined' is brought together in the last song, but in a grim, ironic gesture. Throughout the film, the story world has left no room for the musical's expressiveness, but in the final scene it is forcing itself through in Selma's (or Björk's) characteristic voice — at one and the same time trying to prevent death by postponing her execution (a variation over the convention: 'the show goes on until the music is over'), and showing us that her dream has come true (her son Gene has got his eye-operation), symbolized through the fact that the singing has moved from the imagined diegetical level (Selma's dream world) to the real.

Besides making substantial meta-comments on the musical genre, movies like Luhrmann's and Trier's demonstrate one of the most important aspects of the genre — the fact that the musical has been the laboratory of cinema ever since the sound film's early years. The first talkie, *The Jazz Singer*, was sort of a musical. Busby Berkeley's choreographic cornucopia demanded new and more mobile camera techniques, and the incessant transgressions of the spectacular show acts forced the technical development forward. The basis for today's Hollywood film form is to be found in the history of the musical.

However, the musicals are also film history's dinosaurs. In its old form — the classical movies from the studio-era in the 30's and the 40's — the musical is almost extinct. Movie spectators of today seem to find it difficult to relate to the form, and one cannot help but speculate whether it is the fact that the genre is based on a principle of 'impossibility' regarding integration of narrative and lyricality, of realism and show act, that causes this rejection.

I do not think the cause of death is to be found here. First of all, one should not forget that many musicals have been made where the integration is close to perfect — *West Side Story*, *Hair* and of course later musicals like *Moulin Rouge* and *Chicago*. Nor must we forget the long line of musicals that chose other strategies than the classical integrating model: *Cabaret*, *All That Jazz*, *One from the Heart* and *Dancer in the Dark*.

Instead I think we have to acknowledge that different periods have different means of fascination. The musical evidently belongs to that line in film history Bazin and Kracauer dissociated from when they distinguished the spectacular and fantastic strategy from the realistic line with reference to the claim that the former does not live up to the ideal of cinematographic essence: to depict reality as closely as possible (Bazin 1960 and Karcauer 1956 [1960]). The musical has never related to reality in this sense. It has believed in the picture (to rephrase Bazin), worked intensively with its possibilities and displaced the impact of 'the real' to another level than the immediate. This line is today followed by other spectacular genres such as animation, science fiction, and — especially — action movies. Here, also, emphasis is put on the picture and its possibilities — through choreography, manipulation and experiment. The goal is not to offer an account of the truth of the matter regarding reality as much as to transcend the medium's existing limits.

We are living in an age where wall climbing, detail-choreographed fights, etc., are more fascinating than equilibristic dance and emotional singing. But the connections are obvious. If we were cultural pessimists, we could lament that love and hope have been replaced by hatred and revenge. But we could also — instead — just consider the two different, spectacular genres as expressions of the same strategy. The rhythmically choreographed, stylized and musically supported fight-scenes in e.g. *The Matrix* are not far from the modern musical's raw and expressive dance.

At least it seems like a similar thought has found its way into Takeshi Kitano's samurai movie *Zatoichi* (2003). The musical is indirectly present throughout the film — e.g. through field workers' and craftsmen's rhythmic work in a couple of scenes — and after 1½ hour of bloody samurai-fighting, the film ends with a large celebration of the victory over cruelty, where traditional Japanese drum and mask dance is performed. But gradually it turns into a classical American step act danced in Japanese wooden shoes while the music is being supplemented with horns etc. — as if Kitano wants us to see that even though the action genre has learned a lot from Asian martial arts film in recent years, there is another tradition right behind it which also has had its impact.

In that sense there is still a good deal to do in describing and understanding what the musical does: on its own and when present in other genres.

References

Altman, Rick (1987). *The American Film Musical.* Bloomington: Indiana University Press.

Bazin, André (1960). "The Ontology of the Photographic Image." *Film Quarterly* 134: 4–9.

Cohan, Steven (2002). *Hollywood Musicals. The Film Reader*. London: Routledge.
Dyer, Richard. "Entertainment and Utopia." In: Steven Cohan (ed.). *Hollywood Musicals. The Film Reader*. London & N.Y.: Routledge, 2002, 19–30.
Genette, Gerard (1980). *Narrative Discourse. An Essay in Method*. Ithaca: Cornell University Press.
Hansen, Per Krogh (2008). "Prolegomena: On film musicals and narrative." In: P. K. Hansen (ed.). *Borderlines. Searching the Limits of Narrative and Narratology*. Holte: Medusa.
Jakobson, Roman (1956). "Two Aspects of Language and Two Types of Aphasic Disturbance." In: R. Jakobson and M. Halle (eds.). *Fundamentals of Language*. The Hague, Paris: Mouton.
Kenrick, John (1996–2003). "History of The Musical Stage. 1970s II: Concept Musicals." Retrieved June 20, 2008, from http://www.musicals101.com/1970bway2.htm.
Kracauer, Siegfried (1965 [1960]). *Theory of Film*. London: Oxford University Press.
Marshall, Bill and Robynn J. Stilwell (2000). *Musicals. Hollywood and Beyond*. Exeter, England; Portland, OR: Intellect.
Mast, Gerald (1987). *Can't help singin'. The American Musical on Stage and Screen*. Woodstock, New York: The Overlook Press.
Mordden, Ethan (2003). *One More Kiss. The Broadway Musical in the 1970s*. New York: Palgrave MacMillan.
Mueller, John (1984). "Fred Astaire and the Integrated Musical." *Cinema Journal* 24 1: 28–40.
Roth, Mark (1981). "Some Warner Musicals and the Spirit of the New Deal." In: Rick Altman (ed.). *Genre: The Musical. A Reader*. London et.al.: Routledge & Kegan Paul, 41–56.
Rubin, Martin (1993). *Showstoppers: Busby Berkeley and the tradition of spectacle*. New York: Columbia University Press.
Ulrichsen, Erik and Jørgen Stegelmann (1958). *Showfilmens förvandling*. Stockholm: Wahlström og Widstrand.

Jan Baetens & Mieke Bleyen
(University of Leuven & Lieven Gevaert Centre for Photography, University of Leuven)

Photo Narrative, Sequential Photography, Photonovels

Photography and Narrative

What does it mean to tackle the specific issue of narrative in what is called here "photo narrative"? At first sight, the expression "photo narrative" has at least a double meaning. On the one hand, it can refer to the study of narrative in certain forms–we would like to call them media rather than genres[1]. These forms align series or sequences of photographic images, like the picture-story in photojournalism[2] or the photonovel in the field of fictional photography, a genre to which we will return in the third and fourth part of this article. On the other hand, photo-narrative can also refer to narrativity within photography itself, more precisely within the single photographic image. Although photography is usually considered the representation of a single moment in time, and is thus opposed to the "real narrative" of cinema, popular wisdom tells us that a picture is worth a thousand words. This means that it should be perfectly able to tell a story.

Why do we so often neglect or underestimate the narrative dimension or power of photography? The reasons of this tunnel vision on photography are manifold, but most of them have to do with an essentialist bias in our approach to the medium. Most definitions of photography have indeed a strong tendency to stress two ideas. First, that a "real" photography is a snapshot (it may be useful in this regard to remember the often and systematically quoted words by Henri Cartier-Bresson, which are for many spectators, practitioners, and scholars an ideal summary of the art as a "decisive moment": "To take photographs means to recognize—simul-

---

1 For a discussion of these terms in the context of photographic narration, see Baetens (2000).

2 A picture-story, contrary to the better known photo-essay, rather relies on photographs to tell a single event, for instance the murder of J.F. Kennedy, than on the careful combination of words and images to communicate a message as well as a story, like in W. Eugene Smith's work.

taneously and within a fraction of a second — both the fact itself and the rigorous organization of visually perceived forms that give it meaning. It is putting one's head, one's eye, and one's heart on the same axis" (Cartier-Bresson 1999: 15). Second, that a "real" photography is supposed to have a documentary value, in other words, that it must be an *index* (hence the continuing discussions on the "dangers" of digital photography, which for many jeopardizes the purity of photography.[3] As it should be clear from the examples that we have just given (Cartier-Bresson and digital photography), the idea of photography as being "essentially" about carving out a single moment of time in the real flux of life, is not only a rather narrow one, for there are many images and photographic practices that follow a completely different, less "mainstream" agenda. It is also a rather recent one, for it suffices to have a historically informed look at past forms of photography to notice that the narrative function of photography has been dramatically strong in the first decades of the medium — before this function apparently passed on to the newer medium of cinema. However, and this is where the notion of intermediality comes in, in order to establish this narrative function, one has to know the social and cultural context of photography, which was not isolated from textual media and whose meaning could not be determined outside that interaction with that verbal context. Yet given the fact that our contemporary cultural memory is extremely selective and tends to separate these images from their material context, there is a serious risk of missing the basic narrative function of photography, which was crucial for all the relevant groups — readers, artists, publishers, etc. — in these years.

In order to accept that photography can be narrative — and, in certain exceptional cases, even compete with the narrative impact of cinema (see Baetens 2009) — it is necessary to reject the two theses that photography is "essentially" reduced to single-shot snapshot (or single-moment) photography and that the medium has an intrinsic link with reality. From the very moment there is room for serial or sequential photography, on the one hand, and for fictional photography, on the other hand, the narrative capabilities of the medium come much more to the fore. Moreover, the dismissal of sequential photography and the strong bias against fiction/fictionality are manifestly linked (fiction photography often takes the form of sequential photography, and vice versa), so that the acceptance of sequential photography and the inclusion of fictional images and projects equally reinforce each other.

3 For a critical discussion of these contemporary stereotypes, see André Gunthert 2008.

As is widely known, postmodern photography has radically challenged the mainstream ideas of single-shot and indexical photography, and here too the influence of photography's intermedialization has proven crucial. If recent photography has abandoned the privileged regime of the non-fictional single-shot image, this evolution has undoubtedly been accelerated by the rise of installation art, various other forms of multimedia presentation of the images, the rediscovery of "staged photography" (a taboo in many traditional views of the medium, in spite of the history of the medium: before the use of hand-held cameras, staged photography had been very common!), the greater interest in the representation of time in photography (Méaux, Vanvolsem), the subsequent contestation of Lessing's basic distinction between arts of space and arts of time, and by the frequent blurring of boundaries between the filmic, the pictorial and the photographic image (for a recent survey, see Beckman 2008). Nevertheless, the first question that should be addressed here does not concern the role and place of narrative in the contemporary sequential and fictionalized photography, but the possibility and usefulness of rereading from a narrative point of view the traditional corpus of snapshot images that are generally considered deprived of any major narrative dimension. This discussion will be the starting point of our reflection on photonarrative within traditional photography, i.e. single-frame photography (part 2), before continuing with some remarks on the very idiosyncratic form of the photonovel, which we will analyze first in general (part 3) and then through the close-reading of a challenging example (part 4).

How to read a single image narratively: anything goes?

The major challenge raised by the narrative decoding of a single-shot picture is that such a reading is... always possible. Any image can indeed be seen through a narrative lens, whatever degree of represented mobility or stillness. In the case of "decisive moment" pictures in the tradition of Cartier-Bresson, the narrative translation of the picture's content is easy, but even images whose form and content are purposively static remain perfectly open to narrative interpretations. Take, for instance, a famous picture from Robert Frank's *The Americans* (Frank 1998), *Covered Car-Long Beach, California*, which shows an epitome of immobility: not a car but a covered car, not the road but a place on a parking lot, not a driver or city-dwellers but just a car, not a landscape (always an invitation to the cognitive temporalization of space) but an anonymous wall, a grid, two palm trees, the framing of the image is very clean and regular, nothing reveals the active presence of the photographer, and so on. Nothing seems further away from the beatnik cry for freedom and the fascination of life on the road than a picture like this, and, nevertheless, the narrativization of this very static picture by the spectator eager to do so, is relatively easy. One could convert the notion of immobility in that of "immobilization" and therefore of "a moment of rest between two more dynamic moments." Or one could read the prominent representation of the shadows of the trees on the wall as a symbol of time and therefore, for instance, of the suggestion of a new departure. In other words, since temporality is an inevitable feature of any representation, narrative framing of a picture is part of the set of interpretive tools that are always there to help the spectator to make sense of the picture's content ("this picture shows us this or that event which is part of this or that story") as well as of the picture's making ("this is how I think the photographer has proceeded in order to shoot this picture").

Yet in many cases this narrative interpretation has less to do with the features of the image itself, than with the cognitive stance of the spectator who is "programmed" to look at images in a narrative way, not only because he or she has a universally built-in desire for narrative (Grivel 2004: 28), but also because this desire is often so very rewarding (to read narratively simply helps to better grasp, understand, memorize, communicate, and transform what we see and to make it useful for our own lives). And of course the narrative turn in postmodern photography makes this tendency towards narrativization only grow stronger.

Nevertheless, what seems to proclaim the recent victory of narrative in our appropriation of the photographic medium is not without danger. For the more we read an image narratively, the more we may take for granted narrative as "the" key to the meaning of the image, whose properly visual and material aspects may then be (partly) overlooked. Moreover, many narrative readings of photography rely upon a very broad and excessively vague and general definition of what a story actually is or might be. Most importantly, one can observe a certain confusion between three aspects, which are often mixed up in the practice of so-called narrative readings of single-shot photographs: *duration* (the period or interval of time that corresponds with the represented content), *story* (in the technical sense of the word as used in most narratological approaches), and *meaning* (the final output of the analysis; in the idiosyncratic metalanguage of certain disciplines, words like "meaning" and "story" are often used as synonyms). If these three concepts and semantic fields are intermingled, the narrative reading of a picture ceases to cast clarity and obscures the processing of the image. Finally, if any picture proves open to narrative readings, the concept of narrative can no longer be seen as really productive (if everything is "something," that "something" loses its analytical sharpness and relevance).

For all these reasons, it is important to restrict the very use of the term narrative — and thus the narrative scope itself — in a threefold way (for a very detailed discussion of these ideas, see Baetens 2008).

First of all, narrative analysis in photographs should engage exclusively the kind of pictures that clearly display not just a *duration* of time, but a "real" narrative, which implies features such as 1) a chronological structure (not just "first this, then that," but "first this and then that because of a certain specific link between this and that"), 2) agency (things do not happen by themselves, but because they are caused by an agent, and the various phases of the chronology must be caused by an agent as well). In short, the pictures under analysis should be pictures presenting a story that is *motivated*, a story whose action can be explained by principles of *causality*. These principles can of course be theorized in many ways, but Emma Kafalenos's suggestion in her book *Narrative Causalities* (Kafalenos 2006) to foreground what she calls the "C-function," i.e. the decision taken by an agent to try to alleviate an initial destabilizing event, may offer a good example of what it means to introduce causality and motivation in what could remain otherwise a pure non narrative succession of events.[4] Crucial for the narrative analysis of the single-frame photograph is that in the absence of such a watershed moment (the "function") the image under scrutiny cannot be fully narrative, even if it remains perfectly possible, as in the image by Robert Frank, to add temporal and even narrative elements at the level of the image's interpretation.

A second threshold to be built-in has to do with this tension between what the image displays and what the spectator sees in it. Since we easily take the possibility of a narrative interpretation of nonnarrative material for granted, it is important to ask, if not to claim, that a narrative approach should be restricted to pictures containing their story visibly in the frame itself, instead of being open to pictures telling a story that does not exist outside the mindset of the spectator, such as, for instance, the picture of a pebble on the beach: one can always make up a story in which an agent has put that pebble on the beach with a certain intention or for this or that reason, one can even imagine a story in which the posing of the pebble is the key element of a "C function" (to resort to Kafalenos's terminology), but such an interpretation is merely determined

4 As Kafalenos's "functional" terminology makes clear, her framework is a merger of Propp's syntagmatic organization of narrative functions — the cradle of Greimas's actantial model — and Todorov's more abstract narrative theory — which tends to downsize the wide range of functions and actants to the basic issue of disrupted and restored order.

by the mindset of the spectator and his or her expectations or goals. For a better understanding of what narrative is, these interpretations may be important. Yet they are not very helpful to better understand the narrative aspects of photographs themselves. In an illuminating discussion of this issue, Efrat Biberman makes an interesting distinction between two categories of narrative reading of pictures — her corpus is that of traditional painting — an external reading, in which the spectator associates the visual sign with a literary narrative that is then projected on the painting, and an internal one, in which the act of looking itself produces the narrative meaning. In this situation, the interpretive act of the spectator and the material properties of the image cannot be separated (Biberman 2006). Within the approach defended in this article, which tries to reconcile craving for narrative and taking into account the material properties of the object, it is clear that our sympathy goes to the internal type of reading. The methodology that we would like to develop hereafter should therefore be understood as an attempt to "do narrative" without falling prey to the easy imperialism of savage narrativization which reduces the specific material properties of the object to a mere springboard for narrative reception of unnarrative visual materials.

Third and finally, one should also take into account the fact that reading a single-frame image narratively cannot bypass another basic rule of storytelling. Wolfgang Kemp pertinently points out that a story, at least within an artistic context, is never life "itself," but that it has to be something more or bigger than life. And here is of course where rhetoric comes in:

> It may well be that narrative "is simply there, like life;" but that does not mean that it is like life. It deals (…) with heightened, intensified life. (Kemp 1996: 60; the author is quoting here from Barthes 1966: 7)

Moreover, Kemp rightfully insists that a story necessarily takes the audience into account. A story is told to "move" that audience in one way or another. Kemp's argument goes even further by establishing a kind of analogy between the story's form and content — which obey the basic logic of "subject in search of an object" — and what happens at the level of the story being told. The latter is mainly structured by the fact that a reader or spectator is eagerly waiting for something: the end of the story. To underline this decisive issue, Kemp quotes Evelyn Birge Vitz:

> It is crucial — for there to be a "story" — that the transformation be *awaited*: awaited if only by the narrator and *us*. And it is crucial that it be "the" transformation: not just *any* transformation will do [quotation from Birge Vitz 1989, as given in Kemp 1996: 66 who doesn't mention the original pagination].

The teller wants the reader or spectator to be interested in the story "as such". He or she wants them to be curious about how the story will develop on and how it will end. The suspense element, in other words, is a must. If there is no desire to know how the story will end, the story will not "work" — and will therefore not be recognized and processed as a real story, even if, from a merely technical point of view, it presents all the characteristics that narratologists may consider necessary for the definition of a story.

What does all this mean for photo narrative? How could we apply this triple criterion (i.e. the importance of the representation of duration, the viewer's construction of motivation and causality, and, finally, the foregrounding of the public's interest in the story) to the narrative reading of single-frame photographs? The stance we would like to defend in this article is that a narrative reading can only become fruitful — and have some degree of intersubjective control — if the three abovementioned criteria are all activated, at least to a certain extent. This would mean that a single-frame photograph can only be considered "completely narrative" if it succeeds in piquing the spectator's curiosity with a chronologically and causally organized and motivated visual narrative and making him or her yearn for some ending. If these conditions are not convincingly met, the photograph can perhaps be narrativised by the spectator's imagination, but it will not be a "fully" narrative picture.

Such a stance may seem too narrow, yet we do believe that it will help to bring more clarity in the often very confused debates on the narrative aspects of fixed images. In practice, however, the boundary between "fully" narrative and "partially" narrative (and, why not, even "nonnarrative") pictures will not always be easy to draw.

In a sense, one might say that the decision to replace the single frame photograph by a photo sequence is the easiest solution of the problem of making a real narrative. If single frame pictures remain too ambivalent, if their narrative depends too much on the text that accompanies them, or if the story they tell us is only an "imperfect" story (lacking motivation and causality, presence within the picture itself, suspense and rhetorical power), then why not present a sequence of pictures, which would make things much easier? For in a sequence, causality can be suggested with less effort, narrative agency can be made visible within the frame itself, and tension can be built up without any trouble. All this may be true, but the problem is that it is not *necessarily* true, since in many sequences narrative is missing as well. In that case, what promises to be a real sequence is actually rather a *series* — for instance, a series of portraits (think of August Sander's *People of the 20th Century*), architectural units (think of Bernd and Hilla Becher's documentary work on the industrial landscape), and so on.

The problem then is to decide how to establish the difference between the narrative sequence and the nonnarrative series. This problem is absolutely fascinating. Think of Walker Evans's *American Photographs* (Evans 1938), which definitely have elements of sequential organization, but which are therefore not essentially narrative. The very fact that there are so many cases of hesitation between sequence and series proves that the question whether a work is narrative or not should be asked in a systematic way. The three criteria that we have presented above stay helpful for this kind of discussion as well.

In the case of the photonovel, which is a specific kind of photo sequence, the question whether it is narrative may seem absurd, for the photonovel is obviously a narrative sequence. Yet we will see that 1) the issue of narrative proves much more complex than the simple question of "is it narrative or not?," 2) the kind of narrativity that is being displayed is not necessarily the one that is covered by traditional definitions of narrative, which one can apply to single images.[5]

The photonovel, between text and image, between story and portrait

The photonovel as an institutionalized genre is part of the larger group of sequential photography. Although the difference between both domains is far from being absolute, as we shall see later, one might summarize the distinctive features of the photonovel, as compared with the photo sequence, as follows. First, the photonovel has in principle a high degree of intermediality: contrary to the photo sequence, which is often mute, i.e. textless, a photonovel is characterized by the systematic merging of pictures and words, generally presented as captions or speech balloons. Second, photonovels rely in almost all cases on the notion of the "multiframe" (Van Lier 1988): contrary to the traditional photo sequence where all pictures have the same format and where there is in addition a tendency to present only one image per page or frame, the pictures of a photonovel do not appear alone on the page or in a frame on the wall in the format in which they have originally been printed. Their format may shift and may been cropped and transformed in order to fit the page layout which combines various images within the same frame (generally the pages of a magazine or a book). In this regard—and in this regard only—they

5 Although of course not to all of them, for the narrative reading of images such as Robert Frank's 'Covered Car' supposes a previous 'suspension of nonnarrative disbelief'.

resemble comic books. Third but not least, the photonovel is, sociologically speaking, a part of low culture or mass culture. Its expression and content, which are not unlike the typical representations disseminated by television soaps (at content level: family affairs; at expression level: talking heads) are highly formulaic and, from a political point of view, rather conservative — at least, so goes the story, for historical research has seriously questioned these elitist prejudices against this "inevitably female" form of popular culture (Giet 1997).

What matters here is not "deconstruction" of the distinction between photonovel and photo sequence, which would be too easy and not very productive. More interesting is the genre's intermedial character — a feature deeply rooted in its own history and raising fascinating challenges at a narrative level, for the difficulties in finding a right balance between the verbal and the visual have always hindered the development of the photonovel.

The photonovel appeared in the aftermath of World War II as an original combination of two existing genres, the *illustrated film script* on the one hand and the *graphic novel* on the other hand.[6] One of the most dramatic problems the genre had to face in its early days was the integration of words and images, which led to systematic difficulties and communicational failures at various levels: technical, aesthetic, and narrative. In the first place, the encounter of textual and visual material within the same frame proved to be a *technical* nightmare: texts had to be added in handwritten form, and it was too difficult to obtain a sufficient chromatic contrast between letters and background: often white letters did not stand out enough against a too pale or too grey background, while black letters did not contrast sharply with the dark photographic spaces around them. Moreover, the print quality of the cheap magazines of these years was so poor, the rough paper absorbed so much ink that one had to guess the form and the meaning of the words more than one could read them. The first experiments with colour hardly increased the confidence of the public in the new genre. In the second place, the technical problems appeared also to have a strong aesthetic dimension. Given the fact that the texts were added to already existing photographs, either in the form of speech balloons or in the form of narrative captions, this insertion destroyed in many cases the internal composition of the picture. Furthermore, the very presence of textual material was blamed for preventing the spectator from looking at the pictures themselves (a criticism often addressed at subtitles in film and television). Finally, photonovels were also insecure and vacillating in the synchronicity of their montage of word and images: many im-

6 For a well illustrated, but not very theoretical overview, see Lecoeuvre & Takodjérad 1991

ages were spoiled because the reader did not always know when and where to read the accompanying text, and it was far from easy to "invent" new and smooth forms of reading rhythms in which the verbal and the iconic elements did complete each other without breaking the page lay-out.

These technical problems delayed the breakthrough of the genre as a new cultural form. During the first years of its existence, the photonovel had to compete with other cultural forms such as comic strips, and in this competition the photonovel was rarely victorious. Photonovels, short stories, illustrated instalments, cartoons, comic strips, etc. shared the same place in the specialized feminine press, in which the photonovel first appeared, and it took almost a decade before the photonovel became a culturally established genre. The rise to prominence of the photonovel within the broader field of the popular narrative of the fixed image is clearly linked to the overcoming of the difficulties inherent to the genre's intermediality. In a certain sense, one might, of course, argue that these technical, aesthetic and narrative difficulties were not specific to the genre of the photonovel. A master like Hergé, who replaced the European system of captions placed outside the visual frame by the American system of visually integrated speech balloons in the comics, also needed many years before he succeeded in overcoming the clumsiness of his first attempts. Yet what makes the photonovel so fascinating, in comparison with the comics, is that in its search for solutions to its initial problems the genre has always looked for answers that were not insensitive to the idea of monomediality. Much more than comics, photonovels have always tried to keep words and images as neatly separated as possible, for instance by isolating textual information in special frames (with no further visual information) or by presenting the speech balloons and narrative captions in ways that deliberately prevented interaction with the image. It is very difficult to find experiments in "creative" layout: the typefaces that were used aimed mainly at remaining as invisible as possible and the authors made great efforts to "hide" the composition of the page or the frame from the reader's view. Therefore, it is not absurd to suggest that in its popular forms, the photonovel is an example of partially repressed intermediality, despite its obligation to combine words and images. Even within the traditional photonovel, there is a tendency to "clean" the image as much as possible from textual input, to keep verbal elements outside the frame. In the former case, the photonovel aimed at keeping the verbal information at a distance, for instance by displaying the dialogues as captions beneath the pictures or by inserting text frames between them. In the latter case, photographers deliberately included "empty" spaces in the picture, so that speech balloons could be inserted without destroying the global composition or jeopardizing the visual legibility of the information relevant to the story. Yet without text, it seemed very difficult to tell a story, all the more since the representational and narrative universe of the photonovel was close to the world of the cinema, which was no longer mute at the time of the genre's emergence.

The real leap into textless works had therefore to wait until the development of a new form of photonovel: the minimalist photo sequence. The fate of the more ambitious, high-art photonovel, which was indeed heavily inspired by experiments in conceptual narrative photography in the 1960s (the example of Duane Michals comes immediately to mind), displays these monomedial tendencies with utmost strength and clarity. First, the works of artists such as Marie-Françoise Plissart (Plissart 1998) or Raymond Depardon (Depardon and Bergala 1981) introduce a sharp visual boundary between words and images: textual elements are only tolerated to the extent that they remain on the margins of the photograph. Second, they have a strong preference for textless and wordless stories (the ancient and, of course, very debatable idea of the "decadence" of the visual syntax of silent cinema at the emergence of the talkies is mentioned by several artists working in this field). A good visual story is a story that is told with no other means than purely visual ones, monomediality being considered the ideal form of all serious experiments in the field of sequential photography. Third, if text has to be present, it must be transformed in such a way that all traces of multimediality are wiped out: verbal information is thus no longer added to the image, it is photographed as an intradiegetic text, in order to become itself a visual element of the pictured universe (sometimes at the price of its very readability). As the absolute split of their readership suggests, high-art photonovels may differ from popular photonovels in all possible respects, yet their distinction tends to disappear in their common striving toward monomediality. The distinction becomes even more blurred, if one notices that the absence of textual elements is in many cases very superficial. Even completely textless works like the landmark experiment by Michael Snow, *Cover to cover* (Snow 1975), can be read as an encyclopaedia of indirect textual presence. For if this book has no captions or speech balloons or author's preface or whatsoever, there is a very strong presence of other kinds of texts: the paratext (for instance the title of the book), the diegetized text (i.e. the text as part of the pictured universe), the subtext (for instance verbal puns that one has to grasp in order to make sense of the images), etc.

Nevertheless, in the field of the *high-art* photonovel (Baetens 1993, Ribière 1995) there has always been a strong rejection of the verbal elements, accused of a triple evil. First, textual elements are accused of claiming all of the spectator's attention (just like in subtitled films, it is not easy to follow both words and images). Second, they are also accused of disturbing the pictures' composition (if one has to "add" textual information to an already existing photograph, the composition of the images has a strong liability of losing its internal balance and structure). Finally, they are also accused of preventing images from being in charge of the narrative (the sequential and causal relationships between the various pictures are ruled by the interaction of captions and speech balloons, not, as one would like it to be in the high-art sphere, by the intrinsic qualities of the images themselves). For all these reasons, one understands the fascination exerted by mute, i.e. apparently non-intermedial or non-hybrid stories. The most famous example is undoubtedly the 100-page photographic novel by Marie-Françoise Plissart, *Right of Inspection* (1998; 1st French ed. 1985). Yet, as the "Lecture" by Jacques Derrida, which follows (and completes?) Plissart's pictures, clearly demonstrates, the muteness of the images does not imply vanishing of the words, on the contrary. The more mute images are, Derrida argues, the more they are able to generate (verbal) stories, and therefore, perhaps, to create new forms of intermediality.

A similar point can be made when one looks at the extreme opposite of the high-art photo narrative: the commercial photonovel, a much despised subfield of the romance genre (Lecoeuvre & Takodjérad 1991, Giet 1997). Born in the aftermath of World War II, the photonovel had strong ties with the world of popular cinema and was a typical example of "escapist" literature. Yet although the material structure of this genre seems to be a good illustration of the merging of word and image imposed by the dominant paradigm of the cinema, a closer look reveals that the multimedial collage of pictures, captions and speech balloons, which has become so familiar, may prevent us from seeing the role and place of monomedial features. As Giovanni Fiorentino (1995) has convincingly argued in a study of the photonovel adaptation of Dino Risi's masterpiece of "rose" (i.e. comical) Neo-Realism, *Pane, Amore, e…* (1955), the photonovel's possibilities of multimedial telling were manifestly underused, not just by lack of sophistication (this is the usual argument uttered by photo critics and historians who borrow their categories from Art), but in order to make room for what really mattered: the face of the actors (Sophia Loren and Vittorio De Sica), the emphasis put on their looks (there is not the slightest attempt to achieve a coincidence between the expression of the faces, often showed in profile, and the content of what they are supposed to be saying), and the contrast between the leading actors' mythological universe and the daily (but extremely scenic) setting of Sorrento. Contrary to the film, whose story it "reproduces," the photonovel is, in a certain sense, in pursuit of monomediality. The genre, which appears to be a transposition of the world of the cinema, with its moving images and sound track, to the world of the book, with its fixed images

Figure 1–6: Marie-Françoise Plissart, from the series *Aujourd'hui,* 1993 : 46–51.
Copyright M.F. Plissart.

and texts, turns out to be a continuation of a completely different genre: the (mythical) actor's portrait.

Yet this natural attraction of the photonovel for the implicit genre of portrait photography does not prevent artists from inventing new and medium-sensitive forms of storytelling. This is the phenomenon toward which we are now turning.

The multiple temporalities of a modern photonovel

During the 1980s, the genre of the photonovel has been revolutionized by the Belgian artist Marie-Françoise Plissart, who published various landmark titles, often in collaboration with the writer Benoît Peeters who mixed the traditional form of the photonovel with the elements of the French New Novel and other literary genres, such as the detective novel. One of them, completely textless *Right of Inspection* ("Droit de regards," Plissart 1985) became famous thanks to the essay by Jacques Derrida that accompanied it as its textual counterpart. However, despite the critical praise of these books, they were a commercial failure, and the attempts to reinvent the genre stopped in the 90s. Plissart's last photo narrative, the equally textless "photo story" ("suite photographique"), *Aujourd'hui* ("Today"), can therefore be read as a farewell to a cursed genre.

The title of the book is a statement in favour of a new, narratively inspired vision of photography. In its emphasis on duration ("today" is not "here and now," is not a "slice of time"), it takes a critical stance toward the snapshot ideology of mainstream photography. Through its insistence on the present ("today" is neither yesterday nor tomorrow), it rejects the Barthesian interpretation of photography as thanatography (photography as the essential expression of "what has been," Barthes 1982). The six-page sequence we analyze here (see fig. 1 to 6, which correspond to three double pages in the book) demonstrates that the photonovel offers new uses of temporality and narrativity, which are deeply rooted in the medium-specific employment of general parameters such as layout and montage.

If we start our analysis with the large pictures—the distinction between large and small pictures being a formal stereotype of the photonovel, we notice an almost minimalist sequence that alternates repetitive elements (in the upper and central part: the sky, the sea) and non-repetitive elements (in the lower part: the movements of the characters, who enter and leave what can be read as a "stage"). Yet this first impression is brutally disrupted once the spectator observes the second series that occurs at the background: the movements of a diver. The global symmetry of the images and the pages becomes even more questionable once the spectator becomes aware of a profound tension between the narrative that is taking place in the foreground (the characters "on stage") and the one, slightly hidden due to its smaller dimensions, in the centre.

More specifically, four types of divergence occur. The first concerns the *nature* of the subjects represented: immobile in the foreground, moving in the background — as if the characters were "contaminated" by the material characteristics of their environment: those appearing among the stones are not moving (even when they seem pictured in action, they are manifestly posing); the one surrounded by the water and the air is utterly dynamic. The second difference has to do with the treatment of the movement's *continuity*, which is respected in the action taking place in the foreground, but broken in the diver's scene. In image 2 to 4, the position of this character is almost frozen, whereas the characters in the foreground move from one position to another. In other words, on the level of the photo sequence, *Aujourd'hui* mixes what seems to be mutually incompatible within single images: the freeze frame (on the level of the diver) and the reproduction of the successive moments of a global movement (on the level of the characters in the foreground). The effects of this mixing-up are far-reaching: although the surface of the pictures seems to be very smooth and homogeneous, each photograph is torn between two heterogeneous temporalities and two irreconcilable rhythms. In other words: the features of the photonarrative treatment of the sequence enable the artist to extend dramatically the possibilities of the photographic medium on which it relies. The third opposition concerns differences in *rhythm*, for the way Plissart fragments the successive parts of the two actions is not the same in either part. While looking at the scene with the diver, we notice that time is almost stilled between the successive representations of action (in the central pictures of the sequence, time seems to come to a complete stand-still). While looking at the interchange between the man and the woman in the foreground, the variations in time are much larger. Here again, tension between the two actions included within the same image reinforces the internal dislocation of the photographs. The fourth and last opposition between the two narrative threads within each image concerns the treatment of *chronology*. Whereas the action in the foreground seems to respect the rules of conventional linearity, the six fragments of the diving scene do not obey the same temporal structure (first we see the beginning of action, which is then frozen in the middle, and at the end we see the preparation of the very diving). It remains difficult, however, to give an exact and unique interpretation of the chronological ordering of the diving scene: we may believe that the chronological order is disrupted, but it is no less possible to think that the action starts over again at the end. This increases the degree of temporal manipulation of the whole action, which can be read *simultaneously* as "singulative" and "iterative," as Genette (1972) would call it (in the former case, we have one action, the diving, shown in non chronological order; in the latter case, it is suggested that we have one action that is repeated over and over again). And, inevitably, the temporal, chronological and narrative manoeuvrings that take place in the centre of the photographs will contaminate our reading of what is happening in the foreground, which becomes suddenly less chronological, less ordered, less singulative than it might have appeared at first sight.

This is the first step towards a "creative" reading, which the structural innovations of *Aujourd'hui* encourage us strongly to perform, not only on the level of the temporal dimension of narrative, but also — and given the medium-specificity of Plissart's approach, this aspect is obviously crucial — of its visual and spatial aspects. A possible way of expanding the narrative interpretation of the sequence under analysis is to focus on the representation of the various movements of the characters entering and leaving the frame. These movements rely on a certain number of features while suggesting a combinatory play to which the reader can add new tokens and layers. Two features are central to this play: on the one hand, the orientation of the movement, which can be leftbound or rightbound or going upwards or downwards; on the other hand, the type of off-screen that is involved and which can be either external (out of frame means then: outside the limits of the picture) or internal (out of frame means then: out of sight, i.e. dissimulated by the presence of a screen inside the picture). The diver's movements, for instance, can be described as the result of "verticality" and "internal dissimulation," while the male character moves horizontally from right to left before leaving the stage at the left corner of the photograph. Yet the task of the reader is not only to describe these movements but, given the combinatory possibilities that are opened by the photographic representation, to raise questions about their impact on the interpretation of the image. For the multiplication of temporal possibilities of the image (for instance, the suggestion that the intertwining of the singulative and the iterative may affect the scene in the foreground as well as the one in the middle of the image) can be continued at the level of its spatial organization. If we focus on the figure of the woman who suddenly appears on stage and no less suddenly vanishes in the last picture, our spontaneous reading will be to think that she has entered the frame from the left (where she is then noticed by the man) and will leave it the same way (following the example of the male character?). Yet her own paradoxical "immobility" (although she is not frozen as a character, her position in the picture doesn't change) and the strong opposition between the diver's movements and those by the man in the foreground, make room for different readings, for instance the one that suggests that she is falling from the balustrade into the sea. Such a movement aligns her figure with that of the diver. The splashing waves can then be seen as the diegetic "proof" of this interpretation.

The expansion of the reading to the complete layout of the pages, with their strip of smaller images at the bottom, introduces further subtleties, which all stress the general direction of what has been disclosed on the level of the main pictures. What matters here is the intimate relationship between the specific treatment of the typically photonovelistic features such as sequential arrangement (time) and lay-out (space) and the thorough reinterpretation of our mainstream ideas and uses of photography. Photo narrative is much more than the display of a preformatted or underlying script that is illustrated by a set of images representing each successive step of action. It is first and foremost an invitation to rethink the narrative dimension of photography itself completely, not by internal manipulation of a single image (the pictures by Plissart are very classic), but by the exploration of what it means to insert photography in a framework of spatial and temporal montage. The artist challenges the spectator to interpret the work narratively, without giving the clues of a specific story that is being told. In that sense, the story told by Plissart is a perfect example of radically indeterminate narrativity (Ryan 2004: 14).

References

Audet, René et al. (2007). *Narrativity: How visual arts, cinema and literature are telling the world today.* Paris: Dis Voir.
Baetens, Jan (1993). *Du roman-photo.* Paris-Bruxelles: Les Impressions Nouvelles.
– (2000). "Récit + photo = roman-photo?" *Sincronie,* vol. III.5: 66–173.
– (2006). "Une photographie vaut-elle mille films?" *Protée* 34.2/3: 67–76.
– (2008). "La lecture narrative de l'image photographique." In: Jean-Pierre Montier, Liliane Louvel, Danièle Méaux and Philippe Ortel, eds. *Littérature et photographie.* Rennes: Presses Universitaires de Rennes, 349–358.
– (2009). "Is a Photograph Worth a Thousand Films?" *Visual Studies* 24.2: 143–148.
Barthes, Roland (1966). "Introduction à l'analyse structurale des récits." *Communications* 8: 7–33.
– (1982). *Camera Lucida.* New York: Hill and Wang.
Beckman, Karen and Jean Ma, eds. (2008). *Still Moving: Between Cinema and Photography.* London and Durham: Duke University Press.
Biberman, Efrat (2006). "On Narrativity in the Visual Field: A Psychoanalytic View of Velazquez's *Las Meninas.*" *Narrative* 14.3: 237–253.
Birge Vitz, Evelyn (1989). *Medieval Narratives and Modern Narratology: Subjects and Objects of Desire.* New York: NYU Press.
Cartier-Bresson, Henri (1999). *The Mind's Eye. Writings on Photography and Photographers.* New York: Aperture.

Depardon, Raymond and Alain Bergala (1981). *Correspondance new-yorkaise/Les absences du photographe*. Paris: Libération/Editions de l'Etoile.

Fiorentino, Giovanni (1995). "Seduzione ottiche. L'icona, il fotoromanzo, l'istantanea." In: Fiorentino, G. (ed.). *Luci del Sud. Sorrento un set per Sofia*. Castellammare di Stabia: Eidos, 37–48.

Frank, Robert (1998 [1958]). *The Americans*. New York: Scalo.

Genette, Gérard (1972). *Figures III*. Paris: Seuil.

Giet, Sylvette (1997). *Nous Deux 1947–1977: apprendre la langue du cœur*. Louvain/Paris: Peeters-Vrin.

Grivel, Ch. (2004). "La photocinématographisation". In: Baetens, Jan and Marc Lits (eds). *La novellisation. Du film au livre*, Leuven: Leuven University Press, 21–40.

Gunthert, André (2008). "'Sans retouche'. Histoire d'un mythe photographique." *Etudes photographiques* 22: 56–77.

Kafalenos, Emma (2006). *Narrative Causalities*. Columbus: Ohio State University Press.

Kemp, Wolfgang (1996). "Narrative". In: Nelson, Robert S. and Richard Shiff (eds). *Critical Terms for Art History*. Chicago/London: University of Chicago Press, 58–69.

Lecoeuvre, Fabien and Bruno Takodjérad (1991). *Les années roman-photos*. Paris: Editions Veyrier.

Méaux, Danièle (1997). *La photographie et le temps. Le déroulement du temps dans l'image photographique*. Aix-en-Marseille: PUM.

Plissart, Marie-Françoise (1993). *Right of Inspection: Photographs by Marie-Françoise Plissart, with a Lecture by Jacques Derrida*. Trans. David Wills. New York: Monacelli Press, 1998 (1st French edition: 1985).

– (1993). *Aujourd'hui*. Zelhem: Arboris.

Ribière, Mireille. ed. (1995). "Photo Narrative". Special issue of *History of Photography*. Vol. 19.4.

Ryan, Marie-Laure, ed. (2004). *Narrative across Media: The Languages of Storytelling*. Lincoln: University of Nebraska Press.

Van Lier, Henri (1988). "La Bande dessinée. Une cosmogonie dure." In: Thierry Groensteen, ed. *Bande dessinée, récits et modernité*. Paris: Futuropolis, 5.

Markku Lehtimäki
(University of Tampere)

The Failure of Art: Problems of Verbal and Visual Representation in *Let Us Now Praise Famous Men*

Postmodernism and poststructuralism are often associated with theories of nonrepresentationality. In post-Saussurean linguistics the incapacity of language to reach the world has resulted in the discussions of *impossibility* of representation, producing philosophical claims according to which language and literature are creations rather than re-creations (see Rimmon-Kenan 1996: 11). What especially postmodernist art, either verbal or visual, clearly emphasizes is that the representation and its referent are two different things, that they cannot be in the same place, and finally that the representation in question may even be the opposite to its seeming referent, some object in the "real world." The concept of *re*-presentation in a way supposes, and includes, an idea of the world of objects, on the one hand, and their presentations in a new way in language and in art, on the other.

Art is conscious of and critical toward previous conventions but also toward its own current conventions. Apparently, the artist's exploration of his or her medium and the problems and possibilities of representation is one of the characteristic features of twentieth century modernism. The modernist or postmodernist conception of art often also implies a sense of *failure* in the production and composition of a work that, on some level, aims at the representation of reality.[1] In Colin Falck's words, since Romanticism we have been inclined to mark off a category of artistic failure in our critical language: "The formal failure is a failure, and furthermore *matters*, we tend to argue, because it fails to secure any coherent meaning or comprehension of truth within what purports to be the order of a single artistic work" (1989: 75). As Shlomith Rimmon-Kenan suggests, "the despair that arises from confronting the incapacity of language to 'reach'

1 Compare also: "The 'failure' of the verbal to embrace and fix the visual is used as a constructive principle and steadily thematized by different schools and authors" (Grishakova 2006: 156).

the world is sometimes counteracted by a search for a metalinguistic place from which to speak of the limitations of language and literature," and "this results in metatexts, self-conscious or self-referential literature, works that interrogate or dramatize their own difficulties in representing reality" (1996: 12).[2] This notion brings me to my focal text, *Let Us Now Praise Famous Men* (1941; *FM*), the classic of American photo-documentary genre. It is a book about writer James Agee's and photographer Walker Evans's journey to Alabama in the summer of 1936 to record the lives of three white sharecropper families who were living in desperate conditions during the era of the Great Depression.

Let Us Now Praise Famous Men reflects on its *non*-fictionality yet also on its failure to be "true." In the reflexive acknowledgment of the role his subjectivity, Agee acknowledges both his own limitations and the indeterminacy of a world whose conceptualization resists critical closure (see Hartsock 2000: 185). As Agee writes: "*Failure*, indeed, is almost as strongly an obligation as an inevitability, in [this] work" (*FM*, 215n; my emphasis). If we understand that certain modernist and postmodernist art works are self-reflexive to the extent that the "failure" to succeed is written inside them, we may see that the problem of representation belongs to the *intentional* composition of the work. Therefore, this kind of self-negating and reflection on failure does not necessarily produce an artistic failure, but, at least potentially, a new kind of achievement.[3]

As mentioned, it is a visible sign of modernist and postmodernist art to turn not only toward but also *against* themselves, to critically scrutinize their own textuality, construction, and sense-making. And one of the reasons for this almost self-destructive poetics is a new idea of reality, born in the advent of modernism — a sense of the difficult and ungraspable Real — which can never be represented either in verbal or visual form. What interests me especially here is the complex reality "contract" constructed

2 We may note, for example, that William Faulkner himself referred to his modernist masterpiece *The Sound and the Fury* (1929) as a "failure" because it had not, as it were, reached all its ambitious goals. However, that novel is also "a most splendid failure," showing in its self-reflexivity "a never-completed quest for form and meaning" (Bleikasten 1976: 48, 51). Faulkner reflected on failure as the very destiny of all artistic endeavor: the process of literary production can never find its final completion.

3 This is also what André Bleikasten suggests when discussing Faulkner's novel: in its very failure the novel succeeds, for "even though the gap between text and meaning is always there, the writing process manages to create an order of its own" (1976: 205). We may note that Faulkner, especially his novel connected with the experience of the Depression, *As I Lay Dying* (1930), was one of the central influences on Agee's writing in *Let Us Now Praise Famous Men*. Agee also mentions the sources of this influence: "Details of gesture, landscape, costume, air, action, mystery, and incident throughout the writings of William Faulkner" (*FM*, 399).

in and by documentary literature. The concept of *documentary literature* has usually been understood as an intermediary mode between artistic and non-artistic discourse, but by adopting the term 'documentary prose' Leona Toker argues that it is not the question of any in-between form but of "multifunction objects" (1997: 188). The concept of documentary prose can be adapted to some nonfictional genres, such as biographies and journalistic works, which also need to be studied as a form of art, and whose style and structure can be distinguished from non-literary documentaries. As Toker has it, documentary prose constructs a motivated and symbolically coherent narrative structure, creating "the pattern of motifs within the text" (ibid, 213). However, it appears that many documentary works more or less "fail" in their attempt toward a coherent narrative structure and that sometimes this failure is a crucial part of these works' meaning-making, as seems to be the case in Agee and Evans's *Let Us Now Praise Famous Men*.

As Toker further notes when speaking of documentary narratives as art, "our doubt whether modernist paintings, sculptures, music, or texts are, in fact, works of art is an *integral part* of their aesthetic effect" (1997: 214). Hayden White, speaking of historical representation, suggests that any text can be read, in principle, as a meditation on the impossibility of representation, since "any attempting to grasp any reality through the medium of language or to represent it in that medium raises the specter of the impossibility of the task undertaken" (1987: 206). Thus, according to T. V. Reed, *Let Us Now Praise Famous Men* represents "novel journalism that calls its own representational practices into question," and the book's "questioning of representational capacities within each of the two media [the prose and the photos] is intensified by comparative cross-mediation" (1992: 35, 39). Written mainly against the conventions of the genre inside which it is produced — the thirties documentaries of rural life and their claim to give the reader a real picture of that life — Agee and Evans's book aims at shaking the readers' preconceptions by problematizing the relationship between a verbal/visual text and the harsh realities of the actual world.

By juxtaposing text and photographs, *Let Us Now Praise Famous Men* discusses its own shortcomings in "realistic" representation of poor families in the American countryside while simultaneously foregrounding itself as an artifact. The book makes its presentations in both typographic and photographic form as intimate and immediate as possible. Agee's style of self-negating his own writing, as well as his way of stressing the materiality of the book, is illuminated by his comment on the early pages of the narrative: "If I could do it, I'd do no writing at all here. It would be photographs; the rest would be fragments of cloth, bits of cotton, lumps of earth, records of speech, pictures of wood and iron, phials of odors, plates of food and of excrement" (*FM*, 26). In Reed's words, while the book "at once attempts to bleed the book into reality and to transfigure reality into text (that is, into a self-conscious aesthetic construct)," it simultaneously "injects doubt about any text's ability to achieve immediacy by drawing attention to conventions (including conventions of immediacy) active in the text/world" (1992: 31). The juxtaposition of the prose and the photos, with their equal inability to reach the real, therefore enhances the critical self-reflexivity of the book.[4]

Words and Images

As suggested above, one of the difficulties in *Let Us Now Praise Famous Men* concerns the relationship between words and images, or text and photos, in it, and their respective ways of representing reality. Many theorists have concerned themselves with the similarities and differences between word and image. The structuralist paradigm emphasized visual representations as texts and language systems, and focused on the *reading* of images. Thus, for example, some narratological readings of visual art are still strongly based on employing literary theories for the analysis of films, paintings, or photographs (e.g. Chatman 1978).[5] On the other hand, some theorists stress the crucial differences between words and images, and consequently they are also skeptical toward the application of textual theories to the study of visual art. To some critics, image and text are incompatible to the degree that they cannot merge into an intermedial iconotext. Rather, these critics speak of "mixed texts," implying the semantic distinction between words and images. (See Horstkotte & Pedri 2008: 2–6.) One of the distinctions between visual and verbal images is, therefore, based on the *materiality* of the photograph and the *mentality* of the written word.

---

4 David Minter gives the following description of the book's attempts and generic modes: "It employs a wide range of discourses — ethnographic, sociological, phenomenological, theological, historical, autobiographical, poetic, novelistic — and utilizes an astonishing range of styles — realist, naturalist, impressionist, expressionist, surrealist, cubist, and visionary" (1996: 200). Reed, for his part, labels this almost unclassifiable work as "cubist sociology" and "postmodernist realism" (1992: 35).

5 However, as Marie-Laure Ryan writes from the perspective of postclassical narratology, "the optical notions of point of view, of focalization, of camera-eye narration, and of cinematic montage have provided insights into literary narrative that could not have been reached by limiting the investigator's analytical toolbox to strictly language-based concepts" (2004: 34).

Nevertheless, though interart or intersemiotic studies focus on the differences between verbal and visual "languages," they also chart "a permanent dialogue and exchange between visual and verbal practices" (Grishakova 2006: 179). While an *image* is not a *text*, "the visual and the verbal domains interpenetrate, influence, and inform each other" (Bal 1991: 19). In this intersemiotic and intermedial field, it is helpful to see that while written texts and visual arts represent different ways of producing signs and meanings, those ways are still not necessarily opposed to each other, and that the modes of interpretation we use when "reading" verbal or visual art are basically similar activities. As W. J. T. Mitchell says, "an iconology of the text must also consider the problem of reader response, the claim that some readers visualize and that some texts encourage or discourage mental imagining" (1994: 112). While literary texts are often only metaphorically visual, they may give reasons to visual reading by constructing pictorial spaces and perspectives or by containing allusions to visual art, be it painting, photography, or cinema.

On a certain level, of course, there appears to be a crucial difference between verbal and visual representation. The linguistic sign, as defined by Saussure, has no natural relation to any object in the real world, for this relationship is purely arbitrary, or culturally constructed. Thus the type of sign used in verbal or linguistic representation is usually *symbolic* as opposed to an *iconic* sign, which shares, through resemblance, some traits with whatever it signifies. We may note that visual artifacts differ from written texts in various ways: on the level of material production, on the level of reception and interpretation, and so on. It has been suggested that the nature of photography forms questions of its own. As Peter Brooks suggests, photography appears as a medium "in which the term *representation* might be replaced by 'presentation,' since there is no apparent translation into another code, another system of conventions of representation" (2005: 86). While a photograph is also perceived as resembling that which it depicts, C. S. Peirce noted that a photograph is not only iconic but also *indexical*. The notion of indexicality is the founding element of photographic representation: indexicality links the image to its objects through physical causality or connection. As Geoffrey Batchen notes, "as an index, the photograph is never itself but always, *by its very nature*, a tracing of something else" (1997: 9). Therefore, since the photographic image is an index of the effect of light on photographic emulsion, all unedited photographic and filmic images are, by their nature, indexical — although, of course, conventional practices are always involved in composition, focusing, developing and so on, and obviously recent digital media complicates all things.

As suggested above, structuralist studies of verbal and visual representation have often stressed the pre-eminence of language, but the relationship between the photo-image (or other still pictures) and written text is complicated, and cannot be reduced to some general textuality (see Steiner 2004: 147). It is not enough to read visual representations through verbal paradigms; it is imperative "to attend to the particularized forms of signification that the photograph evinces; to the gamut of genres and modes of narrative practice with which photo-images intersect, as they work within 'photonarrative' constructions; and to the range of intertextual connections with which such constructions are inevitably enmeshed" (Hughes & Noble 2003: 3–4). When we think of photographs from the vantage point of narrative theory, we may recognize their limited, but still potential, storytelling dimensions; yet we need to reflect that the uniqueness of photographic textuality resides in the very referential nature of the photographic entity. Thus, we need to acknowledge that what distinguishes the photo-image from other forms of representation is its material link to reality, just as we have to pay attention to the tension between the culturally fabricated nature of the photograph and its fundamental indexicality, its status as "a trace of the real" (ibid, 4). In other words, "the photograph is a physical trace of (the light reflecting off) that which existed before the camera in the real world" (Horstkotte & Pedri 2008: 12–13). Photographs, in short, differ from other images on the basis of their photochemical process, mechanical production, and indexical connection to reality.[6]

Studies of photographic art aim at foregrounding photographic specificity while relating that specificity to the concerns of a particular cultural and historical climate. John Tagg, in his influential book *The Burden of Representation*, turn his attention from the ontology of the photograph to the historical, social, and cultural contexts in which the *meaning* of photographs is constructed. Tagg stresses the pragmatic, rhetorical, and political aspects of photo-documentary processes, and he distinguishes visual representations from the extratextual reality, which is always more complicated than any framed image (1988: 4). According to Stephen Greenblatt, the established concepts of literary theory — allusion, representation, mimesis and the like — seem inadequate in describing contemporary cultural phenomena in which social energies are charged with aesthetic discourses

---

6 Of course, the question of the photograph's connection to reality remains a complex and difficult one: "Despite [such] obvious conceptual difficulties and despite the recourse to numerous creative techniques that expose as constructed the sense of the photograph's privileged relation to the real (collage, montage, salient examples of framing, posing, retouching, and the use of filters, up to the new possibilities offered by digital manipulation software), the almost automatic association of the photograph with the real, the authentic, and the referent proves difficult to break" (Horstkotte & Pedri 2008: 14).

and vice versa (1989: 11). While I agree with Greenblatt, it seems to me that narratological poetics, with its specific methodological toolbox, can be helpful in enlightening the larger cultural poetics of photonarratives.

An Ethics and Aesthetics of the Depression

The element of documentary representation of the social world — through fiction, poetry, film, photography and so on — is one significant element of American modernism (see Rabinowitz 2005: 264–266), but as the high modernist writers sometimes aimed at objective distance and formal aesthetics, they were, more or less, detached from the actual social concerns of their times. To be sure, actual social reality presented its own difficulties: how in earth to grasp and represent the extreme complexity of American reality, especially the reality of the Great Depression in the 1930s? In 1936, the U. S. government launched a large-scale documentary project called the Farm Security Administration (FSA), which worked hard to make the Depression easier to handle and understand through photographic images (*Figure 1*). It is important to note that the classic phase of American photographic art was born in this context and that these years saw a lot of collaboration between prose writers, poets, and photographers in their joint project to try to depict the events and faces of the Depression era.[7]

In this cultural scheme, *Let Us Now Praise Famous Men* still appears a radically idiosyncratic work. As James Agee believes, the vast amount of verbal and visual documentation of the Depression era, done in the framework of the Farm Security Administration, seemed to have obscured reality rather than clarified it. His book aspires, in Agee's own words, to a "non-artistic" view of its real subjects in an "effort to suspend or destroy imagination," so that without its mediation there may open "before consciousness and within it, a universe luminous, spacious, inculpably rich and wonderful in each detail" (*FM*, 25). Famously, he speaks of his "effort to perceive simply *the cruel radiance of what is*" (*FM*, 24; my emphasis). The book is a verbal and visual record of the daily existence and environ-

---

7 In addition to the collaboration between Agee and Evans, the following are worth mentioning: Margaret Bourke-White and Erskine Caldwell's *You Have Seen Their Faces* (1937); Archibald McLeish's *Land of the Free* (1938), a collection of poems including the work of various photographers; Dorothea Lange and Paul S. Taylor's *An American Exodus* (1939), and Richard Wright and Edwin Rosskam's *Twelve Million Black Voices* (1941). We may also note the influence of the FSA photographs on the narrative style of what may be the most famous of the Depression era novels, John Steinbeck's *The Grapes of Wrath* (1939). Two remarkable studies of the era are Stott (1973) and Dickstein (2009).

Figure 1: Evans, Walker 1935–36. Photograph Albums for *Let Us Now Praise Famous Men* (FSA-OWI Collection, Prints and Photographs Division, Library of Congress, Washington, DC).

ment of three poor families, whose lives Agee attempts to capture in his narrative not so much "by means of art," as he says, but through "open forms." Therefore, *Let Us Now Praise Famous Men* is not so much a book as an "effort in human actuality" (*FM*, 11). Actually, Agee does not want his text to be thought of as a work of art; this is because regarding it as "art" will, in Agee's view, diminish the weight and power of the actual existence of its subject and thus tame the force of reality in the narrative text.

The book shows some serious doubt about any textual artifact's ability to achieve immediacy in its representation, and it makes this constantly by drawing attention to conventions of textual, both verbal and visual, production. According to some of the many definitions Agee gives to his own text, the book is "anti-artistic," "anti-journalistic" and "anti-scientific"; this breaking of conventional frames also means that the text will respect no disciplinary boundaries in its search for "direct experience, emotion, and thought." In the preface of the book Agee writes as follows: "We are trying to deal with our subject not as journalists, sociologists, politicians, entertainers, humanitarians, priests, or artists, but *seriously*" (*FM*, 10; my emphasis). In Agee's view, then, each of these discursive positions remains trapped in one narrow set of conventions, reducing the complex inter-play of language and the world to some single frame of category (see Reed 1992: 34–35). At one point Agee writes:

> I think there is at the middle of this sense of the importance and dignity of actuality and the attempt to reproduce and analyze the actual, and at the middle of this antagonism toward art, something of real importance which is by no means my discovery, far less my private discovery, but which is a sense of 'reality' and of 'values' held by more and more people, and the beginnings of somewhat new forms of, call it art if you must, of which the still and moving cameras are the strongest instruments and symbols. It would be an art and a way of seeing existence (...). (*FM*, 221)

Let Us Now Praise Famous Men has usually been described as either "realist" or "modernist," but these concepts, realism and modernism, themselves are questioned in the text. Agee protests against the flatness of realist representation, but also against modernist art, which "is hermetically sealed away from identification with everyday 'reality'" (*FM*, 217). Discussing the textual means of representation and the handicaps of naturalism and documentary, Agee writes in his characteristically complicated prose style:

> I doubt that the straight 'naturalist' very well understands what music and poetry are about. That would be all right if he understood his materials so intensely that music and poetry seemed less than his intention; but I doubt he does that. That is why his work even at best is never much more than documentary. Not that documentation has not great dignity and value; it has; and as good 'poetry' can be extracted from it as from living itself; but documentation is not itself either poetry or music and it is not, of itself, of any value equivalent to theirs. So that, if you share the naturalist's regard for the 'real' but have this regard for it on a plane which in your mind brings it level in value with music and poetry, which in turn you value as highly as anything on earth, it is important that *your representation of 'reality'* does not sag into, or become one with, naturalism; and in so far as it does, you have sinned, that is, you have fallen short even of the relative truth you have perceived and intended. (*FM*, 215; my emphasis.)

As we may note, Agee regards representation of reality a highly *ethical* act, one that must take as its main goal at least a relative truth, and one that does not sink to the lower depths of naturalist documentation. That Agee mentions "sin" in this context should be seen as meaningful. As Jeffrey J. Folks argues in his essay "Agee's Angelic Ethics," Agee responded instinctively with empathy toward the frail and vulnerable — the poor, the homeless, the sick, all of whom elicited his compassion. He adds that the religious language and imagery of *Let Us Now Praise Famous Men* may lead us to focus on the book's "theological dimensions" and to speak of Agee's "religious vision."[8] However, as Folks further argues, instead of clarity and simplicity, "Agee's conception of ethics always reverted to a messier scenario, one in which motives of loss and destructive rebellion overlapped with professions of responsibility, regret, and religiosity" (2007: 74). According to Agee's Gnostic vision, the people he describes in his book are almost divine in their suffering — and this kind of "angelic ethics" is dangerously close to being unjust to their harsh reality in which there is hardly anything beautiful (see also Entin 2007, 144–147). So, Agee has taken a difficult job in his attempt at an ethical representation of the other, and as he notes, the book must inevitably be a failure. But my question is: how successful *is* Agee's failure, both ethically and aesthetically?

Let us go back to Agee's explicit definition of the aims, purposes, and media of his book:

> The nominal subject is North American cotton tenantry as examined in the daily living of three representative white tenant families. (...) The immediate instruments are two: the motionless camera, and the printed word. The governing instrument — which is also one of the centers of the subject — is individual, anti-authoritative human consciousness. (...) Since it is intended, among other things, as a swindle, an insult, and a corrective, the reader will be wise to bear the nominal subject, and his expectation of its proper treatment, steadily in mind. (*FM*, 10)

Here, the authors (both Agee and Evans) present themselves as documentarists whose working ethics must be considered and negotiated by the readers. What is more, the "nominal" subject of the book — the life of tenant families — both shapes and *is shaped by* the "actual" subject, that is, the flesh-and-blood reality of the real people behind or beyond the text. We may note that Agee changed the names of the three families, not in order to make fiction, but to grant them their dignity and individuality. From this perspective, of course, the title of the book is quite telling.

In a sense the whole of *Let Us Now Praise Famous Men* is an experiential testimony to the difficulty of learning to "feel what wretches feel," as in the quotation from *King Lear*, which serves as a motto of the book (see *FM*, 12). Agee both insists on the reality of the referent and on the inevitable failure of any representation to capture the real. As T. V. Reed notes in his analysis of *Let Us Now Praise Famous Men*, there is no simple

8 We may also note that the book's title alludes to the lines from Ecclesiasticus: "Let us now praise famous men" (see also *FM*, 395). As Gavin Jones suggests, this subtext sets Agee's work "within a familiar Christian dialectic that contrasts wise and powerful men with the silent but blessed poor" (2008: 192n). As a matter of fact, Jones's recent criticism of Agee's much-praised text sees its picture of the poor as rather problematic; to my mind, however, Jones is more convincing as a political historian than as a literary critic.

way out of the aesthetic and political bind of "representation" — that representation is impossible to achieve, and impossible to avoid (see 1992: 23). Daniel Lehman writes that "paying specific attention to specific types of assertions and nonfictional narrative power relationships can teach us about the way truth matters" (1997: 8–9). As he also says, James Agee spoke of this power in *Let Us Now Praise Famous Men*. Here is how Agee writes about George Gudger, the central character of his book:

> George Gudger is a man, et cetera. But obviously, in the effort to tell of him as truthfully as I can, I am limited. I know him only so far as I know him, and only in those terms in which I know him; and all of that depends as fully on who I am as on who he is. (...) The one deeply exciting thing to me about Gudger is that he is actual, he is living, at this instant. He is not some artist's or journalist's or propagandist's invention; he is a human being; and to what degree I am able it is my business to reproduce him as the human being he is; not just to amalgamate him into some invented literary imitation of a human being. (*FM*, 211)

Lehman, constructing his rhetorical and pragmatic theory of nonfictional narrative partly on the basis of James Phelan's related theory of fictional narrative, proposes that "for most forms of nonfiction, the trio of author, text, and reader that Phelan admits into the rhetorical framework must be expanded to admit a fourth player: the actual living or lived beings that make up the subjects of nonfictional narrative" (1997: 23; see also Lehtimäki 2007: 30). As we are reading a documentary book, with real people in it — or, to more precise, factual representations of real people — we can see passages in which not only the author is "reading" the characters but the characters are also "reading" the author. It is the question of confronting another face and the ethical implications in this confrontation; that is, it is the question of showing responsibility toward the other. On a concrete level, some of the characters represented in the book eventually became actual readers of Agee's text, and were eager to question and challenge Agee's representation of them. It is possible that this resistant reception is part of the book's purpose, belonging to the implied author's ethics and aesthetics.

Photographic Textuality

In his essay "A Way of Seeing," written some years after the publication of *Let Us Now Praise Famous Men*, Agee formulated his ideas of writing and photography as follows:

> The actual is not at all transformed; it is reflected and recorded, within the limits of the camera, with all possible accuracy. The artist's task is not to alter the world

as the eye sees it into a world of aesthetic reality, but to perceive the aesthetic reality within the actual world, and to make an undisturbed and faithful record of the instant in which this movement of creativeness achieves its most expressive crystallization. (1965: 4)

Agee's prose in *Let Us Now Praise Famous Men* is filled with realist observation and visual allusions as if he were trying to capture the photographic sharpness with his verbal imagery. Thus, Agee's text contains several allusions to various other media, including poetry, painting, photography, film, theatre, and music. At one point he writes:

> But the music of what is happening is more richly scored than this; and much beyond what I can set down: I can only talk about it: the personality of the room, and of a group of creatures, has undergone a change, as if seen through two different techniques or mediums; what began as 'rembrandt,' deeplighted in gold, in each integer colossally heavily planted, has become a photograph, a record in clean, staring, colorless light, almost without a shadow. (*FM*, 357)

In realist and modernist literature, photography has served as a model for various narrative techniques, including framing, zooming, and detailing objects in the foreground and the background. While Agee's textual self-reflexivity is probably the most visible aspect of his prose, his narrative does contain more descriptive passages as well, as in his photographically realist observations of objects:

> I helped get camera ready and we stood away and I watched what would be trapped, possessed, fertilized, in the leisures and shyness which are a phase of all love for any object: searching out and registering in myself all its planes, stresses of relationship, along diagonals withdrawn and approached, and vertical to the slightly off-centered door, and broadside, and at several distances, and near, examining merely the ways of the wood, and the nails, the three new boards of different lengths that were let in above the left of the door, the staring small white porcelain knob, the solesmoothed stairlifts, the wrung stance of thick steeple, the hewn wood stoblike spike at sky, the old hasp and new padlock, the randomshuttered windowglass whose panes were like the surfaces of springs (...) (*FM*, 49–50).

While Agee aims at photographic style in his description of things, his linguistic consciousness is still foregrounded in his sprawling, Faulknerian sentences and in his Joycean coinage of new words ("solesmoothed stairlifts," "randomshuttered windowglass"). The reader's immersion into the story-world is constantly made complicated.

Let Us Now Praise Famous Men also makes the reader unsure as to where the book itself begins (with the photographs, the narrative text, or the "Preface" placed between them?) and where it ends. In addition to this formal complexity, "the fictive and the factual are as distinct in [the book] as the two sides of a Möbius strip" (Reed 1992: 35). In a Möbius kind of vision the perceiving subject is inside the happenings instead of being only a detached, objective reporter. There is, then, a certain break in modernist art which sees reality as unstable and moving, being viewed from various viewpoints simultaneously. In the age of Cubism and cinema, the objects of the world are no longer understood as "fixed" entities to be perceived by an observing ego from some solid position (cf. Grishakova 2006: 134–141). Consequently, modernism in arts is devoted to reproducing particular perspectives.[9]

While Agee's medium is, finally, written language, Walker Evans, in his photograph of George Gudger (*Figure 2*) and other photos printed in the book, has to establish the sense of relationship between author and character without words. As Reed notes, Evans does so primarily in two ways: by allowing his subjects to compose themselves, and through the use of the family photo album genre (1992: 52–53).[10] While in a painting the artist chooses things that are included (according to his or her aesthetic vision), the photograph can be distinguished from other kinds of visual art in its recording of all the details that are present before the camera's eye:

> The photograph works to alter our perception of the world by drawing attention to a marginal detail, one that would go unnoticed if it were not for the fact that it was photographed and thus framed. Ultimately, the automatic inclusion of daily, ordinary, even banal details within the photograph's frame affects the way the world is seen. Through the everydayness of photographic aesthetics, the familiar (and oftentimes overlooked) aspects of the real world are more readily perceived and thus gain in importance. (Horstkotte & Pedri 2008: 14–15)

The subtle but strong aesthetic composition of the photographs adds dignity and strength to Evans's subjects, those "marginal" human beings and

---

9 As Michael North suggests, there is also something deeply skeptical in the visual culture of modernism, as multiple perspectives visibly demonstrate the partiality of any single point of view. He writes: "Objectivity, in other words, is visibly refuted in many modernist works, and with it goes the reliability of representation. If the camera can lie, as it must if it simultaneously shows two quite different views of the same thing, then how much less reliable is language, which has always been considered even more distant than pictures from the thing itself?" (2005: 187).

10 Marianne Hirsch's book *Family Frames* might be an interesting touchstone here. Hirsch discusses the ways photographs can powerfully shape personal and collective memory. She speaks of the "continuing power and 'burden' of photographic reference," and notes that the camera is an apparatus whose "social functions are integrally tied to the ideology of modern family" (1997: 6, 7). It has been said that photography is instrumental and powerful in its depiction of the family, one of society's most valued and fundamental social groups (Horstkotte & Pedri 2008: 16). There is some irony in that the people depicted by Agee and Evans in their book — with its subtitle *Three Tenant Families*, which is close to its original working title, *Cotton Tenants: Three Families* — formed, in Agee's words, "an undefended and appallingly damaged group of human beings, an ignorant and helpless rural family" (*FM*, 21).

Figure 2: Evans 1935–36, 1:34.

their inglorious daily living. These are finally real people in the pictures, not some artist's imaginative creations.

Let Us Now Praise Famous Men is not an *iconotext* in any pure sense: it is not an artifact where "the verbal and the visual signs mingle to produce rhetoric that depends on the co-presence of words and images," so that text and image were mutually interdependent in their ways of producing meaning (see Wagner 1996: 16). In fact, Evans's photographs are completely separate from Agee's prose in the book's structure, and they are also devoid of all textual features that conventionally accompany this kind of photo-essay: there are no captions, legends, dates, names, locations or any other subtexts or textual guides which would help us to "read" these photographs (cf. Mitchell 1994: 290). One of the questions the reader/viewer of the book must face is in what ways prose and photos are related. Using Barthes's terms, in photonarratives, words can function either as 'anchorage'—helping to identify the scene in the picture and to construct meanings—or as 'relay,' so that images and words work together to produce some larger idea (see Barthes 1977: 38–41; Kafalenos 2005:

429). In the case of *Let Us Now Praise Famous Men*, however, the radical separation of prose and photos from each other suggests that written text cannot capture the otherness of photographs and that words and images are ultimately different ways of depicting the world.

Conventionally, photographs have been located in narrative texts in an illustrative role, so that their own complex textuality, as well as their potentiality of storytelling, has been rendered quite invisible (see Hughes & Noble 2003: 6). It has been suggested that because of their fragmented, discontinuous, and static nature photographic images cannot narrate (see Horstkotte & Pedri 2008: 8). *Let Us Now Praise Famous Men* creates its own demanding photo-textual structure. As the reader opens the book, what she or he finds first is fifty pages of photographs without any text. In his influential book *Picture Theory*, W. J. T. Mitchell argues that the location of Evans's photographs at the front of the volume is an aggressive declaration of photographic independence.[11] It appears that the very organization of the book resists the straightforward collaboration of words and images; in Mitchell's words: "The aestheticizing separation of Evans's images from Agee's text is not simply a formal characteristic but an ethical strategy, a way of preventing easy access to the world they represent" (1994: 295). Here, once again, aesthetics is interconnected with ethics.

As Nancy Pedri argues, an understanding of the photographic documentary needs to reach beyond the notion of the photograph's supposed objectivity, an idea represented by its mechanically produced indexicality or the historical contexts that make its meaning. From a rhetorical and pragmatic aspect, it is also crucial to note the reader's role in the reception of the photo-documentary expression and in the production of its possible, and alternative, meanings. Pedri writes: "Born of an interaction between photographic document and reader, the documentary comes to be that uncertain mixture of fact and fiction that moves readers to belief" (2008: 170). In Agee's words, *Let Us Now Praise Famous Men* is "an effort in human actuality, in which *the reader* is no less centrally involved than the authors and those of whom they tell" (*FM*, 11; my emphasis). In the difficult author-reader contract of the book, the photos seem to draw the reader into an intimate relationship with the person portrayed; but the people in the pictures appear to ask the reader, "in what authority are you entering our lives?" As Agee himself asks in his text: "Who are you who will read these words and study these photographs, and through what

11 Interestingly, Mitchell also suggests that the book might have been influenced by the visual arts of William Blake, in whose work images are independent from texts (1994: 300n). This allusion is plausible since Agee places Blake as the foremost of "unpaid agitators" behind the book's production (see *FM*, 16).

cause, by what chance, and for what purpose, and by what right do you qualify to, and what will you do about it?" (*FM*, 22). As Mitchell suggests, Agee's questions to the reader, as well as his generic requirements, are also predescriptions for a highly alert reader that may not yet exist, that may in fact have to be created (1994: 290). Demanding texts such as *Let Us Now Praise Famous Men* must "teach" its readers, or, in other words, the readers of the book are "schooled" by the text as they read along. Not only writing but also reading (and viewing) is an ethical act.

What is obvious by now is that inside the covers of *Let Us Now Praise Famous Men* we have two different artists working in different ways and with different media but with the same subject matter. Agee sometimes wants to shock the reader, give his readers new perceptions through defamiliarization of objects, while Evans's more simple and austere sensibility leads him to attempt to construct new visions from ordinary or conventional lines of sight. Evans usually refused to move any of the objects he was photographing; instead, he wanted to take pictures of those objects, people and things, in their natural contexts of everyday living; and for the most part he avoided unnatural angles, preferring to shoot from normal height and straightforward angles (see Reed 1992: 48). There is simple poetry in Evans's silent, unmoving images; the style of Agee's text is sometimes similar, sometimes more subjective, angry, and polemic. As John Tagg has argued, instead of a certain manipulative rhetoric of some other Depression era photographs, which aimed at constructing an explicit meaning through spectacle, irony, and symbolization (Tagg's primary example is the aestheticizing art of Margaret Bourke-White), Evans's poetic images are more obscure and more difficult to fix into a definite time, place, and event. Thus, in Evans's photographs, "the relationships of image to image are not those of thesis and antithesis, but of rhyme, repetition, discrepancy, and reversal," "the process of reading is not curtailed in advance," and "no spatial setting is given, no wider explanatory frame, no supporting ground" (2003: 27–28). In Tagg's view, it is precisely *the problem of meaning* that is visible in Evans's photographic art.

Generally, photographs are less discursive and narrative than many paintings; however, as Emma Kafalenos argues from a narratological viewpoint, more than other visual representations of a single scene, photographs lend themselves to being interpreted as an event in a number of different stories (see 2005: 429). Thus, we can read stories, places, events and human experiences *into* Evans's photos, and think about the past, present, and future of the people in pictures. Of course, Agee's prose provides some obviously *ekphrastic* readings of some of those photographs that can be found inside the covers of the book (see below), and still the reader/ viewer can come to quite different interpretations from the writer. Alex

Hughes and Andrea Noble suggest that photographic images make their appeal to the viewer not simply on an intellectual level, since they can work against the culturally consecrated primary of intellect over emotion, or of mind over body; thus, "as we engage with the realm of the photographic we are given access to alternative ways of knowing" (2003: 6). As Mitchell shrewdly puts it, *Let Us Now Praise Famous Men* works against text-image "exchanges" typical of photonarratives, as the book resists the straightforward collaboration of prose and photos. Evans's photographs are bereft of textual and literary elements, and thus they "force us back onto the formal and material features of the images in themselves" (1994: 239). Therefore, the very materiality, as well as indexicality, of the photograph makes it work differently from the written text; it requires the reader to respect the thing in itself.

Things and Truths

Even though words and images work differently, it may still be argued that in *Let Us Now Praise Famous Men*, both prose and photos must face equal problems of reality representation. Both journalistic writing and photographic documentation share the same kind of referential complexity in their nonfictional truth-claiming function (see Pedri 2008: 161). In the production of the book, it appears that both Agee and Evans wanted to challenge their own devices and media by pushing them to certain limits; thus, Evans is experimenting with photographic techniques (lenses, frames, lights, angles, etc.) while Agee painfully — sometimes painfully also for the reader — includes in his prose all the motives and devices of his writing. The result is a book which is "a meditation on the limits of what, among the things we see and recognize, we can directly record or indirectly evoke with images and words" (Minter 1996: 201). As mentioned, sometimes Agee makes clear that he is trying to write "photographically," as if the written word could not reach the complicated real well enough. The "cruel radiance of what is" is the very thing that Agee tries to capture in his prose, even as he knows that perhaps only photography can lighten up that reality.

However, as John Tagg writes in his essay on Evans, there is an ontological distance between the hard material presence of real things and the observing yet subjective photographic eye. In Tagg's phrasing, the "overwhelming thing" and an "unencounterable real" present continuous challenges to verbal and visual representation. As Tagg sees it, questions of the limits of knowledge, of language, and of meaning have belonged to the idea of melancholy, and he writes as follows: "Perhaps a reconsideration

Figure 3: Evans 1935–36, 1:54. See the color illustration on page 338.

of melancholy may help us think about the character of those practices of representation that will not give way to the demand for efficient communication but resist the arrival of meaning, while mourning a real that does not lend itself to representation" (2003: 59).

In this context of reality representation, we may look at a couple of photos by Evans, printed in *Let Us Now Praise Famous Men*. First, we may think that there is an allusion to Vincent van Gogh's famous painting of peasant shoes (1886) in a picture of a tenant farmer's shoes taken exactly fifty years later (*Figure 3*). We may also recall that van Gogh's painting stimulated the great, if controversial, German philosopher Martin Heidegger to write his famous essay "The Origin of the Work of Art" (1935–36), written, as we can see, about at the very moment Evans was taking the picture. In his poetic essay, Heidegger explains the essence of art in terms of the concepts of being and truth. He talks about the viewer's responsibility to consider the variety of questions about the shoes, asking not only about form and matter — the question "what are the shoes made of?" — but bestowing the thing with life by asking of its purpose, that is, "what are the shoes for?" Heidegger writes about art's ability to set up an active struggle between what he calls *earth* and *world*. While "world" in Heidegger's terminology is a passive entity, "earth" is active. The world simply occurs while the earth actively exists. As Heidegger puts it, the parts that clarify and unify the work embody its "world" aspects, while practices that help resist such completion make up its "earth." The earth is resistant; it cannot be fully revealed or explained. This struggle between world and earth takes place within the artwork; but as soon as meaning is pinned down and the work no longer offers resistance to picturing, framing, and rationalization, the struggle is over. (See Heidegger 1971: 39–50.)[12]

The possibility of its earth aspects is due to the fact that the reader of *Let Us Now Praise Famous Men* is able to connect the photograph of the shoes onto the very particular body and existence of a farmer, namely George Gudger (or, actually, Floyd Burroughs, which was the farmer's real name), a man whose specific human weight can be felt in these working shoes. Agee writes of these shoes as if they were a Cubist artwork (and obscure like Charles Bovary's hat), and still firmly rooted into the hard work on cotton fields:

> They are one of the most ordinary types of working shoe: the blucher design, and soft in the prow, lacking the seam across the root of the big toe: covering the ankles: looped straps at the heels: blunt, broad, and rounded at the toe: broad-heeled: made up of the most simple roundnesses and squarings and flats, of dark brown raw thick leathers nailed, and sewn coarsely to one another in courses and patterns of doubled and tripled seams, and such throughout that like many other small objects they have great massiveness and repose and are, as the houses and overalls are, and the feet and legs of the women, who go barefooted so much, fine pieces of architecture. (...) The shoes are worn for work. (*FM*, 241–242)

Of course, Evans's probably intentional allusion to van Gogh's famous painting may also remind us that our vision is being directed aesthetically by the photographer, his choice of framing, angle, and perspective. That is, there is no simple documentary apprehension of these objects *or* of the human being who wears these shoes. Therefore, these real objects and the earth they belong to are artistically transformed to be also something else than what they really are or really were. Still, the contrast between Heidegger's and Evans's "readings" of van Gogh's painting is illuminating, since where Heidegger takes off on a flight of fancy about universal peasantry (and let us not forget his "national" interests), Evans's approach to the painting has the effect of making it appear more concrete and rooted in a specific life (see Reed 1992: 47–48.) In Evans's pictures, just as in Agee's prose, we are made to feel the hard realities and the resistant earth

---

12 Fredric Jameson somewhat clarifies this by saying that Heidegger's theory is "organized around the idea that the work of art emerges within the gap between Earth and World, or what I would prefer to translate as the meaningless materiality of the body and the nature and the meaning endowment of history and of the social." Jameson adds that "Heidegger's account needs to be completed by insistence on the renewed materiality of the work, on the transformation of one form of materiality—the earth itself and its paths and physical objects—into that other materiality of oil paint" (Jameson 2005: 7–8). Jameson also refers to Walker Evans's photograph of the tenant shoes in his own analysis of van Gogh's painting of the peasant shoes.

of the Depression era Alabama, even though neither words nor images really capture that real earth.

Still, if we compare images to words — and here I am speaking of concrete visual images such as photographs — we may recall the photographic medium's necessary indexical complicity with the real. In this sense, Evans's reality referent — be it human faces or objects like shoes — is never totally lost. The indexical nature of "analogical" photography has relation to what Agee calls "unimagined existence" (*FM*, 10), a notion representing his belief that there is an extratextual world, a resistant earth, and nonhuman nature. In Heidegger's style, we can think that Evans's photograph of tenant shoes is still full of earth, existence, and resistance. In a phenomenological sense, in the photograph there remains a kind of natural "being-there" of objects.[13]

While we may trace a certain difference in politics as regards to Heidegger's and Evans's respective philosophies of art, Agee's vision of the world comes rather close to Heidegger's — and there is a historical reason to this, since for example Ralph Waldo Emerson's transcendental views of nature have, more or less, influenced both Heidegger's and Agee's ways of thinking. But let us think about this imaginative relation between Heidegger and Agee through Evans's pictures. In an another photo by Evans, we see a young girl called Louise, daughter of George Gudger, in her harsh everyday reality, but in a way illuminated by the light that also makes this photograph possible (*Figure 4*). Agee seems to be alluding to Evans's photograph when he writes of Louise: "During the week she is always barefooted and wears a wide straw hat in the sun" (*FM*, 249). The light and her large straw hat almost make this photo resemble a medieval hagiographic portratuire (cf. Reed 1992: 48). It is as if there was something very real and, at the same time, something very holy in this picture, and perhaps Auerbach's well-known concept of *figura* might work here: it is an example of figuration, and of a certain kind of blending, which brings heaven and earth together (see Auerbach 1968; cf. White 1999: 94–95; 190n). It may even be said that the style of this image by Evans is a key to the poetics of Agee's text. Still, there are some clear discrepancies between Evans's images and Agee's text, especially when we read them together. Agee sometimes seems to remove, or ignore, the signs of the tenant's literacy and education, which are quite evident in Evans's photographs (see Cosgrove 1995; Jones 2008: 128, 193n). It is as if Agee's intention of

---

13 The photograph is thus connected to the physicality of the past; it is not simply a reconstruction of that past. As Roland Barthes puts it: "In Photography I can never deny that *the thing has been there*. There is a superimposition here: of reality and of the past" (1981: 76).

Figure 4: Evans 1935–36, 1:38.

constructing his subjects both as poor and holy creatures of nature – and thus different from the sophisticated authors and readers of this book – were in contrast to the documentary evidence of Evans's photographs, which show these people rather more like "us."

Thus, Agee writes of Louise Gudger:

> It is hardly to Louise's good fortune that she 'likes' school, school being what it is. Dressed as she is, and bright as she is, and serious and dutiful and well-thought-of as she is, she already has traces of a special sort of complacency which probably must, in time, destroy all in her nature that is magical, indefinable, and matchless: and this though she is one of the stronger persons I have ever known. (*FM*, 278)

In what follows, Agee writes, as if through the photographic medium: "[...] and it is while I am watching you here, Louise, that suddenly yet very quietly I realize a little more clearly that I am probably going to be in love with you: while I am watching you in this precious imposture of a dress, standing up the strength of your father and looking so soberly and so straight into the plexus of the lens through those paralyzing eyes of yours (...)" (*FM*, 328). A ten-year-old Louise becomes both a beautiful child of nature, a Dostoevskyan holy poor, and a kind of Lolita figure in Agee's narrative, and thus a certain *mise en abyme* image of the problems of Agee's ethics and aesthetics.

Agee, according to this "angelic" and "Gnostic" vision, therefore, aims to see things both as real and divine, and he sees transcendental light in common objects, even as he sees grace and dignity in the lives of these uneducated and unprivileged people. In Agee's view, human beings are beautiful because they exist; and even inanimate things and objects are illuminated by light. He writes:

> Plain objects and atmospheres have a sufficient intrinsic beauty and stature that it might be well if the describer become more rather than less shameless: if objects and atmospheres for the secret sake of which it is customary to write a story or poem, and which are chronically relegated to a menial level of decoration or at best illumination, were handled and presented on their own merits without either distortion or apology (*FM*, 216).

Agee believes that the beauty he sees in the natural world is not a human projection or abstraction but inheres in the world he perceives and experiences (see Jones 2008: 128). In a sense, then, what we need to do is to show humble generosity toward the world and its mysteries and remain open to the possibility that even commonest of things have importance. Agee thus writes about "the profoundest and plainest 'beauties,' those of the order of the stars and of solitude in darkened and empty land" (*FM*, 280). Human beings measure their existence between earth and heaven, divines and mortals, as Heidegger would have it.

When Heidegger, in his later writings, calls modernity "the age of the world picture," he means to criticize the act of picturing, of framing, because it distances and subordinates the thing in itself. Heidegger, like many of his deconstructive followers, has a rather negative idea of visuality, since the visual media replaces a real nearness to things with an illusory closeness. Obviously, photography — as a technical, technological, and mechanical phenomenon — has influenced our perception of reality, arguably not only providing us with new ways of seeing but also limiting (through framing) our sense of the world. Thus, modern times have replaced the attitude of *wonder*, which lets things be as they are, with that of *curiosity*, which is based on the desire to know how things can be used for human purposes. As Heidegger believes, the ultimate triumph of curiosity over wonder was an essential component in the hegemony of the technological world-view in the modern era. Technology, in fact, is deeply problematic for Heidegger because it carries to an extreme the distancing of subject and object, or, in visual terms, the thing and its framing through representation. One way to define the opposition between two visual modes in Heidegger's thinking is to make a distinction between the *assertoric* and *aletheic* gaze. The former is abstracted, monocular, inflexible, unmoving, rigid, and *ego*-logical; the latter is multiple, aware of its context, horizonal, caring, and, perhaps, *eco*-logical (see Heidegger 1971; Jay 1993: 270–275; cf. North 2005: 184–185.)

Evans's photographic art hardly represents objectivization of the natural world in its most arrogant and loud version; but what Heidegger especially values, instead of visual framing of the world with the help of modern technology (such as photography), is poetic language and its openness to the mysteries of the world. What Agee probably wants to say is that people, dependent on their language, are too limited in their vision of the world. They are fixed in its material basis, they only view nature in terms of need and use, and thus they fail to see — and represent — the real reality that lies beyond the visible. Art may help us to feel things in a new way, but art, be it verbal or visual, ultimately fails in its ongoing attempts at representing reality as it is.

References

Agee, James, and Walker Evans (2001 [1941]). *Let Us Now Praise Famous Men: Three Tenant Families*. London: Violette Editions.

Agee, James (1965). "A Way of Seeing." In: Levitt, Helen. *A Way of Seeing: Photographs of New York by Helen Levitt with an Essay by James Agee*. New York: Viking.

Auerbach, Erich (1968 [1946]). *Mimesis: The Representation of Reality in Western Literature*. Princeton: Princeton University Press.

Bal, Mieke (1991). *Reading "Rembrandt": Beyond the Word–Image Opposition*. Cambridge: Cambridge University Press.

Barthes, Roland (1977). *Image – Music – Text*. Trans. Stephen Heath. New York: Hill and Wang.

Barthes, Roland (1981). *Camera Lucida: Reflections on Photography*. Trans. Richard Howard. New York: Hill and Wang.

Batchen, Geoffrey (1997). *Burning with Desire: The Conception of Photography*. Cambridge: MIT Press.

Bleikasten, André (1976). *The Most Splendid Failure: Faulkner's The Sound and the Fury*. Bloomington: Indiana University Press.

Brooks, Peter (2005). *Realist Vision*. New Haven & London: Yale UP.

Chatman, Seymour (1978). *Story and Discourse: Narrative Structure in Fiction and Film*. Ithaca: Cornell University Press.

Cosgrove, Peter (1995). "Snapshots of the Absolute: Mediamachia in *Let Us Now Praise Famous Men*." *American Literature* 67.2: 329–357.

Dickstein, Morris (2009). *Dancing in the Dark: A Cultural History of the Great Depression*. New York & London: W. W. Norton & Company.

Entin, Joseph B. (2007). *Sensational Modernism: Experimental Fiction and Photography in Thirties America*. Chapel Hill: The University of North Carolina Press.

Falck, Colin (1989). *Myth, Truth and Literature: Towards a True Post-Modernism*. Cambridge: Cambridge University Press.

Folks, Jeffrey J. (2007). "Agee's Angelic Ethics." In: Lofaro, Michael A. (ed.). *Agee*

Agonistes: Essays on the Life, Legend, and Works of James Agee. Knoxville: The University of Tennessee Press, 73–84.
Greenblatt, Stephen (1989). "Towards a Poetics of Culture." In: Veeser, Aram H. (ed.). *The New Historicism*. New York & London: Routledge, 1–14.
Grishakova, Marina (2006). *The Models of Space, Time and Vision in V. Nabokov's Fiction: Narrative Strategies and Cultural Frames*. Tartu: Tartu University Press.
Hartsock, John C. (2000). *A History of American Literary Journalism: The Emergence of a Modern Narrative Form*. Amherst: The University of Massachusetts Press.
Heidegger, Martin (1971). *Poetry, Language, Thought*. Translated by Albert Hofstadter. New York: Harper, 1971.
Hirsch, Marianne (1997). *Family Frames: Photography, Narrative, and Postmemory*. Cambridge: Harvard University Press.
Horstkotte, Silke, and Nancy Pedri (2008). "Introduction: Photographic Interventions." *Poetics Today* 29.1: 1–29.
Hughes, Alex, and Andrea Noble (2003). "Introduction." In: Hughes, Alex and Andrea Noble (eds.). *Phototextualities: Intersections of Photography and Narrative*. Albuquerque: The University of New Mexico Press, 1–16.
Jameson, Fredric (2005 [1991]). *Postmodernism, Or, the Cultural Logic of Late Capitalism*. Durham: The Duke University Press.
Jay, Martin (1993). *Downcast Eyes: The Denigration of Vision in Twentieth-Century French Thought*. Berkeley: The University of California Press.
Jones, Gavin (2008). *American Hungers: The Problem of Poverty in U. S. Literature, 1840–1945*. Princeton: Princeton University Press.
Kafalenos, Emma (2005). "Photographs." In: Herman, David, Manfred Jahn and Marie-Laure Ryan (eds.). *Routledge Encyclopedia of Narrative Theory*. London & New York: Routledge, 428–430.
Lehman, Daniel W. (1997). *Matters of Fact: Reading Nonfiction over the Edge*. Columbus: The Ohio State University Press.
Lehtimäki, Markku (2007). "The Rhetoric of Literary Nonfiction: The Example of Norman Mailer." In: Lehtimäki, Markku, Simo Leisti and Marja Rytkönen (eds.). *Real Stories, Imagined Realities: Fictionality and Non-fictionality in Literary Constructs and Historical Contexts*. Tampere: Tampere University Press, 29–49.
Minter, David (1996). *A Cultural History of the American Novel: Henry James to William Faulkner*. Cambridge: Cambridge University Press.
Mitchell, W. J. T. (1994). *Picture Theory: Essays on Verbal and Visual Representation*. Chicago: The University of Chicago Press.
North, Michael (2005). "Visual Culture." In: Kalaidjian, Walter (ed.). *The Cambridge Companion to American Modernism*. Cambridge: Cambridge University Press, 177–194.
Pedri, Nancy (2008). "Documenting the Fictions of Reality." *Poetics Today* 29.1: 155–173.
Rabinowitz, Paula (2005). "Social Representations within American Modernism." In: Kalaidjian, Walter (ed.). *The Cambridge Companion to American Modernism*. Cambridge: Cambridge University Press, 261–283.
Reed, T. V. (1992). *Fifteen Jugglers, Five Believers: Literary Politics and the Poetics of American Social Movements*. Berkeley: The University of California Press.
Rimmon-Kenan, Shlomith (1996). *A Glance Beyond Doubt: Narration, Representation, Subjectivity*. Columbus: The Ohio State University Press.

Ryan, Marie-Laure (2004). "Introduction." In: Ryan, Marie-Laure (ed.). *Narrative across Media: Languages of Storytelling.* Lincoln & London: University of Nebraska Press, 1–40.

Steiner, Wendy (2004). "Pictorial Narrativity." In: Ryan, Marie-Laure (ed.). *Narrative across Media: Languages of Storytelling.* Lincoln & London: University of Nebraska Press, 145–177.

Stott, William (1973). *Documentary Expression and Thirties America.* Oxford: Oxford University Press.

Tagg, John (1988). *The Burden of Representation: Essays on Photographies and Histories.* London: Macmillan.

– (2003). "Melancholy Realism: Walker Evans's Resistance to Meaning." *Narrative* 11.1: 3–77.

Toker, Leona (1997). "Toward a Poetics of Documentary Prose—from the Perspective of Gulag Testimonies." *Poetics Today* 18.2: 187–222.

Wagner, Peter (1996). "Introduction: Ekphrasis, Iconotexts, and Intermediality—the State(s) of the Art(s)." In: Wagner, Peter (ed.): *Icons—Texts—Iconotext: Essays on Ekphrasis and Intermediality.* Berlin: de Gruyter, 1–40.

White, Hayden (1987). *The Content of the Form: Narrative Discourse and Historical Representation.* Baltimore: The Johns Hopkins University Press.

White, Hayden (1999). *Figural Realism: Studies in the Mimesis Effect.* Baltimore: The Johns Hopkins University Press.

Ruth Page
(University of Leicester)

Interactivity and Interaction: Text and Talk in Online Communities

Introduction

The interactive properties of digital systems are said to be the characteristic that most distinguishes them from other media. Currently, attempts to classify types of interactivity in the digital domain (Ryan 2006, Walker Rettberg 2003) have focused much of their attention on the interactivity inherent in the text, say as a design principle or the means by which users might navigate digital material. The aim of this essay is to expand existing concepts of interactivity by taking into account the additional interactions that take place between multiple users when stories are told in online contexts. In order to do this, I draw on models of interaction more usually associated with face-to-face narration, thereby bringing together sociolinguistic, discourse-oriented and literary approaches to narrative interaction.

The need to take account of communication between users (writer-reader, reader-reader) in conjunction with human-machine interaction is all the more pressing in the light of the storytelling that is proliferating in what are popularly known as 'web 2.0' contexts. The array of tools used to produce narratives in such contexts includes but is not limited to blogs, social networking sites, wikis and discussion-enriched archives, all of which enable collaboration between multiple users. This storytelling is clearly embedded in a participatory culture (Jenkins 2006) which weaves together channels of text and dialogue in multiple configurations. Without doubt, the communicative interaction that is possible in web 2.0 environments encompasses many kinds of discourse. Crucially, this includes the impulse to tell stories, whether they be autobiographic accounts of personal experience or fictional endeavors. The narrative genres that are beginning to emerge from these contexts are highly varied, but all are shaped significantly by the participatory qualities of their surrounding discourse context. In what follows, I map out the factors which might distinguish between different kinds of narrative interaction in web 2.0 contexts, then examine two examples of storytelling more closely: the evolution of illness narratives on personal blogs and the relationship between editorial intervention and narrative coherence in an experimental wiki novel. To begin, I provide a rationale for integrating discourse-oriented and textual models of interaction.

Text-centred and user-centred models of interaction

The evolution of storytelling communities in the blogosphere, on social networking sites and similar discursive online forums is embedded in wider historical shifts in literacy practices. Although the 'everyday' examples of storytelling (of fans, bloggers, social network users) are usually told in written text,[1] they are situated in interactional contexts which enable readers and writers to communicate with one another online. The affordances of computer mediated communication thus blend the written mode with the conversational style and near instantaneous responsiveness characteristic of oral discourse (Walker Rettberg 2008). The hybrid "spoken-written" quality (Kacandes 2001: 8) of online writing has been theorized in relation to Ong's (1982) concept of secondary orality. This secondary orality contains many of the attributes of primary orality (that is, orality that pre-dates exposure to written cultures), such as its capacity to foster communal connection between participants, but it is "a more deliberate and self-conscious orality, based permanently on the use of writing and print" (Ong 1982: 136).[2]

The distinctive and indissolubly "spoken-written" qualities of online discourse present a fresh challenge for exploring the modal resources of narrative. The convergence that typifies secondary orality means that the qualities of the literate and oral modes cannot be isolated from each other, nor can the analysis of narratives that emerge from this participatory culture rely on models derived from exclusively written or spoken paradigms. Instead, the analysis of stories told in web 2.0 environments must be integrative, able to account for the interactions between texts and users and the dialogic interactions between the many users who participate in online

1 The everyday storytelling is situated alongside other modes of communication such as photo-sharing or skype. However, the main content of the story is conveyed in words.

2 It should be noted that Ong (1982) and later McLuhan use the term 'secondary orality' to refer to the genuine auditory nature of radio and TV, whereas the sense in which I am using it designates the simulation of oral communication through written texts. Other forms of CMC such as Skype, video-logs and voice recognition tools suggest that oral expression may be set to increase again.

storytelling communities. The first, text-centred analysis of interaction has points of similarity with models derived from classical narratology. In contrast, the rather more sociological analysis of human-human interaction is rooted in discourse-oriented fields of study.

Digital narratology has always been interdisciplinary in nature, drawing on work from artificial intelligence, gaming, and semiotics to enrich contemporary narrative theory. It is perhaps all the more surprising then, that for the most part, the study of narratives available in digital media (here taken in its broadest sense) has been influenced by the methodological fissures found in the wider history of narrative studies that have polarised literary-theoretical and sociolinguistic fields of narrative research. Although the founding theorists of narratology conceptualised the project's scope in trans-generic, broad terms as accounting for stories "carried by articulated language, spoken or written, fixed or moving images, gestures, and the ordered mixture of all these substances" (Barthes 1977: 79), in practice, structuralist narratology developed many of the still influential tools of narrative analysis from the study of complex literary texts. At the same time that this literary-theoretical work was burgeoning, sociolinguists began to turn their attention to the empirical analysis of narrative, but trained their attention on spoken data, especially narratives of personal experience (Labov and Waletzky 1967).

Over the decades that followed, the sustained inquiry into the forms and function of narrative developed from both structuralist and sociolinguistic points of inception, travelling on mostly separate but parallel paths. On the one hand, work stemming from classical naratology interrogated texts that were usually written, and embraced a diverse range of literary genres. Where contextual concerns became important, these tended to be of a socio-cultural nature yielding a critical narratology that integrated feminist (Lanser 1986), postcolonial (Aldama 2003) and diachronic scholarship. On the other hand, sociolinguistic work on narrative concentrated on oral stories told in face-to-face contexts such as interviews, meal times (Blum-Kulka 1993) and peer group conversation (Norrick 2000). The analysis of these everyday narratives was interpreted in the light of the social and pragmatic work achieved within localised contexts, for example as stories which performed identity work or managed the interpersonal dynamics between speaker and listener.

The distinctive emphases of these research traditions have been reproduced (at least to some extent) in work on digital media. Digital narratology derived from classical work of the structuralists turned its attention to the artistic endeavours of electronic literature (initially associated with hypertext fiction, but now also including network and flash fiction) and the fictional worlds created in video games and role playing simulations.

This corpus was used as the basis for developing significant models of user-text interaction. Discourse oriented studies of personal narrative instead examined the stories told in computer mediated communication that required little technical expertise and flourished in interactive forums such as discussion boards McLellan 1997), email (Georgakopoulou 2007) and personal blogs (Page 2008). The studies of online personal narratives have retained their contextualist approach, examining storytelling variation due to the speaker identity and social function. The user-user dynamic between actual speakers and their online audience, often evidenced through empirical data, thus plays a crucial interpretive role in delineating the story genres that have been identified in these contexts. The remainder of this essay seeks to open up a dialogue between researchers working in literary-theoretical and discourse-analytic traditions. The guiding assumption is that while the corpus of digital narratives is inescapably heterogenous, such diversity should not lead to disciplinary divides in narrative analysis but rather methodological integration that enriches our understanding of narrative interactivity and interactions in the richly varied world of digital narratives.

Narrative models of interactivity

Interactivity as a general principle is by no means limited to stories told in digital media. Instead, models of communicative interaction underpin the construction of participant roles in many other kinds of narrative. These participant roles are derived from Saussure's idealization of the speech circuit (1983: 11), where the sender and receiver co-participate in transferring a message from one to another, later developed by Jakobson (1960). The structuralist model of transmission accounts for communication events including but not limited to the processes of storytelling. Within narratology, the nomenclature and precise nature of the 'sender' and 'receiver' of the narrative message varies according to medium in which the story is being conveyed and the perspective from which the narrative is being analysed. In treatments of literary text, the sender role distinguishes between authors and narrators, whilst the receivers are narratees and readers.[3] In conversational narratives, the separation of author/narrator is avoided and it is conventional to designate tellers and audience. Regardless of the medium, the communicative framework positions the story as the message being exchanged between participants. In the Saus-

3 See for example the schema outlined by Chatman (1978), reworked by Toolan (2001).

surean speech circuit, the story is not simply passed to a receiver who functions as a passive participant. Rather the audience is anticipated to actively engage with the story in some way, indicated visually in Saussure's model of the speech circuit by the two-way directional trajectory of the lines of telementation between sender and receiver. In practice, the audiences' responses are constituted on numerous and varied levels, from internalised cognitive or emotional reactions to non-verbal physical actions of manipulating a textual interface or verbalised as feedback such as questions, comments and interjections reciprocated to the sender.

Narrative interaction where the story is told using digital technology can be similarly projected using this model, where the reader is positioned as receiving the text in the same way that they might a piece of contemporary literature that "talks" to them (Kacandes 2001). However, there is a wide range of activities that a reader might employ in order to interact with a digital text, many of which are particular to the digital medium. Much discussion has focused on the genres of digital fiction and video games, with their attendant technologies that enable the user to manipulate the textual interface (for example, through the use of keyboards, clicking on a mouse, using a joystick and so on). The necessity of employing these novel physical forms of interaction led early hypertextual critics to endow the reader's navigational responses with creative power, such that Landow renamed them 'wreaders' (1997).

Later work has gone on to distinguish between levels of interactivity that are enabled through digital technology. Ryan (2006) points out that reassembling pre-existing narrative content is not the same as being able to create narrative content itself. She goes on to categorise the qualities of interaction according to four dimensions which she pairs together: internal versus external interaction, exploratory versus ontological interaction. According to these parameters, a reader can participate internally as a member in the storyworld (for example by role-playing an avatar in a simulated story scenario), or they can remain situated outside the storyworld in the external mode. The distinction between exploratory and ontological categories foregrounds navigational interaction. Texts that are structured around exploratory interaction do not allow readers to change the path that narrative events might take: readers can explore the narrative world only. Ontological interaction enables readers to change the course of events within the narrative (for example by choosing one forking path rather than another).

Ryan's model of interactivity, both elegant and widely transferable across forms of digital narrative, is designed for intra-textual forms of interactivity and as such foregrounds the receiver's relationship with the narrative message. Control of the text and the reader's relationship with a created story world lies at the heart of the distinctions in this framework: it was not intended to take into account human-human interactions such as those between the sender and receiver (text creators and audiences). The outcome is that thus far, discussions of interactivity in digital narratology (with its typical focus on electronic literature and gaming) has emphasised the mechanics of navigating the narrative interface and the interpretation of story content, producing a text-immanent model of interaction predicated on the actions of an abstract, individual figure of the (w)reader.[4]

Instead of describing the relationship between users and a narrative world, the interpersonal dynamics of conversational storytelling which might be transferred to computer mediated communication such as the stories told in emails and blogs emphasizes instead the wider, situational context of narration. Thus the analysis of stories told in face-to-face environments focuses much less on the physical means by which narrative production takes place.[5] Social and pragmatic factors also bear on the ways in which an audience might interact with a spoken story. Ryan (2004) points out that "since face-to-face interaction constantly renegotiates the role of the participants, every listener is, at least in principle, a potential storyteller" (41). The audience's contribution to the narrative design is not constrained to waiting to tell a story of their own. Rather, studies of multi-party talk demonstrate the co-constructive participation of listeners in telling stories of shared experience (Georgakopoulou 2007), and that more generally a speaker's awareness of an audience and their face needs can determine the ways in which they makes their story tellable (Labov 1972). The interpersonal and identity work achieved by conversational storytelling may vary according to the speaker's gender, age, ethnicity; the social distance between speaker and listener and the cultural or institutional context in which the story is being told. In contrast to the user-text models of digital narratology, the sociolinguistic analyses of conversational stories are most interested in the connection between storytelling participants (the sender(s) and receiver(s)).

There are good reasons for the differing textual and contextual emphases in digital and conversational treatments of interactivity. Face-to-face and computer-mediated contexts for communication are significantly different from each other. Unlike the shared temporal and physical space of speaker and audience typical of conversational narrative, the asynchronous affordances of online interaction mean that storytelling participants

4 There are empirical studies of actual users' interactions with digital fiction, notably Douglas (1992), Page (2006) and Pope (2007); however, these studies are exceptions to general trends in the treatment of readership in digital narratology.

5 See McNeil and Cassell's (2004) work on gesture as an exception to this.

need not be virtually co-present at the time of communication, nor may speakers necessarily have knowledge of each other from the offline world. Sociolinguistic studies of narrative interaction depend on the identification of speaker variables to delineate contextual information. Empirical studies of online reading interactions (at least of digital fiction) make this kind of speaker identification less easy to establish, first because the profile information of individual readers is not logged simply by visiting a web page and second, the vicissitudes of online representation are such that demographic information is not always reliably indicative of real world speaker attributes.

Despite these medial constraints, the discursive context that emerges from participatory culture means the reader's interaction with the text can now be considered as only one element in the process of storytelling in digital media. While it has always (at least in theory) been possible for readers to communicate directly with the author of a digital narrative, the communicative affordances of web 2.0 technologies (blogs, wikis, social networking sites) provide additional interactive channels that connect authors, readers and other readers. The result is that we need an approach to interaction that examines the reader's relationship with the story content and its digital interface in the wider context of their interactions with other storytelling participants, that is, the other members of the narrative audience and narrative teller.

Narrative interaction and the addition of commentary

The contrast between Ryan's categories of exploratory and ontological interaction signal differing degrees of the reader's influence over the act of narrative production. Exploratory interaction appears to offer only superficial control over determining narrative content, while ontological interaction allows the reader some degree of empowerment.[6] Instead of combining these with internal and external categories, I shift the focus here to explore the differing ways in which exploratory and ontological interaction can be further delineated by drawing on different production-oriented factors which derive from web 2.0 discourse contexts. Consideration of the discourse context is crucial for two reasons. First, these factors provide an additional set of dimensions that can be used to indicate points of commonality and contrast in the increasingly diverse array of narratives

---

6 The extent to which ontological interaction is perceived as empowering by users has been widely contested. See for example Miall (1999).

emerging in digital literature. Second, each of these factors bears on the evolution of a narrative commentary. The commentary may take many forms and be contingent on its source narrative in varying degrees. The potential impact of the user-user created narrative commentary merits further scrutiny.

At first sight, the additional presence of some form of discursive commentary might not appear to be relevant to a typology of narrative interaction. The ability to comment on a story is a well established literary practice, quite distinct from changing or authoring a narrative artefact itself. From this perspective, the reader's contribution to the discourse remains external to and separate from the story text: readers cannot manipulate the content of the narrative which remains under the author's control. Separating narrative from the talk of its discursive context is a model derived from practices of written interaction, where the transaction between author and reader is not situated in a shared, immediate and synchronous discourse context. The discursive capacity of web 2.0 software contrasts with written narrative by creating a dialogic online environment which connects storytelling participants with each other, weaving together the strands of narrative and commentary. Studies of conversational narrative suggest that the co-talk surrounding narrative may shape how the story gets told, and in at least some situations, the contributions to the commentary appear similarly to influence the developing content of digital narratives. The forms that the commentary might take and the extent to which these influence narrative development will vary according to the precise nature of the discourse situation. Three characteristics of the discourse space are of importance here, namely the mechanism used for constructing the commentary, the type of audience involved in the discussion and the qualities of narrative that is being commented on.

Mechanisms for interaction

Although readers may elect not to leave any feedback, many web 2.0 technologies routinely generate templates for readers to send messages to the text author. The feedback can come in many quasi-conversational formats of computer mediated communication, from comments on blog posts, to wall posts on social network sites, to talk pages on a wiki or posts within a discussion forum. These response mechanisms can be distinguished from each other in various ways. The response may either be sent privately to a named individual, or it may be published so that other readers may also see the comment. Relatedly, the response mechanisms may enable either dyadic interaction (for example between a single reader and author) or between multiple parties. Thus a single-authored blog post might attract numerous responses from many different readers while the talk pages of a collaborative project like a wiki enable discussion between many co-writers and their readers. These characteristics combine to form increasingly collaborative opportunities for narrative interaction, where the most open access, multiparty interactions come closest to the workings of participatory culture, while private, dyadic interaction is further away.

The feedback mechanisms used by the reader may be more or less closely tied by thematic content and technical format to the original narrative contribution made by the author. Some environments provide more than one feedback channel for participants. For example in Facebook, an author may post a fragment of their life history in a status update. The audience can respond to the status update in various ways: by privately emailing the author, by filling in a comment slot immediately attached to the update, by posting a separate, public message on the author's 'wall', by engaging in online chat with the author or giving face-to-face feedback at some later point in the offline world. In wikis, the contributors may develop narrative content on the main pages, but discuss that narrative content on talk pages of different kinds (associated either with the content of particular page, or with the profile page of a wiki contributor). The various feedback mechanisms have differing degrees of structural dependency on the original narrative content.

Although all responses can be interpreted as second parts of an adjacency pair initiated by the story segment, the format of some response mechanisms is such that they cannot be divorced from their first part, while other communicative channels are free-standing and can serve multiple purposes. For example, a comment slot (say appended to a blog post) can only be a secondary contribution responding to an original text of some kind. Comment slots are always textually adjacent to the material upon which they comment and cannot exist on their own. In contrast, a wall post in a social networking site, or a post to a discussion forum can be used by a reader to provide feedback on a narrative, but need not be textually adjacent to it and could be used to contribute opinions or requests less directly connected to the narrative content. The outcome is that the commentary may vary in how centrally connected it is to the narrative content. The closer the commentary's textual and thematic connection to the narrative segment, the greater the potential the reader's interaction has to shape the evolving narrative text.

Interactional context: a sense of audience

Studies of face-to-face narration have long recognised the potential influence of the audience's role in shaping the discourse context. Similarly, in online contexts, authors publish their stories with a sense of anticipated audience. But the nature of audiences in networked publics like the internet is unpredictable, being characterised instead by invisibility (boyd 2008). Not all readers will engage with a text or other readers in the same way, and it is misleading to imagine a homogenous textual community. Readers might choose to view a narrative in the public domain but never leave an explicit trace of their identity (other than that tracked by a page view). Given the inequality of online participation (Nielsen 2006), it would seem that the majority of online audiences are lurkers who remain present with but unknowable by the author of an online story.

The extent to which the 'non-lurking' members of the audience makes their identity known to other storytelling participants can also vary. Even when a reader might leave a verbal trace of their interaction with a text, the nature of online representation means that the reader's real world identity need not always be explicitly indicated. Conventions of self disclosure vary considerably from adopting a non-realistic avatar in virtual worlds like Second Life, to use of playful, ironic or deceptive use of pseudonyms in the blogosphere to the high levels of personal authenticity typical in social networking sites like Facebook.

The boundaries that define the nature of the audience range between completely open access to being controlled by privacy settings. In the open access domains, it is impossible for the narrator to estimate accurately who the readers are that might engage with their story. However, if privacy controls are set, then those moderating the site have a clearer picture of their potential audience. The teller's sense of audience also varies according to how far the virtual audience overlaps with people known by the storyteller in offline contexts. For example, the privacy controls available on the social network site, Facebook, mean that users are most likely to tell their life story to a Friend list of individuals they have already met in the offline world (Ellison et al. 2006). In contrast, the open access of the blogosphere means that many readers might never meet in person the tellers of the personal stories they read in online journals. Even if the storyteller has delimited the scope of their readership to persons they know, the audience might still conflate groups of individuals normally segmented in offline contexts. The mismatch between intended and actual audiences coupled with the variation in degrees of narrative interaction presents new contextual challenges for storytelling in networked publics.

However, the demographic nature of the intended and actual audience can significantly influence the socio-pragmatic nature of the story's commentary. Writers clearly draw on a range of discursive strategies in their production and reception of stories that are designed to serve varying functions. The desire to meet the face needs of the other storytelling participants, such as building solidarity between storyteller and audience, or in different contexts to carry out the rather more face-threatening acts such as critiquing another's work are likely to be modified in relation to the extent to which the speaker and audience know each other (or at least perceive that they do). The meta-commentary thus becomes a dialogic space in which the interpersonal work of storytelling is extended and refined.

Narrative characteristics

The interaction provided by readers via the feedback mechanisms can function in many different ways, for example to express disapproval or support for a narrator or their writing, to provide suggestions for further revision or new narrative material. However, the extent to which the commentary created by these interactions actually influences narrative content depends critically on the qualities of the story being told. Above all else, for the ommentary to bear on story content, the narration and its commentary must take place in a serial form that is created over time. Completed narratives that are posted in their entirety are unlikely to be revised and then reposted, even in the light of published review comments. Instead, when stories evolve over time, there are opportunities for the commentary to influence the way that material is developed. The contrast between fanfiction and collaborative writing on wikis illustrates this difference. Thomas's (forthcoming) analysis of Harry Potter fandoms found that although reviewing fanfiction was a crucial dynamic of participating in this storytelling community, the critiques left for individual writers rarely resulted in the writer returning to a story and redrafting it. Perhaps this is in part because the transactional nature of storytelling in fanfiction communities is created not only by exchanging email and reviews but by writing new stories in response to those comments (Kaveney 2005). Nonetheless, it is at least theoretically possible for a fanfiction writer to revise successive drafts of their work, and so it is perhaps surprising that they do not appear to do so. In the case of stories that are written episodically over a period of time, the critique offered by readers during that process is intended to influence revision to existing and development of subsequent narrative material in the same text. The wiki novel talk pages in *A Million Penguins* demonstrate this principle at work, where co-writers put forward multiple (and sometimes conflicting) suggestions for how the content of the novel should emerge. Some of these suggestions were ignored, others were taken up, but regardless, the emergent nature of the narration made intervention via the commentary possible.

The ontological status of the story being told determines both the nature of the interaction provided in the commentary and the subsequent influence of commentary on later narrative reports. It is not only fictional stories that are created in web 2.0 environments. In increasing measure, individuals use web 2.0 technologies to document their lives, telling anecdotes on personal blogs, discussion forums and in fragmented forms through microblogging or social network sites. Typically, autobiographical stories told on the web show their allegiance to offline forms of diary writing and conversation through their use of episodic formats. In online contexts, the serial nature of the discourse creation is assumed to keep approximate pace with the personal events being reported. Thus blogs usually report on the near (rather than distant) past events while status updates of sites like Twitter and Facebook are even closer to the present moment in their public announcement of what the author is doing 'right now'. Of course, the present tense typically found in these autobiographical fragments[7] creates only an illusion of simultaneity between narration and life event: the events are not usually reported exactly in real time. Nonetheless, the relative lack of retrospection typical of many personal narratives found online is important for the impact of commentary. In the absence of a pre-determined narrative design arranged around a fixed teleological focus, the reader's feedback is experienced as an intervention in the present moment which stimulates the ongoing production and anticipation of future updates from the author.

---

7 For example, Facebook updates predominantly favour the present tense combined with the progressive aspect, perhaps because of the template prompt for the update which is framed by the author's name and the verb participle 'is'.

The categories of interaction revisited

User-text interaction	*Contextual factors influencing user-user interation*		
	Feedback mechanism	*Network characteristics*	*Narrative characteristics*
Exploratory	No feedback possible	Degree of open access enabled	Serial narration
Ontological	Degree of public viewing available for feedback (e.g. private email, public wall posts)	Extent to which virtual and offline worlds overlap	Temporal orientation of narrative (e.g. retrospective, prospective etc.)
	Number of participants involved in the feedback (e.g. dyadic interchanges, multiparty interaction)	Perceived demographic profile of network (if known)	Fictional status
	Synchronous / Asynchronous timing of feedback		
	How closely feedback is tied to originating narrative unit (e.g. comment slots, wall posts etc.)		

The facets of web 2.0 feedback mechanisms, networks and narrative characteristics are summarised in Table 1. The user-centred features listed in these three categories operate in addition to the binary distinction between exploratory and ontological interaction (signalled in the first column on the left of the table). The dimensions of user-text and user-user interaction may be combined in open-ended configurations. Thus a given genre may be categorised as exhibiting either exploratory or ontological interaction in conjunction with any number of features drawn from each of the user-centred categories. These combinations might variously emphasise the importance and richness of the discourse context. For example, a genre might be characterised by exploratory interaction (thereby allowing the user minimal navigational control of the narrative content) and combine this with relatively low user-user interaction. The hyperfiction *Cruising* by Ingrid Ankerson and Megan Sapnar illustrates this combination. The hyperfiction scrolls by without intervention from the reader (exploratory interaction). There are no feedback mechanisms for readers to contact the authors or to collaboratively review the piece. By way of contrast, other hyperfictions do allow greater degrees of user-user interaction. *Inanimate Alice* by Kate Pullinger employs similar exploratory interaction (the reader clicks and the animated screens roll). However, there is also an email link inviting readers to 'tell me what you think' about the stories. But this email is dyadic, connecting only one individual with another, located in personal email accounts and isolated from the fictional narrative which, although published episode by episode, does not allow the readers to review its production.

By way of contrast, ontological interaction where the reader may control the content of the narrative itself (both through navigational choices but also adding their own narrative content) might be combined by complex, overt user-user interaction that produces an influential commentary directly impacting the narrative itself. Examples of this kind of user-centred narrative are found in collaborative storytelling communities, of which *Protagonize* is a recent example. Here the readers can both navigate and add to the narrative content in a discursive environment in which publicly viewed feedback between multiple readers is directly linked via comment posts to the story episodes. As the stories are posted in serial fashion, the comment posts not only review existing narrative material, but make suggestions about what should get told next. In addition, although this storytelling community is primarily constituted through virtual connections, it is one in which the participants exhibit a high degree of apparent authenticity in self-representation. Profile pages include uploaded photographs of writers, along with details of their real-world location and other demographic information.

These initial narrative examples should not be taken as posing a fixed, binary opposition between high and low parameters of user-user interaction. Instead, the nuanced range of variation between different kinds of user interactions should be regarded as multifaceted. Thus blogs and fanfiction are characterised by the same exploratory textual interaction where readers can navigate through the archives of textual segments (blog posts, fanfiction) posted by an author, but the readers cannot change the blog post or fanfiction story themselves. Likewise, both blogs and fanfiction have the same level of interactive feedback channels (comments and email), but the nature of the narratives in these environments is quite different. Personal narratives on blogs are serial, prospective and taken to be non-fiction. In contrast, fanfiction is usually posted in its entirety, narrated retrospectively and fictional in nature. Although the personal narratives told on sites like Facebook are similar to blogs in narrative characteristic (personal, serial and prospective), the interactive possibilities of social networking sites are far richer (including online chat, email, public wall posts and comments) than blogs (which offer only comments or email). The networks of the blogosphere and the social networking site are also different. Facebook allows users to set varying degrees of privacy controls, and the user typically also knows their audience in the offline world, whereas blogs may be open to the public whom the blogger might never meet in person. This may not influence the degree to which a reader can navigate a text, but it certainly alters the levels of personal disclosure and tellability in the personal narratives told in each context. The interrelationship between discursive situation, commentary and emergent narrative form is exemplified in more detail in two contexts that serve as a salutary reminder that there is no isomorphic relationship between discourse feature and social function. One case study illustrates how personal narratives of illness are being reworked in the blogosphere, while the other demonstrates the significance of online talk in the evolution of collaborative fiction.

Personal narratives: the importance of comments in cancer blogs

Since the mid–1990s, the blogosphere has provided an increasing environment for writers to share their life experiences, such that personal blogs are now more frequent than other sub-genres of blogs (Herring et al 2004). Autobiographical blog writing can be of many different kinds. Here I focus on one subgenre: the narrative of illness (specifically, cancer). For those confronting the trauma of critical illness, the blogosphere has become both a space for therapeutic self-expression, a source of lay medical information and online support which carries particular import. The relationship between commentary and narrative found in the sample of cancer blogs discussed here should thus be understood within this localised context, rather than typical of all personal blogs. The examples are taken from a fuller study in which over two hundred blog posts from twenty blogs were analysed, equally authored by women and men, all of whom were undergoing treatment for cancer (Page 2008, forthcoming).

Like the majority of personal blogs, the cancer blogs studied here were single authored, openly available in the public domain and enabled feedback from readers by means of a comment appended to individual blog posts. Although the bloggers were writing individually, they told their stories with a clear sense of being connected to an online community. This community was situated in a wider audience unconstrained by privacy controls, open to anyone with access to the internet. However, the linking patterns as indicated through hyperlinks on the blog home pages indicate that the cancer blogs in this sample were densely connected within the blogosphere to the personal writing of other bloggers undergoing similar critical illness. The evidence suggests that the perceived audience for these cancer blogs is primarily a virtual community, brought together around a shared personal concern of dealing with critical illness.

The stories told on the cancer blogs are assumed to be non-fictional representations of actual life experiences.[8] The serial episodes of being diagnosed with, treated for and in some cases recovering from cancer are documented in real time and have a strongly prospective quality as the authors locate their current experiences in relation to anticipated future events (of treatment, death or recovery). Because the personal narratives being reported are assumed to be representations of actual events in the author's lifeworld, the feedback offered by readers is not a critique of the author's writing or suggestions for how the plot might develop. Instead, readers offer opinions, support and advice that appear intended to impact the present and future life experiences of the author. The commentary in this sample contained many responses from readers expressing shared emotional responses to intended to support the authors. For example, one reader commented on the blogger Sylvie Fortman's writing, saying:

> We don't know each other, but I do know what you're going through. What you're doing is called "participating in life"–it's what keeps you alive, keeps you going during this tumultuous time. What you need to know is that this is a special time… a you time (commenter anonymous).

In turn, the commentary clearly shaped what the bloggers chose to write about next, for example to express gratitude for support or to follow up on suggestions, or to anticipate the reader's desire to know how particular events had turned out.

> A few of you wanted me to let you know how things went today, on my first day of chemo. I appreciate your support more than I can explain. I thought I'd let you know how things are going. David Hahn (29 July 2005)

---

8 There was no evidence that any of the authors were engaging in role play. Conventions of authenticity in the blogosphere are such that any breaches are treated rightly in pejorative terms as hoaxes.

As these examples suggest, the readers' comments on personal blogs appear to have a socio-pragmatic influence that extends beyond the formal categories of digital interaction.

There is some evidence that the socio-pragmatic function of the narrative discourse may vary according to the demographic profile of the community in which the storytelling takes place. In the sample of cancer blogs, women were twice as likely to provide comments as were the men, especially added to blog posts written by other women. Although the density of commentary does not directly impact the narrative content, it is notable that patterns of interaction between users also bears on narrative style. In this case, where women readers generated increased levels of supportive commentary, high levels of evaluation (Labov 1972) also appeared in the stories told by women authors (Page 2008 and forthcoming), exaggerating the affective and interpersonal dimension of personal storytelling. The commentary's social function of building solidarity between audience and teller correlates with the story genres typically found in these contexts, such as anecdotes (Martin and Plum 1997), said also to foster a shared sense of connection between speaker and listener.

Collaborative fiction: Commentary in *A Million Penguins*

The ability to collaborate with other readers in online environments is not exclusive to blogs and is also characteristic of wikis. A wiki is a web page that users can edit as well as view. The first example was developed by Ward Cunningham in 1995, who coined the term 'wiki wiki' from the Hawaiian word for 'quickly', reflecting the rapidity with which users could edit content. Wiki design is strongly influenced by open source principles, where the emphasis is on the emerging contribution of a community rather than individual authorship. This is reflected in two factors that are important for evaluating narrative interaction. First, wiki pages are accompanied by discussion areas (either appended comment slots or talk pages) for users to create additional commentary where the development of the wiki pages is charted. Second, authorship of wiki content is not usually named on the main pages by the individual writer. Instead, individual interaction is identified by the page histories that document all revisions to that part of the wiki. The result is a dual layer of narrative interaction. The main pages of the wiki provide a forum where many users can interact with a single text, eventually forming a composite narrative from which it is not always possible (at least on the surface) to identify the precise contributions of individual writers. The discussion pages provide the platform for writers to interact with each other, generating an evolutionary commentary that documents the unfolding story of how the text has been created through the process of collaboration.

Wiki software is not confined to creating a particular text type. Although there are well documented principles of what might constitute a successful wiki (Mader 2008), many different narrative and non-narrative genres might be created using wiki technology. The features of wiki software in general cannot then be mapped uniformly against the text-immanent categories of interaction. For example, the varying degrees of access to a wiki might constrain the user's choice between exploratory or ontological interaction. Wikis offer users varying degrees of participation ranging from read only options (allowing the user to navigate content but not edit the pages) to editing roles (which allows users to edit the content) to administrative roles (which designates authority to disallow access to the text altogether). The distinctive contribution that wiki technology makes to narrative interaction is its editable nature. Other linear collaborative narratives such as 'addventure' [sic] genres offer the user ontological interactivity by enabling them to add new content, but do not allow changes to be made to preceding chapters written by other authors. In contrast, the editing capacity of wikis is far more radical, enabling users to alter any and all content, regardless of the content's position or original authorship.

The editorial interaction afforded by wiki technology would seem to be at odds with the factors which promote the creation of coherent narrative patterns. Narrative design usually operates as a top-down process, where story production unfolds in a linear progression. If stories are told by more than a single author, successful collaboration is associated with a strong social contract between tellers, for example agreeing on common principles regarding overall narrative scope and responsibility or respect for another's contribution to the work (Rettberg, forthcoming). In contrast, the possibilities of wiki editing are not limited by linearity. Earlier story content can be changed or even removed altogether, so that a unified sense of progressive trajectory is undermined and chains of character reference dissolved. The basic narrative requirement that the reader be able to keep track of who is doing what to whom (Longacre 1983) is potentially open to considerable threat. Such risk is amplified when a wiki is public. Co-writers may not know each other, disclose their real identity or have any contact beyond that centered on the wiki. The likelihood of a shared social contract for storytelling, let alone an agreed narrative design is extremely low and the possibility of anarchy and vandalism high. Despite these constraints, world leading publishers Penguin along with faculty from the Institute of Creative Technologies at De Montfort University in the United Kingdom recently ran an ambitious experiment to see whether it was possible to create a narrative in a large-scale, public wiki environment. The result was *A Million Penguins*.

A Million Penguins was launched on February 1st 2007, closing to contributions on March 7th 2007. During that period, it attracted considerable attention, having been viewed by at least 75 000 different people and edited over 11 000 times. Built from an initial sentence taken from *Jane Eyre*, 'There was no possibility of taking a walk that day', the final wiki novel consisted of over 1000 pages, nearly half of which (491) contained some kind of narrative content (Mason and Thomas 2008). The infrastructure of *A Million Penguins* was built using Media wiki software, and contained the usual pages for content (Main pages) and discussion (Talk pages), along with User pages which held information about the writers. Although the software was typical, *A Million Penguins* is an unusual wiki. The presence of a major publishing body is not only a rare intervention in the realm of digital fiction, but also a significant attraction for aspiring writers who might desire a platform to showcase their work (Mason and Thomas 2008), perhaps leading to the international scale of the audience who engaged in some measure with the wiki novel. While not typical of wikis in general, the user interactions with *A Million Penguins* is a rich source of data for exploring how users interacted with the text and each other and for speculating on the impact that such interaction had on narrative form.

Instead of a single wiki novel, *A Million Penguins* is better understood as a space that enabled many kinds of narrative experimentation. The different narratives that emerged in *A Million Penguins* could be distinguished according to their content using conventional generic categories (science fiction, women's writing, choose your own adventure) and also according to the way that users interacted with them. Some of the most productive (and coherent) storylines were created on wiki pages described as 'walled gardens' (Mason and Thomas 2008), that is, areas of the wiki that were not connected via hyperlinks to a range of other main pages. These walled gardens did not exhibit high levels of user-text interaction (page views or edits). In contrast, the most frequently viewed and edited page of the wiki, 'Welcome' was a site where narrative chaos was found in rapidly changing character names and story content.

Increased editing in *A Million Penguins* did not mean that the story was progressively unfolding in a coherent arc of additional, temporally organised events. Rather, the intensive editing was evidence of the constant (and sometimes subversive) revision to an initial textual base from which a coherent narrative could not be generated. The correlation between editing frequency and narrative style in *A Million Penguins* thus appears to be that the higher the level of editorial interaction, the less likelihood that those edits would produce a coherent narrative in this context. The more frequently the main narrative was revised, the more competing users became frustrated and subsequently disengaged with the writing process, as the following two extracts from the commentary on the talk pages illustrate.

> Too late for me. I left for a weekend, and *everything* was different when I got back. Really, only the URL and the underlying software was the same. There's really no point to staying involved if this project moves away from cohesion as it progresses....--*Gamblor856* 00:10, 12 February 2007 (EST)

> WHOA! A whole lot can happen in a day can't it? Seems like a totally different story now, and although I've made relatively few contributions thus far, seeing how much has changed makes me feel weirdly shunted out... hmmm *Beldarin* 15:35, 3 February 2007 (EST)

The correlation between high editorial interaction and low narrative coherence may well be due to the nature of the group of users brought together in the enterprise of this wiki novel. Unlike the success of collaborative ventures between known authors, the lack of a social contract between the writers in *A Million Penguins* was accompanied by moments of tension and conflict over editorial behaviour, referred to by one user as a "tug of war" that was "hard to cope with".[9] The commentary in the talk pages contain many examples where writers took issue with the editorial interventions of another, of which the following example is just one of many:

> am sorry but I frankly think you are missing the point of the whole excercise. If you want to bring people back you can, but you cannot expect others to follow with your idea of how things should go (Alex Bunker – 4 Feb 2007, How many pages)

The group of users contributing to the wiki novel not only failed to share an agreed set of principles for interacting with each other's text, but were in direct conflict with each other, in what one of the editorial team from De Montfort University described as a kind of "wiki war". The correlation between frequency of editorial action and lack of narrative coherence should not then be generalised beyond this context as an inescapable constraint of wiki-type software. Wiki novel experiments between other kinds of communities of writers might produce very different correlations between interaction and narrative production. Whether or not *A Million Penguins* should be regarded as a failed experiment in narrativity depends very much on the perspective taken. As Mason and Thomas (2008) point

---

9 <http://www.amillionpenguins.com/wiki/index.php/Talk:Welcome#How_many_pages>

out, metaphors of Bakhtinian carnivalesque are more productive for understanding the artistic merits of this conceptual experiment. My point here is not to ascribe a value judgement to this wiki novel, but rather to signal the important role that the conflicts signalled in the commentary (user-user interaction) seem to bear on the potential for conventional user-text interactions with the narrative itself.

Conclusion

I have argued that the participatory culture typical of stories told in web 2.0 contexts require an enriched model of interactivity where the individual's manipulation of the textual interface and story content are complimented by analysis of factors in the surrounding discursive context. The feedback channels, the nature of the audience and the episodic nature of the storytelling process all bear on the interactions between tellers and their audiences, which in turn have the potential to influence emerging narrative forms. Factors from the discourse context may combine with either exploratory or ontological interaction in varying, multifaceted configurations. Although these configurations cannot be plotted against each other in fixed oppositions, it is clear that some narrative genres emphasise the influential role of user-user interactions while other genres appear more decontextualised. The brief analyses of interaction in the personal blogs and wiki novel clearly demonstrate that although an enriched approach to interaction can be used to draw comparisons between different types of stories in online contexts, there is no simple correlation between levels of interactive talk between users and a single impact on narrative form. Isomorphic mappings of user-user interaction and pragmatic impact cannot be sustained. In the sample of cancer blog stories, high levels of commentary indicated increased solidarity between teller and audience and were mirrored by the use of story genres that promoted strong social cohesion. In contrast, the high frequency of editorial intervention on the wiki novel *A Million Penguins* was mirrored by heated debates in the wiki talk pages. The conflicts played out in the meta-commentary were symptomatic of the un-collaborative nature of the wiki's open authorship, resulting in the multi-stranded, non-coherent character of the narrative that emerged in the wiki talk pages. Just as stories told in digital media contest the notion of a uniform narrative canon, so the talk that surrounds them can be equally heterogenous in form and function. As new forms of interaction and narrative emerge in the future, no doubt we will need to revise our notions of interactivity once again.

References

A Million Penguins. http://www.Amillionpenguins.com, 2008.

Aldama, Frederick (2003). *Postethnic Narrative Criticism: Magicorealism in Ana Castillo, Hanif Kureishi, Julie Dash, Oscar "Zeta" Acosta, and Salman Rushdie* University of Texas Press.

Ankerson, Ingrid, and Megan Sapnar (2001). "Cruising." http://www.poemsthatgo.com/gallery/spring2001/crusing-launch.html.

Barthes, Roland (1977). *Image-Music-Text*, translated by Stephen Heath, London: Fontana.

Bell, Alice (2010). *The Possible Worlds of Hypertext Fiction*. Basingstoke: Palgrave.

Blum-Kulka, S. (1993). "'You Gotta Know How to Tell a Story': Telling, Tales and Tellers in American and Israeli Narrative Events at Dinner." *Language in Society* 22: 361–402.

boyd, danah m. (2008). "Taken out of context: American teen sociality in networked publics." Ph.D. diss. University of California, Berkeley.

Douglas, Jane Yellowlees (1992). "Print pathways and interactive labyrinths: How hypertext narratives affect the act of reading." PhD diss., New York University, New York.

Ellison, Nicole, Charles Steinfield, and Cliff Lampe (2006). "The Benefits of Facebook 'Friends': Social Capital and College Students' Use of Online Social Network Sites." *JCMC* 12 (4).

Ensslin, Astrid (2007). *Canonizing Hypertext: Explorations and Constructions*. London: Continuum.

Friedman, Susan S. (1996). "Spatialization, Narrative Theory, and Virginia Woolf's The Voyage Out." In: *Ambiguous Discourse: Feminist Narratology and British Women Writers*. Chapel Hill and London: The University of North Carolina Press, 109–136.

Georgakopoulou, Alexandra (2007). *Small Stories, Interaction and Identities*. Amsterdam: Benjamins.

Herring, Susan C., Scheidt, Lois Ann, Bonus, Sabrina and Wright, Elijah (2004). "Bridging the gap: A genre analysis of weblogs." In: *Proceedings of the 37th Hawai'i International Conference on System Sciences* (*HICSS*–37). Los Alamitos: IEEE Computer Society Press.

Hutcheon, Linda (2006). *Adaptation*. London and NY: Routledge.

Jenkins, Henry (2006). *Convergence Culture: Where Old and New Media Collide*. New York and London: New York University Press.

Kacandes, Irene (2001). *Talk Fiction: Literature and the Talk Explosion*. Lincoln: University of Nebraska Press.

Kaveney, Roz (2005). "The Democratic Genre: Fanfiction in a Literary Context by Sheenagh Pugh: The Alternative Universe of Elizabeth Bennet, Blake's 7, and Buffy." In: *The Independent* (online). http://www.independent.co.uk/arts_entertainment/books/reviews/the democratic_genre_fan_fiction_in_a_literary_context_by_Sheenagh_Pugh_509801.html.

Kress, Gunther, and Theo van Leeuwen (2001). *Multimodal Discourse: The Modes and Media of Contemporary Communication*. London: Hodder Arnold.

Labov, William and J. Waletzky (1967). "Narrative Analysis: Oral Versions of Personal Experience." In: J. Helm (ed.) *Essays on the Verbal and Visual Arts: Proceedings of the 1966 Annual Spring Meeting of the American Ethnological Society*. Seattle: University of Washington Press, 12–44.

Labov, William (1972). "The Transformation of Experience in Narrative Syntax." In: *Language in the Inner City*. Philadelphia: University of Pennsylvania Press, 354–96.

Landow, George P. (1997). *Hypertext 2.0: the convergence of contemporary critical theory and technology*. Baltimore: Johns Hopkins University Press (first published 1992).

Lanser, Susan (1986). "Toward a Feminist Narratology." *Style* 20 (3): 341–363.

Longacre, Robert (1983). *The Grammar of Discourse*. New York and London: Plenum.

Mader, S. (2007). *Wikipatterns: A Practical Guide to Improving Productivity and Collaboration in your Organization*. Indianapolis, IN: Wiley.

Martin, Jim and Plum, Gunther A. (1997). "Construing Experience: Some Story Genres." *Journal of Narrative and Life History* 7 (1–4): 299–308.

Mason, Bruce and Thomas, Sue (2008). *A Million Penguins Research Report*. http://www.ioct.dmu.ac.uk/projects/amillionpenguinsreport.pdf.

McLellan, Faith (1997). "'A whole other story': The Electronic Narrative of Illness." *Literature and Medicine* 16 (1): 88–107.

Miall, David (1999). "Trivializing or Liberating? The Limitations of Hypertext Theorizing." *Mosaic* 32: 157–172.

Murray, Janet H. (1997). *Hamlet on the Holodeck: The Future of Narrative in Cyberspace*. Cambridge, Massachusetts: MIT Press.

Nielsen, Jakob (2006). "Participation Inequality: Encouraging More Users to Contribute." *Alertbox*. http://www.useit.com/alertbox/participation_inequality.html.

Norrick, Neal (2000). *Conversational Narrative*. Amsterdam: Benjamins, 2000.

Ong, Walter J. (1982). *Orality and Literacy: The Technologizing of the Word*. London: Methuen.

Page, Ruth (2006). *Literary and Linguistic Approaches to Feminist Narratology*. Basingstoke: Palgrave.

– (2008). "Gender and Genre Revisited: Storyworlds in Personal Blogs." In: Will Slocombe (ed.): *Narratives and New Media* (special issue of *GENRE: Forms of Discourse and Culture*), XII: 151–177.

– (2010). *New Perspectives on Narrative and Multimodality*. London and New York: Routledge.

– (forthcoming). "Blogging on the Body: Gender and Narrative" In: *New Narratives: Stories and Storytelling in the Digital Age*. Ruth Page and Bronwen Thomas (eds.): Lincoln: University of Nebraska Press.

Pope, James A. (2007). How do readers interact with hypertext fiction? An empirical study of readers' reactions to interactive narrative. Unpublished PhD thesis, University of Bournemouth.

Pullinger, Kate and Joseph, Chris. *Inanimate Alice*. http://www.inanimatealice.com/

Rettberg, Scott (forthcoming), "All Together Now: Hypertext, Collective Narratives, and Online Collective Knowledge Communities." In: Ruth Page and Bronwen Thomas (eds.). *New Narratives: Stories and Storytelling in the Digital Age*. Lincoln: University of Nebraska Press.

Ryan, Marie-Laure (2004). *Narrative Across Media: The Languages of Storytelling*. Lincoln: University of Nebraska Press.

– (2006). *Avatars of Story*. Minneapolis: University of Minnesota Press.

– (forthcoming). "The Interactive Onion: Layers of User Participation in Digital Narrative Texts." In: Ruth Page and Bronwen Thomas (eds.). *New Narratives: Stories and Storytelling in the Digital Age*. Lincoln: University of Nebraska Press.

Saussure, Ferdinand de (1983). *Course in General Linguistics.* Translated and annotated by Roy Harris. London: Duckworth.
Thomas, Bronwen (forthcoming). "'Update Soon!' Harry Potter Fanfiction and Narrative as a Participatory Process." In: Ruth Page and Bronwen Thomas (eds.). *New Narratives: Stories and Storytelling in the Digital Age.* Lincoln: University of Nebraska Press.
Toolan, Michael (2001). *Narrative: A Critical Linguistic Introduction.* Second edition. London and NY: Routledge.
Walker Rettberg, Jill (2003). "Fiction and Interaction: How Clicking a Mouse can Make you Part of a Fictional World." D. Art. thesis, Department of Humanistics, University if Bergen.
Walker Rettberg, Jill (2008). *Blogging.* Cambridge: Polity.

David Ciccoricco
(University of Otago)

Games of Interpretation and a Graphophiliac God of War

It is ultra-violent, inescapably sexist, and even contains a bed chamber scene that might be just a few camera frames away from x-rated. Blood is spilled by the barrel, and enemies are ripped apart without mercy and, in some cases, without regard for the laws of physics. According to director David Jaffe, the objective of *God of War* (2005), a third-person action adventure game released by Sony for the PlayStation 2, was to tap into the player's sense of inner rage ("Making" 2005). Kratos, the game's protagonist, is by all appearances an appropriate vehicle for this end. A commander in the Spartan army bound by a dark oath to Ares, the Greek god of war, Kratos slices up his victims by swinging a pair of table-sized blades that are engulfed in flames when in use. They are also attached to chains affixed permanently to his forearms by a searing of the flesh (all part of the oath), allowing him to swing them at a great distance. He does so with a technique that is at once acrobatic and insanely brutal, often with an earth-shuddering roar for added effect. Everything happens in nearly seamless high resolution, the result of some of the most advanced graphical work in the industry at the time. The cutthroat realism, coupled with an award-winning soundtrack, offer what can be an intensely immersive experience of combat and chaos.

But what then are we to make of the moment early on in the game's progression when Kratos, his ship docked at the gates of a war-torn Athens, pauses in front of a book resting open on a pedestal? The player discovers, by calling up a papyrus-styled text that appears at the bottom of screen, that this is "your" journal. We learn that "today's entry" reads: "Hear my prayers Athena. When will these visions end?" Not only is our ruthless hero deeply troubled by chronic psychoses and a profound guilt-complex, he is compelled to regularly take time out of his hectic routine and *write it all down*. What are we to make of this markedly literate moment of self-reflection in one of the most extreme hack and slash video games yet produced?

Perhaps we should be asking a broader question first: what are we doing reflecting on our hero's act of reflection? In creating more realistic and more compelling gaming experiences, *God of War* belongs to a family of games that exploit not just technical affordances but also narrative and, indeed, literary ones. Such titles are not simply video games with appealing stories, but games in which story mechanics and game mechanics are integrated, interdependent, and ultimately inseparable when it comes to understanding how and why we play them.[1] Narratological and exegetical readings of video games work toward this understanding. *God of War* in particular lends itself to a rich narratological and critical analysis. Specifically, this paper uses: 1) familiar theories of narrative discourse to illuminate the highly sophisticated story progression/regression of the game; 2) cognitive-based (or what has come to be called post-classical) narrative theory to produce a reading of the player / player character dynamic; and finally, 3) a critical analysis to reveal the way in which the game's literary self-consciousness is reinforced on a thematic level, an analysis no doubt encouraged by a hero who himself reflects, and writes.

I. Storied Rewards

Familiar concepts from classical narrative theory go a long way toward explaining the narrative mechanics of *God of War*, which are by no means straightforward. The game contains seven embedded flashbacks (or analepses), one culminating series of flashforwards (or prolepses), and one pivotal narrative recursion. These scenes are delivered as pre-rendered cinematic material, commonly called *cinematics* or *cut scenes*, and they

---

1 There has been considerable debate on the place of interpretation and exegesis in games and gaming environments. But it is by now a given that some games place a heavier investment in story dynamics, pursuing what Marie-Laure Ryan (2006: 183) refers to as an "elective affinity" between video games and narrative. Jesper Juul (2005: 132) has also brought more precision to the discussion by dubbing games invested in the presentation of a coherent fictional world "Coherent World Games," a distinction that applies across commercial blockbusters released on popular platforms and art games freely available online. Radical ludology persists, nonetheless, and McKenzie Wark's *Gamer Theory* (2007) is a prime example. A brilliant work that is illuminating both theoretically and rhetorically, *Gamer Theory* does its part to portray an emergent gamer imaginary. In the process, it does not resist the temptation to exclude narrative and the "literary or cinematic imagination" from the realm of what makes video games meaningful. In a discussion of the game *Vice City*, for example, the fictional crime-world is "just a means to discover an algorithm" (120); in a discussion of the game *Rez*, "the storyline is the gamer's alibi" (142) and, later, "the bad faith of the game" (142); and, finally, he states that if we read a game as if it were a novel or a movie "it seems ridiculous" (142). Reading narrative across media is what is at stake, though some of Wark's comments on this matter are unconvincing in their own right: after all, some novels, when read as novels, "seem ridiculous."

are interspersed amid the gameplay as the player progresses through the various levels. The flashbacks, in particular, are in fact cut scenes nested in longer cut scenes that occur in the diegetic present. They consist of representational material, but vary in nature from realistic to surreal; that is, some depict segments of events that one can reasonably assume have happened at some earlier point in the backstory, whereas others depict highly-stylized nightmarish scenes that are better understood as traumatic visions. For example, in one we see Kratos screaming, some 10 years before the diegetic present, as the chains that will allow him to wield his new "Blades of Chaos" are seared permanently into his arms. By contrast, in another we see his wife and daughter against a fiery, groundless backdrop suggesting a place at once everywhere and nowhere, chastising her warrior husband before blood streams forth from her eyes, covering her face in the manner of grotesque time-lapse photography.

Whether or not they explicitly evoke his trauma, all of the flashbacks in the game are at least loosely framed as representations of Kratos' consciousness. The opening cinematic shows a troubled protagonist attempting suicide by leaping off the bluffs overlooking the Aegean Sea. We hear an authorial narrator in voiceover:

> And Kratos cast himself from the highest mountain in all of Greece. After 10 years of suffering, 10 years of endless nightmares, it would finally come to an end. Death would be his escape from madness...
>
> But it had not always been this way. Kratos had once been a champion of the gods...

Before we see the outcome of that decidedly final act, we are transported, via a title card, "3 Weeks Earlier" to "The Aegean Sea." The gameplay proper spans three weeks of "story-time" in Rimmon-Kenan's (1983: 44)[2] sense of the term, but the flashbacks go back much farther, over 10 years, and deliver the defining moments in Kratos' backstory. Each flashback is introduced by a standard cinematic device: a quick zoom to a close-up on one of Kratos' eyes, then "through" it to the analeptic scene or scenes, a device that reinforces the status of these scenes as *his visions*.

Each of these visions, furthermore, is triggered by something in the diegetic present. For example, upon completing the initial combat sequence on a shipwrecked vessel, an in-game cinematic plays. In the cut

---

2 Given that one does not "die" multiple times trying to "win" a novel, a crude extension of Rimmon-Kenan's sibling concept, "text-time" (the time it takes to read a text), would be "game-time," the time it takes to successfully complete a game. Completing *God of War* on the easiest level ("Mortal") can take anywhere from 12 hours (a figure typically found on game review sites) to much longer for the uninitiated.

scene, Kratos kicks open a cabin door to find the scattered bodies of the crew and passengers, butchered by a regiment of undead soldiers who have taken over the ship. The sight triggers a memory of his own sundry savagery in villages across Greece while paying off his eternal debt to Ares. Similarly, when Kratos happens upon a harpy at the foot of the "Cliffs of Madness," he is reminded of the day he makes his oath to Ares, for it was a harpy who delivers his Blades to him direct from the depths of Hades, and we are transported back to that event via another vision. With each flashback, Kratos relives the trauma of those events while the player experiences them for the first time as narrated discourse.

The flashback episodes are also marked by both increasing contiguity and increasing length. The earliest analepsis is a collection of short fragmented scenes, from a few highlights of Spartan brutality to the fleeting image of an elderly village oracle, laughing cryptically. The third analepsis begins to tell the story of the oath, when — in order to avoid certain death at the hand of a barbarian leader — Kratos invokes Ares, who intervenes in exchange for eternal servitude. The fourth follows chronologically from the third and completes that story, and we see Kratos receiving the weapons that will allow him to toil toward that end. The fifth analepsis, moreover, starts to tell the story of how Ares tricks Kratos into killing his own wife and daughter while busy plundering a village outside Athens. But it does not make the identity of these two final victims clear, which is the role of the sixth analepsis, an episode that also serves to explain how Kratos came to endure the curse that gives him his ashen white complexion. Having already warned him to stay away, the elderly village oracle, possibly more upset by the disobedience than the loss of two more villagers, now makes it clear that "[f]rom this night forward, the mark of your terrible deed will be visible to all. The ashes of your wife and child will remain fastened to your skin, never to be removed." Thus, this longer scene marks a return to the fragment of the village oracle in the first flashback and places her laughter in context.

The most dramatic return in *God of War*, however, occurs toward the completion of the game. After Kratos defeats Ares, who had laid siege to Athens and in turn caused a family row of mythological proportions, he receives some bad news from Athena: though the gods are grateful to him for ridding them of the problem god, and they forgive him for his past sins, they still cannot rid him of his visions, for "no man, no god, could ever forget the terrible deeds you have done." A hopeless Kratos decides that the best way to end the visions is to end his life, and we arrive, at a point exactly three weeks later in the diegesis, back at the bluffs where he makes his suicidal leap. That stitch in time is pulled tight with the ensuing narrative recursion, and we see Kratos fall once again, but this time he hits the water below, only to be swept back up in an act of divine intervention to land at the gates of Olympus high above.[3]

The visual recursion is paired with a verbal one, as the narrative voiceover repeats with a variation:

> And Kratos cast himself from the highest mountain in all of Greece. After 10 years of suffering, 10 years of endless nightmares, it would finally come to an end. Death would be his escape from madness…
>
> The fate of Kratos was not as it seemed. The gods had other plans.
> ("Gates of Olympus" episode)

Athena is there to meet him at the gates, where she mentions a position for which Kratos would not likely have thought himself eligible: a new god of war. The empty throne in Olympus is his ultimate reward, and the final act in the gameplay is simply marching the character up the stairs to the palace of the gods to take his place there.

But this is not the final act in terms of the narrative discourse. Indeed, while *God of War* reaches back by about 10 years, it reaches forward by the thousand. As the narrator explains, "From that point forward, throughout the rest of time, whenever men rode forth to battle for good cause or for evil, they did so under the watchful eye of the man who had defeated a god." This voiceover is punctuated by a brief sequence of prolepses, which project a succession of still-frames of future wars in a highly-stylized montage. These represent what look to be major epochs in warfare, ranging from medieval to industrial to modern-day, with each image seen only through a thick veil of flames. With one final close-up shot of the new titular character in his throne, the game concludes. The prolepses thus not only culminate the story of *God of War*, but also its complex temporal staging of it.

The game's temporal contortionism is rendered intelligible in large part through the use of an authorial narrator. Resonant with age and wisdom, her voice not only opens and closes the game's narrative, but also guides the player to and fro, into and out of each analepsis though a series of careful deictic shifts. For example, in the third analepsis, we see Kratos storming into battle, fiercely yet generically. That is, we do not know the time or place of these images, nor are we supposed to. They are establishing shots; as the narrator tell us: "The youngest and boldest captain in the Spartan army, Kratos had inspired fierce loyalty in his men." The past

3 In a game that draws heavily on Greek mythology, it is appropriate to use this narrative framing device, which is also common to Greek and Roman literature. Its prevalence then and now (in postmodernist literature) forms the subject of John Barth's (1984) meditation "Tales Within Tales Within Tales."

perfect "had inspired" indicates an act that occurs for an extended period in the past. But her very next utterance marks a shift: "It had always been enough to carry them through any battle, until this day." Following one more past perfect construction ("had always been"), the deictic marker "this" places us at a particular battle and at a particular time and place. The cut scene shifts accordingly, panning over the battleground of the imminent confrontation of Kratos' army and the barbarian horde, which, as the voiceover details, "numbered in the thousands, and descended on the Spartans without mercy." Similarly, in the fifth analepsis, we see Kratos plundering indiscriminate villages, but then are refocused visually on one in particular. The narrator redirects the discourse in line with the refocused image: "He feared nothing. But there was something about *this* temple, something... forbidden."[4]

Even though the interventions of the narrator enable us to follow the story with more ease, her own status, ironically, is not so easily determined. Given that she has access to past (and future) events, as well as the thoughts of the protagonist, she must be an authorial narrator. But as we learn from the subsequent games in the *God of War* series (which includes, to date, *God of War II*, and *God of War: Chains of Olympus*), this authorial voice belongs to the deity Gaia, who in fact also plays an active part in the storyworld of both of those games. As such, Gaia occupies a rare—and seemingly oxymoronic—narrative situation in any storytelling medium: she is both *homodiegetic* (a character in the storyworld) and *authorially omniscient* (having absolute knowledge of the characters and access to their thoughts).[5] Such narrators are, by default, supernatural. Such an observation is of course predicated on the assumption of reading a continuous narrative across the *God of War* series. But the point is simply that everything makes sense in this gameworld, and Gaia's status justifies how such a narrator would have timeless knowledge (spanning ancient

4 I have transcribed all voiceover quotations, and here attributed emphasis as it is heard in the game. The emphasis, not surprisingly, falls on the deictic word, accentuating both the shift in the game and my own textual explanation of it here.

5 In *God of War II*, after explaining that she has "watched" Kratos up until this point, Gaia intervenes in the storyworld, manifesting for the first time before Kratos—and the player—and telling him that she has decided to help him seek revenge against Zeus. Her voice assumes more of a dual function from this point on. She continues to narrate context and backstory, predominantly during cut scenes though occasionally during gameplay, as if to an implied audience of an unfolding story. But she also instructs Kratos as to what he must do in order to complete his task by way of a dialogue addressed to him directly, thus morphing into the role of character. Her authorial narration moreover decreases as her role in the diegesis becomes more pronounced, until it is phased out completely; there is no authorial voiceover to conclude this game.

Greek history and modern-day warfare) and, in turn, further supports the sense of unified coherence in this "coherent world game" (Juul 2005: 132).

Moments of disjunction do arise, however, not in the narrative coherence of the gameworld proper, but rather on a meta-critical plane, when mapping structuralist narratology on to video game story mechanics. In *God of War*, the familiar concepts of analepsis, prolepsis, and recursion clearly help us understand the temporal dynamics of its narrative discourse, but only to a point. For example, narrative theory supplies several terms for recursive narratives: an embedded narrative is also referred to as a "hypo-narrative," (Bal 1981: 43) and a frame narrative is also referred to as a "matrix" narrative (from the Latin *mater* for "mother" or "womb"). In Rimmon-Kenan's (1983: 91) model, a first-degree narrative is analogous to the frame narrative since it is not contained by any other narrative (at least not in intra-textual terms), a second-degree narrative is embedded in the first, and so on. It would appear, then, that *God of War* makes sense as a frame narrative that nests several second-degree scenes through analepses. But this reading fails in its blanket elision of gameplay, which certainly comprises a first-degree diegesis, even if it is highly problematic to describe "gameplay" as — or, indeed, *reduce it to* — "narrative discourse."

The gameplay, to borrow from Nick Montfort's (2003) constructive vocabulary for Interactive Fictions, is better understood as a "potential narrative." We know, for instance, that the (singular) successful story resolution will involve killing the three-headed hydra on the shipwrecked vessel early on, but we do not know exactly *how* we will do so — how many hacks, slashes, or slips off a platform will be involved. For each player, gameplay comprises infinitely multiple events.

But regardless of what happens and in what way it happens, the gameplay — not to mention the game's reason for being — must always occupy a primary level, even if this level differs not only in degree (of diegesis) but also in kind (as simulated, not represented world). Therefore, the opening cinematic of Kratos jumping off the cliff is not only a suspended present (in more ways than one), it becomes, in a more accurate but still not entirely adequate reading, a second-degree narrative that is framed by the first-degree "potential narrative" of the gameplay.[6] The flashbacks,

6 The game does not allow multiple plot developments depending on the user's actions, and the player character's choices all converge toward the pivotal plot kernels represented in the cut scenes. There is, however, some possible albeit circumscribed divergence in the player character's exploration of the environment. Kratos can explore, for example, a certain nook in a cave that may allow him to collect more of the orbs that increase either his weapon strength or energy store, even though visiting the nook is not essential to complete the level.

Figure 1: Kratos slaying the hydra. © Sony Computer Entertainment America Inc. 2005. Screenshot created by IGN Entertainment. See the color illustration on page 339.

moreover, become third-level narratives. The inherent inadequacy of such a description simply reflects the essential quality of this type of video game as both fictional world and rule-based system. After all, the fictional world of *God of War* can never cohere perfectly with the rule-based system that governs it: the scenario in which the player character dies during the gameplay would (and often does) render the opening scene an impossible narrative, given that Kratos, ironically, would never live long enough to attempt suicide. Or at least the only conceivably "pure diegesis" would be one in which the player character completes the game upon the first attempt without ever dying and starting again.

Notwithstanding the utility and limitations of narrative theory in understanding the story mechanics of *God of War*—or, for that matter, video games in general—there is no doubting the way in which the game privileges narrative in its own right. Typically, action adventure games reward a player's successful completion of a level, which will often follow the defeat of a "boss" character, by expanding their repertoire of weapons, or endowing them with a special magical power, or simply topping up the player character's life meter — at times all of the above. Pre-rendered cinematics are also commonly included in this capacity as incentives for players in between levels (they often serve the instrumental function of allowing game content for the next level to load as well). *God of War* differs somewhat in this respect. Granted, there are plenty of tantalizing cinematics at strategic points in your progress in which many of the familiar faces in the Greek pantheon commend you on your deeds and endow you with magic power for what lies ahead ("Poseidon's Rage," the "Army of Hades," the "Blade of Artemis," and so forth). But the game also rewards you with backstory; it is unique in the way it positions narrative itself as a reward. Intermittent flashbacks reveal crucial plot components, and the story itself becomes motivation for gameplay.

The game engenders "narrative desire," to borrow Peter Brooks' (1984: 37) phrase, albeit one that is bidirectional: the player not only asks, "What will happen in the end?" but also, "What has already happened?" and "How did 'I' come to be this way?" The reward, moreover, consists not simply of more narrative in the strictly *cumulative* sense, but also in the way the analeptic material becomes, as mentioned, longer and more contiguous as the game progresses. In effect, the player is rewarded not just with more narrative, but with more *narrativity* as well. That said, it is not enough to posit that story motivates gameplay without acknowledging that gameplay is the engine that reciprocally drives the narrative discourse. To put it another way, the reward for the player's successes in the domain of simulation amounts to more material in the domain of representation, and, ideally, more emotional engagement with the game in turn.

II. Cogitations in Character

Compelling backstory, however, is still only one of the narratological elements of *God of War* that engage players emotionally. In fact, an even more overt engagement arises through the character of Kratos himself.[7] But in what sense and with what caveats can we treat (or *read*) Kratos as a literary character, which is to say a character that elicits a rich conceptual under-

---

7 As Marie-Laure Ryan (2006: 6) notes, both the story/discourse distinction and the concept of character that comprise the focus of the present essay qualify as narratological categories that apply more or less unproblematically across media.

standing and, often, a complex emotive response?[8] How might a video game character not simply trouble and transcend traditional approaches, but in fact provide a basis by which scholars can extend and enlarge the narratological foundation for a study of character?[9]

The concept of *character*, understandably, goes back as far the conception of narrative poetics. But from Aristotelian poetics, in which characters exist solely as the "agents" of a given performance (*Poetics* 1982: 51) through to those of earlier 20th century structuralism, the concept has been subordinated to *action* or *plot*. In order to focus on verb-centric grammars, for example, Vladimir Propp (1928, cited in Rimmon-Kenan 1983: 34) reduces characters to the roles that they would undertake in what he called "spheres of action"; Boris Tomashevsky likewise describes characters as "connecting thread[s] helping us to orient ourselves amid the piling-up of details, an auxiliary means for classing and ordering particular motives" (cited in Chatman 1978: 111); and for A. J. Greimas (1979) characters are "actants" who either accomplish or submit to an act, and fit into one of six categories underlying all narrative (cited in Rimmon-Kenan 1983: 34). Seymour Chatman's (1978: 126) conception is more amenable to the mutually informing status of plot and character. Drawing on Barthes' (1974) seminal discussion of Balzac's "Sarrasine," he describes character as a code of traits, which may or may not be stated explicitly in a text, that provide the material by which the reader constructs a characterization. Chatman's model is still nonetheless governed by linguistic analogy, with the vertical paradigm of character traits interrelated to the horizontal syntagm of plot.

The subordination of characters to their plots is no longer pervasive in narrative theory for several related reasons. The past few decades have been marked by a narrative turn in the social sciences and an explosive interest in narrative in and across disciplines (Herman 2007: 4), which has led to both more and more nuanced studies of just about every narrative category imaginable. In addition, the field has reorganized itself internally,

---

8 Ralf Schneider (2001) uses the term "literary character" in his article outlining a cognitive approach to characters in narrative print fiction, and my adoption of the term is deliberate. I am indebted to Schneider's scholarship for prompting my own consideration of the ways in which a cognitive approach might work for a study of characters in such coherent video game worlds.

9 The focus of these questions remains limited here to characters in third-person coherent world games, in which the player typically assumes the role of an existing character and is able to learn more about that character during gameplay. Multiplayer role-playing games raise different questions given the player's ability to customize or configure their avatar. I use the term "player character" as opposed to "avatar" for the same reason. "Avatar," with its origins in role-playing games, connotes such configurability.

reforming in relation to rather than underneath the "pilot-science" of linguistics (2007: 14). At the same time, the object of analysis has changed as well: a preponderance of postmodernist narratives on the heels of narratology's heyday encouraged not necessarily a reversal of the character/plot binary, but rather a demonstration of texts in which characters are privileged over and above their role in a given story plot, or — to put it simply — characters that do not really go anywhere or do anything. A further disentangling of *narrative* from the narrower concept of *story* has occurred in turn, with the term "narrative" understood to encompass more than simply the plot-centric, causally unified material of a story and serving instead as a larger marker for story, discourse, and narration, and including non-representational elements such as pattern and mood. Such a development is especially necessary and productive in light of participatory media that problematize story (in the singular sense) with narratives that are multiple, and/or "potential."

That is not to say that there is a consensus regarding the study of character and characterization in narrative, but rather a better and broader range of approaches. Uri Margolin (2007: 64–79) outlines three dominant theories of character: 1) character as artifice, that is, a textual and artistic product created by some author; 2) character as a "non-actual" individual populating a hypothetical fictional domain or "possible world"; and 3) character as a mental construct in the reader's mind, a theory invested in the highly varied and inferential *process* of understanding a literary character. The grouping is conceivably diachronic as well as synchronic, with the character as artifice model most aligned with traditional structuralism, the character as non-actual individual model coinciding with the emergence of a literary Possible Worlds Theory in late 1970s, and the character as readerly mental construct model closest to the cognitive narrative theory of the last few decades. The cognitively-informed approach is powerful not only because it integrates and builds on the theories that precede it, but also because of one of its governing premises: that the study of fictional minds can tell us more about the minds of readers. [10] As David Herman (2007: 245) writes, "analyzing fictional minds [...] entails giving an account of

10 Cognitive narratology is powerful albeit contestable. Much like earlier structuralist narratology, it entertains universals — though rooted now in science of the mind — at least as a starting point to better understand literature, and reading and writing more generally. In addition, it has the potential to be seen by its detractors as a further encroachment on the literary arts by sciences and a scientific method. At the same time, among interdisciplinary borrowings it may have a distinct advantage as a genuinely *mutual* one: not just a case of narrative theory appropriating cognitive science, but also cognitive science appropriating narrative theory to better understand human behavior and the human mind.

readers' minds too—of how readers interpret particular textual details as information about characters' attempts to make sense of the world around them." It is both possible and productive to extend this reciprocal study of mind between character and reader to that of character and *player*, but not without first addressing the immediate disjunctions that arise.

Video game characters complicate narratological readings of character in obvious ways. For Mieke Bal (1997: 115), character is "intuitively the most crucial category of narrative," but also "the one subject to the most fallacies," the first problem arising with trying to "draw a clear dividing line between human person and character." The problem, of course, is even greater when it comes to the "dividing line" between player and player character, given that the design goal of many first-person and third-person action adventures is some form of fusion between the two. The gamer becomes part of a cybernetic loop, engaged with the game character not just emotionally, but also representationally (the player is figured in the fictional world) and proprioceptively (the player controls this figure through physical input). Emotional engagement with the player character is, arguably, a fortunate byproduct of gameplay and by no means essential to it. Then again, by the same logic, emotional engagement with a character in a novel is by no means essential to reading it, but may well be necessary for it to be a successful and compelling work of art. Thus, we can accept that coherent world games aspire to be successful if not in the same way as a literary work then at least by some of the same means, such as, in this case, an emotionally engaging character.

Yet other complications arise when treating game characters as literary ones. Given their lack of a singular, fixed linear progression, game environments complicate character development. Notwithstanding some inventive exceptions,[11] it is difficult to develop a character according to a story arc if no such arc exists. Furthermore, often the player character's *technical* development is privileged over his or her *dramatic* development. Such technical development is manifest in the incremental increase of skill and power and paralleled by the player's own increasing skill level in playing the game. This privileging clearly speaks to the goal-directed nature of gameplay. The creation of an elaborate backstory and the use of in-game cinematics are common ways to counter the difficulty of dramatic

11 In Fumito Ueda's (2005) *Shadow of the Colossus*, the protagonist similarly makes a pact with an evil entity, compelling him to slay 16 colossi with the hope of bringing a lost lover back to life, and his appearance degenerates as the levels increase. He becomes more and more pale, and even sprouts small horns for the final level. Kratos does undergo one dramatic change in appearance during the course of the game's (back)story: the curse that turns him ashen white, which is subsequently lifted after the defeat of Ares.

development of game characters, though, as David Freeman (2004: 416) points out, such techniques tend to be overused as well. A more intimate somatic union of player and player character, coupled with a potentially less intimate dramatic union, contribute to the need for a further revision of the already slippery notion of emotional identification. Ralf Schneider (2001: 5) suggests that "empathy" is a more adequate term than the more common "identification" when working toward a cognitive paradigm of literary character:

> Unlike identification, empathy does not require readers to share, or want to share, any number of traits with the character, nor does it require them to give up the position of an observer.

The player, however, by definition, forgoes the position of observer, and they take on the player character's traits by way of a voluntary and temporary inheritance. In the game, identification and empathy must sit in relation to agency and action.

A final and perhaps the most obvious way in which video game characters differ from literary characters is their status as visual and not textual "beings"; they are always already more than a "mental construct" because, like a character in film, we can see them on the screen. For Chatman (1978: 101) the filmic "story-space" affords a "standard vision" of a character. At the same time, it does not suffice to think of game characters as filmic characters given that our control of them precludes the same standard vision. Put simply, even though we all see the "same" Kratos, I can decide to make him jump up and down for no particular reason, and this may or may not allow you, or me, to interpret him as being happy.

Nevertheless, Kratos is still a fictional character, one that players must reconstruct, not in the act of reading, but rather during, in between, and after gameplay. In fact, many of the same reasons that make video game characters problematic for narrative theory also make them promising in the opportunities they open for post-classical narratology. More specifically, the dynamic relationship of player and character has direct implications for a cognitive theory of literary character. The genre of third-person action adventure, where players see their character acting in the storyworld, has some unique advantages in this regard as well. It acts as a limit case in between, on the one hand, film and print literature, where characters are observed at a distance so to speak, and, on the other hand, role-playing games and first-person shooters, albeit for different reasons. That is, role-playing games, such as *World of Warcraft*, deliberately pursue a deeper merging of identity between the player and avatar via configurability, whereas first-person shooters eschew the player's ability to visually register their player character beyond an appendage with a weapon or a

Figure 2: Kratos up close. © Sony Computer Entertainment America Inc. 2005.
See the color illustration on page 340.

rear over-the-shoulder point of view, thus effectively de-emphasizing that character's status as someone or something "other." Because they stage participation in a pre-existing world via a pre-existing character who has a pre-existing story, third-person video games allow for not just perspectival distance in how we see this fictional world and our player character, but also a critical distance in how we interpret them.

In *God of War*, players reconstruct the character of Kratos according to information that they gather from varied sources throughout their experience of the game. Processing this information — continually updating and synthesizing it — equates to the "bottom-up" mode of character reception common across cognitive modes of textual reception. There is of course the information gleaned immediately by the physical appearance and expressiveness of Kratos in the game, and through what his (flashback) visions reveal directly about his past experiences — and how those experiences shape his present mental state. But in addition to these more overt means, players learn about Kratos through an array of verbal and textual sources. The narrator provides information not just about his background, but also his state of mind: for instance, she can reveal information about his "instincts" just before he enters the forbidden temple, or his "intentions" when he manages to halt his rapid descent into Hades. Players also learn about Kratos through what he says, either to himself or to other characters. The opening line falls into this former category: "The gods of Olympus have abandoned me. Now there is no hope." These asides, though rare, are significant because they show an otherwise combat-preoccupied Kratos in moments that are both private and introspective. The scene in which he consults his journal en route to Athens would qualify similarly as an aside, albeit one in which his own writing, and his own interiority, is depicted in textual form.

Perhaps the most emotive moments supporting this character's development, however, involve those in which Kratos interacts with other non-player characters (or NPCs). Such interactions occur during short present-tense cinematics that are interspersed throughout the gameplay and extend it diegetically. One such scene occurs early in the game after Kratos defeats the three-headed hydra, shortly after it swallows the ship's captain. Upon hearing a faint cry from within the central, and largest, serpentine head, he investigates by walking into the open mouth of the monster. There he finds the captain hanging on to a fleshy ledge somewhere in the throat of the beast, precipitously close to dropping down into its stomach. "Thank the gods you came back for me," he says, as Kratos reaches out toward him. "I didn't come back for you," is the reply, as our protagonist rips the master key from off the captain's neck and hastens his departure into an intestinal abyss with a swift kick. The scene is telling for what it says about Kratos' capacity for compassion, and its placement serves to establish crucial character information early on.

In another short scene on the same ship, Kratos encounters a jailed crewman. As you approach the bars of the cell, the man recognizes you, recoils, and says: "Stay away from me. Stay away. I know who you are Spartan. I know what you've done. I'd rather die than be saved by you." The non-player character dialogue is the only interaction that transpires here. You/Kratos cannot free the man, even if you wanted to, nor can you kill him for his affront; rather, you simply have to stand there until he is done telling you how horrible he thinks you are. The only option available is to go back and listen to it again. The exchange allows us to update our understanding of Kratos as character, but the emotive effect is heightened with the player experiencing the admonition as a direct address. Indeed, even though Kratos is plagued by personal, subjective visions, which form a dominant part of the game's discursive fabric, he nonetheless operates in an elaborate socio-interactional network. His interactions, however brief, can have a substantial emotive impact on the player, and they become defining moments with which to assemble Kratos as mental construct. Such observations, furthermore, gesture toward a socio-cognitive analysis of character, an analysis both challenged and enriched by the added dimension of the player/character relationship peculiar to video games.[12]

The same observation also marks a clear demonstration of where bottom-up character reception intersects with a top-down mode, an opposing but complementary mode that, in the broadest sense, involves bringing our stored knowledge to bear on a given text. When it comes to lived experience, those working in the domains of psychology, cognitive science, and Artificial Intelligence have long employed a set of diverse yet interrelated constructs in order to describe and discuss such stored knowledge in a systematic way. These constructs fall under the branch of cognitive science known as schema theory, and include *schemata* and *scripts*. Both schemata and scripts are, in Herman's phrase, "repertoires of expectations" (1997: 1047) that allow us to organize and interpret our current experience. But the two differ in that scripts are a more localized, smaller scale description of expectations, or what Catherine Emmott calls "stereotypical action sequences" (2003: 310), which serve to import a ready-made knowledge structure and cue our reaction accordingly. In contrast to schemata, scripts are also dynamic; they are all about how we process event sequences *in their unfolding*.

Like scripts, schemata draw on stored knowledge but refer to a more generalized process of importing broad frameworks that allow us to readily process the background and context—or in the case of fiction, the *genre*—of a given narrative experience.[13] Indeed, such knowledge and memory structures apply equally to artistic and literary experiences that we glean from reading novels, watching movies, or playing certain video games. And though researchers have tended to use rudimentary stories to test the presence and influence of scripts and schemata, more recently many of those same researchers and those working in narrative and literary theory have explored the relevance of schema theory in underpinning our comprehension and processing of longer, more complex, and more literary texts. Scripts and schemata are never *in* the story, but act always as a backdrop to it, and both are heavily context-based; that is, a restaurant experience will cue a different set of scripts than that of a Greek tragedy. For the same reasons they will always play into a top-down mode of interpretation, whether of an entire narrative or a single character.

---

12 For a longer discussion of socio-cognitive dynamics in print narratives, see Catherine Emmott's "Constructing Social Space: Sociocognitive Factors in the Interpretation of Character Relations." In: *Narrative Theory and the Cognitive Sciences*. Ed. David Herman. Stanford: CSLI Publications, 2003 (295–321).

13 A foundational text on scripts in schema theory is Schank and Abelson's (1977) *Scripts, Plans, Goals and Understanding: An Inquiry into Human Knowledge Structures*.

Scripts can help players recognize and process the dialogic exchanges in *God of War.* For example, the scene in which Kratos reaches out to the ship's captain as he is about to fall into the hydra's digestive system cues one script (among several, and possibly concurrent ones), which suggests that this is the scene in which some sort of repartee counterbalances the gravity of a life or death situation, and the hero will act his part as the hero—or not. The outcome of the scene in conjunction with our (high drama action-adventure) script running in the background further helps us organize the portrayal of good and evil in the game and how Kratos rides this divide. Although the commercial game industry is often criticized for its uninventive reliance on Hollywood on matters of this kind,[14] *God of War* manages to do its part to inject some ambiguity into the good/evil binary (at the expense of the ship's captain). Ironically, though most players will indeed take their cue, so to speak, from Hollywood action pulp, the prototypical laconic exchange over a precipitous matter of life and death actually owes a lot to the Spartans themselves: *laconic* derives from the name of the district around Sparta in ancient Greece, and today remains an etymological testament to their habit of being terse and to the point. But whatever our individual store of scripts entails, we inevitably bring to the game our own preconceptions of what is socially acceptable and what is not, and in this case, we can revel in Kratos' profound embrace of social unacceptability as we contemplate his hero versus anti-hero status.

Players enact a top-down mode of character reception in the game also in the form of more generalized schemata. *God of War* activates two of the most powerful and celebrated frameworks in the history of Western civilization, drawing on the world of ancient Greece while simultaneously animating its mythological belief system. The game is populated with the gods of Olympus who share the topography of the game's vision of ancient Greece. Kratos' home village sits outside Sparta while the gods are housed atop Mount Olympus and a "Desert of Lost Souls"—crawled eternally by Cronus the Titan—stretches out somewhere in between them. And there are the countless monsters, among them hydra, Minotaur, Cyclops, gorgons, wraiths, harpies, sirens, Cerberus, centaurs, satyrs, and a bottomless pit of undead legionnaires, all of whom, at least when counting limbs and heads, approximate their Greek mythological counterparts. All at once, the awesome graphical spectacle that is *God of War* can activate

14 See for instance, Chris Crawford (2003: 182) on "Hollywood Envy."

Figure 3: The bloodsport of one Spartan general.
© Sony Computer Entertainment America Inc. 2005.
Screenshot created by IGN Entertainment.
See the color illustration on page 341.

the architectural grandeur of Athens, the magic and minutiae of the Greek gods, and the bloodsport of one Spartan general.

It is often the combination and subversion of schemata, however, that elicits an affective response from a reader or viewer; that is, often stories are compelling precisely because they are unpredictable, and they proceed under the guise of one schema for the sole purpose of destabilizing it with the intrusion of another. As Herman writes, "stories stand in a certain relation to what their readers or auditors know, focusing attention on the unusual or the remarkable against a backdrop made up of patterns of belief and expectation" (1997: 1048). It is no different for the player of *God of War*, as the game draws on schemata only to subvert them, to great effect, by having Kratos assume the throne of a god as a mortal. In the mold of Heracles, Kratos' ascension renders his own status ambiguous, his relationship to the godly and earthly realm, and indeed what lies below them, a matter of debate.[15] The role of these schemata, however, is clear in the application of a top-down conception of Kratos, allowing us to place him geo-historically and ideologically.

With regard to the game as spectacle, the claim for Kratos as a compelling character in a visual, participatory medium raises further questions. In dealing with character reception in film, for example, it is necessary to recognize how both sound and moving image contribute to, if not dominate, an emotive presentation (and reception) of character. Sound and the moving image, two elements known to prey on the viewer's affective vulnerabilities, are of course unavailable to the print novel. *God of War* obviously indulges in both, but it is notable in the way it pursues two other techniques that are more closely aligned with prose fiction: namely the use of authorial narration and the illusion of unfettered access to a fictional mind. Given that gamers in some sense also *share* the mind to which they have access, it is in the latter technique that we can further consider what a cognitive theory of character can tell us about the genre of third-person video games, and Kratos in particular.

God of War uses Kratos as its point of departure in an exploration of the Spartan cultural mystique. The cultivation of a warrior class that essentially outsourced its manual and intellectual labor makes Spartan culture a popular object of inquiry. From Aristotle (1962: 304), who in his *Politics* chastises the Spartans for "[putting] their young to excessive military training [and]...rendering them vulgar and uneducated," to modern day movie-goers who marvel at Leonidas on the big screen for his embrace of the same one-dimensional, unconditional value system, Spartans fascinate us.[16] This exploration can only serve as a point of departure, however, for Kratos is not your average Spartan general, having taken an oath of eternal servitude to a god then tricked by that same god into killing his own family. Kratos is aggrieved to say the least. But tapping into the player's sense of inner rage, to use Jaffe's terms, is still only part of the story. Kratos is by all accounts an insanely angry man, but the point is that he is in no way *simply* an insanely angry man. More specifically, *God of War* is a meditation on calculated rage, a meditation that has media-specific implications. The player, indulging both a surrogate body and mind in Kratos, quickly

15 Kratos mirrors Heracles also on matters of paternity as players discover in the game's sequel.

16 Underscoring this fascination are deeper questions about the Spartan mindset that are fodder for studies of emotion and emotion discourse, which, as Herman (2007: 255) notes, can provide valuable resources for narrative understanding. Were Spartan warriors simply extreme in their emotional constitution and their fearlessness in particular? Or did their society culturally construct men for whom fear was something categorically and experientially different from what we typically assume to be a universal emotion?

realizes that there is much more to the game than dicing up the enemy. Our actions alternate between the murderous and the methodical, the need to battle and the need to puzzle-solve. From the earliest level on the shipwrecked vessel, for example, the player finds out that charging the row of undead archers on one of the ship's upper decks will result in piercing pain; but (with some in-game instruction) we learn that we can push a large wooden crate along the lower deck in front of us, which acts as a shield for the offending arrows. Once we safely reach the upper deck, the same crate becomes the means by which we climb up to the archers and dispose of them.

These action puzzles[17] grow ever more difficult as the game progresses, the player negotiating them at the same time as they negotiate the tension between "good frustration and bad frustration" (Freeman 2004: 337). Help is always only a website away, with the publication of puzzle solutions a common feature on game review and independent gamer sites. The following is an example of a solution to a more advanced puzzle that appears during the "Challenge of Hades" level:

> So you dodged all those massive fireballs and made it to the other side. And what did you find in that room? NOTHING! So how do you get out of this area?
>
> There are four doors on the left side and four on the right of this massive fireball corridor.
>
> The door to exit this room is the third one on the left. Time your evasion and open that door as quickly as possible and enter before a fireball tramples you down![18]

Clearly, rage alone connotes the absence of careful thought, but even a cursory experience of Kratos' world demonstrates that his inner rage is tempered by a constantly calculating mind.

Furthermore, the act of *playing Kratos*, by extension, invites a reflexive comment on his calculated rage. In playing his character, one enacts a dialectic of rage and control, given that you need to stay in control on both the fictional and meta-fictional plane in order to dispatch your rage efficaciously. Some of the most epic combat finales require an intricate combination of buttons on the PlayStation console. Kratos, for instance, is at the peak of his fury when he is dealing with the Cyclops, but only a measured manipulation of buttons and analog sticks on the gaming console will ensure a successful result. It is possible to suggest that coher-

17 The term is standard in game studies.
18 The site is authored by VampireHorde, and the text is "God of War, Scrabble of the Gods—Puzzle Solutions Guide" at http://www.gamefaqs.com/console/ps2/file/919864/36093, visited June 1, 2009.

ent world games are all, in a sense, meta-fictional comments on control. As Stephen Poole writes in his *Trigger Happy*, characters give us pleasure "through a joyously exaggerated sense of control, or amplification of input" (2000: 148). Significantly, his popular audience investigation of video games and the entertainment revolution gestures toward a cognitive universal on this same point when he describes such amplification of input as

> one very basic attraction of all types of interactivity, and [...] a near-universal pleasure among humans in the modern industrialized world. Why do people enjoy driving cars? Amplification of input: you just lower your foot and suddenly you are moving at exhilarating speed. (2000: 148)

Nevertheless, in articulating the pleasures of *God of War*, it is clear that a model integrating both cinematic diegesis and gameplay can work productively toward a more complete understanding of both the characters who populate gameworlds and those at the controls. Margolin (2007: 69) refers to the "totally unnatural access to other's minds [as] one of the hallmarks of literary versus factual modes of characterization, and a major source of readerly interest in, and learning from, what are ultimately 'paper people'." We can say the same when referring to what are ultimately "pixelated people" as well.

III. Blade of Chaos, or Quill of Contemplation?

When *God of War* was released in 2005, it lent itself to a reading that would have been decidedly "against the grain," that is, an analysis that would reveal the highly wrought narrative and literary quality of the game *in spite of* its status as a blockbuster title in the PlayStation mainstream. It would have been an analysis that gave added support to Steven Johnson's (2006: 9) notion of the "Sleeper Curve," a phenomenon in which we see "the most debased forms of mass diversion — video games and violent television dramas and juvenile sitcoms — turn out to be nutritional after all." Such an analysis would have *started* with the premise that the complex intellectual and emotional demand of playing Kratos would in itself be a reason to "read into" the game. For as Freeman (2004: 368) points out, "complex" and "engrossing" are by no means necessarily related but are often so, an observation that tends to hold more strongly in artistic and literary works — even defining them as such.

But in the few years since its release, the interpretive community has already taken that first step in establishing *God of War*'s expressly "literary" status, a community that includes everyone from those voting for the game on fan forum review websites to those legislating against it court.

Indeed, *God of War* was cited in the Illinois district court as an example of "a game with literary merit whose access would likely be unconstitutionally prohibited to minors" under that state's laws regulating sexually explicit content (Smith et al. 2006: n.p., fn. 29). Meanwhile, the game continues to amass critical acclaim. Having won over 50 awards, including 12 "Game of the Year" awards and four awards specifically for categories honoring "best character," it is now available as a "Platinum" title, a status reserved for Sony's top-selling games. Seven of its accolades came at the 2006 Annual Interactive Achievement Awards, widely considered to be the Oscars of the video game industry. In 2007, it was voted the best PlayStation 2 game of all time by video game review giant Imagine Games Network, better known as IGN (IGN 2007). The fact that *God of War* has attracted so much critical attention in the industry, however, by no means preempts the need for critical attention in a scholarly vein. Rather, the fact that it no longer warrants such a reading against the grain means that the work is now open to a *finer-grained* theoretical analysis, an analysis that can dispense with a lengthy justification of the game's cultural and artistic significance.

But *God of War* is not just literary in its approach to narrative discourse, temporality, and character, it is self-consciously so, and this self-consciousness is reinforced on a thematic level. The game is full of texts. Some are artifacts represented in the diegesis, from Kratos' journal to the cryptic manuals belonging to the mad architect, Pathos Verdes III, who has designed so much of the world in which the protagonist finds himself. Others are extra-diegetic, such as the text box instructions that appear (in the same papyrus-styled text box as the journal entry) during gameplay, conveying which button combinations will help you get out of a combat quandary.[19] There is also the curious one-word commentary that appears after Kratos has tallied up a high number of "hits" on an opponent. This commentary (in the form of adjectives, such as "Vicious!" and "Inhuman!") appears in the "HUD," or Heads Up Display, where a character's vital statistics and weapon situation are displayed in the gaming interface. And of course, some texts sit on the boundary between these two ontological realms, such as Gaia's authorial narration itself, which guides us through the shifting scenes omnisciently yet anonymously, at least until the game's sequel.

---

19 These instructions — or, in Montfort's (2003) IF parlance, *directives* — involve tips on button combinations to use in combat situations, and are of course addressed directly to the player rather than the player character (given that Kratos does not have a gaming console).

Figure 4: An epigraph at the start of one of the game's promotional trailers. © Sony Computer Entertainment America Inc. 2005.

The game is remarkable, moreover, for the kind of texts that it engenders in the broader gaming community. There is still the expected rubric of reviews, walkthroughs, plot summaries, game cheats, and game guides. But in other, less customary textual moments there are further signs that the game's literary self-consciousness is transferred to the gamer. Consider one player's apology at the end of a rather extended review shortly after the game's release: "I'm sorry this review is so long, but what was I going to do? I kept writing and *I just couldn't stop*" [*emphasis in original*].[20] Or another who writes, "recently, I borrowed God of War from a buddy of mine. The storyline intrigued me so much I decided to write a plot summary of the game." He then goes on to thank several people, including "The Man Upstairs, for giving me the skills to work on my writing."[21] Another blogger goes into great detail regarding his moral reservations about getting too close to his character:

> … I was grateful for the third-person perspective in games. I could disassociate myself from the horrors that Kratos performed, since they grew from his char-

20 The site from which this text was retrieved (December 2007) is no longer online, but the page can be accessed using the "Wayback machine" Internet Archive site here: http://web.archive.org/web/20051218191739/http://www.damnedmachines.com/archives/2005/04/index.html, viewed June 5, 2009).

21 Posted by "headcrook" on December 12, 2005, at http://au.faqs.ign.com/articles/675/675093p1.html, viewed June 5, 2009.

acter, and not from mine. The story was already laid, had already unfolded, had already occurred—I was just experiencing it.

> Because you see, the people of Ancient Greece were almost completely alien to our own sense of morality; they treasured might and strength and honor where many of us believe in self-sacrifice and helping others. Cronus, Zeus' father, attempts to maintain his throne by *eating his own children*, and Zeus attains his throne by cutting open his father's stomach to retrieve his siblings. And as terrible as their myths were, their entertainments contained similar themes: Euripides' *The Bacchae* and *Medea* offer denouements where mothers destroy their children. In Sophocles' *Oedipus Rex*, Oedipus puts out his own eyes. These are brutal events, tragic events, and they flow from the savage, passionate characters who personified the human condition for the Greeks.
> [*emphasis in original*] (Douville 2005)

The author's comments here speak both to the conscious decision to disavow the surrogate mind and body of Kratos and to the cultural mystique inspired by Sparta. But more generally, they speak to the fact that the story of Kratos wants to be retold by those who share his experience, be it intimately or at a safe distance.[22]

If these gamer scribes seem unlikely then they are no different than their hero, a graphophiliac god of war whose "only solace," we are told, is the sea, but nonetheless finds time to pause at a journal that appears not only full, but overflowing. Its pages scattered across the floor of the ship's cabin, an undeniable metaphor for its author's state of mind, the journal reminds us that there is no way to completely separate the experience of "reading" the game from the experience of playing it, and it encourages us to rage on, reflectively.

All in all, we do not have to read into this game, or read it as a narrative, just as we do not have to read Kratos' open journal, which has no function in the strictly ludological sense. But there is something instructive about the fact that the journal is delivered to us via the same stylized text box — the same mechanism — that delivers the extra-diegetic clues on how to play the game. That is, it may give us a clue as to how we might experience this game both as a game and as a fictional world. In this article, I have endeavored to speak to an audience inspired by recent trends in narrative theory and its potential to help us understand both fictional and non-fictional beings, which is also to say aesthetic and everyday

---

22 Even the Wikipedia entry for the game was flagged for months after its creation, not surprisingly, for containing "a plot summary that may be overly long." The page, located at http://en.wikipedia.org/wiki/God_of_War_(video_game) (viewed June 5, 2009), has since been edited and the summary streamlined, but the sprawling text can still be found, along with the editorial rebuke, on sites that harvest Wikipedia articles and have not been updated for years.

experience. As my own reading demonstrates — with some support from a community of gamer scribes — it is not only possible but immensely productive to apply these narrative-theoretical frameworks to certain video games, and at the same time avoid losing sight of the specificity of the gaming experience.

References

Aristotle (1982). *Poetics*. Trans. and intro. James Hutton. New York: W.W. Norton & Company.

– (1962). *Politics*. Ringwood, Victoria, Australia: Penguin Books.

Barth, John (1984). "Tales within Tales within Tales." In: *The Friday Book*, Baltimore: Johns Hopkins University Press, 218–38.

Barthes, Roland (1974). *S/Z: An Essay*. Trans. Richard Miller. New York: Hill and Wang.

Bal, Mieke (1981). "Notes on Narrative Embedding." In: *Poetics Today* 2: 41–59.

– (1997). *Narratology: Introduction to the Theory of Narrative*. 2nd Edition. Toronto: University of Toronto Press.

Brooks, Peter (1984). *Reading for the Plot*. New York: Alfred A. Knopf.

Chatman, Seymour (1978). *Story and Discourse: Narrative Structure in Fiction and Film*. Ithaca: Cornell University Press.

Crawford, Chris (2003). *Chris Crawford on Game Design*. Berkeley: New Riders Publishing.

Douville, Brett (2005). "Sacrifice: God of War." Blog post dated October 01, 2005. "Brett's Footnotes" http://www.brettdouville.com/mt-archives/2005/10/sacrifice_god_o.html, viewed June 5, 2009.

Emmott, Catherine (2003). "Constructing Social Space: Sociocognitive Factors in the Interpretation of Character Relations." In: *Narrative Theory and the Cognitive Sciences*, ed. David Herman. Stanford: CSLI Publications, 295–321.

Freeman, David (2004). *Creating Emotion in Games*. Berkeley: New Riders Publishing.

God of War. 2005. Sony Computer Entertainment America, Inc.

Herman, David (1997). "Scripts, Sequences, and Stories: Elements of a Postclassical Narratology." *PMLA* 112.5: 1046–1059.

– (2003). "Stories as a Tool for Thinking." In: *Narrative Theory and the Cognitive Sciences*. Stanford, CA: Center for the Study of Language and Information (CSLI) Publications, 163–194.

– (2007). "Cognition, Emotion, and Consciousness." In: *The Cambridge Companion to Narrative*, ed. David Herman. Cambridge: Cambridge University Press, 245–259.

IGN PlayStation Team (2007). "The Top 25 PS2 Games of All Time" http://au.ps2.ign.com/articles/772/772296p3.html, viewed June 5, 2009.

Johnson, Steven (2005). *Everything Bad Is Good for You: How Today's Popular Culture Is Actually Making Us Smarter*. New York: Riverhead Books.

Juul, Jesper (2005). *Half-Real: Video Games between Real Rules and Fictional Worlds*. Cambridge, Mass: MIT Press.

"Making *God of War*" (2005). *God of War* DVD Extra Features. Sony Computer Entertainment America, Inc.

Margolin, Uri (2003). "Cognitive Science, the Thinking Mind, and Literary Narrative." In: *Narrative Theory and the Cognitive Sciences.* Stanford, CA: Center for the Study of Language and Information (CSLI) Publications, 271–294.

Margolin, Uri (2007). "Character." In: *The Cambridge Companion to Narrative*, ed. by David Herman. Cambridge: Cambridge University Press, 66–79.

Montfort, Nick (2009). "Toward a Theory of Interactive Fiction." December 19. First published 8 January 2002. http://nickm.com/if/toward.html, viewed June 5, 2009.

Poole, Stephen (2000). *Trigger Happy: Videogames and the Entertainment Revolution.* New York: Arcade Publishing.

Rimmon-Kenan, Shlomith (1983). *Narrative Fiction.* New York: Methuen.

Ryan, Marie-Laure (2006). *Avatars of Story.* Minneapolis, MN: University of Minnesota Press.

Schank, Roger & Abelson, Robert (1977). *Scripts, Plans, Goals and Understanding: An Inquiry into Human Knowledge Structures.* Hillsdale, NJ: Lawrence Erlbaum.

Schneider, Ralf (2001). "Toward a Cognitive Theory of Literary Character: The Dynamics of Mental-Model Construction." *Style* 35.4: 607–40. Available online: http://findarticles.com/p/articles/mi_m2342/is_4_35/ai_97114241/, viewed June 5, 2009.

Smith, Paul (2006). "Attack on Violent Video Games." *Communications Lawyer* 24.1.

Wark, McKenzie (2007). *Gamer Theory.* Cambridge, Mass.: Harvard University Press.

Elsa Simões Lucas Freitas
(Universidade Fernando Pessoa)

Advertising the Medium: On the Narrative Worlds of a Multimedia Promotional Campaign for a Public Service Television Channel[1]

> Advertising has become too various and vast an activity for any study to be comprehensive. (Cook 1992)

> There is inherent drama in every product. Our No.1 job is to dig for it and capitalize on it.
> (Leo Burnett, as quoted by David Ogilvy 1983)

Introduction

By definition, advertising messages can function as privileged means for storytelling and for the conveyance of abridged narrative formats, regardless of the medium used to broadcast them. Media such as television offer increased possibilities for the explicit depiction of the constitutive elements of a narrative format, with the added advantage that they are able to reproduce the passage of time inherent to the telling of a sequence of events. However, other media such as radio and magazines also encase storytelling possibilities, with the presentation of prototypical narratives.

It is the purpose of this chapter to analyze a multimodal advertising campaign broadcast in Portugal, whose aim was to promote a number of programmes of a public service television channel. In this specific case, the medium that divulged the advertising message was, simultaneously, (1) the channel used for conveying it and (2) the object of the advertising message itself. In this instance, there is effective conflation of narrative modes and therefore (at least in the case of the television commercials), the medium becomes the story.

---

1 I would like to thank Marina Ramos (RTP1) and Brandia Central advertising agency for kindly allowing the reproduction of their ad campaign in this chapter.

The campaign to be analyzed under this perspective is constituted by television commercials, outdoor ads and radio spots, broadcast during the period October 2008 — January 2009, promoting a number of emblematic programmes of the Portuguese public service channel (RTP1), which stressed the innovative nature of these programmes and, more importantly, the breath of fresh air they represented for this television channel.

The complexity of this multimedia campaign and the intertextual and self-reflexive nature of each of its ads provide insights into the process of intermediality (verbal/visual interaction within each ad but also intermedial thematic congruence within the campaign), narrative (shifts in narrative point of view and mise-en-abîme portrayal of plot and characters in the ads) and storytelling (with non-linearity and montage effects so as to create «stories within stories» that maximize parody and self-referentiality in many of these ads).

1. The different roles of advertising

Advertising text can be broadly and imperfectly described as communication with an agenda. Although it can be argued that every piece of communication has a purpose of some kind, ads do present a number of distinctive characteristics, when cumulatively considered: they are paid for by the entities who issue them, are conveyed by mass media, and have been deliberately overloaded with meaning in order to convince the receiving audiences to undertake action of some kind (Wells et al. 1998: 12–13). Communication in ads is a process where every element has to be carefully planned, anticipated, adjusted and readjusted to achieve success, i.e. to be able to influence the public in the desired manner:

> Successful communication is accomplished when the marketer selects an appropriate source, develops an effective message or appeal that is encoded properly, and then selects the channel or media that will best reach the target audience so that the message can be effectively decoded and delivered. (Belch and Belch, 2004: 145)

The presence of a substantial financial investment at the sender's end of the process introduces the extra motivation element in this specific communicative circuit, and, very often, this perceived premeditation taints it with a social connotation of intrusion, insincerity and undesirability amidst a world made up of other more clearly defined discourses and narratives:

> In this respect, advertising is one of the most controversial of all contemporary discourse types, partly because it is relatively new, but also because it is closely

> associated with the values of the competitive high-growth market economy in which it thrives. In a world beset by social and ecological problems, advertising can be seen as urging people to consume more by making them feel dissatisfied or inadequate, by appealing to greed, worry and ambition. On the other hand, it may be argued that many ads are skilful, clever and amusing, and that it is unjust to make them a scapegoat for all the sorrows of the modern world. (Cook 1992: 16)

Despite the mistrust that advertising in general and its after-effects seem to fuel, ads are generally acknowledged to be complex and mythical in their appeal to the imaginary dimension (Barthes 1977: 169), creative and seductive (MacCannell 1987: 524; Goddard 1998: 2–3) — hence their presumed danger.

Especially in contemporary society, they are often criticized for not being straightforward about their purposes and deceptive in their skilful appropriation of other discourses to camouflage their true mercenary nature (Williamson 1978: 165). This lack of clearly defined boundaries (what is advertising? and what is *not* advertising?) constitutes perhaps advertising's original sin for its detractors. On the other hand, this inherent lack of innocence and purity accounts for the complexity and richness of a discourse planned and executed by the co-operative efforts of many people, resulting in a message composed of multiple layers of characteristics borrowed (or vampirised, as some would say) from other discourses, in an effort to overcome the cluttered media space and the audience's indifference and, most importantly, to enhance the ad's entertainment possibilities (Gulas and Weinberger 2006: 16–27), namely through the use of narrative sequences and storytelling more or less related to the product or service at stake.

2. Narrative and storytelling in ads as creative strategies

Advertising messages have to be attractive and compelling to the consumer – and several different tactics can be used to achieve that goal. There are some factors that seem to positively influence people's awareness of ads, which have to do with either the intrinsic novelty of the product or service advertised, the unusualness of the ad's approach, the relevance the ad may have for the viewer's individual situation or, lastly, the sheer number of repetitions the viewer has been exposed to (Yeshin 2006: 284–285). In a world where it is increasingly difficult to market products with few distinctive features and where ad repetition can easily backfire, it is often the message's function to address the issue of excessive clutter in all the media:

> It is important to stress (...) that ads don't just sell commodities, they give meanings to brands. There is a difference between these two aims. Some tactics that have immediate and demonstrable effects on sales can actually work against the long-term interests of the brand. (...) Changing frequently the style of ads for the product could promote awareness of the advertising and short-term sales but disrupt and weaken the long-term perception of the brand. This is where some ad agencies would see themselves as coming in – as guardians of the meanings associated with the brand (...) (Myers 1999: 7–8)

Typically, this aim of defending and maintaining the brand's image is undertaken by means of two main classical approaches to advertising messages: either the «hard-sell» (also known as «straight-sell») or the «soft-sell» type (Cook 1992: 10) — although elements of both types can be found in a single ad, since the difference between them is not totally clear-cut: appeals to rationality and emotions are often carefully balanced within the space of an advertising message (Yeshin 2006: 286). Although soft-sell approaches are perhaps more widely used nowadays, ads emphasising factual information are still very common during commercial breaks and in print media, since they seem to be rather convincing when it comes to prompting audiences into immediate action (Wells et al. 1998: 402)

Normally it can be said that, whereas hard-sell is more focused on logical arguments about the intrinsic and distinctive characteristics of the product and stresses the need for immediate acquisition, the soft-sell approach is much more indirect, with the main aim of building and reinforcing the brand's image. Therefore, it does not usually foreground specific features of the product, but rather works on the association of a set of images and concepts with the product or service advertised. Ideally, the audience will eventually come to associate these images and concepts to the brand itself, thus creating a more positive awareness of it (Yeshin 2006: 285)

Narrative is one among the various possibilities used by ads to attract viewers' attention and to lend a defined personality and a storyline to an otherwise lifeless product or service. Different kinds of narratives and storytelling formats can be used in ads, either in soft-sell or hard-sell approaches, very often developing according to stereotypical models used in advertising. The most commonly employed are perhaps slice of life, fantasies, dramatisations and stories about and around the product or service.

Virtual or proto-narratives (where narrative possibilities are hinted at or implied rather than explicitly depicted) can be embedded within frames of testimonials by prototypical experts in their fields or showbiz celebrities (Freitas 2008: 187) — as in the specific case of the campaign we will be analysing at a later point. Combinations of these creative executions are frequent, and they can be made even more complex with the use of humour, music and animation.

The use of drama, under any of the above mentioned forms, offers plenty of possibilities for the conveyance of advertising messages, and it has been a favourite format with advertisers for a long time. David Ogilvy considered it as above average in ability to alter their brand preference:

> In these commercials one actor argues with another about the merits of a product, in a setting which roughly approximates real life. In the end, the doubter is converted – your toothpaste really does give children healthier teeth.
> These playlets have been successful in case after case. Copywriters detest them because most of them are so corny – and because they have been in such a wide use for such a long time. But some agencies have succeeded in producing slices which are not only effective at the cash register, but realistic and charming. (1983: 105)

These dramas are especially successful when it comes to making the audiences relate on personal terms with what they are looking at, turning them into a part of the action, instead of being mere bystanders listening to a demonstration of the product or service's qualities delivered to their benefit:

> A drama is a form of indirect address, like a movie or a play. In a drama the characters speak to each other, not to the audience. In fact, they usually behave as though the audience were not there. Members of the audience observe and sometimes even participate vicariously in the events unfolding in the story. They are «eavesdroppers». Like fairy tales, movies, novels, parables and myths, advertising dramas are essentially stories about the how the world works. Viewers learn from these commercial dramas by inferring lessons from them and by applying those lessons to their everyday lives. (Wells et al. 1998: 403)

Slice-of-life formats very often combine the problem/solution approach with the dramatisation of an everyday life scene, where the product appears as the perfect — and only — form of effectively overcoming the problem faced (Belch and Belch 2004: 278–279). In this case, it is important for the situation created to be believable, since this format is normally aimed at obtaining an effect of proximity and familiarity (Yeshin 2006: 291) — although exceptions are possible when schema disruption is intended, especially for humorous effects, in which case contrived or unusual scenarios might be used, either since the beginning of the ad or, for a more surprising effect, introduced at some point during the process of storytelling.

At the other end of the spectrum, fantasy formats can sometimes totally dispense with narrative structures. In these cases, there is no temporal or spatial progression: the ad becomes a contemplation object by itself. We have then a static object that tells no story apart from its own physic limits and existence broadcast by the media (González Requena and Ortiz de Zárate 1995: 23). Whereas normally in ads we witness an exercise on the expansion of meanings, by means of explicit or implied narrative structures (among other possibilities), in this case there is deliberate contention of possible readings. This is a common creative execution for upscale cosmetic ads, striving to inspire very specific brand associations (Belch and Belch 2004: 281), or even obtain an effect of mirror-image between the onlooker and the projected image, so as to present a total identification between the *I* of the ad and the *you* who observes it. Since such a structure totally dispenses with other elements of the communicative process (such as the *other* who the narrative might be about) and no progression exists, the ad becomes a narcissistic instance, where nothing outside this closed universe is of interest:

> In *Civilization and Its Discontents*, Freud argues that the price of culture is the voluntary relinquishing of essential archaic emotions. Cultural archetypes (perfection, cleanness, harmony and order) serve as the substitutes for natural pains and pleasures. These surrogate pleasures are actively exploited by the mass advertisement industry. The symbols of comfort, security, cleanness, efficiency, prestige, sexuality, etc., form the "archetypes" of consumption mythology and turn the advertised object into a marketable commodity. Advertisement seeks to meet the consumer's psychical needs and ideological dispositions. *Thus, advertising and mass media channel and influence the consumer's perception, yet they reach their goals by proclaiming their power to satisfy the consumer's deep wishes and expectations, i.e. by creating a "mirror image" of the consumer.* (Grishakova 2006: 275, my italics).

This "mirrored image" that characterises some ads means the negation of the very notion of narrative, by definition always *about* something (González Requena and Ortiz de Zárate 1995: 22).

2.1. Advertisements as tokens of virtual narratives

As we have seen, advertisements are particularly resistant to straightforward characterization (Goddard 1998: 6). Because of their ability to plunder desirable characteristics from totally unrelated types of text, they question the very notion of discourse type (Cook 1992: 34).

Ads are made up of all kinds of substances and have the ability to incorporate anything that can prove useful to their purpose — be that promoting sales (as in the case of most commercial ads), reinforcing a positive brand image (as in institutional ads) or even coaxing audiences into altering dangerous behaviours and adopting more socially responsible ones — which is the purpose of non-commercial advertising in general (Yeshin 2006: 6).

Therefore, when considered as narratives, their composite and interactive nature forces us to revaluate the classical instances of narratology when applied to analyses of their narrative structures and effects:

> Narrative advertisements are an important object of analysis because they have to raise the product's selling point within the limits of a temporally and spatially restricted storyline. Because of these restrictions many aspects of the narrative message can often only be implied or suggested… (Bezuidenhout-Raath 2008: 7)

Because of these limitations, rather than telling the whole story, very often the ad will suggest the possibility that, at some decisive points, the narrative can fork out into a number of different stories, which adds to the narrative complexity and, possibly, to the increased interest on the part of the audiences. Even when the narrative paths are well defined and closure is provided, the audience will consider the alternative paths that were hinted at during the storytelling process (Ryan 2008c: 628), which presents obvious advantages for a discourse that thrives on indeterminacy and suggestion (Cook 1992: 45). In fact, time and space limitations — which, at a first glance, might be seen as major drawbacks to the telling of a coherent story — can work to the advantage of the advertising message, introducing a number of gaps that will have to be fulfilled by the viewers, who have to invest their individuality, but also their shared knowledge in the tale being told: co-authoring — a necessity in variable degrees for all texts — is foregrounded in advertising narratives:

> It is what is not said in a discourse — because everyone in the society knows it — which is most important. (…) There is a strong assumption that people who address us are saying things which are coherent. (…) We *make* sense even when there is none, using some unstated cultural assumptions to fill in the gaps. People are reluctant to suppose that the sender cannot see the sense of his or her own discourse and assume that the fault must be their own. Discourse has to be conspicuously and extensively nonsensical before it is perceived as such (Cook 1992: 176–177)

Ad texts are highly charged with meanings, conveyed by different channels, usually converging towards a final unified message. Gapping is necessary, because of time and space constraints, as we have seen, but also convenient for the ad's purposes: firstly, in such a complexly planned and financially expensive message such as this one, the audience is likely to assume that it has to make sense, fully applying Grice's Maxim of Cooperation to it; secondly, the audience's willingness to fill the gaps will be oriented towards the direction intended by other conveyors of meaning such as music, gesture and facial expressions. In this sense, gap-filling will rely on individuality up to a point, but will be also conditioned so as to avoid unsatisfactory or irrelevant readings (Spolsky 2008: 193).

Cohesive devices that structure narrative in ads of a linguistic nature — repetition of important words and terms, use of rhetorical devices, pronouns, ellipsis and conjunctions and referring expressions (Cook 1992: 148–149) — are commonly employed so as to provide an economic but also effective form of guaranteeing the necessary sense relations. However, as ad texts are always constituted by more than just linguistic matter, they have the possibility of using other channels to establish or reinforce cohesion.

Another advantage of delegating some of the responsibility for cohesion on non-linguistic channels has to do with the type of relationship advertising discourse establishes with its audiences — a one-to-one, familiar and intimate one. In fact, this does not correspond to the real communication process at stake: the audience does not know the actual sender of a message concocted by so many people and which aims to convey a highly individualised meaning to millions of people at the same time (Myers 1994: 78). Therefore, phatic cohesive elements meant to reinforce politeness and that are characteristic of more respectful relationships are dispensed with in advertising discourse, where closeness is taken for granted:

> Where the relation is already established and secure, there may be less need for politeness strategies. This accounts for a similarity in behaviour of marked power difference on the one hand (say, police officer and suspect) and of equality and intimacy on the other (say, close friends or partners) (...) Both generate bald statements and commands, physical proximity without apology, the broaching of intimate subject matter, interruption and abrupt topic switch. (Cook 1992: 151)

Different visual elements, often metaphorical or metonymic in nature (Kress and van Leeuwen 1996: 17–18; Messaris 1997: xviii), gesturing (Goffman 1979: 3; McGregor 2008: 205), facial expressions (Freitas 2008: 137), musical background (Blake 1997: 228; Baldry 2004: 91; Wolf 2008: 255) and sound effects (Cook 1992: 48), or even silences during a dialogue (Freitas 2008: 139, 151) can all function as effective non-linguistic gap-fillers, appealing to common knowledge and more or less predictable schemata to complete storytelling, perfectly mimicking the dynamics of narrative in a conversation between close friends, where turn-taking and interaction is essential.

2.2. The narrative, the ad and the medium: definition problems and constraints

Generally speaking, the message in the ad is largely determined by the medium chosen to convey it (Cook 1992: 9; Ryan 2008a: 289). Narrative structures in advertising messages are easier to convey in media such as television or radio, where the temporal progression of the ad reproduces at a smaller scale the elapsing of time that corresponds to the unfolding of the events depicted (Bezuidenhout-Raath 2008: 7), although narrative structures and storytelling effects can also be suggested in static media such as print ads (Freitas 2008: 69) or even, to a lesser extent, in outdoor advertising.

When the corpus to be analysed is constituted by ads, regardless of the medium used to convey them, a major concern of a practical nature has to be dealt with from the start: how to effectively transcribe ads (i.e. immobilise their characteristics on paper in order to be able pinpoint and study them), while respecting the dynamism and the flow of movement that are largely responsible for the meanings conveyed (Baldry 2004: 84)? This concern is obviously more pressing in television commercials. David Ogilvy already voiced this difficulty when explaining how he undertook the task:

> Everyone who writes about television commercials faces the same insoluble problem: it is impossible to show them on the pages of a book. All I can do is reproduce some storyboards which illustrate my points, and pray you can decipher them. (1983: 103).

However, the problems associated with transcription are also an issue in print ads or even radio spots:

> While the words in this book can put the words of an ad on the page, they can only hint at the nature of its music and pictures, for these cannot be written down 'as themselves' but only as something else — words. (...) Yet even in analyses of printed ads the problems are legion. To use too many accompanying reproductions alters the character of a written analysis, leaving the writing swamped by the ads themselves. Reproduction, moreover, is unlikely to do justice to such factors as size, colour and position within accompanying discourses. (Cook 1992: 37)

In fact, individual ads in every medium can be described as «self-contained systems in flux» (O'Halloran 2004: 109), which could be seen as a threat to the logic of continuity that normally characterizes narrative processes.

Another difficulty has to do with the fact that ads do not appear in isolation, and they are embedded in a multitude of other mini-narratives, belonging to the same discourse genre (as in the case of other commercials during the same break) or other discourse types (for instance, articles in the adjacent pages of a magazine). Therefore, to single them out for the purpose of analysing them will inevitably introduce alterations to the way they are normally viewed by audiences: very often as interruptions to what the person is effectively doing and not worth paying a lot of attention to (Myers 1999: 204). After all, audiences are quite familiar with advertising's hidden agenda, and their meaning is not usually difficult to grasp by their target publics. Thus, narratives in ads have to beware of these additional constraints and, what is more, to make the most of them. Unlike what happens in other discourses, ads will not have people's undivided attention; they will have to count on people talking during the ad, about more or less unrelated things the ad reminded them of, about the celebrity endorsing the product (and how much they are earning for doing it), but seldom about the real benefits of the product or service at stake. Hence the need for stressing the message through the different channels available: if the talking in the living-room stops people from actually hearing what the actors are saying, the music and sound effects will convey the right mood; or if the TV is set to mute during the break, hopefully the gesturing and facial expressions will be able to tell the story as well. The sheer number of repetitions will also guarantee with a reasonable degree of certainty that at least once or twice the right target audience will be exposed to the ad in full — making it possible for them to identify the ad at stake in later exposures, even if these exposures are only partial.

Apart from this reinforcement of the overall meaning achieved by the joint effort of the channels involved in the making of a single ad, and the repetition of number of exposures in the same medium (usually quite high), ad messages also try to achieve ubiquity by simultaneously appearing in several media. In the case of multimedia campaigns, the overall message is semiotically translated so as to convey the same impression on its audience, when adapted to the specific characteristics of the medium used to broadcast it. Although it is possible in some cases to make use, for instance, of the same text that what used for the television commercial in the corresponding radio spot, there is usually some effort to adapt each ad in the campaign to the medium where it is going to be broadcast, maximising its potential while keeping in sight an equivalence effect (Eco and Nergaard 2001: 219–220). These repetitions (*in toto* and in semiotic overall effect) are a part of the functioning of the advertising system and correspond to a circular effect: on the one hand, audiences know that ads will be repeated, so it is not worth paying them a lot of attention; on the other hand, advertisers are aware of this, so they will study ways in which the content of the message can be repeatedly stressed without upsetting the very delicate balance between enough exposures to prompt action and tiredness on the part of the viewers:

> As we have seen, the process of interpretation of the ad by the audience is, in fact, a process of translation through which the viewer integrates a specific ad in an advertising campaign into an overall concept — almost like working with a puzzle, where every single piece makes sense. This ability to interpret a given element in one code as equivalent to another in a different code is achieved by means of the encyclopaedic and linguistic competence that enables a language user to determine 'equivalence' in pragmatic terms. (…) In practical terms, a viewer with the right background and experience will be predisposed to look for equivalence in an object that was conceived with the aim of achieving that equivalence. (Freitas 2004: 309)

Although this can also apply to other discourses, ad narratives are meant to be repeated (*ad nauseam*, some would say) and that need for repetition (due to pragmatic reasons) becomes a structural characteristic of ads and advertising campaigns. Their repetitive nature implies that they are relatively unimportant — and maybe that is why their economic and social effects are ponderous and relevant in the long run (Rose 2001: 95)

3. Intermediality and storytelling in ads: the case of the RTP 1 campaign

As we have previously seen, the apposition of narrative effects in ad texts is a strategy to transform a product or service into an entity that is both meaningful and active, which seems to be quite effective, provided the storyline is related to what is being advertised. Also, the technical possibilities of the medium being used will necessarily shape the kind of narrative that will unfold. This does not mean that a narrative format cannot be maintained across the all spectrum of media chosen to broadcast a specific campaign: however, it will be shaped according to the technical possibilities afforded by each medium.

In the specific case of the campaign chosen for analysis in this chapter, we find a situation where medium and message are superimposed, up to a point: in fact, one of the media selected to advertise television programmes for the new season on a given channel was television – and all the television commercials were broadcast in the same channel where the new programmes would shortly be appearing. These television commercials exemplify the notion of conflation of roles of the media — as the conveyors but also the repository of meanings:

> Because of the configuring action of the medium, however, it is not always possible to distinguish an encoded object from the act of encoding. In the live

> broadcasts of television, for instance, the object to be sent is created through the act of recording itself. Insofar as they present their own affordances, channel-type media can be simultaneously modes of transmission and semiotic means of expression. It is in this second capacity that they impact narrative form and meaning. (Ryan 2008a: 289)

The ads that will be analysed in this chapter represent a good example of the complex intermedial relationships that can be found within the space of a single advertising campaign. In fact, it is not the *same* narrative plot that is recreated in the different media. In the case of the campaigns analyzed here, each ad is identified as a prototype of the ads of that campaign: for instance, all the ads in the campaign for *A Minha Geração* will feature the programme's presenter as the narrative link, whereas in the campaign for the football broadcasts, it is the ball that literally invades celebrities' lives and provides the narrative thread.

In broad terms, each of these ads, in each of the media used, promotes one programme selected from the new programmes of a television channel. With a few exceptions (the radio ads and, to a lesser degree, the outdoor ads, which clearly have a subsidiary role), their function is complementary, rather than repetitive, which is understandable, since their aim is to promote the totality of the programmes, and not just one in particular.

3.1. The ads and the media used in the RTP1 campaign

The self-promotional campaign broadcast by RTP1 between October 2008 and January 2009 used the following media for divulging its ads: television, outdoors and radio. Since only new seasons of specific programmes were being promoted, and no new programmes were being introduced, all the ads could appeal to prior knowledge on the part of the audience as to actors, presenters and journalists displayed. For all the above media, the ads were very much based on familiar and prototypical features of the programmes, to make them easier to identify at first glance. As we will see, this previous familiarity with the programmes and their formats has important implications for the type of narrative structures that we will find in the campaigns analysed.

The following chart classifies the programmes being promoted and the media used for each of them. For some of the programmes, a few more ads in each of these media were broadcast during the same time period. However, for reasons of space, only these mentioned in the chart were selected for discussion, since the ones that were not included present no relevant differences in terms of message content and approach:

Programme	*Television*	*Outdoors*	*Radio*
Conta-me como foi (soap/comedy based on historical facts of the 60s)	1 commercial		1 spot
A Minha Geração (music show, entertainment, interviews, based on musical hits of the past)	3 commercials	3 outdoors	
Prós e Contras (interviews, current affairs, politics)	1 commercial		
Olha quem dança (musical show, audience participation for dance contests)	1 commercial		
Football broadcasts (live sports, sports commentary)	1 commercial	3 outdoors	

A general overview of all these ads reveals a flagrant similarity between them — as befits a campaign for promoting one television channel: they are every bit as entertaining as the programmes they aim to publicise. For this purpose, they condense the main characteristics of each programme (briefly described in the chart above), in very much the same dynamic and agile way we normally expect to see in a film trailer at the cinema. This is a common tendency in television ads nowadays:

> In fact, ads have come to assume the same bright reality that characterises the majority of television programmes that compete for audiences during prime time (…), thus blurring the frontiers of genre between what is the entertainment part and what are the buying-inducing bits. This hybridism makes it easier to turn them into objects of aesthetic pleasure and to downplay the fact that the ultimate aim of ads is to sell (…) (Freitas 2008: 127)

All these ads are part of a joint brand-building effort — if we consider this television channel as a «brand», with a separate and clearly identifiable identity — instead of a mere sum of individual ads. This notion is further reinforced by the closing line in all the ads: «*On Friday nights/ weekends /…* (depending on the day the programme is broadcast) *leave your routine and enter RTP1*», in a clear boost for the channel and not just for the programme at stake: apart from reinforcing the audience rates for each of the programmes, this campaign is effectively promoting a global entertainment service for the forthcoming season.

Therefore, it is possible to say that the narrativity detectable in these campaigns is also the result of the cumulative effect of the programmes and campaigns that refer to them. In fact, most of the narrative threads pre-exist the ads: it is the programmes advertised which are narrative in structure (with the possible exception of the football broadcasts and *Prós e Contras*), in which case the ad will take advantage of the storylines that already exist in order to create a clean, economic and condensed formula with maximal reference to another narrative. Taken together, programme and respective campaign achieve a full sense of narrative, where previous knowledge on the programme and the new inputs brought by the promotional ad converge into one coherent story:

> Narratives are more than temporary drafts in the theatre of the mind, more than transitory firings of neurons in the brain along individual pathways; they are solidified, conscious representations produced by the convergence of many different mental processes that operate both within and outside stories. (Ryan 2006: 12)

In this case — and unlike what would usually happens in a traditional novel or a short story, programme and ad split the narrative effort between themselves: we can say that it is the programme that provides the «telling» of a given narrative (giving it its backbone, overall coherence and spatial and temporal development), while the ads, in their turn, will guarantee the «showing» of the narrative characteristics of that same programme — as a small sample of what we will get if we let the ad persuade us into becoming spectators of the full-blown stories presented in prime time. Ads play, then, an ancillary role (Ryan 2008b: 316) to the more complex narrative function of the programmes. Literally, they illustrate what comes next, creating a mouth-watering effect that seduces viewers into becoming engaged participants in a universe of programmes full of storytelling possibilities.

3.1.1. The RTP1 campaign: the television commercials

Television as a medium offers the possibility of immediate high impact in their target audiences, mainly because of the complex ways it combines visual and audio materials. Its dramatic capacities are also very high, in that it can recreate life scenes in a credible and complete way (Wells et al. 1998: 343). Since there is a more widespread sensorial appeal than with other media, it is also more likely that there will be an increase in attention levels and higher emotional investment on the part of the viewers (Freitas 2008: 9–10).

In the specific case of the television commercials in this campaign, the pinpointing of the intended audience (which is something difficult to achieve in a medium that is generalist) is possible and made easier by the fact that the people who are meant to adhere to this new season of

Figure 1: Frames from *Conta-me como* foi television commercial
See the color illustration on page 342.

programmes have probably been clients of long standing — and nothing would be easier for them than to go on doing what they have already been doing up to that point. Hence the word play of the ads' closing line, proposing that routine-breaking action will be undertaken by the service provider, and not by the viewers.

The television commercial for *Conta-me como foi* [*Tell me how it was back then*] is perhaps the most rewarding of the television lot in terms of intermedial, intertextual and storytelling readings. Also, it is the one which provides the most evident narrative structure and relies more strongly on non-linguistic channels to provide all the necessary cohesive links.

This commercial publicises the forthcoming third season of a hugely popular programme in Portugal, which narrates the family life of a low-middle class traditional family living in Lisbon during the 1960s and early 70s. Its cast is mostly composed of well-known actors, and the clothes, hairdos, ways of speaking and household objects are recreated with minute detail. The television set is an important part of the family life, where it functions as source of entertainment, news and outraged comments from the older members of the family about the latest prevailing tendencies in arts, ways of dressing and behaviour, political developments in the country and the state of the world in general. Whenever comments like these occur, the present day viewers of *Conta-me Como Foi* enter the television screen just like the characters who are watching it, and are shown real images of those decades, shown in black and white shots, always slightly out of focus. Apart from image quality, they are easy to identify as documental images from the RTP archives because of the peculiar elocution style of television newscasters and variety show presenters of the 1960s and early 1970s.

This commercial mimics the usual structure of the programme, by including a mini-version of all these details and managing to achieve a light-hearted and humorous tone that is also similar to the comedy undertones of the series. It begins with a black and white domestic sequence that looks exactly like a television commercial of the 1960s, where the label of a box of detergent that is being handled by the actress/singer reads *Conta-me Como Foi*. At the same time she twirls and swirls around the room, displaying the box with waltz-like gestures and a posed smile, she sings, with a choir of two male voices, a lively, very sixties tune that explains that this "new product", which is "the best in the market of the television channels" has finally arrived, and that it has come back because of popular demand, since "everyone has missed the Lopes family so, so much." As this "commercial" is reaching the end, the camera moves back, so as to encompass two people sitting on a sofa, watching the commercial and looking at each other with a puzzled expression on their faces. The image is now in colour and the living room used in the series is now recognisable. The man and the woman on the sofa are the main characters of the series. The woman stares blankly at the man and asks: "What on earth is this?", and he responds, shrugging his shoulders: "How should I know? Some modern fancy, I guess."

As we can see from the brief description above (which, as was inevitable, is unable to capture the rhythm and liveliness of some many layers of meaning interacting at the same time), this commercial explores to the full the mise-en-abîme effect the programme consistently uses — but in reverse: the viewers are plunged *in medias res* within a scene of the programme, which is, after all, an ad advertising it. However, the main characters seem unable to recognise any of the references to it, and even classify it as something so modern as to be incomprehensible. This successive jumping in and out of the fictional status of the narrative creates an effect of surprise or even incongruity, with an increased humorous effect arising from it (Raskin 1985: 31–32).

As it were, the sixties-like ad would be adequate and effective in publicising the third series, without the need for the closing gambit. Comparing the programme to a box of detergent that is back in the market because of widespread popular demand would probably cause laughter just because of the disruption of normal detergent ad scripts. However, the introduction of another frame (represented by the characters' dialogue) between the "commercial" and the real viewers further mediates the telling of the story by the actress, foregrounding even more its fictional status of a (doubly fictional) narrative embedded within another (fictional) narrative.

The television commercials for *A Minha Geração* [*My Generation*] are much less complex, although they also condense in an effective manner what the essence of the programme is, i.e. to talk about and remind people of high points of several decades in different areas, with an emphasis on arts and entertainment in general, but also discussing major events in politics and religion, for instance.

Therefore, with so many disparate areas to contemplate, a series of different ads were devised, with a very flimsy narrative thread: the viewers are invited to imagine the presenter of the programme as if she were really living the situations referred to in the programme — instead of just discussing them with the people that she interviews. This proposal of total immersion is achieved by visual strategies. A number of easily identifiable scenes in black and white are shown in the ads, and Catarina Furtado (the presenter) is there as well — not as a contemporary woman who just observes it from afar, but as someone who plays an active role in every situation. For this purpose, the images are doctored so as to accommodate her presence in pre-existing classical scenes. In order to deepen the impression that she is a part of that decade, her clothes, hair and make-up are also carefully adapted to each of the situations depicted. As she becomes the only element to guarantee cohesion in this set of commercials, her attitude is similar in all of them: her expression and facial gestures are always a bit contrived and poised, in a display of joy and awe, obviously rendering conspicuous her happiness to be sharing that moment — be that being spoken to by Frank Sinatra, dancing frantically with a Euro-Festival Song Contest finalist or even watching John F. Kennedy delivering his famous speech in Berlin. In this case, possible narrative developments are suggested, rather than displayed, and they become possible by means of intertextual interpretations, where reality and fiction will mix.

The television commercial for *Prós e Contras* [*Pros and Cons*] dramatises the aim of the programme it is publicising by structuring its visual functioning around a metaphorical reading of a literal expression: "verbal argument = taking opposite sides = war" (Lakoff and Johnson 1980: 51). The commercial depicts people clearly standing on opposite sides – on the one side are the police forces, and on the other people in protest.

Figure 2: Frames from three television commercials of *A Minha Geração.*

Their facial expressions and gestures express deep-seated disagreement and resentment towards the opposite side of the barricade.

This scenery of the conflict, filmed in dramatic black and white images, cut by close shots of faces with clenched teeth and arms picking up stones and aiming guns, once again metaphorically describes the heated arguments sustained by the participants in this programme, whereas the helmets and protective devices worn by the parties in conflict represent the vast array of documents prepared in advance by the participants and the numerous pre-emptive statements in defence of their respective positions.

An important element, however, is that there is confrontation in this battle (the one in the ad, but also the many battles fought during the programme), but not a real physical conflict. At the height of provocation, the two groups swap sides: the protesters become policemen and the policemen are the ones protesting now — perhaps due to the presence of the female journalist who presents it, and whose hand-drawn face on a billboard appears as the closing scene. At the same time, a female voice-over tells us that before we take sides, we have to know the arguments of

Figure 3: Frames from the television commercial of *Prós e Contras.*

the others first, explaining that *Prós e Contras* is the programs were both sides are always heard. As in the previous case, it is the easily recognisable presenter of the programme that establishes the necessary interpretative link with the images shown in the ad and who firmly relates them to the programme that is being publicised.

The commercial for *Olha Quem Dança* [*Look Who's Dancing*] is built around a sequence of mini-narratives which make sense on their own, but also acquire a cumulative meaning at the final scene. We see different people, none of them very young or elegant, performing their serious, boring or repetitive jobs, dressed as if to participate in a dance contest of some kind. The internal coherence of this commercial is established by the repetition of parallel visual scenes, which convey regularity but, perhaps even more importantly, by the Latino dance music that accompanies all the scenes and whose rhythm matches the body movement of all these actors, thus creating a link between scenes that could have only been juxtaposed. The final connection appears under a linguistic form, as a female voice-over which invites viewers to come and dance with them on Friday

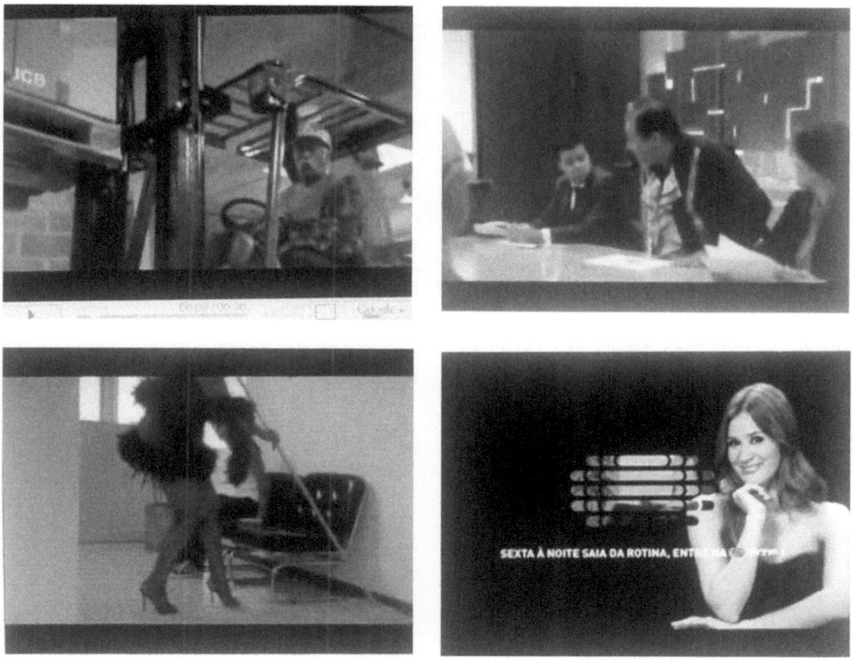

Figure 4: Frames from the television commercial of *Olha Quem Dança.*

nights, and also visually, with the image of the female presenter of the programme in the closing scene, as if saying that all these narratives suggested are possible and likely, and need not remain encased inside people's minds.

The commercial for the promotion of football broadcasts does not have a clearly identifiable narrative structure, since it is the ball that provides a cohesive focus for the whole sequence. In fact, it could be said that the ball functions as a disruptor of possible ongoing narratives, since it interrupts familiar faces of this channel, while they are at work. It is the music (stately, leisurely and whimsical) that unites the scenes, filmed in the settings these professionals use for working during the day. Therefore, whatever narratives are going on, they are at least put on hold for a while when the ball is at play: perhaps an invitation to the viewers to do the same while important games are being broadcast during the weekends?

Figure 5: Frames from the television commercial of the football broadcasts

3.1.2. The RTP1 campaign: the outdoor ads

Outdoors have as their main advantage the possibility of targeting people who are on the move (Belch and Belch 2004: 433) — which could constitute an immediate disadvantage as well, since people will only give them a passing glance because they will not have time to look for detail. This implies that, generally, outdoor ads will have only a few words and powerful and striking images.

As we have seen in the first chart, two of the television ads discussed in the previous point have corresponding outdoor ads. Beginning with the outdoor for *A Minha Geração*, we can see that they have a clearly supportive role in relation to television: whereas the commercials try to encompass the diversity of fields covered by the programme, the outdoors are limited to the field of music. Once again, it is the programme presenter who provides the visual link between the three outdoors, becoming not only a part of the record cover that identifies the decade, but the singer of the music, once again confirming the ad's immersion in the sixties that

Figure 6: Outdoor ad for *A Minha Geração*. See the color illustration on page 343.

had already been explored in the television commercials. Therefore, what in the commercial was music and image in motion is here recovered in terms of equivalence by the protagonist role assured by the (static) cover of the record, which, however, encases limitless musical possibilities that could be activated in the minds of the public.

The outdoor ads for the football broadcasts on the weekends use a similar strategy to the one we have already seen in the television ad, i.e. showing well-known professionals of this television channels from non-sports areas. However, we can postulate a complementary role between the commercials and these outdoors, in that some narrative thread could be suggested between them.

If we consider that, in the commercials analysed in the previous section, the interruption caused by the ball left most of the professionals indifferent, we can read the individualised outdoor ads as a sort of conversion to the importance of the ball (and football's importance, more specifically): in these three outdoor ads, we have a female journalist, a stand-up comedian and a presenter portrayed as major figures in the world of football, as if we were being told that even they, in spite of their busy professional lives and success in their chosen careers, had acknowledged the magic of football – so why not the viewer as well? This also constitutes

Figure 7: Outdoor ads for A Minha Geração

an ingenious form of advertising them back, as well, and the real roles they fulfil in the television channel, in an intertextual web of criss-crossed promotion.

3.1.3. The RTP1 campaign: the radio spots

In the case of the only radio spot selected from this campaign, the advertisers have opted for one solution that does not always work in an effective manner, i.e. to maintain the audio elements on the corresponding television commercials and reproduce them without any alteration in the radio spot.

This means that there was a deliberate decision to use the former as a supporting device for the television commercial, by reducing it to few of its semiotic elements. This ends up being effective in the present case mainly for one reason: the television commercial is so rich and overcharged with meanings of the semantic area of «sixtiness» that only a few of them would be enough to activate approximately the same readings. As we have seen in the analysis of the television commercial, it was the compelling and harmonious song that did the necessary explaining about the third series and also set the tone for the ad. The male voice-over that

Figure 8: Outdoor ad for Football Broadcasts.
See the color illustration on page 344.

Figure 9: Outdoor ads for Football Broadcasts.
See the color illustrations on page 345 and 346.

closes the television ad, with its careful and contrived form of speaking also helps to define the decade. Therefore, taken together, these two elements are enough to make the radio spot work as a reminder of the main ad of the campaign — as they would be sufficient for identification if the intended public were not paying attention to the television commercial and only its audio part were heard.

Conclusion

Contemporary ads can yield valuable information about the way narratives function and about the way they can be told in very economic forms with the help of the media involved in the broadcast of these ads. Ad campaigns have to be considered as global efforts, instead of being considered in isolation, since some of their storytelling possibilities are encased in the intertextual crossing of references, both within the universe of a single campaign, but very often in the recalling of other discourses that will activate, in their turn, other more or less individual readings. In ads, what we very often see is not the telling of a whole story with clear boundaries, but the sketching of one narrative which will make sense on its own, with the suggestion of many others, which the viewers will continue (or not) according to their individuality. This freedom in the elaboration of possible narratives is not exclusive of advertising discourse — but it constitutes one of its most evident characteristics and it is a part of its inner functioning.

As we have seen in the advertising campaign briefly analysed in the previous points, due to constraints related with lack of time, the process of story-telling in ads recuperates basic narrative devices such as gesturing or facial expressions to convey the enchainment of events and compensate for the gapping that is a characteristic of advertising discourse. These elliptical forms make these condensed narratives brisk, effective, fluent, and engaging, since so much cooperation is expected from the viewers, who have to supply the missing elements by using their own schemata to fill any blanks. In most cases, the medium used to convey the story constitutes one of the elements of narrative process, i.e. the channel used by the narrator to reach the narratee. However, — as in the case of one of the commercial spots analysed in this chapter — the role of the medium is foregrounded and comes to assume narratorial expression in the story that is being told.

Contemporary ads emphasise interactivity and continuous flow of meanings in the stories they choose to tell us. Linear paths in ad narratives are not common, which is something that also characterises contemporary societies, where stories of every type are constantly being told, overheard, interrupted, retold and commented on, with further layers of meaning being added to them all the time. All these turns of the screw make narratives more appealing, even if it becomes more challenging to establish the necessary connections between so many different storylines.

Narrative has undeniable human appeal and it is clearly a form of imposing a sense of continuity, enjoyment and tellability to the events depicted in the ad — and, paraphrasing Terence, we can say that nothing that is human can be, all in all, alien to advertising.

References

Baldry, Anthony P. (2004). "Phase and transition, type and instance: patterns in media texts as seen through a multimodal concordancer." In: O'Halloran, Kay L. (ed.). *Multimodal Discourse Analysis: Systemic Functional Perspectives*. London: Continuum, 83–108.

Barthes, Roland (1977). "Change the object itself: Mythology today." In: Barthes, Roland. *Image Music Text* (trans. Stephen Heath). London: Fontana Press, 165–169.

Belch, George E., and Michael A. Belch (2004). *Advertising and Promotion: An Integrated Marketing Communications Perspective*. New York: McGraw Hill.

Bezuidenhout-Raath, Ilze (2008 [2005]). "Advertisements." In: Herman, David, Manfred Jahn and Marie-Laure Ryan (eds.). *Routledge Encyclopedia of Narrative Theory*. London and New York: Routledge, 7–8.

Blake, Andrew (1997). "Listen to Britain: music, advertising and postmodern culture." In: Nava, Mica, Blake, Andrew, MacRury, Iain and Barry Richards (eds.). *Buy this Book: Studies in Advertising and Consumption*. London and New York: Routledge, 224–238.

Cook, Guy (1992). *The Discourse of Advertising*. London and New York: Routledge.

Eco, Umberto, and Siri Neergard (2001 [1998]). "Semiotic approaches." In: Baker, M. (ed). *Routledge Encyclopedia of Translation Studies*. London and New York: Routledge, 218–222.

Freitas, Elsa Simões Lucas (2004). "Similar concepts, different channels: intersemiotic translation in three Portuguese advertising campaigns." In: Adab, Beverly, and Cristina Valdès (eds.). *Key Debates in the Translation of Advertising Material*. Manchester: St Jerome Publishing. *The Translator*, 10(2):291–311.

– (2008). *Taboo in Advertising*. Amsterdam and Philadelphia: John Benjamins.

Goddard, Angela (1998). *The Language of Advertising*. London and New York: Routledge.

Goffman, Erving (1979 [1976]). *Gender Advertisements*. London and Basingstoke: Macmillan.

González Requena, Jesús and Amaya Ortiz de Zárate (1995). *El Espot Pubicitario: Las metamorforsis del deseo*. Madrid: Cátedra.

Grishakova, Marina (2006). *The Models of Space, Time and Vision in V. Nabokov's Fiction: Narrative Strategies and Cultural Frames*. Tartu: Tartu University Press.

Gulas, Charles S., and Mark G. Weinberger (2006). *Humor in Advertising: a comprehensive analysis*. New York: M.E.Sharpe.

Kress, Gunther and Theo van Leeuwen (1996). *Reading Images: the grammar of visual design*. London and New York: Routledge.
Lakoff, George and Mark Johnson (1980). *Metaphors We Live By*. Chicago and London: The University of Chicago Press.
MacCannell, Dean (1987). "'Sex Sells': Comment on Gender Images and Myth in Advertising." In: Umiker-Sebeok, Jean (ed.). *Marketing and Semiotics: New Directions in the Study of Signs for Sale*. Berlin: Mouton de Gruyter, 521–531.
McGregor, William (2008 [2005]). "Gesture." In: Herman David, Manfred Jahn and Marie-Laure Ryan (eds.). *Routledge Encyclopedia of Narrative Theory*. London and New York: Routledge, 205–207.
Messaris, Paul (1997). *Visual Persuasion: the role of images in advertising*. London: Sage.
Myers, Greg (1994). *Words in Ads*. London: Edward Arnold.
– (1999). *Ad Worlds: Brands, Media, Audience*. London: Arnold.
O'Halloran, Kay L. (2004). "Visual Semiosis in Film." In: O'Halloran, Kay L. (ed.). *Multimodal Discourse Analysis: Systemic Functional Perspectives*. London: Continuum, 109–130.
Ogilvy, David (1983). *Ogilvy on Advertising*. London: Prion Books.
Raskin, Victor (1985). *Semantic Mechanisms of Humor*. Dordrecht, Holland: D. Reidel Publishing Company.
Rose, Gillian (2001). *Visual Methodologies: An Introduction to the Interpretation of Visual Materials*. London: Sage.
Ryan, Marie-Laure (2006). *Avatars of Story*. Minneapolis and London: University of Minnesota Press.
– (2008a). "Media and Narrative." In: Herman David, Manfred Jahn and Marie-Laure Ryan (eds.). *Routledge Encyclopedia of Narrative Theory*. London and New York: Routledge, 288–292.
– (2008b). "Mode." In: Herman David, Manfred Jahn and Marie-Laure Ryan (eds.). *Routledge Encyclopedia of Narrative Theory*. London and New York: Routledge, 315–316.
– (2008c) "Virtuality." In: Herman David, Manfred Jahn and Marie-Laure Ryan (eds.). *Routledge Encyclopedia of Narrative Theory*. London and New York: Routledge, 627–629.
Spolsky, Ellen (2008). "Gapping." In: Herman David, Manfred Jahn and Marie-Laure Ryan (eds.). *Routledge Encyclopedia of Narrative Theory*. London and New York: Routledge, 193–194.
Wells, William, Burnett, John and Sandra Moriarty (1998). *Advertising: Principles & Practice*. New Jersey: Prentice-Hall.
Williamson, Judith (1978). *Decoding Advertisements*. London and Boston, Massachusetts.
Wolf, Werner (2008). "Intermediality." In: Herman David, Manfred Jahn and Marie-Laure Ryan (eds.). *Routledge Encyclopedia of Narrative Theory*. London and New York: Routledge, 252–256.
Yeshin, Tony (2006). *Advertising*. London: Thomson.

Alison Gibbons
(De Montfort University, Leicester)

The Narrative Worlds and Multimodal Figures of *House of Leaves*: "—find your own words; I have no more"

As academic pursuits, both multimodality and intermediality can be seen to have launched in the 1990s, although it should be acknowledged that intermediality stems from the more established tradition of interart studies. While to some extent, the youth of these disciplines makes them exciting fields of research, it nevertheless also leads to a certain degree of intersection and overlap between the two. Indeed, one of the prerequisites faced by critics working in intermediality studies is the necessity of definition. That is, since intermediality is acknowledged as an "umbrella-term" (Rajewsky 2005: 44), subject to varying uses and interpretations and often used interchangeably with other related terms such as intertextuality and multimediality amongst others, it is essential to identify one's critical position. I will therefore outline what is understood by the term in the next section, refining my usage of it throughout.

This article is structured in eight parts with a conclusion. The first three sections function as introductions; to intermediality, multimodality, and *House of Leaves* by Mark Z. Danielewski, respectively. In section 4, I consider the intermediality of the novel as embedded in its narrative layers while in section 5, I offer an analysis of an extract which shows up both multimodality and intermediality at work. Section 6 presents a less well-known form of intermediality, namely intermediality as ontological experience, while the final two sections examine this concept in relation to *House of Leaves*.

1. Intermediality

Intermedial research first thrived in the academic circles of Europe, and Germany in particular, before gathering the more international recognition it holds today. In its development, critics have strived to demarcate the field by creating taxonomies of intermediality (for instance, see Balme 2001, and for overviews see Rajewsky 2005, Wolf 2005), yet there seems to be no universal or indeed unified understanding. Tackling the critical problem of definition, Rajewsky (2005) suggests:

> Trying to reduce to a common denominator the host of current conceptions of intermediality and the vast range of subject-matter they cover, we are forced to appeal to a very broadly conceived concept which would be limited neither to specific phenomena or media, nor to specific research objectives. In this sense, intermediality may serve foremost as a generic term for all those phenomena that (as indicated by the prefix *inter*) in some way take place *between* media. "Intermedial" therefore designates those configurations which have to do with a crossing of borders between media… (2005: 46; her italics)

Furthermore, as can be seen in Rajewsky's own articulation, the term is heavily reliant upon the free morpheme 'media'. This in itself suffers from problems of definition, as Wolf (2005) notes:

> A plethora of meanings has been connected with this notion ranging from a very narrow conception as a technical channel for transmitting information to an extremely wide definition in which 'medium' designates all 'extensions of man', be it of the body or the consciousness (Wolf 2005: 253).

Wolf suggests that both extremities of understanding of the term 'media' are unhelpful for intermedial studies and that the range of designations for the term 'intermedial' is partly due to its interdisciplinary scope.

Taking Rajewsky's (2005) and Wolf's (2005) classifications, intermediality can be subjected to further formal classification for analytical clarity. As such, four categories emerge: transmediality, intermedial transposition, intermedial reference, and plurimediality. Transmediality (Wolf 2005: 253) applies to phenomena which can exist in more than one media, and tends to be restricted to formal devices such as metalepsis or narrative itself. Intermedial transposition (Wolf 2005: 254; termed 'medial transposition' by Rajewsky 2005: 52) refers to the transformation of a text in one media into another form of media product such as film adaptations of novels, while intermedial reference (Rajewsky 2005: 52; Wolf 2005: 254–5) works like intertextual reference but across media, for instance when a book refers to a film.

The final category, plurimediality (Wolf 2005, 254; termed 'media combination' by Rajewsky 2005: 52) I have left until last since it meets with considerably overlap with another more commonly used term, multimodality. I engage with this in the next section.

2. Plurimediality / Multimodality

Plurimediality, or multimediality, is defined by Wolf (2005: 254) as occurring "whenever two or more media are overtly present in a given semiotic entity at least in one instance", while multimodality is defined by the term's originators Kress and van Leeuwen (1996: 183) as existing in "any text whose meanings are realized through more than one semiotic mode". The slippage between the meanings of these two terms is therefore immediately apparent. The crucial difference is the emphasis on either media or mode respectively, but regrettably, this only returns us to Wolf's insightful explication of the scope of 'media' itself. On one hand, it is tempting to use 'media' as a reference to the narrow more technical conception mentioned by Wolf while 'mode' would take on a more encompassing dimension. However, looking at the types of texts cited by Wolf and Rajewsky as plurimedial (opera, illuminated manuscripts, comics) and Kress and van Leeuwen as multimodal (newspapers, film, magazines, webpages, comics), no such clarity emerges. In this article, I adopt the term multimodality. I do this partly because of the term's popularity, but also because I take a cognitive approach to the intermedial. Thus, the term multi*modal* suggest both media forms as well as sensory modality, enabling the medial and the modal to be connected to the ways in which human subjects perceive and interact with intermediality.

The focus of the article is an example of multimodal printed literature, a noves which utilises a plurality of semiotic modes (primarily verbal, visual, and kinetic) in the communication and progression of its narrative. The different modes of expression are located on the page not in an autonomous or separate fashion, but in such a way that, while these modes have distinct means of communicating, they constantly interact in the production of textual meaning. As such, one mode is not privileged, but rather narrative content, type-face, type-setting, graphic design, white-space, and images all have a role to play. Since multimodal literature is still an emerging area of academic interest (see Gibbons 2008; 2010, forthcoming 2010; Nørgaard 2010), it is worth outlining some of the formal features that consistently appear in multimodal novels (taking the inclusion of images for granted):

(1) Unusual textual layouts and page design.
(2) Varied typography.
(3) Use of colour in both type and imagistic content.
(4) Concrete realisation of text to create images, as in concrete poetry.
(5) Devices that draw attention to the text's materiality, including metafictive writing.

(6) Footnotes and self-interrogative critical voices.
(7) Flip book sections.
(8) Mixing of genres, both in literary terms (e.g. horror, romance) and in terms of visual effect (e.g. newspaper clippings, play dialogue).

Such novels are highly sophisticated art forms, both in terms of their self-consciousness (using metafictional, intertextual, and intermedial reference, foregrounding materiality, innovative typographical textual layouts) and the invitations and demands they issue to readers. Indeed, multimodal novels often emphasise the dynamic and embodied nature of reading.

3. *House of Leaves* by Mark Z. Danielewski

Mark Z. Danielewski's *House of Leaves by Zampanò with introduction and notes by Johnny Truant* is a central example of a multimodal fiction, having achieved 'bestseller' status soon after its publication (see Bray/ Gibbons forthcoming 2010). As a multimodal object, *House of Leaves* is brimming with typographical trickery and inventive visual designs that share many commonalities with concrete poetry. In many of the novel's narrative sequences, text traverses the page, frequently changing direction and page-location or forming imagistic designs, all of which bear relevance to the narrative action within the present moment of reading. The material reality of the novel is also a point of emphasis, since the book is an epic 700 page read, its almost square-like shape making it a 'door-stop' of a book that is heavy in a reader's hands. Indeed, these features lead Hayles to speak of *House of Leaves* as "so profound it becomes a new kind of form and artefact" (2002: 112) when compared to so-called 'traditional' printed literature. Importantly, the multimodal attributes (foregrounded visual designs and white space used in combination with verbal text) of *House of Leaves* are vital both to its narrative and to the reader's cognitive experience of the novel.

House of Leaves is not only challenging in terms of its multimodality and materiality, but it is narratologically intricate. It weaves multiple storylines together into a recursive narrative structure composed of embedded or nested worlds. In interview with Cottrell, Danielewski admits, "I believe the structure of *House of Leaves* is far more difficult to explain than it is to read" (no date). As such, my summary of the novel's complicated plot is accompanied by illustrative diagram (see figure 1).

At the heart of *House of Leaves* is the central plot of "The Navidson Record". Will Navidson is a Pulitzer Prize winning photojournalist who decides to create a film documenting his family's move to, and new life in, their new home on Ash Tree Lane. However, all is not as it seems, and the video takes a sinister turn when the internal measurements of the house appear to grow and an unfamiliar door opening into a dim corridor emerges in the master bedroom. A series of explorations into these strange and shifting proportions take place, conducted by Navidson, his brother Tom, and friend Bill Reston, as well as a team of professional hunter/explorers — Holloway, Jed, and Wax. "The Navidson Record" is the name of the video, documenting the mysterious occurrences in the house through 'big-brother'-style house-cameras as well as through camera footage taken during the explorations of its dark interior.

Since "The Navidson Record" is a docu-film, the reader does not, of course, have direct access to it. Although it forms a narrative layer in terms of the novel's ontological landscape, this layer is not concrete or tangible, but rather one that is recovered through narrative mediation. In fact, the reader learns of "The Navidson Record" through a character named Zampanò. Zampanò is an old blind man who documents the video through written narrative description and academic commentary, the completed manuscript of which is also named "The Navidson Record". It is worth mentioning that Zampanò's visual disability troubles the video's ontological status (Does it really exist? How could the old man have ever *seen* it?).

Zampanò's commentary is itself encased within the narrative of Johnny Truant, a crude tattooist with a Los Angeles lifestyle who, after Zampanò is found dead in his apartment, becomes the owner of the manuscript compiling Zampanò's reflections on "The Navidson Record". Truant's narrative begins in the novel's *Introduction*, after which it exists in the form of footnotes, sometimes brief and sometimes spiralling into large passages of text that take over the narrative for several pages.

Framing Truant's narrative is the text of the anonymous editors, who occasionally add footnoted remarks, often pertaining to the fact- or fictionality of the book and/or functioning in a similar way to a disclaimer. For instance, their words appear on the text's actual copyright page, they author the short foreword, and an example of their commentary within the novel can be found on page 54: "[66]Mr. Truant declined to comment further on this particular passage. – Ed." (Danielewski 2000: 54). To differentiate the latter three authors and layers of narrative, each is assigned a different typeface. Pressman explains:

> Each of these narrative voices is identified by a different font and associated with a specific medium: Zampanò's academic commentary appears in Times Roman, the font associated with newspapers and the linotype; Truant's footnotes are in Courier, imitate a typewriter's inscription, and thematically identify him as the

"courier" of the manuscript; the terse notations from the Ed. are aptly presented in Bookman. (Pressman 2006)

One might view this as a form of intermedial reference with the visual dynamic of font choice signalling the character's voice.

In addition to the above-mentioned narrative worlds, *House of Leaves* also contains three appendices, the contents of which are attributed to the three storyworld authors respectively, and, unusually for a novel, an index. Figure 1 depicts the relationship(s) between these and the more central narratives with dotted connecting lines originating from the border of the narrative world that claims ownership.

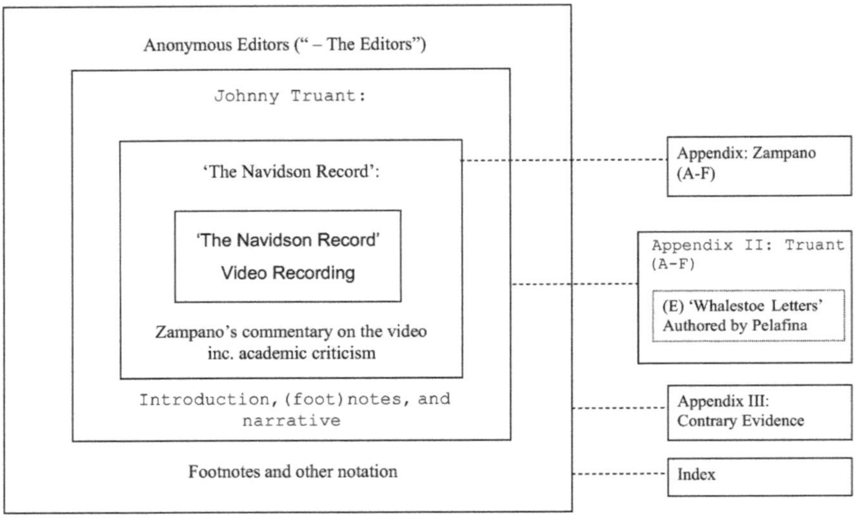

Figure 1: Narrative Levels of Danielewski (2000) House of Leaves

Due to the recursive narrative structure of the novel, characters in framing worlds have narrative access to the appendices of the world(s) they encase. For instance, both Truant and "- The Editors" have ontological access to Zampanò's appendix, but only "- The Editors" have access to Truant's appendix. Those who have access are thus able to comment upon these lower level appendices, such as "- The Editors" note at the beginning of 'The Three Attic Whalestoe Institute Letters' in part E. of Truant's Appendix. Not insignificantly, 'The Three Attic Whalestoe Institute Letters' are a collection of letters to Truant from his mother Pelafina. Pelafina's letters introduce, therefore, another author to *House of Leaves* who also has her own font and narrative voice.

4. Narrating the Film of "The Navidson Record"

In the previous outline of the complex narrative structure of *House of Leaves*, it was mentioned that Zampanò's narrative is a document of the video of "The Navidson Record". As such, this narrative mediation of the albeit fictional film is itself intermedial. Firstly, it is a form of (faux) intermedial reference, using the medium of written narrative in what we might think of as a form of filmic ekphrasis. There is also another form of intermedial reference at work in the novel. Throughout "The Navidson Record", there are repeated references to the images of the docu-film. For instance, Zampanò uses frequent colloquial collocations such as "As we can see…" (Danielewski 2000: 127), both drawing on the inclusive 'we' to evoke a sense of authenticity and solidarity with his intended narrative audience and highlighting the visuality of the original medium. There are also meta-references to the technological apparatus of film: "the camera blips on again" (Daniewski 2000: 128), "Using 16mm motion picture (colour and B/W) and 35mm stills" (Daniewski 2000: 154).

Of most interest, however, is the way in which the novel attempts to capture and re-present filmic qualities and techniques through the multimodal combination of word and image. Wolf (2005: 255) calls this 'evocation', where one medium 'imitates the effects of another medium". An excellent example of such explicit intermedial reference occurs in Exploration #4, the first of the final two highly multimodal explorations. The exploration is full of dramatic tension, with Holloway, the lead explorer, seemingly going mad and turning on his team, thus requiring Navidson and Reston to also venture into the dark interior on a rescue mission. However, Navidson is left stranded and alone at the bottom of what appears to be an impossibly long stairway. The narrative informs the reader that this is "the final shot of the section" (Danielewski 2000: 304) before providing Navidson's desperate direct speech. The narrative continues in the following way (see table 1).

Page no:	Words on Page	Realisation
307	The film runs out here,	Located bottom right of R page
308	Leaving nothing else behind but an unremarkable	Located bottom. Additional spaces between words
309	White	Placed just above the centre of the page
310		Page is completely blank

Page no:	Words on Page	Realisation
311	Screen	Placed just above the centre of the page
312	•	Placed just above the centre of the page

Table 1: (Danielewski 2000: 307–312)

Navidson seems hopeless, heightening narrative tension leading up to the final words of the chapter in question. The film reaching its end is depicted through intermedial means. This is made explicit through the opening clause 'The film runs out here', a meta-statement which serves to make sense for the reader of the forthcoming multimodal representation. The "white / / screen" that is left behind is realised in a number of ways. First of all, both modifying adjective and noun are placed on individual pages, emphasising the blank mass of white page on which they sit, and thus complementing the verbal description both in terms of colour and comparative emptiness. Furthermore, in between the two words sits a single completely blank page. This page therefore visually enacts the verbal description, recasting the white screen as the empty page of *House of Leaves*. Finally, the last page in the sequence, which features a single black dot, is suggestive of the way in which old television screens shut down, the colour or light fading out of the screen briefly leaving behind a single point of light.

The example of intermedial reference through evocation discussed above is by no means an isolated occurrence in *House of Leaves*, with Danielewski frequently exploiting the material capacities of the novel format to represent filmic effects. There are also other instances of intermedial reference, which can be seen in the inclusions of genres such as dramatic transcripts (Danielewski 2000: 254–273; 354–365) and sheet musical (Danielewski 2000: 477–479). By evoking other media in *House of Leaves*, Danielewski enhances its status as a multimodal literary artefact. Moreover, while the evocation of the film medium in written narrative is always illusory in that it takes on what Rajewsky (2005) and Wolf (2005) acknowledge as an 'as if' quality, it nevertheless works to instill the impression of viewing 'The Navidson Record' while reading the novel. Thus, Zampanò's use of the inclusive pronoun 'we' in collocations such as "As we can see…" positions the reader as his intended fictional narratee heightening the readerly sense of involvement in and experience of the *House of Leaves*.

5. Exploring the Multimodal House

In this section, I continue to consider how readers experience the novel by undertaking a cognitive-poetic analysis of the multimodality of an extract from *House of Leaves*. Cognitive poetics (see Gavins/ Steen 2003; Stockwell 2002) is a discipline concerned with developing a greater understanding of the mental processes involved in the act of reading, imagining, and comprehending literature. To achieve this, it studies form, style and language while drawing on work in the cognitive sciences, such as neuroscience, cognitive psychology, and cognitive linguistics. This enables a reception-sensitive approach offering a dynamic account of reading and focusing not simply on "the artifice of the literary text alone, or the reader alone, but the more natural process of reading when one is engaged with the other" (Stockwell 2002: 2). Cognitive-poetic frameworks and terms will be introduced and explained as they arise in analysis.

I have selected pages 440–441 for analysis, since the multimodal spatial arrangement is particularly striking and thus provides a valuable point of analytical departure.

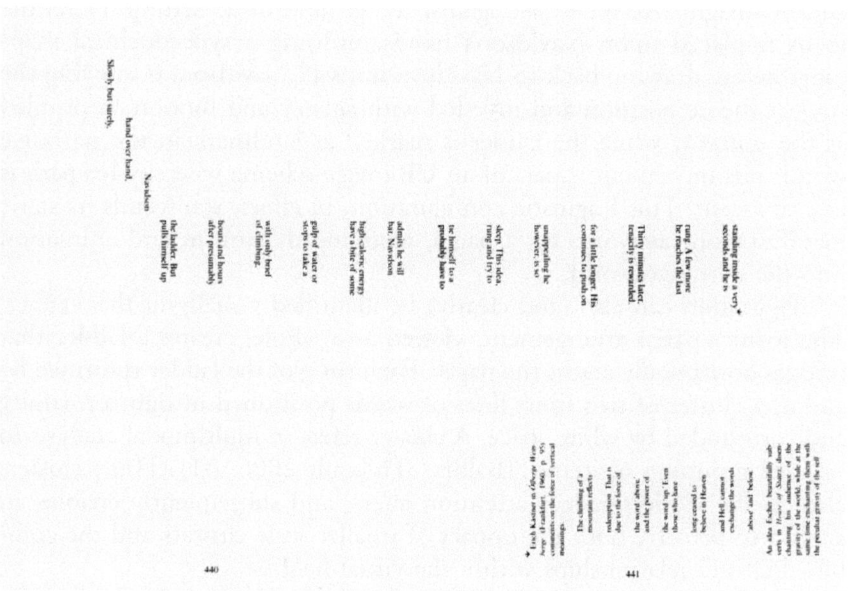

Figure 2: Danielewski (2000) House of Leaves: 440–1. Reprinted by permission of The Random House Group Ltd.

These pages feature an episode from Exploration #5, which Navidson takes alone after the team of professional explorers have all become lost inside or devoured (literally or metaphorically) by the house's interior darkness. Arranged across a double page spread, the words sit vertically, meaning that the book must be rotated in order for the pages to be read. The narrative delivers the following episode:

> Slowly but surely, hand over hand, Navidson pulls himself up the ladder. But after presumably hours and hours of climbing with only brief stops to take a gulp of water or have a bite of some high-caloric energy bar, Navidson admits he will probably have to tie himself to a rung and try to sleep. This idea, however, is so unappealing he continues to push on for a little longer. His tenacity is rewarded. Thirty minutes later, he reaches the last rung. A few more seconds and he is standing inside a very… (Danielewski 2000: 440–1)

At this point, the narrative stops and the reader must turn the page to continue the sentence and find out where Navidson is standing.

The first sentence immediately creates what is known in cognitive poetics as figure and ground relations. Figure and ground is a cognitive poetic framework which stems from visual perception. A figure is a prominent, foregrounded entity which captures attention and becomes a visual and/or imaginative focus, set against the ground of its setting. Here, the focus is placed upon Navidson's hands, utilising a synecdochical mapping, before drawing back to Navidson himself. Navidson, occupying the subject theme position and invested with agency and motion, is profiled as the trajector while the ladder is marked as landmark in the narrative world. His movement is part of an UP image schema whereby his path is one of ascent. This linguistic configuration, in effect, transcends its static manifestation (as words on a page), instilling dynamism and animation into the narrative world.

Figuration can also (and clearly) be identified visually in this extract. The iconic spatial arrangement, viewed as a whole, creates a ladder that bridges horizontally across the pages. Each rung of the ladder is formed by and as a cluster of two short lines of words positioned in tight proximity and surrounded by white space. A cluster refers in multimodal analysis to "a local grouping of items" (Baldry/ Thibault 2006: 31). Thus, clusters alter as the viewer/reader's attention alters, and subsequently enables an analyst to perceive both the impact of smaller-scale clusters and the combined cluster relationships within the visual field.

The words, printed in dark black type, stand prominent against the pale scape of blank page, just as in life a real ladder would occupy the figural position when leant against a wall. The act of reading, generally, facilitates several levels of visual figure-ground organisation. In accord with currency of attention, the primary figure is the word being focused upon in a given moment. In this extract, these levels recede through individual clusters, sentences (which, similar to poetic enjambment, continue across clusters), to the printed ladder as a whole. In the visual periphery is the page spread and any glimpses of the actual world past the frame of the book.

The ladder, its sequence of words and their spatial location, dictates the reading path that must be taken. Even when the book has been rotated, the apparent starting point is in its original top left corner. However, the physical revolution of the book forces a less familiar eye motion. The first three lines, each moving horizontally from left to right toward the next, create vectors that signal reading direction. In multimodal studies, a 'vector' harnesses properties such as dynamic force, directionality, and orientation (Baldry/ Thibault 2006: 35–6) influencing reading/viewing paths. These 'stairs' demonstrate this, pushing the eyes' path upward, step by step, toward the rungs of the ladder where the unconventional rising of textual fragments makes for a somewhat uncomfortable and awkward reading process. This ascendant design results in a deviant reading path. The upward accumulation of rungs, another vectorial patterning, forces the eye to leap across the spaces, visually 'cluster hopping' (Baldry/ Thibault 2006: 26) despite the linearity of verbal narrative.

In the process of cluster hopping, the eyes perform a kind of 'kinetic occlusion' (Gibson 1966: 203–206). The notion of kinetic occlusion originates in the work of perceptual and ecological psychologist, J. J. Gibson (1966: 203–206) and refers to the passing of one surface over another. Gibson gives the example of a picture dropping from a wall. In doing so, he comments on the process in an eloquent articulation which focuses upon the visual processing of the surrounding environment:

> In terms of optical texture, there occurs a *wiping-out* at the leading border, an *unwiping* at the trailing border, and a *shearing* of texture at the lateral border of the figure in the array. These aspects of transformation involve a rupture of the continuity of texture... (1966: 203; his italics)

Scarry (2001: 12–13) also refers to kinetic occlusion and her explanation adds the movement of her hand across her face (2001: 13) to Gibson's example. In both examples, it is a case of one surface or object temporarily 'wiping out' that which lies beneath from view. Nevertheless, there is a crucial difference between Gibson's (1966) and Scarry's (2001) accounts of kinetic occlusion. Gibson is interested in visual processing while Scarry focuses on literary experience and is therefore interested in imaginative processing. In applying the notion of kinetic occlusion to the multimodality of *House of Leaves,* I am therefore utilising a combination of Gibson's and Scarry's theories.

Starting with the imagined narrative world of *House of Leaves*, Navidson's climbing movement involves "hand over hand" on alternate rungs of the ladder. From an objective side-view, as the forehand passes before the back hand to reach for the higher tier, there would arise within the text-world a brief instance of kinetic occlusion where the forehand blocks the rear from sight. Returning to *House of Leaves*' visual structure, each rung of the ladder, as it is read, attracts the reader's attention, throwing the previous into relief. Unlike the literal process of kinetic occlusion (Gibson 1966), that is of seeing one object pass before another object, these rungs create occlusion through the eyes' motion, as the rung being presently read, the currency of that cluster, overshadows the former. This process, as Scarry points out, "specifies durability" (2001: 13): the previous rungs, while no longer in focus, continue to exist below, and in the eyes' journey to the top of the ladder, create a layering, an accumulation of lower tiers. Additionally, one may perceive the grammatical constructions of "Slowly but surely", "hand over hand", and "hours and hours" as creating a similar effect, using lexical repetition, parallelism, and sound patterning to echo this layering and emphasise Navidson's monotonous climbing activity, continuous throughout the lengthy temporal duration.

The reading path involved in this extract creates a subjective resonance. The reader's eyes and the character Navidson become counterparts through upward motion and discomfort. The reader's physical and visual encounter with the text parallels the narrative depiction of climbing and by extension the actual exercise in the real world. This visual representation, enhanced by the linguistic use of present tense, thus forces the eyes to enact a conceptual metaphor. Conceptual Metaphor Theory (see Lakoff/Johnson 1980) suggests that human conceptual patterns are metaphorical by nature. As such, conceptual metaphors permeate language. Were I to pause now and ask, somewhat colloquially, 'Do you see what I mean?', my phrasing is reliant upon the conceptual metaphor KNOWING IS SEEING, a metaphor that must unconsciously be activated in order to comprehend my intended meaning.Conceptual metaphors consist of a source domain and a target domain whereby conceptual elements from the source are transferred through metaphoric connection to the target which is often re-characterised as a result. In this way, conceptual metaphors provide a means for understanding abstract concepts (the target) by comparison to a basic-level domain (the source) grounded in bodily and/or everyday experience.

The conceptual metaphor at work here is LITERARY EXPERIENCE IS PHYSICAL MOVEMENT. This links neatly to Gerrig's (1993) idea of narrative experience as akin to transportation. Gerrig's model of the imaginative process of reading is based on the transportation metaphor. He speaks of the reader "*being transported* by virtue of *performing* that narrative" (1993: 2; his italics). This is, therefore, by no means a newly-revealed conceptual metaphor yet, I believe, the performance of this metaphor in *House of Leaves* is distinct. By 'performance', Gerrig refers to the purely imaginative and emotional endeavour of immersion or transportation into a fictional world whereas this reading path adds another performative dimension, that of literal ocular movement and participation parallel to that in the world of the text. The manifestation of this conceptual metaphor, produced by the interplay of word and image, is the shared endeavour of the writer, deciding and organising the visual layout according to narrative content, and the reader whose optical journey realises LITERARY EXPERIENCE IS PHYSICAL MOVEMENT. Had the visual aspect of this extract not been taken into account, the performance of this visual conceptual metaphor might not have been considered.

Moving to the right hand page of the extract, there is a second ladder. Positioned at the top of the larger primary ladder, the book must again be rotated in order to facilitate reading. Running left to right from the top downwards, this ladder including the top and bottom platform reads:

> Erich Kästner… comments on the force of vertical meanings:
>
> The climbing of a mountain reflects redemption. That is due to the force of the word 'above,' and the power of the word 'up.' Even those who have long ceased to believe in Heaven and Hell, cannot exchange the words 'above' and 'below.'
>
> An idea Escher beautifully subverts in *House of Stairs*; disenchanting his audience of the gravity of the world, while at the same time enchanting them with the peculiar gravity of the self. (Danielewski 2000: 441)

The reflection upon the words 'up', 'above', and 'below', is essentially a meditation on the related conceptual metaphors GOOD IS UP and BAD IS DOWN in which psychological judgements are explained via reference to the experience of elevation. The discussion of the 'power' and 'force' of these words implies their importance in the structuring of thought. In other words, GOOD IS UP and BAD IS DOWN have become constitutive metaphors, and are vital to the process of human understanding. This visual ladder and the reading pattern it implements generate a twist in the construal of this observation. GOOD IS UP suggests a cognitive expectation concerning what happens when one reaches the top of a ladder. Conversely, the reading path journeys downwards, thus creating a paradox. The disparity between the verbal and the visual spawns a tension of meaning: does the directionality of reading invert the meaning of the linguistic content? Furthermore, before turning the page to discover Navidson's next location, the ladders have taken the reader upwards and downwards respectively. This conflict, left unresolved, creates a 'cliff-hanger' effect, raising anxiety over the nature of the page-turning location overleaf. It is worth noting that such narrative anxiety was here triggered not by a seamless multimodal integration but by the tensional differences between the verbal and visual modes. This effect can perhaps thus be seen as *intra*-medial multimodal effect. While tension occurs within the novel medium, it also emerges from the divergence of two semiotic modes, verbal and visual communication.

The above quotation also reveals an interesting intermedial reference to Escher's (1951) famous painting *House of Stairs.* Not only is there a connection in the lexical and syntactic repetitions of the title to Escher's painting and Danielewski's novel. The reference suggests an implicit form of intermedial evocation. Escher's *House of Stairs* is apt in relation to an episode in *House of Leaves* which creates visual 'stairs' from the arrangement of its text. Similarly, while Daniewski's ladders traverse the page in different directions, so too do Escher's stairs. Furthermore, Escher's painting plays around with visual perspective. The planes of the stairs he depicts exhibit paradoxical angles, and consequently appear to be gravity defying. Thus, for reader's familiar with Escher's painting, Danielewski's intermedial reference uses Escher's *House of Stairs* to subvert the conceptual metaphors of GOOD IS UP and BAD IS DOWN, as without gravity, the bodily experience which structures them has no bearing.

At the top of each ladder on pages 440–441 can be seen two small arrows. Both point back down their respective ladders. These seem not to be directing the reader to a particular object. Neither do they signal reading direction as the reader's first encounter with an arrow is at the top of the central ladder that s/he has just 'climbed'. One possibility is that they are in fact connected with reading direction, but acting more like visual vectors, the first pushing the reader's eye toward the top of the second ladder from where to begin reading in the direction the second arrow points. Another possibility is that the arrow at the top of the first ladder, pointing downward to the floor so to speak, is designed to act as a diagrammatic reminder of the possibility of falling. This cognitive possibility, when contemplated, coupled with the vectorial instinct to follow the direction pointed to by the arrow-head, may influence the reader's eye to journey back down the ladder in a form of literary 'freefall'. In this case the arrow has, along with the reader's complicit optical descent, stood in for the snake in the popular children's game *Snakes and Ladders*. This displays the innovative and playful nature of the novel, yet it also functions to heighten narrative anxiety, suggesting the dangerous route that Navidson, and through a parallel relation the reader too, has taken.

This extract demonstrates multimodal meaning-making at work, and continues to show connections between multimodality and intermediality, including the impact on the reader's experience of the text. In the next section, I consider a further form of intermediality, hitherto unmentioned, namely an ontological intermediality, before extending my analysis with this in mind to further explore the way in which readers experience *House of Leaves* as a multimodal and intermedial object.

6. The Ontology of the In-between

In his (2003) article 'Sens(*a*)ble Intermediality and *Interesse*: Towards an Ontology of the In-Between', Oosterling considers "the experience of the "inter" that is enhanced in intermedial art practices" (2003: 31). For Oosterling, this is a philosophical pursuit, focusing upon the "specific quality of the experience of the "inter" [...]the unstable and non-discursive quality of the being (*esse*) of this in-between (inter) as inter-*esse*" (Oosterling 2003: 31; his italics). Oosterling offers a comparative glance at French post-structuralist criticism and the aesthetics of the sublime to conclude that the intermedial experience is perhaps less unique to the art world and more characteristic in contemporary times of global living where both intermedial and multimodal experiences are prevalent. While presenting an interesting take on twenty-first century culture and critical thinking, Oosterling unfortunately provides neither a replicable approach to art objects which lend themselves to intermediality nor an outline of the intermedial aesthetic experience.

A more concrete approach is taken by Chapple/ Kattenbelt (2006) who are also interested in the experiential and ontological dimension of intermediality. They consider intermediality specifically in relation to theatre and performance, suggesting:

> Although at first sight, intermediality might appear to be a technologically driven phenomenon it actually operates, at times, without any technology being present. Intermediality is about changes in theatre practice and thus changing perceptions of performance, which become visible through the process of staging. We locate intermediality at a meeting-point between the different realities that the performance creates. (Chapple/ Kattenbelt 2006: 12)

Although Chapple/ Kattenbelt's words refer to theatre studies, I believe such changes in both practice and perception are also evident in the novel, and in particular in the multimodal novel, feeding into what Wolf briefly refers to as "the 'intermedial turn' in Western culture since modernism" (2005: 256). Chapple/ Kattenbelt (2006) continue:

> The intermedial inhabits a space in-between the different realities that the performance creates and thus it becomes, at the minimum, a tripartite phenomenon. Intermediality is a powerful and potentially radical force, which operates in-between performer and audience; in-between theatre, performance and other media; and in-between realities – with theatre providing a staging space for the performance of intermediality. (Chapple/ Kattenbelt 2006: 12)

The idea of an experiential, performative and transformative intermediality is significant, and its worth goes beyond theatrical events. Multimodal novels foreground both their own materiality and the reader's embodied participation in the process of literary experience. In some cases, embodied participation goes beyond the expected and often habitual turning of pages and can take on a more performative dimension. As such, I suggest that when multimodality in literature works to position readers in what seems to be an ontological in-between (of the virtual and the actual), intermedial spaces are created. In the next two sections, I further explore the relationships between multimodality and intermediality in relation to Mark Z. Danielewski's multimodal novel *House of Leaves*. In doing so, I demonstrate the ways in which multimodal literature can position readers in the in-between spaces of intermedial aesthetic experience.

7. The Figured Trans-World and Intermedial Space

The reader's physical interaction with the book, in terms of the need to rotate it to facilitate reading, is a product of the novel's multimodal arrangement. As with the extract analysed, throughout the explorations featured in the novel's narrative, the words on the page replicate the shifting architecture of the house's dark interior and as a result the characters' journeys through it too. In pages 440–441, it was Navidson's solo expedition that was represented and followed by the reader. This pursuit creates parallel relations between the reader and the character Navidson. By this means, I argue, a form of doubly deictic subjectivity is created. My conception of doubly deictic subjectivity is an extension of Herman's definition of doubly deictic *you* in which;

> the audience will find itself more or less subject to conflation with the fictional self addressed by *you*. The deictic force of *you* is double; or to put it another way, the scope of the discourse context embedding the description is indeterminate, as is the domain of participants in principle specified or picked out by *you*. (1994: 399)

According to the latter sentence of Herman's articulation, the ambiguous reference of *you* is at the heart of this subjective conflation. In pages

440–441, the second-person pronoun is not in use, yet a convergence of character and reader does nevertheless transpire. While I cannot therefore call this an instance of doubly deictic *you* per se, I advocate it as an example of doubly deictic subjectivity, built upon a similar "superimposition of virtuality (the fictional protagonist) and actuality (the reader)" (Herman 1994: 387), only in this case it is triggered not by pronominal polysemous reference but by multimodal imposition. The reader is at once both an observer of the fiction and powerfully involved in that fiction.

The combination of physical activity with doubly deictic involvement can perhaps itself be seen as intermedial evocation, with the kinetic movement carried out by the reader translating the narrative description of Navidson's journey into real-world action. As a consequence of this, the customary creation and experience of the text-world in *House of Leaves* is altered. To provide a brief definition, Text World Theory (See Werth 1999; Gavins 2007) is a discourse framework, focusing on how linguistic structures trigger different and various text-worlds. The theory uses the powerful TEXT AS WORLD conceptual metaphor to articulate the way in which readers construct any given discourse by producing a cognitive realisation of it, an imaginative construct which may appear so vivid as to take on a world-like quality. A text-world is therefore a mental construct which is the joint production of producer and recipient. Moreover, there are a number of conceptual levels within which these worlds operate. The preliminary level is the context in which the communicative event takes place. This is called the 'discourse-world', referring to the external and immediate situation of the participants. The second level is the 'text-world' itself which, as mentioned, is the cognitive representation of the communication. In the passage analysed, the central ladder is the prominent text-world, as shown in figure 3. The smaller ladder, holding academic commentary, creates a second separate text-world with a further embedded text-world in the form of direct quotation from Erich Kästner. Further to this is the presence of an intermedial reference world.

Due to the corresponding visual designs of the ladders, among other factors, the reader makes cross-world inferences, that is Erich Kästner's comments on the words 'above' and 'below' influence the reader's understanding and interpretation of Navidson's climbing of the ladder in the prominent text-world, as demonstrated in the earlier analysis. In figure 3, the larger arrows represent the way in which meanings from text-world 2 and text-world 3 feed into the prominent text-world.

In terms of the extract's text-world structure, I am most interested, however, in how a multimodal novel like *House of Leaves* creates further ontological layers and indeed intermedial spaces. As a multimodal novel, *House of Leaves* accentuates the reader's involvement in text-world creation,

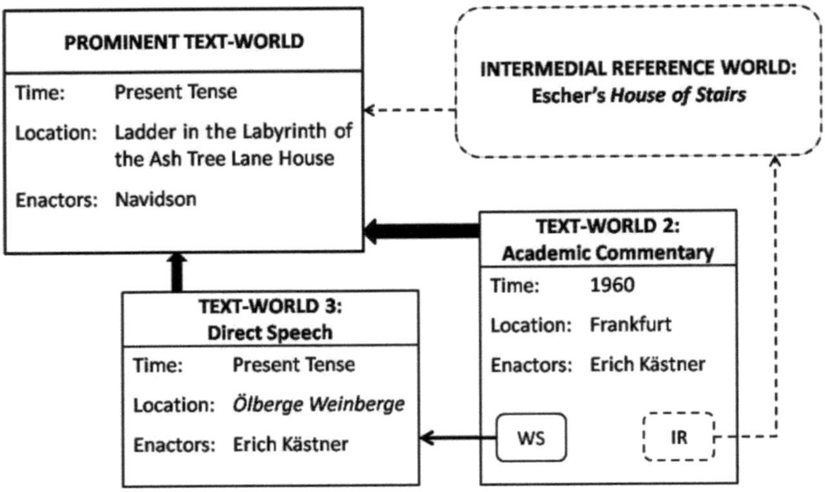

Figure 3: Text-Worlds of Danielewski (2000) House of Leaves: 440–441

demanding physical interaction with the book as object and positioning the reader doubly deictically through a subjective resonance with the character of Navidson. Unlike theories of literary identification that claim readers may imaginatively assume the role of a character, I am arguing that only a partial identification with Navidson is encouraged by Danielewski, since the text also dramatises the reader as participant. The reader is not just projecting into the world of the text, but playing a more active and corporeal role.

In an article on multimodality and imagination, Hall suggests that multimodal children's books affect the relative positioning of the imaginative domain to the actual text, since the imagination no longer operates in "a separate and bounded world" (2008: 137). Rather, Hall speaks of "imagination as action, triggered not through words or looking into receptacles but through deep commitment to an object" (2008: 138). *House of Leaves* requires such deep commitment from its readers too, the impact of which leads to the construction of what I term a 'figured trans-world'.

The concept of the figured trans-world stems from Holland et al.'s (1998) studies of identity construction in cultural environments as well as one of their sources, Vygotsky's (1978) work in the arena of children's play. Holland et al.'s study makes a case for the existence of cultural worlds in which identities are constructed through collective imaginings and active participation. These worlds are called 'figured worlds'. Holland et al. provide the following definition:

> By "figured world," then, we mean a socially and culturally constructed realm of interpretation in which particular characters and actors are recognized, significance is assigned to certain acts, and particular outcomes are valued over others. [...] These collective "as-if" worlds are sociohistoric, contrived interpretations or imaginations that mediate behavior and so, from the perspective of heuristic development, inform participants' outlooks. The ability to sense (see, hear, touch, taste, feel) the figured world becomes embodied over time, through continual participation. (1998: 52–3)

Although perceived as a culturally embodied practice, the notion of figured worlds is not totally removed from the activity of reading since Holland et al., in the opening to their chapter on figured worlds, acknowledge reading as a human endeavour tied to imaginative world creation and thus related, though not tantamount to, these socially constructed "as-if" worlds.

Material objects and artefacts are central to figured worlds, acting as 'pivots' in Vygotsky's (1978) terms. Holland et al. summarise Vygotsky's hypothesis:

> Describing how children develop the ability to enter into an imagined world, Vygotsky speaks of a "pivot", a mediating or symbolic device that the child uses not just to organise a particular response but to pivot or shift into the frame of a different world. (1998: 50)

With regard to figured worlds, pivots are employed synonymously: "Artifacts 'open up' figured worlds" (Holland et al. 1998: 61). In reference to literature, the book as an object is a mediating artefact that evokes, and enables a shift into, its imaginative world. However, it does not generate a figured world since, although literature is a cultural and collective endeavour, it does not produce an analogous shared experience, nor does it depend upon equivalent active participation and/or performance. Multimodal texts, however, emphasise the embodied nature of the reading experience. As Kress, in his book *Literacy in the New Media Age*, articulates, "imagination in the sense that it is required by the demands of design — the imposition of order on the representational world — is a move towards action in the outer world" (2003: 60).

The concept of the figured trans-world that I am presenting here is not identical with Holland et al.'s socially grounded notion of figured worlds. In my conception, a figured trans-world is generated when the reader is required and/or directed by the text into a performative role in the discourse-world, a role that calls upon corporeal activity and insinuates, to greater or lesser extent, active reader involvement in the narrative. For the figured trans-world to be activated, the reader *must* take up that role. In the 'ladder' extract from *House of Leaves*, the multimodal design of the book results in it being rotated and handled as an object. Executing these affordances of the book is a performance that emulates Navidson's movements, creating doubly deictic subjectivity. Used thus, the book as a material artefact acts a pivot, opening up the text-world for figuration. Crucially, this process forges a concretised form of trans-world projection for the reader, an embodied connection between participant and enactor.

As a *trans*-world, this idea has the benefit of maintaining the rigid ontological boundaries between text- and discourse-world that are fundamental to Text World Theory. The figured trans-world encompasses the reader's performance in the discourse-world, that is their figured representation of the action in the narrative of the text-world without assuming absolute 'transportation' or compression of worlds.

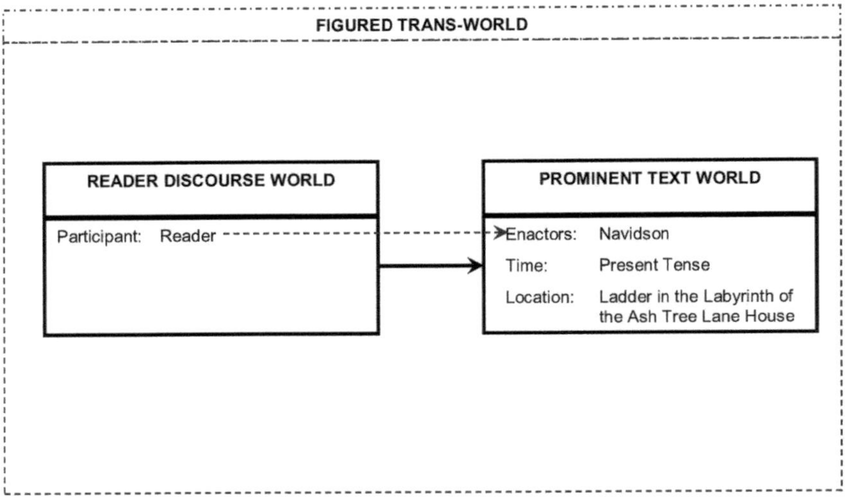

Figure 4: Figured Trans-world of Danielewski (2000) House of Leaves: 440–441

Crucially, it accounts for the reader's self-awareness and heightened involvement with the book as object, as narrative and as literary experience.

The figured trans-world, seeming to collapse the distance between discourse-world and text-world, can itself be seen as an intermedial space arising in relation to *House of Leaves* as an effect of the semiotic combinations of word, image, and readerly kinetic activity. Experientially, the reader has a sense of being situated somewhere in-between their own reality and the storyworld. Chapple/ Kattenbelt (2006) assert;

> the intermedial is a space where the boundaries soften – and we are in-between and within a mixing of spaces, media and realities. Thus, intermediality becomes a process of transformation of thoughts and processes where something different is formed through performance. In our concept of intermediality, we draw our history of ideas to locate intermediality as a re-perception of the whole, which is re-constructed through performance. (2006: 12)

Although Chapple/ Kattenbelt refer specifically to theatrical performance, the *perfomative* dimension demanded in *multimodal* literary experience, along with doubly deictic subjectivity and the creation of a figured trans-world, creates such softening of ontological boundaries. In *Postmodernist Fiction*, McHale discusses the notion of 'semipermeable membranes' (1987: 34–6), referring to the flexible boundaries between narrative worlds. The figured trans-world is an infringement of the semipermeable membrane between fiction and reality and is by its very nature an intermedial space.

Speaking of doubly deictic *you*, Herman suggests that fictions which utilise the effect of double deictics, "by formally encoding (features of) the contexts in which they are or might be read, in turn prompt reflection on how contexts permeate and modify the narrative structures anchored in them" (2002: 350). The figured trans-world itself can be seen as vital to this effect, since although text- and discourse-world maintain their ontological separation, the readerly impression of enactive participation augments the blurring of the boundary or, in other words, the membrane itself. The discourse-world and the text-world are distinct worlds in ontological terms, yet by dramatising the reader's relationship with the book through performance, Danielewski provokes concretised trans-world projection, making the boundary itself seem almost indistinguishable. The reader of *House of Leaves* does not just 'read' the novel. Like Navidson, and aligned with him through subjective and corporeal resonance, in this intermedial space s/he seems to actively explore it. In the next section, I continue to develop the concept of the figured trans-world as intermedial space by considering another way in which readers are directed into a performative role in the narrative – that of narrative inscription.

8. Reading and Writing in-between the lines

Danielewski toys with the positioning of the reader in relation to the novel. The active, and indeed bodily, role that the reader takes in the process of reading *House of Leaves* is accounted for by the concept of the figured trans-world, detailed above. Figured trans-worlds, and the embodied projection relations between reader and character(s) they create, do not only arise within the explorations of The Navidson Record, but can be seen to occur in other layers of the narrative and throughout the novel as a whole. In narrative terms, Pelafina's letters to Johnny Truant, collected in appendix E, also invite the reader to participate in a figured trans-world. Unlike the previous example, the figured trans-world that is generated here is not the product of readerly movement that evokes narrative action. This instance, therefore, provides further details of the figured trans-world, its creation and the "potentially radical force" (Chapple/ Kattenbelt 2006: 12) of the intermedial space.

The Whalestoe Letters are written by Pelafina, Truant's mother, who at the time of writing was a committed patient at the psychiatric facility, The Whalestoe Institute, and date from 1982 until 1989 when Pelafina dies from "self-inflicted asphyxiation" (Danielewski 2000: 643). The letters begin as tender communications from mother to son, but as they progress, Pelafina becomes increasingly paranoid about the institute's new director to the extent that she suggests he may murder her. Her paranoia culminates in a brief letter dated April 27, 1987, when she writes (Danielewski 2000: 619);

> Dear, dear Johnny,
> Pay attention: the next letter I will encode as follows: use the first letter of each word to build subsequent words and phrases: your exquisite intuition will help sort out the spaces: I've sent this via a night nurse: our secret will be safe
> Tenderly,
> Mom

This letter provides Johnny and the reader with a cipher with which to decode the next letter (Danielewski 2000: 620–3), indeed encrypted as Pelafina describes.

The next letter read by its surface text, that is, in its coded form, makes little semantic sense. Thus in order to recover meaning the reader must make use of the cipher to translate the letter. This is a relatively undemanding process that, although I am reluctant to disclose the exact text, reveals a disturbing message concerning Pelafina's experiences in the Whalestoe Institute. What is interesting from the perspective of this study is the necessity of reader participation for the narrative exposé.

While in the previous extract the multimodal arrangement acted as a guiding tool, in Pelafina's letters the reader is provided with instructions in the form of the cipher; 'use the first letter of each word to build subsequent words and phrases'. In actively deciphering Pelafina's letter, the reader enters into a figured trans-world. Rather than merely reading

Truant's letters from his mother, the reader performs the decoding operation, in the process suggesting a doubly deictic subjectivity aligned with Truant. Crucially, the reader acts upon the text, paying attention to its surface, and inscribing the secret message to create an alternative surface, written in the reader's own hand. This is another form of figured trans-world, since it involves the reader being actively engaged with the text in relation to the narrative. It is also an intermedial space, since although the reader translates the written text of the novel into his or her own written text, it is an act of medial creation, one which suggests differing medial conditions between the two written artefacts, the published and personal.

Figured involvements in intermedial spaces founded in textual inscription, as in decoding Pelafina's letters, were hinted at in the description of the book that Truant provides in the *Introduction*. After an exhaustive and at points conflicting list of features possessed by the novel, Truant resignedly writes, "- find your own words; I have no more" (Danielewski 2000: xvii). From what appears to be a flippant comment, there emerges a poignant truth, one whose meaning is an implicit directive for the generation of a figured trans-world. Technically, in deciphering Pelafina's letter, the reader is finding Pelafina's words, rather than his own. Yet in doing so how does one keep track of Pelafina's horrific admission? Perhaps it is scrawled into the thick margins of Appendix E; perhaps it is scribbled on a scrap of paper, a leaf, and then folded into the pages of the book. Furthermore, considering figured involvement in the novel as a whole, as academics, students, or inspired readers willing to take on Truant's challenge, temptation may have us writing notes into the empty spaces of the page. While such a reaction may seem more closely aligned to an academic readership, 'real' readers of the novel have confessed to also behaving in this way. For instance, in an amazon.com review of the book, a customer named Laura A. admits, "Only a few pages in (hooked), I made the executive decision to arm myself with those little page-marker sticky notes so I could go back and re-visit things of interest" (see website 1 in references). As readers who do perform the act of writing, both Pelafina's secret message and our own annotations, we lend a greater intensity to Truant's words. The possessive second-person pronoun in "- find your own words" is apostrophic, a direct address suggesting the performance of intermedial transposition. That is, the real reader takes up the position addressed by the pronoun, and as part of the process of reading *House of Leaves*, brings a new more personal written mode into being.

The full title to Danielewski's novel is *House of Leaves, by Zampanò with introduction and notes by Johnny Truant*. Truant's footnotes interspersed throughout the novel, presumably sprawled onto the pages of Zampanò's manuscript, are his textual inscriptions. If we mark our copy of the book with literary and/or personal comment, we create a doubly deictic alignment with Truant and therefore another figured trans-world. In short, we do add our own words; we carry out Johnny's plea. In the process, we create an additional layer to the novel (shown in figure 5), a highly subjective intermedial space. It becomes *our* rendered copy of a book *introduced* and *noted* by Truant, and *written* by Zampanò. In many novels, this act would not carry the same semantic weight, but *House of Leaves*, with its recursive narrative structure and multiple authors, turns this act into a significant narrative event. As 'writers', we are caught up in constructing a further narrative encasing, through doubly deictic involvement in a figured trans-world, in which we do have a degree of agency. The content of our scribblings is not dictated but highly individual, more so because the discourse-world of the reader is brought into play, and the act of reading and interpreting is itself dramatised by the narrative. As Brick puts it, "*Personal experience* is at the heart of Danielewski's book" (2004; his italics).

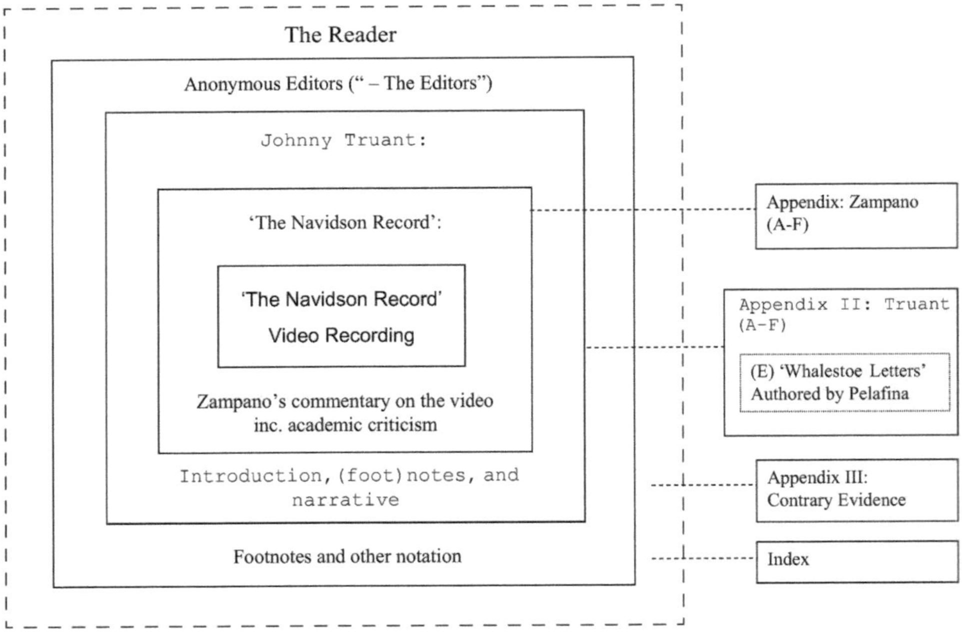

Figure 5: Narrative Levels of *House of Leaves*, including readerly 'figured' layer

Interestingly, in the intermedial space of a figured trans-world created through textual inscription, the reader is not just placed in-between realities in an ontological sense. S/he is also in-between roles as they become not just a reader of *House of Leaves*, but also one of its many writers.

Conclusion

In this article, I have been exploring the relationship between the multimodal printed novel and the intermedial aesthetic experience. *House of Leaves* plays with its intermedial boundaries, both in terms of intermedial reference and evocation as well as creating intermedial ontologies. Multimodality evokes doubly deictic subjectivity and figured trans-worlds, both of which serve to dislocate the reader, unsettling actual and fictional realities. As such, the boundaries between the text- and the discourse-world are obscured in a way that implicates readers in the materiality and the narrative structure of the novel. In consequence, it is as though we, as readers, become the next in line of a legacy, as "The Navidson Record" is 'shown' to us through description and the manuscript is passed from Zampanò to Truant to us. The intermedial space we find ourselves in, the figured trans-world of each reader's own actions and writings, appears to manifest this literary interpretation of textual inheritance as part of an overwhelming reality — the writing upon the book has occurred in relation to the text-world, as part of a figured trans-world and, vitally, as the reader's indelible action in the discourse-world.

In their description of intermedial spaces, Chapple and Kattenbelt (2006: 12) emphasise the potential for transformation and re-perception. The multimodal and performative generation of intermedial spaces in reading *House of Leaves* reveals this to be true, since each and every reader of the novel will be part of a unique intermedial aesthetic experience, dependent of the extent to which he or she enters into figured trans-worlds and his or her familiarity with intermedial references such as Escher's *House of Stairs*. While there are always differences in reader interpretations of literary texts, the enhanced experience of the in-between in relation to *House of Leaves* transforms each reader's textual perception: the novel and its narrative comes to be viewed as an intimately personal encounter.

References

Baldry, Anthony and Paul Thibault (2006). *Multimodal Transciption and Text Analysis: A multimedia toolkit and coursebook*. London: Equinox.

Balme, Christopher B. (2001). "Lepage und die Zukunft des Theaters im Medienzeitalter." In: Leeker, Martine (ed.). *Maschinen, Medien, Performances: Theater an der Schnittstelle zu digitalen Welten*. Berlin: Alexander Verlag, 668–683.

Bray, Joe and Alison Gibbons, eds. (forthcoming 2100). *Mark Z. Danielewski*. Manchester: Manchester University Press.

Brick, Martin (2004). "Blueprint(s): rubric for a deconstructd age in *House of Leaves*." *Philament* 2. Online, Retrieved August 2006 from http://www.arts.usyd.edu.au/publications/philament/issue2_Critique_Brick.htm, 2004: no pagination.

Chapple, Freda and Chiel Kattenbelt (2006). "Key Issues in Intermediality in Theatre and Performance." In: Chapple, Freda and Chiel Kattenbelt (eds). *Intermediality in Theatre and Performance*. Amsterdam; New York: Rodopi, 11–25.

Cottrell, Sophie (no date). "Bold Type Interview: a conversation with Mark Z. Danielewski." Online, Retrieved September 2007 from http://www.randomhouse.com/boldtype/0400/danielewski/interview.html, no pagination.

Danielewski, Mark Z. (2000). *House of Leaves by Zampanò with introduction and notes by Johnny Truant*. London; New York: Doubleday.

Escher, M. C. (1951). *House of Stairs*, Lithograph.

Gavins, Joanna (2007). *Text World Theory: An Introduction*. Edinburgh: Edinburgh University Press.

Gavins, Joanna and Gerard Steen (2003). *Cognitive Poetics in Practice*. London: Routledge.

Gerrig, Richard (1993). *Experiencing Narrative Worlds: On the Psychological Activities of Reading*. New Haven: Yale University Press.

Gibbons, Alison (2008). "Multimodal Literature 'moves' us: Dynamic Movement and Embodiment in *VAS: An Opera In Flatland*." In: *HERMES* Journal of *Language and Communication Studies* 41: 107–124.

– (2010). "'I contain multitudes': Narrative multimodality and the book that bleeds." In: Page, Ruth (ed.). *New Perspectives on Narrative and Multimodality*. Abingdon: Routledge, 99–114.

– (forthcoming 2010). *Multimodality, Cognition, and Experimental Literature*. London; New York: Routledge.

Gibson, J. J. (1966). *The Senses Considered as Perceptual Systems*. London: George Allen & Unwin Ltd.

Hall, Christine (2008). "Imagination and Multimodality: reading, picturebooks and anxieties about childhood." In: Sipes, Lawrence R. and Sylvia Pantaleo (eds.). *Postmodern Picturebooks: Play, Parody, and Self-Referentiality*. New York; London: Routledge, 130–146.

Hayles, N. Katherine (2002). *Writing Machines*. Cambridge: The MIT Press.

Herman, David (1994). "Textual You and Double Deixus in Edna O'Brien's *A Pagan Place*." *Style* 28(3): 378–410.

– (2002). *Story Logic: Problems and Possibilities of Narrative*. Lincoln; London: University of Nebraska Press.

Holland, Dorothy and William Lachicotte, Jr., Debra Skinner and Carole Cain (1998). *Identity and Agency in Cultural Worlds*. Cambridge; London: Harvard University Press.

Kress, Gunther (2003). *Literacy in the New Media Age*. London: New York: Routledge.
Kress, Gunther and Theo van Leeuwen (1996). *Reading Images: The Grammar of Visual Design*. London: Routledge.
Lakoff, George and Mark Johnson (1980). *Metaphors We Live By*. Chicago; London: University of Chicago Press.
McHale, Brian (1987). *Postmodernist Fiction*. London; New York: Routledge.
McLuhan, Marshall (1964). *Understanding Media: The Extensions of Man*. New York: McGraw-Hill.
Nørgaard, Nina (2010). "Multimodality and the literary text: making sense of Safran Foer's *Extremely Loud & Incredibly Close*." In: Page, Ruth (ed.). *New Perspectives on Narrative and Multimodality*. Abingdon: Routledge, 115–126.
Oosterling, Henk (2003). "Sens(a)ble Intermediality and *Interesse*." *Intermédialités* 1, 29–46.
Pressman, Jessica (2006). "House of Leaves: Reading the Networked Novel." In: *Studies in American Fiction* 34(1). Online, Retrieved February 2007 from http://gateway.proquest.com/openurl?ctx_ver=Z39.88–2003&xri:pqil:res_ver=0.2&res_id=xri:lion&rft_id=xri:lion:ft:abell:R03944197:0, no pagination.
Rajewsky, Irina O. (2005). "Intermediality, Intertextuality, and Remediation: A Literary Perspective on Intermediality." *Intermédialités* 5: 43–64.
Scarry, Elaine (2001). *Dreaming by the Book*. Princeton: Princeton University Press.
Stockwell, Peter (2002). *Cognitive Poetics: An Introduction*. London: Routledge.
Vygotsky, L. S. (1978). *Mind in Society: The Development of Higher Psychological Processes*. Cambridge: Harvard University Press.
Werth, Paul (1999). *Text Worlds: Representing Conceptual Space in Discourse*. London: Longman.
Wolf, Werner (2005). 'Intermediality'. In Herman, David/ Manfred Jahn and Marie-Laure Ryan (eds). *Routledge Encyclopedia of Narrative Theory*. London; New York: Routledge, 252–256.
Website 1. Laura A. "Obsessive House of Horrors." In: Amazon.co.uk, Customer Reviews for *House of Leaves*. Online, Retrieved May 2008, from http://www.amazon.com/review/product/038560310X/ref=cm_cr_pr_link_3?_encoding=UTF8&pageNumber=3&sortBy=bySubmissionDateDescending, no date: no pagination.

Marina Grishakova
(University of Tartu)

Intermedial Metarepresentations

Introduction

Simonides' definition of painting as "mute poetry" and poetry as "speaking picture" naturally suggests the complementarity of verbal and visual media, pointing as it does to the natural presence of poetry in painting and vice versa. From this viewpoint, verbal and visual media are partially co-extensive. To the contrary, Leonardo da Vinci's dictum on painting as mute poetry and poetry as blind painting from the *Treatise on Painting* highlights dissimilarity, making synthesis of the two arts problematical. In this case, the "deficiency" of each art ("muteness" of painting and "blindness" of poetry) is seen as its constitutive principle. Verbal art aspires to the state of visuality and sensory presence, hence the topos of writing as "seeing" — as a mere aspiration or unattainable goal: "Verbal art achieves whatever iconicity and presence it can claim through relational, diagrammatic means, or, problematically, through metaphors" (Steiner 1982: 22). The "failure" of the verbal to capture the visual is often thematized by different schools and authors (see Grishakova 2006; Lehtimäki, in this volume). Likewise, visual art resorts to indexical and symbolic means of signification to be articulated. Whereas verbal art aspires towards the state of sensory presence, visual art aspires towards full articulation. Insofar as neither reaches its ideal, there remains a meaningful gap between them.

Over the last four decades there have emerged a number of theories of vision that take the meaning-generating gap between vision and word, "the rift between [...] the seeable and the sayable" (Mitchell 1994: 12), as their starting point. These theories highlight the inherently mixed nature of media — the resistance of the visual to the verbal within the same "iconotext," an admixture of iconic and symbolic (continuous and discontinuous) elements within the same medium. The simultaneously contrasting and complementary natures of visual and verbal media have become objects of study in semiotics. According to Joseph Courtés, there is no stable equivalence between visual signs and their presumed meanings (Courtés 1995: 243). Courtés notes that reducing visual signs to the system of equivalences, analogous to linguistic signification, would be erroneous: before and irrespective of any semantization, visual signs belong to perceptual order. However, they are able to form loose configurations with the elements of other (pragmatic, thymic or cognitive) orders. In Juri Lotman's opinion, discrete and continuous languages are mutually untranslatable; only an approximate equivalence can be established between discrete units (symbolic signs) and continuous semantic entities (such as painting, cinema screen, dream, dance, ritual behavior, etc.), where a meaning is "smeared" over the *n*-dimensional textual space. "Translation" from visual languages to verbal ones or vice versa leads to considerable displacements of meaning and sense-generating shifts (Lotman 1981: 9–10).

Tension between word and image is particularly obvious in the case of "metapictures" (Mitchell 1994) or pictorial paradoxes, where the very conditions of visual representation and perception are called into question. The destabilizing effect of the metapicture, its "wildness" and resistance to interpretation demonstrate both "the impossibility of a strict metalanguage," which would provide an adequate description of the metapicture and "the imbrication of visual and verbal experience" (Mitchell 1994: 83). Such "metapictorialism" is characteristic of modernist and avant-garde art in general. Winfried Nöth distinquishes between "metapictures" (pictures about pictures or pictures of pictures which include quotation or other forms of intertextual reference) and "self-referential pictures" (pictures that refer to themselves) (Nöth 2007). He argues that the two categories only partially overlap, yet the difference between them has been ignored by Mitchell, whose definition covers both metapictures and self-referential pictures. Nöth illustrates the difference between two types of pictures by means of analogy with the lingustic concepts of metalanguage (a "second-order" language, a language of a higher order of abstraction and description) and self-referential language (a self-reflexive "first-order" language).

However, Mitchell's "metapicture" as both an artefact and a form of metareflection is a visual analogue of "metafiction," where the first- and the second-order languages co-exist, rather than an equvalent to "metalanguage". On one hand, "metapicture" demonstrates the *impossibility* of a strict metalanguage, on the other hand, it almost naturally translates into metareflexive description.

In contrast to "metalanguage" and "self-referential language," the concepts of metafiction and self-reflexive fiction are employed interchangeably as synonyms and refer to the phenomenon of self-reflexiveness that lays bare conventions of fictional representation and tells us something about fictionality in general. Likewise, any "metapicture" tells us something about pictorialism and, consequently, reflects on itself and other pictures. Both metafictionality and metapictorialism combine self-referentiality with metadescription. However, whereas Mitchell's "metapicture" applies to pictorial meta- and self-reflexive representation, the terms "metavisual" and "metaverbal," coined by myself (see Grishakova 2004), refer to *intermedial* metarepresentation.

Obviously there exist verbal analogues to Mitchell's "metapictures" — self-reflexive verbal "metatexts," where conditions of verbal representation are laid bare or called into question. Whereas the metavisual text appeals to verbal representation, the metaverbal text evokes visual representation to compensate for the lack or inadequacy of verbal information. Pseudo-sensory images that are triggered by textual cues and are unstable by their very essence supplement verbal representation (see Mitchell 1986; Esrock 1994; Aldrich 1972; Hester 1972). Both metavisual and metaverbal texts belong to the category of metarepresentations.

"Metarepresentation," as used in cognitive linguistics and psychology, applies to a (mental, implicit, or public, explicitly manifested or materialized) representation of a representation: "a higher-order representation with a lower-order representation embedded within it" (Wilson 2000: 411). In this usage, "metarepresentation" already refers to the intermedial transfer — for instance, a mental representation represented in the sound or graphic substance or vice versa (Nöth's classification includes only public representations of public representations in the visual medium). As such, "metarepresentation" may be extended also to other forms of intermedial representation.[1] Insofar as intermedial (visual-verbal) transfer and translation results in a system of approximate, loose equivalences established between the iconic and symbolic signs, between verbal and visual representation, the intermedial metarepresentation reveals tension between these components and, simultaneously, highlights the incapacity of a separate medium to capture the multimodal nature of perception. Potentially, any verbal or visual text is an "imagetext" or "iconotext," where either

1 See also Wolf 2009. Werner Wolf suggests using the term "metareference" instead of "metarepresentation" since, being, presumably, devoid of specifically linguistic connotations, the former "does not create problems when applied to non-representational or non-textual (i.e., non-verbal) media" (Wolf 2009: 16). However, "reference" is also a linguistically biased concept: only language (or combination of language and pointing gesture) can unambgiously attract attention to a specific object. Within the Fregean opposition of "sense" and "refrence", it pertains to the relation between the sign and and the extralingual world, whereas "representation" (as it is used by Sperber) belongs to the cognitivist and constructivist agenda and functions as a mediator between mental world models and discursive practices.

iconic or symbolic signs predominate and both kinds of signs are in a state of more or less explicit mutual tension. Yet intermedial metarepresentation, such as Magritte's famous inscription, "This is not a pipe," referring to the pictorial representation of a pipe, makes their mutual resistance the object of representation. The metaverbal text (e.g. an ekphrastic text, cine-novel, or graphic poetry) reflects on the incomplete nature of verbal medium by probing the limits of verbal representation and appealing to the visual forms (graphic elements, real or virtual film shots, works of art, dreams, hallucinations, mental imagery, etc.). The metavisual text reflects on the incomplete nature of visual representation by juxtaposing image with verbal message and revealing their discrepancy (Russian Formalists pointed to the tautological structure of the talkies and warned that sound would ruin the film poetics; however, tautology of the image and sound proved to be an illusion).

Whereas tension between the symbolic and iconic elements in visual arts, particularly in painting, is a well-studied topic, the elusive nature of mental images is resistant to description and has been less studied. The first possible source of tension between the verbal and the visual within the fictional text is the twofold nature of the fictionalizing act, a discrepancy between the mimetic and diegetic aspects of narrative presentation, between "what is shown" and "what is told", or, in Greimas' terms, between the performative and cognitive aspects of narration. Any work of fiction is both a text and a fictional world. Reading involves adaptation between the verbal expression and the visual mode of perception, i.e. mental images of the storyworld inferred by readers (see Esrock 1994). The reader is in a privileged position in comparison to the fictional character because of his (her) "surplus" of vision, which embraces multiple perspectives and evokes a mental image of the fictional world. There is a meaningful gap between schematic referential frames provided by text and synthetic images of the fictional world evoked in reader's consciousness. What I call the "image of the fictional world" roughly corresponds to Roman Ingarden's "concretization." According to Ingarden, the work of art is a "schematic formation" containing "places of indeterminacy", which are partially fleshed out ("concretized") by the individual reading. Reconstruction of imaginary scenes is especially active on the level of "schematized aspects" and "represented entities." "Schematized aspects" are "visual, auditory, or other aspects via which the characters and places represented in the work may be 'quasi-sensorially' apprehended," and "represented entities" are objects, events, and states of affairs that form the characters and plot of the literary work (*Stanford Encyclopedia* 2004; Ingarden 1973).

The second source of tension between the verbal and the visual is a discrepancy between the narrative functions of telling and observation, or in Greimas's words, the performative and the cognitive aspect of narration. This discrepancy is at its most obvious in first-person homodiegetic narration ("character narration"), which combines authorial and character functions: "The curious hybrid, part actor, part reporter, the narrator is one of the points where fiction and narration strangely intersect" (Ricardou 2002: 182). The first-person homodiegetic narrator (witness-participant) has the privilege of seeing others in the fictional world while remaining himself partially "invisible". He is seen from the outside only as modeled by the Other and from the inside only as the "language of inner experience" (Bakhtin).

The notion of authorial omniscience and the traditional likening of knowing to seeing have sometimes led to the naturalistic reading of the metaphor of authorial vision. Some Foucault-influenced critics have even scolded the realist author for the "police control" he exercises over the characters by means of "panoptic vision." As Dorrit Cohn justly observes, Foucault's power relations exist only between acting subjects or "ontological equals;" their application to narrative agencies is unmotivated. Further, she points out that panoptical vision is a means of *external* manipulation: "The guardian [...] can only perceive his subjects' manifest behaviour, which he can punish or reward" (Cohn 1995: 9, 13; reprinted in Cohn 1999). However, external manipulation or physical coercion is for Foucault part of the broader process of "normalisation," in which power structures not only control the body but are also interiorized into the subject's mind and language. Cohn refers to the Genettian idea of narration as a *restriction* on the authorial omniscience: the authorial full vision of the fictional world is restricted through the acts of focalization, i.e. characters' perceptions. The scheme is naturalistic and indeed resembles the Foucauldian picture of control, the more so since novelists themselves often playfully underscore their characters' dependence on the authorial will. If, however, the fictional text is placed into a broader cognitive perspective of double communication between the author and reader, narrator and narratee, the storyworld as an effect of "a revelatory vision that provides imagined beings with an imagined inner life" (Cohn 1995: 13) might be considered as a form of "appresentation" — participant observation and constitution of the Other as part of the self, which leads to the *extension* of the cognitive perspective on the world and the growth of knowledge. From this viewpoint, the author does not possess full knowledge: on the contrary, (s)he uses narrative agency to extend his (her) comprehension and knowledge in the process of narration. Narration is a process of sense-making rather than a transfer of a ready package of information from the author to the reader, hence the effect of surprise, which a work in progress often evokes in its author, e.g. when Tolstoy is astonished at Anna Karenina's "unexpected" behavior.

The authorial functions are distributed between mediating narrative agencies. The function of physical vision, i.e. vision within the fictional world, is delegated to the homodiegetic narrator or a character. Classical narratology (Genette, Chatman) has always tended to separate verbalization from vision, "narration" from "focalization". It seems that both approaches–the straightforward identification of authorial omniscience with vision, and the strict separation of authorial verbalization from the character's vision–need further refining.

Obviously, the author-narrator is not able to (physically) "see" the storyworld. However, as early narratology puts it, the authorial narrator may adopt character's vision or "simulate" vision from the deictic center, i.e. from an imaginable point in the storyworld ("hypothetical focalization;" see Herman 1994). Any "verbal icon" is just a blueprint for creating images, not the image itself. It is a sign of verbalized perception, which has at least a minimal spatio-temporal localization *within* the storyworld and therefore is subjectively tinged. Even impersonal (extradiegetic, third-person narration) comprises indices of the narrator's simulated "presence" in the storyworld (deictic expressions, the distribution of the "given" and "new" information, or rheme and theme; modal and evaluative words; see e.g. Uspensky 1970, Boldyrev 2000, Lenz 2003, Schmid 2005 and others). Hence the authorial narrator's "quasi-sensory" perception duplicates the "physical" vision of the character and simulates the narrator's presence within the storyworld. This double focalization stems from the dissociation of the represented or extraverted and representing or introverted consciousness as a distinctive feature of fictional representation (Chafe 1994).

The first-person homodiegetic narrator, who occupies an intermediary position between the author and the character, embodies tension between word and vision, mimetic and diegetic aspects of representation. The narrator's "specular desire" for "full vision" is impeded because of the limited access to knowledge: it stimulates the resistance of the visual to the verbal, a suspense or blockage of verbalization. The latter entails an increasing degree of textual indeterminacy.

Metavisual texts

Portraits form a large group of metavisual texts. On one hand, portraiture, although inscribed into aesthetic and cultural conventions of its age, is subjected to the *resemblance pact*, i.e. a requirement of similarity between the portrayed and the representation. The resemblance pact includes *pos-*

ing. In his talk at the inaugural conference of the European Society for Aesthetics, Paolo Spinicci defined pose, as a condition of portraiture, in the following terms: "a kind of intentional behavior which consists in disposing face and body according to a design which is exclusively determined by the awareness of being observed and by the desire to appear in a particular way — the way one has chosen — to an observer" (Spinicci 2009). Though pose may be staged by the artist (the author of the portrait), it is attributed to and authorized by the portrayed person: the pose is meant to render the portrayed person's identity. This fact, as Spinicci argues, turns portraits into first-person narratives. The portrait comprises tension between iconic and symbolic-indexical (narrative) components. The latter (pose, attributes — books, maps, tools etc., clothes, uniform and awards on official portraits, setting and background) function as deictics: they are meant to be read and projected upon a certain reality. Therefore the portrait is a window onto the reality, even such a stylized portrait as Julie Heffernan's "Self-Portrait as Post Script 2007," where the artist poses naked, surrounded by hunting trophies (birds, animals and sea creatures, e.g. a giant squid), her head and body embellished by peacock's feathers and flower garlands, reminiscent of Rococo paintings.

Application of narratological terminology in visual studies (such as narrator, focalization, metanarration etc.), proves to be successful only if accepted critically as usage of metaphorical *ad hoc* concepts in the domain, different from their initial application (see Grishakova 2006). The film narrator has been identified with the camera, the filmic composition device (M. Jahn), the "organizational and sending agency" behind the film (Chatman) or, finally, the narratorial function has been entrusted to the viewer (Bordwell). Indeed, the interplay between the seemingly anonymous camera work and the whole framework of (human and machine) interactions governing film shooting allows for various attributions of authorship and narrative agency.

Hitchcock's *Rear Window* (1954) exemplifies the character-observer's search for a meaning of the visible and the struggle for narrative control over the situation. As Hitchcock's critics have already noted, the "window" in Hitchcock's film is actually a "mirror" (Fawell 2001; Wood 1991). All the events, or rather different life stories, in the apartment house opposite the character's window reflect, to a greater or lesser extent, the "hidden" story of the protagonist and his fiancée Lisa — the story that unfolds on the level of subconscious impulses and drives. Thus the life seen through the "rear window" reveals what is hidden or suppressed in the rather conventional or ambiguous conversation of the characters — the "creatures trapped in the habits of their existence" (Fawell 2001: 2).

The observation, the role of the witness or the "eye," is a natural thematization of the protagonist's profession. Jeff (played by James Stewart) is a reporter-photographer who is unwillingly placed in the witness' position: he is practically immobile due to his broken leg. To compensate for his immobility Jeff submerses into intense, continuous observation. He also uses women, whose curiosity he manipulates, and optical devices as prostheses to interact with the observable. *Rear Window* is a self-reflexive film, modeled on filmmaking and film viewing. Critics have pointed out Hitchcock's obsessive use of the photo-camera throughout the film (see e.g. Fawell 2001: 22). The protagonist himself plays the role of the camera while observing the life stories in neighbor's windows. Jeff may be identified as the "narrator" of the embedded stories (other characters' life stories), whose development is given almost exclusively through his eyes. Though the camera preserves a degree of independence while "narrating" the story of the murder (it is "scanning" the windows and the yard when Jeff falls asleep or does not look through the window), Jeff's window serves as the main point of reference: even while using the "objective camera," Hitchcock gives additional information to the viewer from the point of view of Jeff's window (Fawell 2001: 46).

Jeff's nurse Stella, who blames him for his paranoid watching, is inclined to see the situation of involuntary voyeurism as typical: "we've become a race of Peeping Toms. People ought to get outside and look in for a change." Critics spare no effort to find the cause of Jeff's "strange" behavior, his passion for "peeping" and unwillingness to marry. They have referred to his egoism, repressed homosexuality, impotence, melancholy and neurosis. Yet hypothetical signs of Jeff's latent homosexuality or impotence may be actually read in many different ways, though indeed sexual puns and hints abound in the movie.

The women, Stella and Lisa, judge Jeff from the commonsense point of view. They are initially presented as an obstacle for his observation: they consider his behavior abnormal and try to divert his attention from an almost paranoiac looking through the window by involving him in a conventional talk and interrupting him when he himself is trying to speak. Jeff reacts to the women as "conventional" and rather aggressive creatures (critics and biographers sometimes refer to Hitchcock's misogyny, see e.g. Spoto 1983). However, Stella and Lisa themselves become involved in the game of looking when the sinister patterns of Thorwald's behavior discovered by Jeff finally engage their attention. Hitchcock uses the poetics of mystery and silence to break everyday patterns of life and stereotypical behavior. The function of the "primeval" power of vision is central in this breakthrough. There is always a tinge of professional passion in Jeff's observations. Thus the question about various ways of cutting up a body (read by critics as a parallel between sex and violence) is not devoid of cinematographic interest: it is essentially the problem of editing and montage.

The visual pattern is in overt conflict with conversation. If in Hitchock's films the sound track competes with the images or even "steals the show" (Fawell 2001: 5), the dialogue has its own function within the sound track. In *Rear Window*, speech manifests inner disharmony between the verbal and the visual: it is strained, hostile or ambivalent, and harsh or anxious intonations are prevalent. The voice stands out against the background of natural sounds and music that support and emphasize the images or are contrapuntal to them. Moreover, in Hitchcock's *metavisual* text, there is a suppressed verbal counterpart, i.e. the words, which remain unsaid. This verbal counterpart is brought to the surface by hints and harsh intonations as well as screams, sighs and mysterious sounds in the surroundings of Jeff's apartment. The viewer has every reason to suspect that this "invisible speech" is in principle not amenable to full verbalization.

The conflict of vision and verbaliztion is the main axis of the film, onto which other oppositions and patterns (feminine-masculine, conventional-nonconventional, etc.) are superimposed. Hitchcock learned a great deal from the early silent cinema, especially from German expressionism. In *Rear Window*, the strategy of supplying visual information with its subsequent confirmation or disconfirmation through verbal comment (Bordwell 1997: 41) is modeled upon silent film structure (alternation of scenes and intertitles). On the other hand, the linkage between the film and photography is made evident: it reminds the viewer of the secondary nature of the "talkies" and the principal discrepancy between vision and word inherent in the cinema text.

The British thriller *Peeping Tom* (1960) directed by Michael Powell abounds in Hitchockian allusions and reminiscences. Powell's film has been associated with *Psycho*, *Vertigo*, and *Rope*, yet its most obvious pre-text is *Rear Window*. "Peeping" as a general disease of the post-Freudian age becomes the central focus in Powell's movie. The motif of the presumable complicity between the observer and the observed implicit in *Rear Window* is explicitly thematized by Powell. Powell's film displays the murderous power of camera (as the author's substitute, cf. Rothman 1982): here, the camera functions as a tool of observation and murder. The couple, a voyeuristic observer and a murderer, typical of Hitchcock films, merges into the single person. The protagonist Mark Lewis, a photographer working in a film studio, kills women with a blade attached to the leg of his portable camera. He films the murders, trying to capture pre-mortem expressions of horror on his victims' faces. Later he records police working on the crime scene, creating a series of inset stories within the main story—"films within the film." Tension between the verbal (vain effort to capture and explain) and the visual (mysterious, incomprehensible, horrible, but irresistibly attracting) becomes even more irresolvable. It is, again, a woman who epitomizes the Freudian dialectics of repulsion-attraction, leading to madness and murder on the one hand, while on the other hand belonging to the world of stereotypical behavior and conventional talk where mysteries are explained away.

Establishing shots introduce a sinister episode: Mark filming a prostitute, approaching her with camera. The viewer can see the expression of increasing horror on her face before an invisible danger, hear her screams and watch the close-up of her open mouth — shots reminiscent of the famous episode in the shower in Hitchcock's *Psycho*, where the camera also violates the female body. However, both the murder and the murderer remain beyond the frame in Powell's film: a shot-reverse shot sequence is interrupted by long subjective camera shots, whereas the cameraman (Mark) stays invisible, as if detached from his camera.

The contrasting episode of the birthday party displays the other side of the filmic reality: the innocent and conventional "daily life." Mark's role is, again, ambiguous: the "objective camera" shows him peeping through the window in the room where his tenant Helen celebrates her birthday. Helen meets Mark downstairs to invite him to join the party. Her speech is sustained in a very conventional, polite manner; her intonation is very distinct and intense: "I'm Helen Stephens. I'm having a party — and the other tenants are there. And a few friends... We'd like you to join us. Please, come in; you'll meet the others who live here." Later Helen knocks at Mark's door to give him a slice of the birthday cake. A very conventional and polite talk is in sharp contrast with the establishing episode and the film show in Mark's room (he has been watching the film shot in the morning at the place of murder). Helen asks Mark about his occupation and requests to show her what he works at. Instead, Mark shows her a documentary shot by his father for the purpose of psychological study of fear. The film spectator is only able to see film fragments: the camera focus alternates between Helen's face, as if registering her reactions (amazement, anxiety, fear etc.), and the screen. This strategy implicates the spectator in Mark's voyeurism and makes him Mark's accomplice, insofar as Helen is a potential victim of Mark's compulsion to kill. Helen is unable to capture the whole meaning of Mark's father's sinister experiments. She is well-intentioned, innocent and obviously unsuspecting or ignorant about evil powers that govern Mark's life. While detecting the presence of evil, she reacts with moral indignation — a rational reaction to irrational powers. The following dialogue between Helen and Mark accompanies the film show:

HELEN: Mark, what a beautiful little boy! Who is he?
MARK: Me.

HELEN: Of course, it is! Then, who took this film?
MARK: My father.
HELEN: What a wonderful idea! You'll be able to show it to your own chil… [Reacting to the close shot of the terrified, crying boy] You must have had a bad dream… [Commenting on the boy climbing the garden wall to see a kissing couple beyond it] Whatever are you after? A naughty boy. I hope you were spanked. [Commenting on the episode when the father awakens the boy at night and puts a lizard on his bed] Mark, what a strange thing for your father to photograph! Mark, this isn't some sort of joke, isn't it?

Helen's questions are becoming more insistent and aggressive: "Please, help me to understand this thing! All right now, Mark, what was that all about? That was a lizard. How did it get there? Wouldn't you try to explain? I like to understand what I'm shown!" In turn, Mark becomes more emotional, his replies more brisk and fragmentary: he runs the film with increased speed until Helen switches off the projector. The episode introduces the film's basic dilemma: the limitedness of the verbal, its inability to capture the overwhelming complexity of the perceptual world. Mark himself seems to be unaware of the subliminal motives of his behavior: he is driven by opposite impulses that mirror dark and light sides of his personality. Helen is only able to solve Mark's mystery in the very end of the story, before his suicide, in which he reproduces his usual method of murder by killing himself with the blade attached to his camera. In both Hitchcock's and Powell's film, a discrepancy arises between the viewer's (external) and character's (internal) perspective: verbalization is lagging behind the visual information supplied to the viewer and paces the process of narration.

In the visual medium, metafictional and metanarrational devices transposed from the verbal medium perform new functions and produce different effects. Thus, the metaleptic contacts of authors and characters in fiction usually produce the effect of character's "hyperrealization" — the character being promoted to the rank of the real author's ontological equal, whereas the author acts, ambiguously, in creative deity's or real person's capacity. In Nabokov's novel *Bend Sinister*, the character hears "the cautious crackling of a page" thrown into the author's wastebasket (the page of the novel in which the character itself is created) and, being shot to death in the fictional world, is nevertheless saved on the highest, extradiegetic level of reality. In *Lolita*, the "real" (fictional) Lolita dies in childbirth, whereas Lolita as a figment of author's imagination is saved by the immortal power of art. In Mark Forster's movie *Stranger than Fiction* (2006), the author's metafictional intrusion into her character's life and the character's meeting with the author result, on the contrary, in author's relegation from the rank of the extra-textual invisible deity (Forster's author Karen Eiffel is famous for killing her main characters in various ways; her role in the character's destiny is that of a supernatural power) to the role of a "real", embodied human creature. Upon the meeting with the main character of her novel in progress, Karen Eiffel is forced to cancel the planned death of the character and change the ending of the story simply because the character is not any more a "paper man," and she is unable to kill a real human being.

Metaverbal texts

Whereas the *metavisual* text refers to an inadequate or virtual verbal counterpart of the visual representation, the excess of verbalization in the *metaverbal* text is meant to compensate for a lack of visual representation — what the narrator and the characters are trying but unable to see, or what they are only imagining to be real. This is the case of the governess in Henry James' *Turn of the Screw* — a text which actively evokes images of virtual worlds and beings. As Christine Brooke-Rose observes, James's text "invites the critics unconsciously to 'act out' the governess dilemma" (Brooke-Rose 1981: 128). She shows how critics start re-writing the story and adding missing details. Similarly, the governess verbalizes the story to compensate for the impeded visualization. The comparison of the ghosts with "letters," i.e. the letters of the story the governess herself is writing ("I saw him as I see the letters I form on this page;" James 1996: 654), points to the metafictional meaning of the story as a thematization of the discrepancy between narration and observation.

Felman and Brooke-Rose highlighted the role of vision and mirror structures in James's story (Felman 1977; Brooke-Rose 1981). The governess is looking for the "mirror contact," i.e. exchange of glances, which would permit to recognize the Other as the "Self" and thus to regain visual control over the Other, which, roughly speaking, corresponds to the second (narcissistic) stage of the Lacanian "mirror phase." Looking seems to be the most reliable source of information for the governess: "to see" means "to know" and thus to verbalize (e.g.: "I only asked that he should *know*; and the only way to be sure he knew would be to see it;" James 1996: 652). However, there is a "surplus" of vision, which is beyond the governess's reach and resistant to verbalization.

The main story comprises reverberations of the events mentioned in the frame: they repeat in the main narrative in a subversive or regressive form. A number of perfect mirror contacts, i.e. recognitions of the Self in the Other, are established in the frame. The mother sees what the child sees; the first-person narrator "reads" Douglas's thoughts in his gaze; the governess sees what Douglas sees and he sees that she sees it; etc. The governess' story, on the contrary, degenerates into a series of dubious reflections and imperfect visual contacts. According to the governess's "mirror theory", contact with ghosts should have left a visible "imprint" on the children. Yet the children are mirrors that do not reflect anything, the ghosts most often avoid direct visual contact with the governess, and the housekeeper Mrs. Grose seems to be an imperfect mirror. Thus the reader is left in incertitude, not knowing whether there is, indeed, anything "on the other side of the mirror," i.e. the governess.

The frame of the story with its triple narrative mediation (the governess, Douglas, and the first-person narrator) already introduces a number of discrepancies between word and vision. The beginning of the narration is deferred. Preliminary information is scarce, yet Douglas hints that it will not be much fuller in the future either: "The story won't tell" (ibid, 637). Despite, or rather thanks to, the elusive substance of the story, the governess's desire to see and to know grows over the course of the narration. As a result, the governess starts verbalizing the virtual speech of other characters, i.e. she acts out the story, taking over the role of the author.

The governess's first talk with the housekeeper assumes the form of "prodigious and gratified looks" and "obscure and roundabout allusions." The opportunities for verbalization are limited by the employer's injunction "not to report," by the reserved manners of the housekeeper, and by the presumed resistance and rejection of full contact on the children's part. An additional restriction is introduced by the housekeeper's illiteracy, her inability to read the letter sent by the schoolmaster and thus to play the role of the governess's mirror double. The first apparition is metonymically linked to the letters in the governess's manuscript. This is also the first case when "to see" does not mean "to know," where verbalization is blocked. "Like the letters, the ghosts, too, are essentially figures of *silence*" (Felman 1977: 149). The housekeeper's assumption that Miles stole letters at school and for that reason was expelled establishes metaphorical connection between letters and secret corruption. Instead, as it turns out, Miles "said things," i.e. verbalized things, which are not to be verbalized.

For the governess, the first apparition epitomizes the usurpation of control over vision: she has been observed by a stranger. Further, the feeling of being observed is projected onto the children: their behavior gives the governess the suspicion "of being watched from under cover" (James1996: 695). The feeling culminates in the lake episode when Flora appears "to read and accuse, and judge" the governess (ibid, 720). The second apparition makes it obvious that it is not the governess that the ghosts are looking for. As if to compensate for the absence of the "mirror contact" and lack of control, the governess takes the place of the ghost on the other side of the window and applies her face to the glass as the ghost did before her. Further, the mirror reversal is repeated twice (Miles on the lawn looking at the tower, Flora at the opposite shore of the lake; see Brooke-Rose 1981). The feeling of the uncontrollable "surplus" of vision beyond the governess's reach intensifies after the new apparition emerges: "I scarce know how to put my story into words that shall be a credible picture of my state of mind"; "I can give no intelligible account of how I fought out the interval" (James 1996: 667, 670).

The governess assumes the role of the "screen" between the children and the ghosts: "the more I saw, the less they would" (ibid, 668). However, she feels she is an imperfect screen since she does not see enough. The governess needs to see the ghosts to retain control over visual contacts, to reach "full vision" (ibid, 671). She is worried that the children may see more that she does: "not seeing enough" produces an impression of obscurity, lying, and "theatralization" on the children's part. The communion between the children and the ghosts presumably takes place behind the governess's back, beyond her field of vision.

To compensate for the lack of contact with ghosts the governess is tempted to demand full confession (verbalization) from the children: "Why not frankly confess it to me, so that we may at least live with it together and learn perhaps, in the strangeness of our fate, where we are and what it means?" (ibid, 685). She suspects that the children imitate the bad servants' speech without her knowledge and makes guesses about the character of this verbalization. Further the necessity of verbalization plays a more and more significant role. Finally the desperate governess starts talking with the ghost of the other governess and verbalizes the ghost's hypothetical speech for the housekeper (ibid, 705, 707). Thus the narrator's desire for visual control instigates her struggle for verbal control, i.e. for "narrative authority".

The tension between vision and word in James's story is related to the struggle for narrative authority. As Wayne Booth has pointed out, James often transformed the narrator from a "mere reflector" into a full-fledged actor. Some of his stories are double-focused as a result of an incomplete fusion of the two types of narrators (Booth 1983: 346). Yet the situation in the *Turn of the Screw* is more complicated. James consciously employed visual and theatrical metaphors to explain his method of writing. For him the act of novel-writing was "a negotiation between the viewer and the viewed" (Hale 1998: 86). *Turn of the Screw* provokes "visual" reading, and the governess as the storyteller is supposed to maintain control of the story. However, while striving for control over verbalization and access to other characters' minds, she is permanently relegated to the role of a helpless onlooker because of either inadequacy or distorted character of her vision.

Nabokov's novella *The Eye* overtly thematizes the struggle for the narrative authority as a struggle for "vision." The first-person narrator splits into two agents (narrator vs. observer) and performs the movement along the "Möbius strip" of the narrative to look at himself as a character from its "obverse side." Thus the privileged position of the first-person narrator, who observes others in the fictional world while remaining "invisible" himself, is turned "inside out."

In Nabokov's novella, the first-person narrator commits suicide, yet his mental self lives on and creates the surrounding world anew. The self (the "I") has the function of the onlooker, witness, observer, i.e. the invisible "presence" or the mobile point of view in the world created, although it also retains a bodily presence. The other half of the "I" exists under Smurov's name as a "body" within the diegetic world. Smurov is made visible by means of his mirror reflections in the other characters' minds. The "I" is the object of vision in the first part of the story and the subject of vision in the second part, where its alter ego Smurov is detached and placed among the other characters. Then the "I" sees the self as the Other, yet this "visible side" is verbalized in the language of the other characters' experience. The "I", the Lacanian subject "that does not function as the center of human thought and action, but which inhabits the mind as an elusive agency, controlling yet uncontrollable" (Nobus 2003: 61), is always pervaded by the Other and becomes visible as the "Other." The narrator is, to use Bakhtin's words, translated from the language of inner experience to the language of outward expression. The "I" (Eye) conducts an investigation, looking for the real, "original" Smurov among his multiple copies in the other characters' minds. The fusion of the two halves occurs in the end.

The first part of the story comprises a series of frozen stills, *tableaux vivants*, photos or frescoes with the "I" as an empty center (which corresponds to the Smurov's image cut out from Vanya's photograph in the second part): I and Matilda, I and the boys, I and the melodramatic villain and jealous husband Kashmarin, etc. Nabokov refers to the principal "incompleteness" of the photographic image as a fragment of life torn from the context, from its live organic texture (a quality to which Walter Benjamin and Roland Barthes also pointed). The second part comprises Smurov's images in other people's minds: he is a "parasitic" image, a "tenacious parasite" (Nabokov 1965: 113), retained by their visual memory.

The identity of protagonist and narrator is established through the mirror reflection in the end of the novella. However, the "I" observing and the "I" acting or observed remain distinct throughout the narration. The difference is supported grammatically as the first- and the third-person positions. The first-person narrator is the authorial agent to the same extent as it is the protagonist's alter ego. As Ricœur argues, every narrative act already involves reflection upon the events narrated: "[N]arrative 'grasping together' carries with it the capacity for distancing itself from its own production and in this way dividing itself in two" (Ricœur 1990, 2: 61).

The "I" (the first-person narrator) placed within the diegetic world can be seen only from the inside — in the language of inner experience — and is thus partially disembodied. It is always an appeal to the reader's participatory observation and "concretization", i.e. fleshing out a schematic entity. By contrast, the outside "I" is presented as the Other, alienated from its inner experience.

A literary tradition to which Nabokov's novella undoubtedly refers is that of confessional prose (Rousseau, Dostoevsky and their followers). In *The Eye,* the cliché of the narrator's confessional "sincerity" is dramatized. The "I" of the story, the protagonist and the unreliable narrator, is, as usual in Dostoevsky, diffident, hesitating between megalomania and an inferiority complex, anxiously looking for his "reflections" in other people. He is also the author of the story who "can accelerate or retard" the motions of characters, "or distribute them in different groups, or arrange them in various patterns": "for me, their entire existence has been merely a shimmer on a screen" (Nabokov 1965: 100). The narrator observes the events from the outside, but also enters the fictional world either as a character or as a ghost; he may "recruit" characters as his agents, merge with a character, detach himself from the character or stop observing him altogether. Finally, he is the author's alter ego: it is the author who, according to fictional conventions, is not supposed to speak "sincerely" and has to be shielded by his oblique "reflections" within the text.

Although the final, complete fusion of the protagonist and the narrator never takes place in *The Eye,* at least grammatically, and the mutual mirroring of the two stories is still partial and distorted, there are multiple signs disseminated over the text indicating the relative symmetry of the two stories, that of the "I" and that of Smurov, and therefore pointing at their implied identity. Pairs of characters standing like atlantes on either side of the door steadily form the "frame" for the protagonist: the boys in the first story, Khrushchov and Mukhin in the second one (ibid, 24, 42). The book *Ariane, jeune fille russe* (a novel by Jean Schopfer, who published under the penname Claude Anet) appears in both stories. Even if the reality of the suicidal shot in the first part remains hypothetical, the wound makes itself felt in its mirror counterpart: "For several days already I had felt a strange discomfort in my bullet-punctured chest, a sensation resembling a draft in a dark room. I went to see a Russian doctor" (ibid, 72).

Thus, in Nabokov's novella, the garrulous narrator typical of confessional prose and the image of the protagonist as a poseur, a prattler, are in contrast with the elusiveness of narrator-character's "real" image shielded by the "I," the "empty center" of the story. The text is built as a system of verbal mirrors aimed at capturing this elusive image and unable to succeed.

Nabokov's novella anticipates Robbe-Grillet's strategy of the "absent (hidden, invisible) story" (in *Le Voyeur* and *La Jalousie*), which could have been focalised through a witness's eyes, yet as the witness's account proves to be unreliable or purely hypothetical, it remains resistant to reconstruction and is only inferred from the "surface" narration. Martin Amis also experimented with this technique in *Other People* (1981). The story of the female protagonist, amnesiac Mary Lamb (alias Amy Hide), presents a challenge to the reader who is used to "read[ing a] character's mind" and to reconstruct a character's inner life on the basis of its external manifestations (the "third-person perspective"). Paradoxically, the absence of the "first-person perspective" drastically reduces the opportunity of such reconstruction: Mary's mind is blank; she has neither past nor future. Mary's story is a double-deck story, however. The surface story of Mary's aimless wanderings in the world, which her "blank" consciousness carelessly mirrors, comprises traces of the sadistic murder of Amy Hide and the intruding presence of the murderer, whom the reader has every reason to identify with the narrator. Amis's manipulative authorial narrator "tortures the characters into life" and finally annihilates them (Finney 1995: 3). This second, deep-level story is hidden under surface and practically invisible for the reader.

As it seems, these narratives are so *effective* — in terms of the reader's (viewer's) response — not only due to the elements of the ghost, mystery or detective story they comprise, but also because they necessitate reader's active support, concretization and desire to examine the story "from the obverse side of the narrative" — as E. Wilson puts it (Wilson 1969:121), to see what is "on the back of the tapestry" (James 1996: 689).

Conclusion

In a broader cultural perspective, tension between the verbal and visual is an aspect of the struggle for knowledge, a contest of rival epistemologies: "The history of culture is in part the story of a protracted struggle for dominance between pictorial and linguistic signs, each claiming for itself certain proprietary rights on a 'nature' to which only it has access" (Mitchell 1986: 43). Metarepresentational narratives illustrate the process of hypothesis formation in the situations of indeterminacy, limited access to knowledge, or limited possibility of capturing and verbalizing the observable. Human cognition is multimodal: multiple clues of different origins (verbal, visual, aural, olfactory, etc.) form our knowledge of the surrounding world and stimulate hypothesis formation, yet the meaning of these clues may not be immediately apparent, and the clues themselves are appropriated by different readers or viewers in very different ways. As Bordwell writes, "the spectator could 'go beyond the information given' in ways unforeseen by the filmmakers" (Bordwell 2008: 149). This is true of any work of art, both verbal and visual, which opens new perspectives, more extensive than the work's immediate communicative content, and provides access to new meanings beyond the immediately available. Intermedial metarepesentation — be it verbal representation of a visual representation, mental imagery translated into the verbal language or, on the contrary, mental imagery triggered by the verbal language, — serves as a tool of human navigation in the surrounding world and a bridge between perception and knowledge.

References

Aldrich, Virgil C. (1972). "Pictorial meaning, picture thinking, and Wittgenstein's theory of aspects." In: Shibles, W. (ed.). *Essays on Metaphor*. Whitewater: Language Press, 93–103.

Boldyrev=Болдырев, Николай (2000). "Отражение пространства деятеля и пространства наблюдателя в высказывании". *Логический анализ языка. Языки пространств*. Москва: Языки русской культуры, 212–216.

Booth, Wayne C. (1983). *The Rhetoric of Fiction*. Harmondsworth: Penguin, 1983.

Bordwell, David (1997). *Narration in the Fiction Film*. London: Routledge.

– (2008). *Poetics of Cinema*. New York–London: Routlegde.

Brooke-Rose, Christine (1981). *A Rhetoric of the Unreal. Studies in narrative and structure, especially of the fantastic*. Cambridge: Cambridge University Press.

Chafe, Wallace (1994). *Discourse, Consciousness, and Time. The Flow and Displacement of Conscious Experience in Speaking and Writing*. Chicago: Chicago University Press.

Cohn, Dorrit (1995). "Optics and Power in the Novel." *New Literary History* 26: 3–20.

– (1999). *The Distinction of Fiction*. The Johns Hopkins University Press: Baltimore and London.

Courtés, Joseph (1995). *Du lisible au visible*. Bruxelles: De Boeck Université, 1995.

Esrock, Ellen J. (1994). *The Reader's Eye: Visual Imaging as Reader Response*. Baltimore, MD: Johns Hopkins University Press.

Fawell, John (2001). *Hitchcock's* Rear Window. *The Well-Made Film*. Carbondale and Edwardsville: Southern Illinois University Press.

Felman, Shoshana (1977). "Turning the Screw of Interpretation." *Yale French Studies* vol. 55/ 56: 95–207.

Finney, Brian (1995). "Narrative and Narrated Homicide in Martin Amis' *Other People* and *London Fields*." *Critique* 37: 3–15.

Grishakova, Marina (2004). "Vision and Word: The Seat of the Semiotic Conflict (H. James, V. Nabokov, A. Hitchcock)." In: Grishakova M. and Lehtimäki M. (eds.). *Intertextuality and Intersemiosis*. Tartu: Tartu University Press, 115–133.

– (2006). *The Models of Space, Time and Vision in V. Nabokov's Fiction: Narrative Strategies and Cultural Frames*. Tartu Semiotics Library 5. Tartu: Tartu University Press.

Hale, Dorothy J. (1998). "Henry James and the Invention of Novel Theory." In: Freedman, J. (ed.). *The Cambridge Companion to Henry James*. Cambridge: Cambridge University Press, 79–101.

Herman, David (1994). "Hypothetical Focalization." *Narrative* 2.3: 230–253.

Hester, Marcus B. (1972). "Metaphor and aspect seeing." In: Shibles, W. (ed.). *Essays on Metaphor*. Whitewater: Language Press, 111–123.

Ingarden, Roman (1973). *The Literary Work of Art*. Evanston: Northwestern University Press.

Jacobs, Karen (2001). *The Eye's Mind. Literary Modernism and Visual Culture*. Ithaca and London: Cornell University Press.

James, Henry (1996). *Complete Stories. 1892–1898*. New York: The Library of America.

Lenz, Friedrich, ed. (2003). *Deictic Conceptualisation of Space, Time and Person*. Amsterdam–Philadelphia: John Benjamins.

Lotman=Лотман, Юрий (1981). "Риторика." В: Структура и семиотика художественного текста. *Труды по знаковым системам* XII. Тарту: Издательство Тартуского университета, 8–28.

Mitchell, W. J. T. (1986). *Iconology: Image, Text, Ideology*. Chicago and London: University of Chicago Press.

– (1994). *Picture Theory. Essays on Verbal and Visual Representation*. Chicago & London: The University of Chicago Press.

Nabokov, Vladimir (1965). *The Eye*. New York: Phaedra.

Nobus, Dany (2003). "Lacan's science of the subject: between linguistics and topology". In: Rabaté, Jean-Michel (ed.). *The Cambridge Companion to Lacan*. Cambridge: The Cambridge University Press, 50–68.

Nöth, Winfried (2007). "Metapictures and self-referential pictures." In: Nöth, W. and N. Bishara (eds.). *Self-Reference in the Media*. Mouton de Gruyter: Berlin-New York, 61–78.

Ricardou, Jean (2002). "Text Generation." In: Richardson, Brian (ed.). *Narrative Dynamics. Essays on Time, Plot, Closure, and Frames*. Columbus: The Ohio State University, 179–190.

Ricœur, Paul (1990). *Time and Narrative*, vol. I-III. Chicago: The University of Chicago Press.

Rothman, William (1982). *Hitchcock: The Murderous Gaze*. Cambridge: Harvard University Press.

Schmid, Wolf (2005). *Elemente der Narratologie*. Berlin & New York: Walter de Gruyter.

Spinicci, Paolo (2009). *The Nature of Portraits: Some Phenomenological Remarks*. Paper delivered at the inaugural conference of the European Society for Aesthetics, April 4–5, 2009, Fribourg.

Spoto, Donald (1983). *The Dark Side of Genius: The Life of Alfred Hitchcock*. New York: Ballantine Books.

Stanford Encyclopedia of Philosophy 2004, ed. E. N. Zalta. http://plato.stanford.edu/archives/spring2004/entries/ingarden

Steiner, Wendy (1982). *The Colors of Rhetoric: Problems in the Relation between Modern Literature and Painting.* Chicago: University of Chicago Press.

Uspensky=Успенский, Борис (1970). *Поэтика композиции.* Москва: Искусство.

Wagner, Peter, ed. (1996). *Icons — Texts — Iconotexts. Essays on Ekphrasis and Intermediality.* Berlin–New York: Walter de Gruyter.

Wilson, Deirdre (2000). "Metarepresentation in Linguistic Communication." In: Sperber, Dan (ed.). *Metarepresentations. A Multidisciplinary Perspective.* Oxford-New York: Oxford University Press.

Wilson, Edmund (1969). "The Ambiguity of Henry James." In: Willen, Gerald (ed.). A *Casebook on Henry James's "The Turn of the Screw".* New York: Thomas W. Crowell Company, 115–153.

Wolf, Werner (2009). "Metareference across Media: The Concept, its Transmedial Potentials and Problems, Main Forms and Functions." In: Wolf, W. in collaboration with K. Banthleon and J. Thoss (eds.). *Metareference across Media. Theory and Case Studies.* Dedicated to Walter Bernhart on the Occasion of his Retirement. Amsterdam-New York, NY: Rodopi, 1–85.

Wood, Robin (1991). *Hitchcock's Films Revisited.* London–Boston: Faber&Faber.

Color illustrations

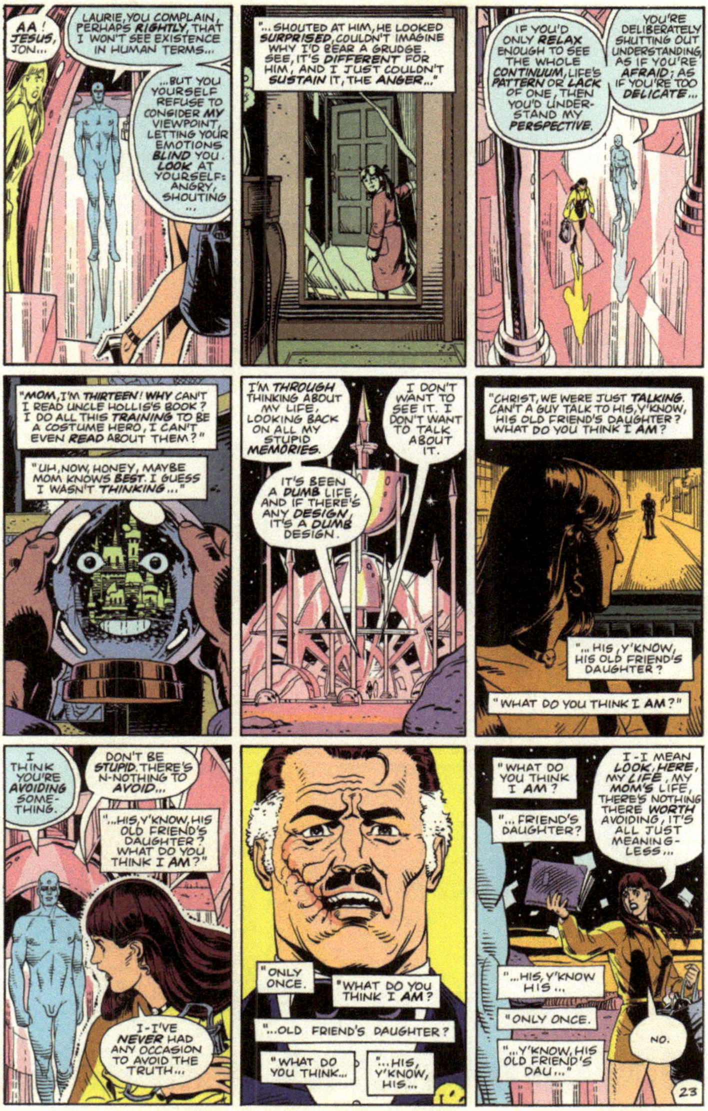

Figure 1: The Comics Page as Metonymic Space. "The Darkness of Mere Being." (Moore and Gibbons 1986: IX.23. By permission of DC Comics).

Figure 2: Sequence and Synthesis. "Look On My Works, Ye Mighty..." (Moore and Gibbons 1986: XI.1. By permission of DC Comics).

Figure 4: Recursion and Page Layout. "Day at the Circuits" (Spiegelman 2008. Originally printed in Spiegelman 1975. By generous permission of Art Spiegelman).

Figure 3: Evans 1935–36, 1:54.

Figure 1: Kratos slaying the hydra. © Sony Computer Entertainment America Inc. 2005. Screenshot created by IGN Entertainment.

Figure 2: Kratos up close. © Sony Computer Entertainment America Inc. 2005.

Figure 3: The bloodsport of one Spartan general. © Sony Computer Entertainment America Inc. 2005. Screenshot created by IGN Entertainment.

Figure 1: Frames from *Conta-me como* foi television commercial.

Figure 6: Outdoor ad for *A Minha Geração.*

Figure 8: Outdoor ad for Football Broadcasts.

Figure 9: Outdoor ads for Football Broadcasts.

Figure 9: Outdoor ads for Football Broadcasts.

Index

Bei Fragen zur Produktsicherheit wenden Sie sich bitte an:
If you have any questions regarding product safety,
please contact:

Walter de Gruyter GmbH
Genthiner Straße 13
10785 Berlin
productsafety@degruyterbrill.com